True American

TRUE AMERICAN

*Language, Identity, and
the Education of Immigrant Children*

ROSEMARY C. SALOMONE

*Harvard University Press
Cambridge, Massachusetts, and London, England   2010*

Library of Congress Cataloging-in-Publication Data

Salomone, Rosemary C.
  True American : language, identity, and the education of immigrant children /
Rosemary C. Salomone.
    p. cm.
  Includes bibliographical references and index.
  ISBN 978-0-674-04652-8 (cloth : alk. paper)   1. Immigrant children—
Education—United States.   2. Immigrant children—United States—Language.
3. Immigrant children—United States—Ethnic identity.   4. Bilingual education—
United States.   5. Americanization.   6. United states—Ethnic relations.
7. United States—Emigration and immigration.   I. Title.
    LC3731.S24   2010
    371.82′691—dc22   2009035780

To the memory of my grandparents
with love and gratitude

Language is the only homeland.

— CZESLAW MILOSZ

Contents

Preface

Writing a book is a mind-altering journey. Embarking with a general idea of where one's thoughts will lead, one ends up in quite another place, having been detoured by new ideas and questions one had not anticipated at the outset. So it was with this project. But the journey here was not just intellectual; it was very personal, in fact more personal than I could have imagined. It also was most timely, as the immigration issue heated up in the United States, assimilation and integration assumed unprecedented proportions in the national debate, language took center stage, and the education of what are now called "English language learners" took disturbing twists and turns, all challenging conventional notions of what it means to be American. At the same time, terrorism from abroad provoked heightened fears of foreigners, especially those whose values depart from the American mainstream, while a global economic crisis made clear that the world is shrinking before our eyes.

In the process I realized why the immigrant experience had always fascinated me. It was one I had lived through, not as a participant but as a close and keen observer, beginning in childhood and through my early career working with immigrant children and their families. In a most gratifying way, this book took me back to when my ancestors first sailed to America in the 1880s, others trailing behind, some returning and some remaining over the course of the next quarter century. It carried me through my childhood and to the community in which I spent my formative years: one densely populated by Irish, Italians, Poles, and Greeks, with smaller pockets of Norwegians, Lebanese, Syrians, and Eastern European Jews fanning out along the periphery. Almost every childhood friend had a grandparent or parent who had arrived in the States in the massive wave of migration in the early twentieth century. Ours was a world of lingering ethnic churches, food stores, and holiday rituals set against the backdrop of mid-twentieth-century assimilated America portrayed on our television screens and in movie theaters as the idealized life to which we all should aspire.

Growing up in the shadow of World War II and the reconstruction of postwar Europe, we considered ourselves fortunate compared to the distant relatives who had stayed behind, known to us only through their sporadic letters written in a foreign language, and our packages of medicines and outgrown clothing sent in return. For our families, we were the "true American" generation. We would speak English fluently and exclusively. Most of us heard grandparents regularly converse in their native language, our parents haltingly making the connection. That was their "inside" world from which the third generation would remain deliberately excluded and, from the parents' point of view, protected. Little did they or we foresee that many of us, as young adults impassioned with newly fashionable ethnicity, would return to the "old country" searching for our roots in both "high" and "low" culture. As the years passed, our identities became increasingly American until the only remaining vestiges of our families' immigrant pasts, beyond perhaps our surnames, were fond memories of family and community celebrations now considered quaint.

Those childhood years of watching my maternal grandparents strive to blend the old with the new, and hearing my mother's childhood stories of navigating the world for them through a maze of school officials insensitive to immigrant families, left an indelible mark on me. And so it was no surprise that my early career led me to teaching English to foreign students and immigrants in Columbia University's American Language Program, and then to designing and overseeing French-Haitian, Italian, and Spanish bilingual education programs in two of the most impoverished communities in New York City. I soon discovered that learning English was just one of many concerns weighing on the daily lives of these students. From that vantage point, I saw the bilingual education movement grow practically from the ground up, as I implemented the very laws and regulations about which I now write. At the same time I wrestled with theoretical and empirical questions in my doctoral research, examining language learning and language use among bilingual children and their families.

I was sailing on uncharted waters on both counts. Not only were there few experiences or instructional materials to draw on in this reformist view of immigrant education, but there was little research to back it up. Despite the inevitable frustrations, I gained invaluable insights into educational governance, language policy, cultural integration, and identity politics. The limited power of education in the face of overwhelming social problems soon propelled me into law school. An initial academic appointment at the Harvard Graduate School of Education, along with the chance to help create the first International High School in New York, allowed me once again to join theory and practice. In the twenty-plus years since then, I have stood on the sidelines watching events unfold and issues ripen while dissecting them with scores of law students, many of them immigrants or the children of immigrants. In the meantime, immigration has become a burning international issue, and the education of English language learners remains a point of contention.

In researching this book, I have tried to remain objective as I look through the lens of these early experiences. My present thinking has been richly informed by discussions with immigrant and refugee groups, community leaders, advocates, lawyers, scholars, students, school administrators, teachers, parents, and others too numerous to identify, not to exclude the many anonymous taxi drivers, shopkeepers, and hotel workers, on both sides of the Atlantic, who were willing to respond to my pointed questions on the immigrant experience and its impact on language, identity, and schooling.

The final product has benefited greatly from helpful comments and suggestions from participants in various symposia, including the 11th Meeting of the International Academy of Linguistic Law in Galway in 2006, the IMISCOE Cluster B5 meeting sponsored by the University of Lisbon in 2007, Law and Society Association meetings in Berlin and Montreal, and the Second Days of Language Rights conference in 2008 at the University of Teramo, Italy, where I presented related papers. I further thank the administrators, teachers, students, and parents at the Oyster-Adams Dual-Language Immersion School in Washington, D.C., and at the International High School in Long Island City, New York, for allowing me to observe each school's workings at close range and for sharing their hopes and understandings. The same goes for the students at St. John's University School of Law who graciously spent time discussing with me the joys and angst of growing up in immigrant families. Words of gratitude for generous research support go to the Spencer Foundation, to the Faculty Research Program at St. John's University School of Law, and to the Wang family, whose own migration to America is a remarkably powerful story.

A book of this interdisciplinary and comparative scope could never come together without the good counsel of relevant scholars. And so I thank the following individuals who carefully read and commented on individual chapters: Courtney Cazden, James Crawford, Fernand de Varennes, Guus Extra, Nancy Foner, Christine Hélot, Mark Movsesian, Michael Olivas, Concha Maiztegui Oñate, Robert Phillipson, Diane Ravitch, Rosa Santibáñez, Harold Schiffman, Tove Skutnabb-Kangas, and my husband, Joseph Viteritti. Any errors or misjudgments are totally my own. I also thank the students who assisted me on this project over the years: Stefanie Beyer, Vanessa Fang, Peter Le Piane, Kelly McMahon, Rasheeja Page, and Felicia Rovegno. Special thanks go to my son Andrew Viteritti for sharing with me his wealth of knowledge on immigration in Europe and for never tiring of our intense discussions; to my mother, Louise Salomone, for her poignant memories of "Americanization Past"; and to my husband, for viewing with me countless films on the immigrant experience. Words of thanks also go to the dedicated and talented staff of St. John's Law Library, particularly Barbara Traub, interim director and head of Reference and Instructional Services, who skillfully mined a broad terrain of data bases, William Manz, senior research librarian, who met endless requests for interlibrary loans, and Aru Satkalmi, senior research librarian, who provided me with a steady flow of information on education. Finally, much gratitude goes to my editor at Harvard University Press, Elizabeth Knoll, whose gentle editorial suggestions, encouragement, and belief in this project have kept it moving along through the most daunting of times.

Most important, I dedicate this book to the memory of my grandparents, Catarina Di Fiore and Francesco Sansone, who gave me a treasured look at the immigrant longing to become a "true American" with all its anxieties and triumphs.

True American

CHAPTER ONE

The Symbolic and the Salient

I N THE SPRING of 2006, the news media were abuzz with talk of "Nuestro Himno" ("Our Anthem"), a Spanish version of "The Star Spangled Banner." Sung by Latin pop stars and loosely translating the English lyrics, within hours of its release the song triggered a firestorm of negative reactions from news commentators, bloggers, and the general public. The original version, written in 1814 in the throes of battle against the British, brought to mind images of war's devastation and patriotic fervor; the new one suggested a nonviolent struggle for freedom, with reference to a "sacred flag."

For many Americans, the stir was a bit perplexing. In the grand scheme of concerns weighing on the country, modifying the national anthem seemed relatively benign. It was certainly not a novel undertaking. Over the years, at least 300 different versions had been produced in musical styles ranging from rock and roll, to rap, country, and classical. As the storm gathered force, it soon became clear that what was causing the uproar was not the words or the style; it was the particular language itself. More precisely, the language in which the anthem was being sung on Spanish radio stations, nationwide, was the native language of more than twenty-eight million Americans, and this fanned fears that the United States was becoming a bilingual nation with all the attendant conflicts.

The song's British producer rushed to defend it. The intent, he claimed, was merely to help those who do not speak English "fully understand the character of the [anthem], the American flag, and the ideals of freedom that they represent." Others saw it differently. Some called it an act of musical vandalism, a sign of disrespect, a dangerous turn toward cultural divisiveness. A resolution proposed in Congress "remind[ed] the country" why the anthem should be sung exactly as written. Even President George W. Bush joined in, telling the press, "I think that people who want to be a citizen of this country . . . ought to learn to sing the national anthem in English."[1] These words were striking coming from Bush, a native Texan who had unequivocally embraced Spanish and Hispanics throughout his political career. His own State Department had posted four Spanish versions of the "Star Spangled Banner" on its website.

Fast-forward to the spring of 2007, and we see language again caught in yet another maelstrom capturing worldwide media coverage. This time it was New York City's plan to open an Arabic public school, the Khalil Gibran International Academy. Named after the Christian Lebanese poet, the school would be dedicated to teaching the Arabic language and Middle Eastern history and culture along with the standard citywide curriculum. There was nothing unique about the idea of a dual language school combining English- and non-English-speaking students. The city already operated over sixty such programs, with more on the drawing board, in a wide range of languages, such as Spanish, Chinese, Russian, French, and Haitian Creole. The approach, in fact, was appealing to many educators and middle-class parents across the country.

But there was something critically different about this school, and the difference had all to do with Arabic and its association with Islam. The school's religiously diverse board and the fact that its namesake was Christian seemed irrelevant. Critics immediately took exception. The school, they charged, would become a vehicle for political ideology, a potential breeding ground for militant Islamic terrorists. Over the following months, religious and community leaders and city officials publicly staked their ground in the debate. Supporters across the religious spectrum hailed the school's mission to promote tolerance and intercultural understanding. Opponents pounded the media, attacking the school's acting principal, Debbie Almontaser, a Muslim immigrant from Yemen with a long record in city schools and interfaith organizing. Bloggers drew political inferences from her style of dress, posting photos of her in traditional or modified head scarf, with or without jewelry. They referred to her by her Arabic name, Dhabah, which she had not used since childhood.[2] There were news headlines like "Madrassa Grows in Brooklyn," and claims that Arabic language instruction would be "inevitably laden with . . . Islamist baggage."[3] Website postings speculated that students in gym class would be taught "how to wire their bomb vests."[4] Others more tactfully urged caution in view of the "sad reality" that today's terrorism comes largely from "a particular community" and "that's a reality" we must face.[5]

Prominent New Yorkers, including rabbis and the Jewish press, defended the principal and decried the smear campaign waged against her, but to no avail. By the following September, Almontaser had handed in her resignation over an unfortunate misstep that threatened the school's future. She had defended, as a mere expression of female power, the term "intifada" (commonly used in reference to the Palestinian uprising against Israel) printed on a T-shirt sold by a local Arab women's organization. Her attempt to recant her words came too late for her detractors. She later sued the school district to regain her position, but to no avail. On opening day, an interim principal greeted the fifty-five sixth-grade children enrolled in the school, located just a few subway stops from Ground Zero in a Brooklyn neighborhood long noted for its Arab residents, food stores, and restaurants. The students entered the building under police guard, with American and foreign reporters documenting the event. Parents, some mothers wearing head scarves, nervously looked on. Only six of the students could speak Arabic. The rest were English-speaking African-Americans. The student profile hardly suggested an insular haven for children of fanatical Muslim immigrants. In the months that followed, Debbie Almontaser met defeat in federal court and city officials appointed a new principal for the school.[6]

One decade earlier, who would have thought that a translation of the national anthem or a school language program could provoke such deep-seated rancor? But the intervening years had brought seismic changes, and for many Americans the world seemed to be shifting under their feet. In both scenarios, timing and context were crucial. The release of "Nuestro Himno" came on a Friday in the midst of a congressional impasse over immigration reform, with Hispanics taking to the streets and threatening a nationwide boycott of schools and workplaces the following Monday. The debate in Washington centered on protecting the nation's porous borders while addressing the status of the estimated twelve million undocumented immigrants already in the country, most of them from Latin America. At the same time, Congress was wrangling over proposals declaring English the "national" or "unifying" language, similar to laws passed in over half the states. Language had become a flashpoint in the national discussion on immigration. In the case of the Arabic school, the horrific attacks of September 11, 2001, followed by terrorist bombings in London, Paris, and Madrid, along with Arab hostility over U.S. involvement in Iraq, had made New Yorkers particularly fearful of the dangers of Islamic fundamentalism and wary of the city's growing Muslim population.

Both controversies reveal a basic historical truth. In turbulent times, language is often merely a proxy for race, national origin, or religion. Individually and together, these personal points of reference evoke deep anxieties over the effects of immigration on a society's ability to maintain its culture and institutions in the face of changing conditions, what European scholars in the 1990s termed "societal security."[7] In the two situations at hand, it was not simply respect for the national anthem, or the possibility that Spanish was gaining ground, or the undeniable link between Arabic and militant Islamic terrorism that drove these conflicts. Especially in the anthem case, as Web postings and quotes in popular news media made clear, there was a growing sense of discomfort with the "indelible foreignness," a gnawing sense of "otherness," that languages other than English represented to many Americans and a palpable unease that the American "way of life" might dramatically change.[8] Would the country's cafeteria-style menu of "diversity lite" transform into a more normative multilingual and multicultural society? In both instances, though more markedly in the case of Arabic, the conscious promotion of a foreign language and culture engendered, in many Americans, fears of disloyalty to the political principles on which the nation stands. Could foreigners with lifestyles, values, and religious beliefs outwardly different from the mainstream integrate into the American polity as we know it?

These issues have gained national attention as diverse populations of immigrants increasingly preserve their ethnic and linguistic identities in ways large and small. Directly challenging the American canon of assimilation, they give political pundits and public intellectuals ample cause to ponder the pointed question, "Who are we?"[9] With the number of foreign-born in the United States estimated at around thirty-eight million, accounting for nearly 13 percent of the population and growing by about one million each year, this question has no easy answer. The problem is not confined to the United States. Western European countries, in particular, are similarly struggling with mass migration, cultural diversity, and integration. Large numbers of their foreign-born population are Muslims from Turkey or from former European colonies. For them, interrelated matters of race, religion, and language are of critical importance.

This brings us back to New York's Arabic school and the heart of what this book is about. No doubt it is easy to overstate the identification of Arabic with Islam. Nonetheless, the extreme cultural differences that Islam presents to Western societies and the concerns those differences now raise in a post-9/11 world place in stark relief the key role that schooling and language, and their cultural associations, separately and collectively play in shaping individual, group, and particularly national identity. Save perhaps for the Muslim issue, these seemingly intuitive connections often get lost in the immigration debate on both sides of the Atlantic. The oversight is indeed confounding.

Schooling by its very nature is a prime vehicle for indoctrinating the young in a common core of values and political principles. Thirteen state constitutions expressly declare that a central purpose of their educational system is to promote good citizenship, democracy, and free government.[10] In recent decades, the United States Supreme Court has joined the chorus, reminding us that schools are the mechanism through which society "inculcate[s] the habits and manners of civility as . . . indispensable to the practice of self-government," that they are "vitally important for inculcating fundamental values necessary to the maintenance of a democratic political system," and that they are "the most pervasive means for promoting our common destiny."[11] In case after case, the Court has reaffirmed the crucial role that public education plays as "a most vital civic institution for the preservation of a democratic system of government."[12] For the United States, a nation built on abstract ideals of liberty, equality, and republicanism, the public schools have served as the engine for familiarizing successive waves of newcomers, some seemingly more foreign than others, with American ideals and social practices. Cultural and political transformation, including the acquisition of a common language and a new "American" identity, has been part of the implicit agreement and considered critical to the success of that project.[13]

That being said, the sheer effort and necessity to maintain a shared medium of communication, reinforced by a sense of American "exceptionalism," has created a national blind spot regarding other languages and an almost ideological embrace of English monolingualism. Like other "settler societies," including Australia and Argentina, ambivalence over our very diversity and fear of multilingualism's potential to cause ethnic strife have generated a steady centripetal force toward the dominant colonial language and culture to the exclusion of all others.[14] Unlike many other countries, however, the United States has never declared an "official" language. For more than two centuries, the Constitution has remained silent on this question, implicitly leaving the matter to state and local discretion. Meanwhile a covert national policy favoring English and only English has developed, in fact if not in federal law, through an intricate web of customs, institutions, and programs promoting the use of English in all areas of public life.[15]

The nation's Founders themselves were operating within a late eighteenth-century European worldview where the equation of language and national identity was only beginning to take root. As John Marshall, the fourth chief justice of the U.S. Supreme Court, noted in a letter to Noah Webster, geographic and social mobility, rather than public laws, would create "an identity of language through[out] the United States."[16] Even today, the few rights to language use or accommodations found in the law are generally bootstrapped onto antidiscrimination principles founded on race and national origin. But it was Noah Webster, through his reference works promoting a unifying language distinct from British English, who is credited with drawing the conscious connection between language and American identity.[17] "Language," he wrote in 1828, "is the expression of ideas; and if the people of one country cannot preserve an identity of ideas, they cannot retain an identity of language."[18] To Webster's mind, the fate of the republic was "tied inextricably" to the fate of American English.[19] This unofficial commitment to English language dominance laid the ground for the future. For some it was a distinctly American brand pragmatically peppered with linguistic diversity.

In the ensuing years, policies toward other languages have developed gradually as a patchwork quilt of accommodation, tolerance, discrimination, and even repression, much of it focused on schooling. Over the past four decades, in particular, state and federal court decisions, legislative pronouncements, and administrative rulings have largely addressed language as a matter of education policy. Lacking a clear pattern, these indecisive and at times conflicting statements reflect popular attitudes toward immigrants, and particular ethnic groups, whatever those attitudes happen to be at any given time. The more the mainstream has found the group culturally alien, or politically or economically threatening, the more hostile and harsh the official response has been. The truth of this observation has become even more evident in recent years. English Only groups have again achieved political force, primarily in response to the growing visibility of Spanish speakers, many, though not all, of them immigrants or the children of immigrants.

Economic consequences, including job losses and tax burdens, undeniably drive some of the opposition to immigration. Calls for declaring English the official language or for limiting the use of other native languages in schools reflect even deeper anxieties over cultural differences and the overwhelming desire to preserve from further ethnic erosion the Anglo-Saxon core and sense of social solidarity that English both symbolizes and affirms. "Can you speak Spanish in public and still be a real American?" seems to be the burning question. Efforts to officially establish English are also about avoiding those feelings of linguistic and cultural dissonance that bilingual road and store signs, or telephone commands to press "one for English" and "dos para español," engender in a society that warmly embraces monolingualism despite the rhetoric of diversity and the reality of growing multilingualism, especially among immigrants. Though today's politicians, bent on garnering votes, readily understand that Spanish is the "language of politics," the "politics of language" is far more complicated.

The Spanish question and the controversy it has generated draw from differing narratives of *conquest* and *migration* that quietly roil beneath the surface of the debate over language and schooling. Often overlooked in the central immigration story are the more coercive measures that were taken by the government to acquire land and consequently incorporate the inhabitants who spoke languages other than English. For today's Mexican and Native Americans, who have deep ancestral roots in this country, the language debate is especially contentious, at times giving rise to demands for special language entitlements and accommodations. For both groups, becoming "American" was initially not a matter of free choice. Prior to European colonization and westward expansion, both inhabited territory that became absorbed into the United States. With statehood granted to Texas in 1845, the annexation of New Mexico, Arizona, and California three years later, and the exodus created by the Mexican Revolution of 1910, the stage was set for an intermittent flow of Mexican migration, which reached unforeseen proportions in the next century. The original Spanish-speaking inhabitants became a minority group within a nation that one day would find their language and culture threatening as it spread across the continent.

As demonstrated by the disputes over the Spanish anthem and the Arabic school, language carries political baggage and inherent conflicts that weigh heavily in the school setting in a contradictory way. Preserving the native language and culture of newcomers runs counter to the traditional socializing mission of public education. At the same time, forcing children to completely abandon their first language and culture seems morally unjust, developmentally unwise, and politically shortsighted by some contemporary understandings. These tensions are not completely new, but they have been playing out most forcefully in the polarized debate over "bilingual education." The term itself has become more a "political code word" suggesting competing views, rather than a defined set of policies or practices, on educating immigrant-origin students and the use of their native languages.[20] That debate was nationally launched in the federal Bilingual Education Act of 1968, which allocated funds on a competitive basis. The idea was for local school districts to initiate innovative programs designed to counter the effects of poverty and limited English proficiency. Inspired by the civil rights movement, educators and policy makers at that time saw the need to address alarmingly low academic achievement and high dropout rates, particularly among Mexican Americans, although the legislation applied to all language groups.

The poverty factor (dropped in subsequent amendments) and the underlying "deficit" rationale (focusing on a lack of English proficiency as a minus, rather than on potential bilingualism as a plus) proved politically effective in the 1960s world of compensatory education. Yet both also cast a stigma from which the approach would never recover. With no clear vision in the original law as to why or how bilingual education would be provided or what the concept really meant, it soon became apparent that the federal program's goal, grounded in assimilation thinking, was to develop English language skills and not bilingual proficiency. By the same token, state laws expressly mandating bilingual instruction assumed the "deficit" view of difference. Federal court decisions, administrative rulings, and government statements likewise built on the premise that linguistic minority students had a "handicap" to be overcome, a problem to be remedied. Defining legal rights to education in terms like "appropriate" and "effective," federal judges, administrators, and policy makers commonly avoided taking a clear position on the child's native language and culture, deferring to state and local school officials. When they did take a supportive stand, the result proved politically volatile and legally questionable. Even the Supreme Court's 1974 decision in *Lau v. Nichols*, considered the high-water mark of language rights in schooling, called for a "meaningful" education without an affirmative definition.[21] Bilingual programs thus became "educational medicine" for the poor and the disadvantaged rather than a tool for developing the linguistic abilities of all students.

Beginning in the late 1970s, growing concerns over immigration from Latin America, together with reports of students trapped for years in bilingual classrooms without adequately learning English, created a backlash against using, and particularly developing, the child's native language in the schools. The fear was, and still is, that we were creating a permanent language minority with no incentive to acquire the English skills necessary to succeed economically or participate politically in American society. The achievement gap, particularly between Hispanic and white students, continued to widen. Transitional bilingual programs that used the native language merely as a bridge to English instruction came under fire, despite their serving just a small fraction of English language learners (ELLs). Most of these students were still being educated in mainstream classrooms with several hours per week of small-group English as a Second Language support. The one factor the critique often ignored was the obvious effect of poverty on academic achievement. In any case, as English Only proposals gained traction in state policy circles, and educational accountability and high-stakes testing placed a premium on standardized English reading scores, bilingual education lost public and professional support, save for a small core of linguists, researchers, and legal advocates and a shrinking number of immigrant parents. Between 1992 and 2002, enrollment in bilingual programs declined from 37 percent to 17 percent of English language learners, despite an increase of 72 percent in their overall number.

Contributing to the loss were state voter initiatives in California, Arizona, and Massachusetts aimed at replacing bilingual instruction with structured (or sheltered) English immersion. The first uses both English and the student's home language to teach content areas like math and social studies. In the second, materials and instruction are in English but the curriculum is specially designed, and the instruction is linguistically modified, to make English content understandable to ELL students with varying levels of English proficiency. The axe all but completely fell in 2002 when the federal No Child Left Behind Act effectively dismantled the original 1968 law. Although it did not expressly prohibit or mandate any one instructional method, the Act offered pointed incentives for state and local school officials to move students swiftly and exclusively toward English proficiency. At the same time, the legal right to education for ELLs had devolved into a "what works" standard, with neither express mandates nor limits on native language and culture.

Against this convoluted backdrop, many of the arguments now popularly advanced against bilingual education prove mistakenly overworked and outdated. Caught in a pedagogical and sociological time warp, they often unfold as if the immigrant population were static and monolithic, parental preferences were irrelevant, family ties were inconsequential, native language development allowed no nuances or instructional alternatives, language were separable from culture and individual identity, and schools still educated students for a life bounded by national borders. The term itself is becoming obsolete, more often replaced by the less emotionally charged phrase "dual language acquisition."

Upward of twelve million, or 22 percent, of school-age children nationwide are now from immigrant families, more than triple the proportion in 1970. Only about one-quarter of them are foreign-born. Among their families, over half come from Mexico, other Latin American countries, or the Caribbean. Another quarter come from Asia, and about 4 percent from Africa. It has been estimated that by the year 2010, 25 percent of students in kindergarten through grade twelve will be children of immigrants. As of 2007, 21 percent of children aged five to seventeen spoke a language other than English at home. That figure ran as high as 45 percent in California and 32 percent in Arizona.[22] Upward of 5.1 million students fall into the English language learner category, and their numbers are increasing at close to seven times the rate of the total school population.[23] Close to 80 percent of them speak Spanish.

The impact of these numbers on public schooling is striking and, in some cases, unanticipated. While six states—Arizona, California, Florida, Illinois, New York, and Texas—continue to educate about two-thirds of the nation's ELL students, states like North Carolina and Nevada are facing a record number who lack proficiency in English.[24] At least among Hispanics, foreign-born students are more likely than the native-born to live either in these new immigrant states or in emerging ones like Arkansas and Wisconsin, forcing school officials to quickly get up to speed on best practices for educating them.[25]

Two-thirds of ELLs come from families with incomes that fall below 200 percent of the poverty line and have parents who themselves are the products of inadequate schooling, whether in their home countries or in the United States. Many ELLs have significant gaps in their education. Even among those born in the United States, many have not resided continuously in the country or have experienced inconsistent schooling as the result of frequent family relocations or the lack of coherent language instruction within and across the schools attended.[26] The most devastating evidence that public schools are failing these children lies in the end result. Only half of ELLs graduate from high school on time with a regular diploma.[27] On the 2007 National Assessment of Educational Progress (NAEP), fourth-grade ELLs scored thirty-six points below non-ELLs in reading and twenty-five points below them in math. At the eighth-grade level the gaps were even wider—forty-two points in reading and thirty-seven points in math.[28] Especially among Hispanics and certain Asian groups, populations most vulnerable to academic failure, dropout rates remain inordinately high and graduations rates low.

The numbers and diversity of ELL students are daunting even for the United States, a nation with a long history of educating the foreign-born and their children. Sociologists look to the twentieth century's experience integrating the masses of southern and eastern European immigrants as a benchmark for measuring the educational and economic integration of those who have arrived since 1965, when new immigration policies re-opened the nation's borders. The underlying assumption is that, despite excesses at the margins, society's efforts to Americanize earlier groups were reasonably effective in achieving what the schools and other institutions had set out to do. Many Americans heartily embrace that experience as a model for educators to follow now. As the "old" immigrants and their children abandoned their language and culture, the familiar argument goes, so should the "new," and the schools should expect nothing less of them. "Why can't they learn English the way my parents and grandparents did?" is a rhetorical question commonly asked across the country. As reasonable as the question may initially appear, bilingual advocates and others view that period less favorably, using it as a cautionary tale of attitudes and practices that were constraining at best and damaging at worst to many immigrant children. Beyond the psychological and sociological harms, they emphasize, is the dramatic loss in linguistic and cultural resources which, had matters developed otherwise, would have proved valuable to the United States as it emerged as a world leader in the mid-twentieth century.

Over the past forty years, schools irrefutably have become more sensitized to cultural differences among immigrant students. Unlike the Americanizers of the past, educators have adopted various approaches to develop English language skills while encouraging students to be proud of their ethnic heritage. The social studies curriculum has broadened to include the contributions and experiences of additional peoples and historical figures. Schools more commonly sponsor programs and festivals celebrating the ethnic backgrounds of their diverse student populations. The growing backlash to immigration, language accommodations, and multiculturalism, nonetheless, has blurred these sensitivities and provoked sharp disagreements that merely suggest a political dimension to immigrant integration without squarely addressing it. And though the educational establishment has attempted to accommodate differences more or less, the public discourse has remained locked in the cultural assimilation mode of times past. Some, echoing the late Samuel Huntington, still maintain that what unites Americans is an Anglo-Protestant culture and bedrock Christianity.[29] That proposition undeniably ignores the changing demographics of the immigrant population. It also belies a more inclusive acceptance of cultural diversity along with the recognition that immigration is a significant part of American identity.

A number of critical features distinguish the "new" (post-1965) immigrants from the "old." They vary by countries of origin and are more religiously diverse. More directly, racial differences and resulting issues of discrimination hamper their ability to blend into the American mainstream. They also move in a world that has vastly changed the immigrant experience, rendering it far less an abrupt break with the past. Advances in technology and transportation, along with new opportunities for dual citizenship, facilitate transnational activities and dual identities that were far less possible a hundred or even fifty years ago. The recognition afforded ethnic ties in the wake of the civil rights movement has further created a climate where young people from immigrant families now feel free to forge their own sense of what it means to be American. For them, the old melting-pot metaphor is irrelevant to their vision of the present and the future. It also runs counter to the needs of a nation struggling to maintain its place in a changing world.

Global developments, most notably the rise in terrorism from the Middle East and the rapid economic growth of nations like China, have transformed attitudes toward certain foreign languages and cultures, creating an urgent need for individuals with linguistic skills and cultural sensitivities to help navigate the turbulent waters of international affairs. It is not mere happenstance that, since 2001, the number of public schools offering full-time Arabic instruction has quadrupled while enrollment in university Arabic programs has increased by 150 percent.[30] In 2005, congressional resolutions and a presidential proclamation acknowledged the "Year of Languages," promoting foreign language study in the interests of national security and the economy. The following year the federal government launched the National Security Languages Initiative, which is aimed at increasing the number of Americans with advanced proficiency in "strategic languages" critical in addressing global terrorism and the global economy. Arabic and Chinese are high on the list. Yet the same concerns also have heightened fears and distrust of foreigners, their languages, and their ways of life, as the controversy surrounding the Spanish version of the U.S. national anthem and particularly the Arabic school vividly reveal. Language is now viewed socially and politically as both a skill of international necessity and a symbol of national threat, especially when that language is Spanish or Arabic, or the speakers are Muslim, though for different reasons.

In this book, I address these themes, tensions, and developments. I use the ongoing debate over educating children of the "new" immigrants as a prism for exploring the connection between language and identity in an age of globalization, transnationalism, and difference. From there I suggest how this new reality should in turn influence policy and practice. Looking at immigrant education as it has evolved over the past century— from language as a problem, then as a right, and most recently and tentatively as a resource—and using language as a barometer of attitudes toward immigrants, I examine three broad issues: how a fixed assimilative notion of what it means to be American, and its inherent ambiguities, have largely shaped the debate regarding the preservation of immigrant languages; how identities embraced by post-1965 immigrants and their offspring, along with developments beyond the nation's borders, are challenging that notion and its time-worn assumptions; and how legal mandates, policies, and teaching methods might strike a more reasoned balance between the developmental and educational interests of immigrant children and the national interest in maintaining political unity, economic competitiveness, and international esteem in a world that is becoming smaller by the second.

I begin by traveling back in time, debunking the myths of former halcyon days of immigrant schooling in America. Despite persuasive findings to the contrary, those myths have colored present-day perspectives and policies on the education of today's newcomers, the appropriate place of language and culture in their lives, and the identity they are expected to assume. I include beneath the immigrant umbrella both children born abroad and the second generation, many of whom lack sufficient English proficiency to succeed in mainstream classrooms. Digging beneath more recent debates over Official English, transnational lifestyles, and immigrant assimilation, I expose the common misconception that immigrants and their children are resistant to learning English. In doing so, I open the discussion beyond English language learners to address immigrant offspring who are proficient in English but who are exposed to a "heritage language" in their home and may even speak it to some extent. I dismiss the idea that competency in two languages inevitably burdens cognitive development among immigrant children. I suggest that we consider instead the alternative reality of intergenerational bilingualism as a positive secondary trend, one that middle-class immigrant communities have long supported with private resources and that public schools should affirmatively foster for all students who claim a non-English home language.

Unpacking fears of national danger and social disunity that other languages evoke, I attempt to find a more individualized middle ground between the 1970s group-based claims to native language development and the current categorical push toward English Only instruction. I acknowledge the inherent difficulties with legal entitlements to a particular type of education. Yet I also reject legal constraints that deny parents a voice in choosing what is most appropriate for their children in the absence of compelling justifications to the contrary. Without dismissing concerns over the poor academic performance among certain immigrant groups, or denying the weaknesses in early bilingual education efforts, or endorsing a specific education model, I suggest that the lessons of the past, the reality of immigrant lives in the present, and the inevitably growing global demands of the near and distant future, all move us to consider the interests of immigrant children in a "meaningful" education that addresses both the practical need for English proficiency and the long-ignored personal benefits in maintaining ties to the home language and culture.

At the same time, I recognize an equally important concern that bears on national identity but remains remarkably absent from discussions on language and schooling. To the extent that opposition to linguistic diversity stems from fear and uncertainty as to what Americans might talk, think, and act like in the years to come, and where their allegiances might lie, I suggest that schools consciously turn that seeming threat into an opportunity to promote a more inclusive sense of citizenship as they help write the next chapter in the ongoing immigration saga.

Reaching across the Atlantic, I compare the American question of language, identity, and schooling with issues raised, and responses formulated, among western European countries facing a similarly diverse yet somewhat different profile of immigrant students set against a united Europe in the making. The fears evoked in the Arabic school controversy in New York are especially relevant here. Juxtaposing these contrasting pictures, I examine how history and politics shape national discourses and policies on immigrants and their languages. The comparison sheds light on the American landscape, the nuances of assimilation versus integration, and the possibilities and limitations for changing education practices in the United States and abroad. It also exposes the misguided notion, now rejected especially by European Union leaders, that monolingualism promotes economic growth while multilingualism threatens national unity and identity.

In the end, sorting out what is symbolic from what is now salient, raising timely questions in both historical and international perspectives, this book aims to reframe the discussion on the role that public schooling can best play in creating a synergy between language, with its deep associations, and the most current iteration of what it means to be a "true American."

CHAPTER TWO

Americanization Past

ALL TOO OFTEN the educational philosophy and practices of the past are implicitly invoked as a model for the present. Third- and fourth-generation Americans proudly declare that their grandparents or great-grandparents "made it" without any cultural affirmation or acknowledgment. Opposition to language accommodation is justified partly on that premise. Yet this story is overly sentimentalized in popular memory. The narrative, more universally uplifting than factual, both understates and overstates the commonalities between past and present periods of intense immigration.

That being said, many of today's fears and anxieties echo those from a century ago when the United States faced an even more overwhelming influx of newcomers whose cultural differences proved foreign and frightening. At that time, the federal commissioner of education, P. P. Claxton, warned that those immigrants had "little kinship with the older stocks of our population, either in blood, language, methods of thought, traditions, manners, or customs," knew "little of our political and civic life," and were "unused to our social ideals."[1] These words sound hauntingly familiar. Then as now, language was a lightning rod for concerns about unassimilated foreigners, raising calls for extreme measures. Then, as now, public schools were the prime arena for resolving the short- and long-term impacts of mass migration on national unity and identity. Teaching immigrants English was key to that project—though political and "racial" differences, now veiled as linguistic deficiencies, were at least as pressing and more explicitly discussed than today's post-civil-rights sensitivities allow.

A look back at that earlier time can provide a reality check on the "old" immigration, the events that immediately preceded it, and its successes and failures. In retrospect we can see the role that schooling and language together played in Americanization by promoting a particular view of assimilation. That view became engrafted on the psyche of earlier immigrants and carried over to their assimilated offspring who now shape the mainstream consensus on the very same questions. For all those individuals whose ancestors arguably "succeeded," this hopefully will be an eye-opener.

The Old Immigrants

In the mid-1800s, when the common-school crusaders began spreading their message throughout the land, Americans were predominantly mainstream Protestant and English-speaking. That is not to overlook the large numbers of African slaves and Native Americans whose education remained outside the political pale. Up to that time there was a measure of tolerance for the languages of early colonizers in territories not originally settled by the British, including Dutch in New York, French in what became Louisiana, German in Pennsylvania, and Spanish in the southwest.[2] In 1839 Ohio passed a law authorizing German-English instruction upon the request of parents. Louisiana adopted similar legislation in 1847 for French. As late as 1857, school reports in Indiana and Pennsylvania were still published in German. By 1870 the U.S. commissioner of education was heard to declare: "The German language has actually become the second language of our Republic, and a knowledge of German is now considered essential to a finished education."[3]

This apparent acceptance of linguistic diversity would soon change with the inrush of new and different immigrants. Just as the idea of state-operated schools began to gain ground, a combination of economic depression, famine, and political upheavals in northwestern Europe triggered a mass migration that continued for three-quarters of a century, dramatically shaping the mission and substance of American schooling and the place of language in that project. As railroads were built across Europe and the United States, and steamships replaced the old sailing vessels, travel within and between the two continents became more accessible. Europe's poor could make their way to the ports, find low-cost, no-frills travel across the Atlantic, and even work their way into the heartland of America. Together with a continuing flow of British nationals, new settlers from Germany and Scandinavia joined the larger numbers of Irish Catholics coming in the wake of the potato famine. They came with experience in self-government and a high rate of literacy, thus proving more compatible with mainstream U.S. society than the eastern and southern Europeans who followed. Meanwhile, the discovery of gold in California in 1849, combined with depressed agricultural production northwest of Hong Kong, brought three hundred thousand Chinese immigrants, mostly male, over the next several decades.[4] The 1898 annexation of Hawaii freed thousands of Japanese contract laborers from sugar plantations, generating yet another spurt of Asian migration.

In the wake of this flood, tolerance began to be replaced by hostility. What started out as a tacit English-first policy in the early days of the nation's founding gradually transformed into overt English-only laws among the states. Debates over the 1879 revisions to the original 1849 California constitution, for example, revealed common beliefs that Spanish speakers had "ample time to be conversant in the English language if they desired to do so."[5] The changes essentially eliminated Spanish language rights. Meanwhile, the surge in immigration from Germany and other European countries, the intense pressure from Germans to maintain their language in both public and church-run schools, German immigrants' repeatedly unsuccessful requests for federal laws and other documents to be printed in German, and the spread of the German press and cultural institutions, all provoked a rise in nativism. Legislative efforts to limit the use of foreign languages, particularly German, in the schools became widespread. In 1889 and 1890 alone, Illinois, Kansas, Nebraska, New York, North Dakota, Ohio, South Dakota, and Wisconsin all faced similar attempts.[6] Prior to that time, it was not language but rather religious and racial differences that had fomented nativist activities.

Around 1870 a new set of coalescing forces once again changed the face and intensity of immigration. The need for human capital for industrialization pulled a new wave of immigrants to America's shores as economic inequalities, political instability, and religious oppression pushed them to leave Europe. The captains of American industry in the North saw the new immigrants as a ready source of cheap labor. Between 1873 and 1910, an estimated 9.3 million southern and eastern Europeans migrated to the United States, along with much smaller numbers of Arabs, mostly Christian, from Syria and Lebanon.[7] According to 1910 census records, immigrants and their children made up three-quarters of the population of New York, Boston, Chicago, Detroit, and Cleveland. Reestablishing their customs within self-contained and densely populated communities offered the newcomers a level of Old World familiarity and comfort. It also isolated them from the mainstream, giving them an aura of ineradicable difference.

Close to 70 percent of those entering the country between 1900 and 1910 were male.[8] Many were single. Because they left children behind, initially these immigrants placed little burden on local schools. Employed seasonally in low-skilled construction jobs or farming, or in factories, mills, and mines, they traveled back and forth, not unlike today's migrant laborers, treating the Atlantic somewhat like a lake to be crossed to and from work.[9] Their goal was to support their families or buy farmland back home. They lived in squalid boarding houses or labor camps. They typically had little opportunity to interact with Americans, learn English, and assimilate. Some found the living and working conditions unduly harsh and, where politics permitted, returned home, not unlike immigrants of today.[10]

Those who stayed were welcomed by American industry for their labors, but American society became increasingly uneasy with their social practices, low living standards, inability to speak English, high rates of illiteracy, and unfamiliarity with democratic government. Mostly Roman Catholic, members of Eastern Orthodox rites, or Jewish, these immigrants did not share the beliefs of mainstream Protestantism, and their poverty threatened the middle-class social structure. The two went hand in hand. Many of these immigrants had a distinct physical appearance that made them unable to blend invisibly into mainstream society. The developing discipline of sociology, along with social Darwinism and the pseudoscience of eugenics, legitimized the popular belief that genetically based racial differences accounted for the immigrants' undesirable social characteristics or behavior. Poverty was merely a symptom of racial degeneracy, it was thought, and poverty was rampant among them. Implicitly reinforcing those beliefs, beginning in 1899 the U.S. government categorized all newcomers in terms of thirty-six different races, which had less to do with skin color and far more to do with geographic origin, language, and alleged innate attributes.

In 1902, Woodrow Wilson, then a professor of government at Princeton University, declared with certitude that the immigrant stock had altered into "multitudes of men of the lowest class from the south of Italy and men of the meaner sort out of Hungary and Poland, men out of the ranks where there was neither skill nor energy nor any initiative or quick intelligence."[11] A 1903 cartoon in *Judge* magazine entitled "The High Tide of Immigration—A National Menace" graphically captured the depths of those sentiments. In the cartoon, a helpless Uncle Sam clutches the American flag as he leans against a high rock and looks down fearfully at a sea of brown-faced males washing up on the shore in a high tide of "Riff-Raff Immigration." The men wear hats with the labels *anarchist, pauper, illiterate, outlaw, mafia, criminal,* and *degenerate.* Carved into the rock are the words, "Danger to American Ideas and Institutions."[12] These fears crystallized in the work of anti-immigrant organizations, one of the most notable being the Immigration Restriction League, founded in 1894 by Boston Brahmin Harvard graduates. The IRL waged a tireless public information campaign against the menace of unbridled immigration and relentlessly lobbied Congress for legal restrictions.[13]

A federal immigration commission report presented to Congress in 1911 strengthened the restrictionist cause. Named after its chairman, Senator William P. Dillingham of Vermont, the Dillingham Report was an ambitious work of forty-two volumes covering the potential impact of immigration on the American economy and workers. One particularly revealing volume, *Dictionary of the Races or Peoples,* made repeated references to the changing "source" and "character" of immigration and the overwhelming predominance of Italians, Jews, and Slavs. The authors described the new immigrants as "far less intelligent [as a class] than the old, approximately one-third of all those over fourteen years of age when admitted being illiterate." They distinguished between the old immigrants and the new, the former having come "to be a part of the country," and the latter merely intending to "profit" monetarily and then return back home.[14] The report identified forty-five races or peoples among the immigrants, thirty-six indigenous to Europe. And while it claimed to use "race" in the "broad sense" of language and geography, it built on a taxonomy of physical, intellectual, and attitudinal "difference" suggesting a hierarchy of individual worth.[15] This was pure grist for the eugenicist mill.

As commentators have noted, the "realities of race" had taken on an "almost casual quality."[16] Yet such "dehumanizing stereotypes" that confused nature and culture kept American racism from facing the "dirty secret" of its social construction.[17] The report clearly forecast how whiteness and assimilation would become central to immigration policy over the coming decade. In the end, the commission recommended a literacy test as the "most feasible single method" for limiting immigration.[18]

Competing Views

Amid this crescendo to stop the flow of immigrants into the country, others focused on "Americanization," a term that has come to describe the effort in the first two decades of the twentieth century to acculturate those already here. Yet there was widespread disagreement as to what Americanization meant—its underlying purpose, its ultimate vision of

America, and what governmental and social institutions, most notably the public schools, should do to achieve the desired end. Motives ran from repressive and somewhat xenophobic interests to magnanimous desires to help the immigrants adjust and overcome the hardships they faced.

In the early twentieth century, the renowned professor Elwood P. Cubberley of Stanford University was notorious among educators for espousing a nativist view toward newcomers. Like those advocating immigration restrictions, Cubberley believed that the newly arrived immigrants were intrinsically different from the northern Europeans who had preceded them. "Illiterate, docile, lacking in self-reliance and initiative, and not possessing the Anglo-Teutonic conceptions of law, order, and government," he noted, "their coming has served to dilute tremendously our national stock, and to corrupt our civic life." The task of educators, he declared, was to "break up these groups or settlements, to assimilate and amalgamate these people as part of our American race, and to implant in their children, so far as can be done, the Anglo-Saxon conception of righteousness, law and order, and popular government."[19] There was no room in the United States for "hyphenated" Americans.[20] That belief, though perhaps not so harshly or explicitly stated, would prevail for the next half century until openly challenged in the wake of the civil rights movement.

Yet even as more diverse peoples sought economic and political refuge in America, other writers and scholars offered a more sentimental view of immigration's transformative experience. Some of them foreigners themselves, they presented a vision of American identity drawn not from fixed Anglo-Saxon traditions but from a dynamic amalgamation that was forming as the immigrants intersected with each other and with the larger society. For them, no one race would form the unique standard; society would progress in a constant state of flux. Such was the implicit message of Israel Zangwill's play, *The Melting Pot*. First performed in Washington, D.C., in October 1908, the title provided the metaphor that forever shaped American discourse and debate on immigration and ethnicity.[21] Over time, Zangwill's work invited a steady stream of rebuttals that continue to the present day.

Use of the imagery of "melting" for regeneration or rebirth was not new. In his 1782 *Letters from an American Farmer*, Frenchman J. Hector St. John de Crèvecoeur observed, "Here individuals of all nations are melted into a new race, whose labors and posterity will one day cause great changes in the world."[22] In a small sense Crèvecoeur was right. The shedding of Old World constraints—poverty, slavery, superstition, patriarchy, caste, and such—is still a forceful part of the American mythology. Yet Crèvecoeur also assumed that assimilation was fast and that it was easy. On that count, history would ultimately prove him overly optimistic. Toward the close of the next century, a young historian, Frederick Jackson Turner, took Crèvecoeur's metaphor in a new direction. Turner proposed that it was the western frontier and not the forces within eastern cities, or the country's European heritage, that was shaping the template for a new American character and society.[23] But it should not be forgotten that, compared to today's newcomers, the earlier immigrants of Turner's grand fusing were more similar to each other and to the original Anglo-Saxon settlers in culture, political ideals, and physical characteristics.

Zangwill, an English Jew himself, not only recaptured the metaphor from the western frontier, but boldly added to the mix the variegated lot of newly arrived immigrants, fusing them all into a singular new national identity. He even intimated Divine intervention with a hint of American exceptionalism. As proclaimed by the play's protagonist, a young Russian Jewish immigrant, "Germans and Frenchmen, Irishmen and Englishmen, Jews and Russians—into the Crucible with you all! God is making the American . . . He will be the fusion of all races, the coming superman."[24] In the end, former identities would be abandoned as all races and groups made an equal contribution to a new American sense of self. As historian John Higham pointed out, the play draws up "a riptide of conflicting values and emotions." The "melting pot" metaphor itself suggests that assimilation does not occur naturally but instead needs someone to control or supervise it. Meanwhile, the industrial imagery— "fraught with the menacing heat and the flaming intensity of a steel mill"—implies that the process is not without pain, but is totally worth it.[25]

Zangwill dedicated his work to Theodore Roosevelt, who hailed it as "a great play." Although Roosevelt acknowledged that immigrants willing to assimilate should be treated as equals with all others, he repeatedly railed against the "hyphenated" American. "The sooner he returns to the country of his allegiance, the better," he declared.[26] At the close of the war, fearful that Americans would revive their foreign associations, Roosevelt warned, "We have room for but one flag, the American flag. . . for but one language . . . the English language, for we intend to see that the crucible turns our people out as Americans, and . . . not as dwellers in a polyglot boarding house; and we have room for but one . . . loyalty to the American people."[27]

Zangwill's play quickly engaged the public imagination. Some spoke glowingly of the melting pot. It would create an implicitly superior human being, different and better than the individual nationalities that went into it. Yet the idea gave little immediate comfort to the national consciousness. Verbal attacks on immigrants became progressively more bitter and racist, while social workers, educators, and scholars ran to the immigrants' defense. In a litany of articles in popular magazines and journals, sympathetic voices maintained that the problem was not the immigrants' ethnic makeup but instead overly rapid urbanization and society's failure to constructively help them adjust to their new home. If anything was to be feared, they warned, it was the fact that the children of the foreign-born were assimilating too fast, adopting some of the less desirable features of American life.[28]

When the more repressive side of Americanization took hold in the war years, those with sympathetic views more affirmatively validated the immigrants as individuals and as members of defined cultural groups. Responding with some fear to the outbursts of excessive chauvinism and reactionary nationalism, others argued that to irrevocably grant one race—Anglo-Saxons—the right to define the American character, simply on the basis of "priority of habitation," defied the fundamental spirit of American democracy. In that view, becoming American was about adopting certain social ideals that had nothing to do with dress or speech. Abandoning other languages, traditions, and "spiritual allegiances" was not essential to the task.[29]

Two whose voices especially stood out were Horace Kallen and Randolph Bourne. Writing in *The Nation* in 1915, Kallen proposed that new Americans should be encouraged to keep the best of their distinct ancestral traditions, which in turn would contribute to mainstream American life. Kallen was not merely looking for ethnic differences to be tolerated; he expected them to be affirmed. For him, "the right to be equal did not contradict the right to be different."[30] In his 1924 book, *Culture and Democracy in the United States,* he introduced the phrase *cultural pluralism.* Although barely recognized in its time, Kallen's work is now considered a direct ancestor to modern-day multiculturalism.

Bourne, admittedly influenced by Kallen, developed the idea of "multiple citizenship" in a 1916 landmark essay published in the *Atlantic Monthly.* To his mind, the diverse nationalistic feelings that some immigrants were expressing in response to the war suggested that the "melting pot" was failing. In its stead, Bourne envisioned a more dynamic "transnational" America where the polity was constantly in a state of re-creation. America, he predicted, would be what the immigrants, and not what the "ruling class" of British stock, wanted it to be. For Bourne, the immigrants' culture and European attachments presented an outstanding opportunity to create a richer and more cosmopolitan ethos that would be a model for other nations.[31] Bourne is credited with having sown the intellectual seeds for modern-day views on transnationalism. But even those who ascribed to this bold idealism were realistic enough to question whether the "dominant classes" really wanted such a society.[32] With Americans marching off to war against immigrants' homelands, and radically left-leaning views migrating from across the Atlantic, cries for 100 percent Americanism became louder and more certain.

In 1920, as the United States was emerging from a wartime mentality, two full-length explorations of immigrant assimilation, though not totally of the same mind as Kallen's, gave new support to the concept of cultural pluralism. Both were far ahead of their time. The first, by Isaac Berkson, extolled the benefits of bilingualism, biculturalism, and "double allegiances." Giving particular attention to the Jews, Berkson maintained that knowledge of an additional language and culture gives perspective, not only enriching the individual personality but opening the mind to understanding differences among nations and perhaps even removing tendencies toward war. Berkson recognized the possibilities for conflicting political loyalties, but seemed confident that compulsory schooling would go far in mitigating the potential dangers.[33] Julius Draschler went even further, suggesting that the state become actively involved in promoting "cultural democracy," whereby the public schools would affirmatively offer programs emphasizing the cultural backgrounds of the nation's diverse population.[34] Though these arguments bore no visible influence on education policy of the day, they resurfaced decades later to support contemporary views on bilingual education, heritage language programs, and multicultural studies.

Education for Americanization

Throughout this period, the overall numbers, diversity, and continuous flow of immigrant children into the schools were disheartening and disruptive. In 1909, 58 percent of the students in thirty-seven of the country's largest cities had foreign-born parents. In Boston it was 64 percent, in Chicago 67 percent, and in New York a stunning 72 percent. Nationally they represented sixty distinct ethnic groups.[35] These newcomers sent school enrollments soaring. Between 1899 and 1914, the school population of New York increased by 60 percent. On any day following a steamship rolling into the harbor, school officials could find a hundred new arrivals on their doorstep.[36] Classrooms designed for twenty students often had to accommodate three times that many. Students commonly sat two, sometimes three, to a desk, causing illnesses to spread like wildfire.[37] Some children settling into new communities never even reached the schools. If there was no record of their arrival, there was no way the authorities could enforce compulsory education laws.

State governments and professional organizations began to weigh in on local school committees. As early as 1891, the National Education Association (NEA) declared the "right of the child to an elementary education in the language of the nation, and the duty of the State to secure him that right." NEA leaders loudly sounded the alarm that "foreign colonies" were forming with "a purpose of preserving foreign languages and traditions and . . . destroying distinctive Americanism."[38] Three-quarters of a century later the same group would do an about-face and lay the foundation for federal legislation recognizing the child's home language and culture. Yet as the century was coming to a close, the NEA, like other professional groups, viewed public education as a key force in maintaining political cohesion above social diversity.

The task of converting newcomers into virtuous citizens, speaking one language and pledging allegiance to one flag, demanded both a more activist role for the state and a more expanded role for the schools.[39] The child seemingly belonged more to the state and less to the family, a fact that many foreign parents, especially those from rural backgrounds and unaccustomed to schooling, found difficult to accept. For some groups, truancy and dropout rates were especially high. Teachers and school administrators found themselves dealing with problems for which their Normal School training had not prepared them: bathing students to remove lice; teaching good manners, standards of cleanliness, and appropriate dress; accommodating older students with limited or no prior schooling either in their native country or in the United States; providing lunch to children who were poorly nourished; navigating foreign cultures and attitudes toward formal education; overcoming the immigrants' suspicion toward government institutions; communicating with parents who could not speak English. The tasks were endless. In one school in New York City, a thousand baths were administered in one week. As one visitor reported, "In nearly every classroom that I entered the atmosphere was foul. Sometimes even the assembly hall and the corridors were distinctly offensive."[40] As the school struggled to transform the immigrants, the immigrants were transforming the school and in ways that educators resisted and resented.

Meanwhile, as historian Diane Ravitch notes, "Early twentieth-century public schools performed no miracles for first- and second-generation children of European descent . . . The curriculum was rigid and irrelevant to children's lives, the classes were overcrowded, and the teachers (many of them second- or third-generation Irish or Germans) had no special affection for the immigrant children or for their parents' strange culture."[41] Not unlike today, many of the youngest children who spoke no English when they entered school were actually born in the United States but lived in ethnic enclaves where only their home language was spoken.

When the federal Bureau of Education initiated a national investigation into immigrant education in 1914, it found that with the exception of New Jersey, state funding for immigrant classes was nonexistent.[42] Some local school systems, like those of New York, Cleveland, and Detroit, initiated special classes, variously called "steamer" or "C" classes. These essentially were immigrant reception centers intended to allow non-English-speaking children a period of time, anywhere from six weeks to six months, to learn enough English to function, however haltingly, in the regular program. They were a rough approximation of today's "structured English immersion." Though progressive for their day, the "C" classes served but a small number of students. In New York, where they originated, they never exceeded 2 percent of the total school enrollment, a result of severe overcrowding, limited resources, and inertia and opposition among teachers and principals.[43]

Undoubtedly this was a vast improvement over placing all new arrivals, regardless of age, into the lowest grades with the idea that this would enable them to more efficiently and effectively learn English—a practice both distressing for the over-age immigrants and unsettling for the English-speaking children who were of appropriate age.[44] Even worse was the practice of placing immigrant students in classes for the mentally deficient. A more typical strategy was total "submersion" in a classroom combining English- and foreign-speaking students with a teacher who spoke only English. It was not uncommon for schools to hold students back repeatedly in the same grade, which merely encouraged them to drop out at an early age. In 1911 it was reported that, among children of foreign-born fathers who belonged to a non-English-speaking "race," 43.4 percent were identified as "retarded," that is, older than the normal age for his or her grade.[45]

For southern and eastern European immigrants, the school situation was often uncaring and thoughtless. For Native American children as well as Asian immigrant children, particularly on the West Coast, it was totally unjust. In 1885 the state of California had adopted a constitutional provision, amended in 1893 and not repealed until 1947, allowing school districts to segregate children of Asian and Native American heritage. On that authority, the San Francisco School Board in 1905 passed a resolution establishing separate schools for Chinese and Japanese students. Board members believed that the "co-mingling of such pupils with Caucasian children" was "baneful and demoralizing in the extreme," their "ideas" being "widely divergent from those of Americans." The following year, the board ordered all ninety-three Japanese children to attend the segregated Chinese school in Chinatown. Only under threat of legal action from the federal government did the board agree to rescind its segregation order.[46] For Mexican children, the law was less clearly defined but equally unjust. School districts in California and Texas commonly segregated them under the guise of addressing their language differences, a practice that remained until struck down by a federal court in 1946 in a precursor to *Brown v. Board of Education.*[47]

Of the European immigrants, many were eager to enjoy the opportunities America had to offer, but some were reluctant to abandon tradition. Yet as Oscar Handlin has noted, tradition was "embedded in a remote and irrecoverable place" not easily accessible to their children who had never been there. And so they sought surrogates in religion and language.[48] In a number of cities, Roman Catholic churches established Polish, Lithuanian, German, and to a lesser extent Italian bilingual schools staffed by religious orders whose members themselves were typically foreign-born. Sparing children the cultural alienation of public schooling, these parochial schools were often more successful in keeping students enrolled beyond the sixth grade.[49] Many native-born Americans failed to comprehend this close association between language and religious devotion. For some immigrants, though, past repressions that had threatened that association made it all the more intimate. For central Europeans who had experienced nationalization efforts in their conquered homelands, language itself was a defining group symbol.

This was not a phenomenon unique to those newly arrived. Germans in the Midwest and French Canadians in the upper New England states, fearing that losing their language meant losing their faith and identity, had long maintained religion-based language schools. Lutheran congregations, predominantly German but also Scandinavian, as well as Greek Orthodox churches made similar efforts to preserve the language and culture in their children. The first permanent Greek day school in the country opened in Chicago in 1908.[50] Minnesota alone had more than 350 church-run schools as late as 1917. In less than one-third of them were students taught in English.[51] Not all religious leaders, however, supported cultural maintenance. Most Roman Catholic clergy, predominantly of Irish descent, firmly believed that immigrants should quickly assimilate. Between 1911 and 1918, the number of Japanese language schools grew from one in San Francisco to eighty nationwide, with more than two thousand students, in addition to forty-seven kindergartens with more than a thousand students.[52] These schools, which were not tied to religion, taught not only the Japanese language but the culture and traditional values that Japanese parents wanted to pass on to the next generation.

Foreign-language schools, however, served only a minute fraction of immigrant children. Some of the programs were not even full-time but merely met after the regular school day. The vast majority of children could be found in the public schools, which became incubators for social and cultural adaptation. Administrators and teachers presented a common front, expecting children to quickly conform to American, or more specifically Anglo, social standards. They unquestioningly and dispassionately Anglicized the newcomers' given names, their tastes in food, their dress, and their outlook on life. As Julia Richman, a New York City district superintendent, told the NEA in 1905, the immigrants "must be made to realize that in forsaking the land of their birth, they were also forsaking the customs and the traditions of that land; and they must be made to realize an obligation, in adopting a new country, to adopt the language and customs of that country."[53]

So eager were many of the immigrants to propel their children into the American mainstream that they showed little direct resistance to the "cultural evangelism of the school."[54] If they could not transform themselves, at least the public schools would transform their children into the total Americans they themselves could never hope to be. Some, particularly eastern Europeans, had left homelands where they were persecuted or excluded from schooling or denied basic rights, and so they were immensely grateful for whatever the public schools had to offer. Educators of the day noted how intent many of the foreigners were, regarding their children's elementary education in particular. Contrary to what one would assume, children of the foreign-born had one-third the illiteracy rate of native-born Americans.[55] Even when parents discouraged their children from continuing in school, usually it was not from animosity toward the American "creed" but from more practical economic necessity.

Not unlike today, some children left in frustration, realizing the gap between the school's rhetoric of equal opportunity and the reality of ethnic ascription.[56] Truancy rates were staggeringly high. Compulsory attendance laws were unevenly enforced. Children as young as ten worked in factories or mills. Some, having dropped out of secondary school, attended part-time continuation schools that provided vocational skills training. Educators often made scarce efforts to encourage them otherwise. Even when school officials tried to intervene, they met opposition from families in need of the meager sums of money their young children could bring into the home. Among the children of immigrants from non-English-speaking countries, high school enrollment was staggeringly low as compared with children of native-born whites—13 versus 32 percent in New York City, 18 versus 42 percent in Chicago.[57]

Whereas the day schools did little to consciously ease the children's transition or ensure their academic success, the night programs were more proactive in offering classes in English skills and American principles to the children's parents. Reformers warned that it was impossible to educate children in American "language, ideals and habits" if in the evening they returned to an ethnically isolated community and a home where they heard no English and had no contact with American mores.[58] Evening schools taught the immigrants more than English to increase their earning power; they put them closer to the American way of life and taught them tolerance and respect for people's differences. In 1905 the Chicago evening schools were reportedly bringing together forty-seven nationalities.[59] Programs were largely local initiatives, at times begun at the request of the immigrants themselves.[60] Meanwhile, with financial support from the Committee for Immigrants in America, the federal Bureau of Education established a Division of Immigrant Education with investigators and other staff to study the Americanization question.[61]

The schools were not alone in their efforts to integrate immigrant children and their families into the social fabric of America. Liberal Progressives, particularly settlement house workers, along with middle-class immigrant leaders, worked tirelessly at prodding the immigrants to study the English language, American history, and political institutions and to become familiar with the economic system. Both groups presented a humanistic and democratic alternative to harsher Americanization concepts of assimilation, although they parted ways on their ultimate goals.

Beginning in the 1890s, young social reformers, college-educated and from middle-class Protestant backgrounds, many of whom were women, pushed for legislation that acknowledged the cultural contributions newcomers could make to their adopted land, assuring them that, at least in the short-run, they need not abandon the past to become American. Their most lasting legacy was the establishment of settlement houses in urban areas. Living among the poor, they tried to bridge the cultural divide between the immigrants and the larger society. Their inspirational and organizational leader was Jane Addams, founder of Hull House in

Chicago, who imagined a national identity that could continually renew and transform itself as the immigrants engaged in a vibrant interchange with American culture.[62] But she and her Progressive colleagues also worked to inculcate mainstream Protestant republican virtues, which they believed were essential to a unified society. For them, ethnic solidarity and segregation were merely a temporary state, a period of adjustment, that would continue to flourish until assimilation gradually but inevitably ran its course.

Together with liberal Progressive thinkers, the settlement houses played a crucial role in reforming the public schools.[63] For philosopher and educator John Dewey, whose influence on the Progressive movement in education still provokes debate, the hyphen should connect rather than separate.[64] Education, broadly defined and across generations, was a key element. It was the responsibility of the schools, he maintained, to "teach each [ethnic] factor to respect every other, and . . . to enlighten all as to the great contributions of every strain in our composite make-up." Yet Addams and her colleagues also saw the harsher side of common or public schooling. As Addams observed, urban schools, in trying to present to immigrant children a standard of how "normal" Americans and their families looked and acted, in the end merely confirmed, rather than challenged, these children's feelings of marginality. Such feelings were a prerequisite for what she called the "American process of elimination," a "negative process of Americanization" wherein what one acquired was less important than what one left behind and forgot.[65] If, as Horace Mann had stated, the common school would be "the great [economic] equalizer of the conditions of men—the balance-wheel of the social machinery," it was also reducing diversity to the least common denominator.[66]

Immigrant middle-class organizers similarly established community centers staffed by foreign-born social workers and educators. The idea was that those who shared the immigrants' language and culture could best be entrusted with brokering and implementing ethnic policies and assimilation. Unlike the liberal Progressives, ethnic-group leaders embraced the idea of "unity within diversity" along with a hyphenated Americanism, establishing their rights as a group and not just as individual citizens. The survival of ethnic identity was the final shape of American society, not just a means but an end in itself. For them, "partial acculturation without assimilation" was the preferred pattern for immigrants in adapting to their new home. While they should become Americanized in dress, speech, and even politics, and cooperate with other groups, they should remain socially distinct. Immigrant-run community centers actively promoted ethnic art, history, music, drama, and language.[67] Of course, one can easily question the underlying motives. By preserving ethnic attachments, immigrant leaders were no doubt ensuring not just a collective "American future" for their people but their own positions of influence.[68]

Wartime Patriotism

Despite their differences, settlement workers and ethnic leaders recognized the immigrants' distinct qualities. Other activists and reformers were less sensitive and patient and therefore less tolerant. They looked for immediate results, demanding a revolution in the life of the immigrant, seemingly unaware of their own families' evolution over several generations. Again there was a sense that the immigrants' inability to speak English and to follow American customs placed them on a lower plane mentally and morally than the native-born. Between 1910 and 1914, groups like the North American Civic League for Immigration, along with state agencies and the federal Bureaus of Education and Naturalization, affirmatively promoted English language and citizenship classes to assimilate the immigrants. The League's affiliate organization, the Committee for Immigrants in America, soon set the campaign on a national scale, supplying funds to the federal Bureau of Education to support Americanization programs in the schools.

These intertwined public and private initiatives, while undeniably necessary, laid the groundwork for a more nationalistic side to Americanization that took off full-throttle during and following World War I. At that point the country was being swept by both patriotic fervor and panic about immigration, as many Americans began to fear that national unity could be undermined by immigrants' conflicting loyalties. Reports that immigrants, some already naturalized, were returning to their homelands to join the fight revealed the potential dangers of dual citizenship and dual allegiances and shocked complacent Americans into action. The Russian Revolution in 1917, the birth of the Communist Party of America two years later, and the increasing involvement of immigrants in labor disputes in New England and elsewhere gave added urgency to the national movement for Americanization. As the war put in question the loyalties of Germans in particular, fear of anarchist strains among the foreign-born in general made their languages, cultures, and social institutions all the more threatening. Transforming immigrants into narrowly defined "Americans" became a national obsession.

A critical point came in May 1915 when the Committee for Immigrants in America formed a National Americanization Day Committee. The chief purpose was "to promote a national movement to bring American citizens, foreign-born and native alike, together on July 4, national Independence Day, to celebrate the common privileges and define the common loyalties of all Americans wherever born." The demands for Americanization activities quickly escalated, moving the group to change its name to the National Americanization Committee (NAC) until it dissolved in 1919.[69] In October 1915 the *New York Times* carried the front-page headline "Eminent Citizens Join a Patriot Band." The article reported on the group's official formation at a dinner hosted by Mr. and Mrs. Vincent Astor. The guest list included Mrs. Cornelius Vanderbilt, Thomas A. Edison, Columbia University President Nicholas Murray Butler, and the federal commissioner of education, P. P. Claxton. The "haves" were taking up the cause of the newly arrived "have-nots" in the hope of "welding the immigrants into a single nation."[70] With growing discomfort over the war in Europe and a rising sense of patriotism, the NAC set three points as the cornerstone of its "America First" campaign: the English language, American citizenship, and American standards of living. The group's goals were clear and unequivocal: to assimilate, naturalize, and educate the immigrant. As Nathan Glazer put it, "This was the melting pot in operation, with a vengeance."[71]

In her 1916 book *Straight America*, NAC director Frances Kellor argued that Americanization was essential to a more vital nationalism. A critical component of that effort was a common language. In its absence, she warned, the immigrant and the native-born American could not come together in a "common Americanism." A key strategy in the NAC's "English First" campaign was to engage industry. Beginning with a well-planned citywide experiment in Detroit, the NAC convinced employers to provide inducements for workers to attend evening classes. Some employers threatened to fire workers who did not attend. Others offered minimal wage increases as a reward for attendance. Still others merely made it clear that they preferred workers who were trying to learn English.[72] A *Detroit News* editorial touted the political and social benefits: "As soon as a reasonable command of the language is acquired the natural prejudice that exists between the native born and the foreign born fades away because the English-speaking alien appears to be one of us, having yielded to the process of complete assimilation."[73]

The NAC initially presented Americanization in terms of mutual obligations: the foreign-born would adopt the English language and American ways, and the native-born would accept the immigrants as equal partners in a common destiny. When the country entered the war in

1917, the NAC turned over nearly its entire staff and equipment to the national government. At that point, the group's rhetoric became more overtly nationalistic, as did the tone of the country. The fact that one out of three immigrants had come from nations fighting the Allies provoked fears of divided loyalties. Reports that 70 percent of the ten million men who had registered for the draft, most of whom were immigrants, were totally illiterate, unable to even sign their names, was a wake-up call to the nation and especially to school officials as to how critical the language question had become.[74] For those reasons the federal government began pressuring religiously based bilingual schools to emphasize English language skills.[75]

The following year the government placed "Americanization as a War Measure" before the American people. In his opening remarks to a conference convened in 1918, Secretary of Interior Franklin K. Lane invoked Americanization as a religious crusade. Calling his audience "prophets of a new day," the "missionaries who are to go forth," he urged them to "preach Americanism," which he described as "something mystical," the "most advanced spirit that has come to man's spirit from above." He cautioned the nation's leaders that the recent downfall of Russia, with no sense of nationality, high illiteracy, and no means of appreciating democracy among its people, should serve as a warning lest a similar fate befall America. Among the resolutions passed was a recommendation that all schools conduct all elementary instruction only in English. At the group's urging, Lane appointed a committee to lobby Congress for federal leadership in promoting the teaching of English along with "systematic instruction" in American ideals, standards, and citizenship."[76] The Bureau of Education distributed thousands of circulars, newsletters, bulletins, pamphlets, and "America First" posters offering suggestions on how to carry forth the crusade to Americanize the immigrants.[77] Later that year, in his annual report to the secretary of the interior, the commissioner of education called the teaching of English the "first step" in the "fusing process" of Americanization. That process required "every bit of school machinery" to accomplish the task.[78]

The end of hostilities in Europe the following November should have put the Americanization campaign to rest. But the "Red Scare," and the fact that some immigrants were sympathetic to the Bolsheviks, kept the movement's spirit alive just as it was beginning to expire. By the close of 1919, the federal Department of Justice had arrested nearly five thousand individuals, and 2,635 aliens faced deportation for actions against the government. The following June, Congress passed legislation authorizing the exclusion and deportation of all alien anarchists and others who advocated overthrow of the U.S. government by force. Fear of aliens some-times resulted in mob actions.[79] Patriotic elements publicly displayed the Constitution as the symbol of American democracy. Others sought to put First Amendment freedoms of thought and expression on hold in the in-terests of national security. The paradox was striking, though not un-thinkable in hindsight, as calls for suppression of free speech during "wartime" have become common up to the present day.[80]

Some educators and child advocates, on the other hand, sensed that the Americanization campaign defied fundamental American ideals. In a 1918 address sponsored by the National Security League, Arthur Somers, president of the New York City Board of Education, warned that Ameri-canization would not succeed unless the country recognized what immi-grants bring and not merely what it could offer them, and unless local communities invited immigrants into their activities "not in a spirit of pa-tronage, but in the spirit of fellowship for which America stands."[81] He underscored the importance of learning English, echoing his remarks from earlier in the year when he had called English a "common lan-guage," the "crux . . . that binds nations together and makes men and women love each other."[82]

The final Americanization conference met in 1919 under the auspices of the Americanization Division of the Bureau of Education. The pro-gram highlighted distinct differences between the nationalistic concerns of government officials, despite conciliatory rhetoric to the contrary, and the immigrant-oriented views of educators, community organizers, and others. The language question took center stage. The remarks made at the conference would lead one to think that Americanization was largely a matter of learning English, and that all the other problems immigrants faced—such as poor housing, inadequate health care, and labor exploita-tion—were of less significance in their struggle to adjust to their new en-vironment.

Near the outset, Commissioner of Education P. P. Claxton asserted, "English is the language of the United States . . . It is the common means of expression; it is the air that we breathe, and without a knowledge of English one can never begin to know the American people and Ameri-can ideals." He urged that public, private, and parochial schools must all teach English and that their work "must be done" in English. Al-though he said that immigrants need not "forget their own language," he stopped short of suggesting that the state should in any way help them preserve or develop their native tongues. He urged the schools to teach the foreign-born the "ideals and history" of the country and the "fun-damental meaning of democracy," including "equality of opportunity."

Somewhat ambiguously he suggested that, in the process of transforming immigrants into "good Americans," "[we will] broaden our own ideals, and enrich our own material and aesthetic lives."[83]

Others expressed a similar but more affirmatively additive view of Americanization, suggesting that immigrants could merely add English to their linguistic repertoire rather than abandon their home language. The executive director of the Educational Alliance, a New York group working with Jewish immigrants, called it a process of "reciprocal adjustment." As the immigrants were changing their point of view, enlarging their experiences, adding a new language, and strengthening their understanding of American political ideals and structure, he explained, they were likewise influencing native-born Americans in comparable ways.[84] The president of the Slovak League was more direct, warning that to "forc[e] the English language on the immigrants by law" would be counterproductive. It would merely remind them of the very oppression that had driven them from their homelands. Becoming a "true American patriot," he advised, meant embracing American ideals, and this could be accomplished "without the full mastery of English."[85] A sociology professor from Oberlin College called for English to stand as "our medium of opportunity and not as an instrument of annihilation."[86]

In the end, as one observer recalled, the conference revealed how fragmented the Americanization project had become.[87] By the following autumn, with no funds forthcoming from Congress, the Bureau of Education was forced to close its Americanization Division and abandon its role in the Americanization movement. Feeling defeated in what had become her life's work, Frances Kellor lamented that "[b]eyond the slogans of 'a common language and a common citizenship'. . . . America, the greatest country in the world, has no national domestic policy whatsoever and no organization as a government for dealing with race assimilation, its most delicate and fundamental problem."[88]

The following year, many states overtly demanded conformity among foreign-speaking immigrants, underscoring the deep fears the war had evoked. Many passed legislation calling for the creation of evening classes in English and citizenship for immigrant adults, as well as courses in civics and American democracy for their children.[89] Several states required all persons between the ages of sixteen and twenty-one who could not speak, read, or write English on a fifth-grade level to attend evening classes for four to eight hours a week. Some states, including Rhode Island and Utah, fined those who failed to attend. In a page that could have been torn from today's newspapers, the Illinois law best defined the rationale underlying these rules: immigrants should learn English "because the English language is the common as well as official language of our country, and because it is essential to good citizenship that each citizen shall have or speedily acquire, as his natural tongue, the language in which the laws of the land, the decrees of the courts, and the announcements and pronouncements of its officials are made, and shall easily and naturally think in the language in which the obligations of his citizenship are defined."[90]

In a sweeping 1918 proclamation declaring English the official language of the country and the state, W. L. Harding, governor of Iowa, mandated not only English as the medium of instruction in all Iowa public and private schools, but that conversation in all public places in the state—on trains, on the telephone, in public addresses and church worship—should be in English.[91] In 1920, Nebraska was the first state to establish English as an official language by constitutional amendment. Three years later, Illinois was the first to declare "American" (changed to "English" in 1969) the official language by way of statute. As the preamble to the version reported by the Illinois Senate Judiciary Committee stated, "The name of the language of a country has a powerful psychological influence upon the minds of the people in stimulating and preserving national solidarity." Like the citizens of England who spoke English and those of France who spoke French, Americans would speak "American."

Shaped largely by American isolationism, anti-German feelings, and anxieties over massive immigration, public discourse during and immediately following World War I constructed proficiency in any language other than English as dangerous and "incompatible with American identity" for newly arrived immigrants and as an "inconsequential luxury" for middle- and upper-class American citizens.[92] A resolution adopted in 1918 by the National Education Association Commission on the National Emergency in Education declared "the practice of giving instruction to children in the common branches in a foreign tongue to be un-American and unpatriotic."[93] By 1923 a total of thirty-four states—up from fourteen in 1903, and seventeen in 1913—had enacted legislation mandating English as the sole language of instruction either in public schools only or in both public and private schools.[94] Fifteen of the laws were enacted in 1919, the year the American Legion was founded and its National Americanization Commission gave high priority to making English the mandated language of instruction in public schools.[95] Some states, like Texas and Nebraska, even imposed criminal penalties on teachers found using a language other than English in the classroom. Some, including Indiana, Louisiana, and Ohio, expressly singled out German, prohibiting its use as a medium of instruction in elementary and secondary schools.[96] Such radical efforts to stamp out any trace of foreign background, especially language, engendered resentment and hostility among many immigrants who up to that time had been eager to learn English in order to advance economically.

Laws restricting the teaching of foreign languages were largely overturned in 1923 in the Supreme Court's decision in *Meyer v. Nebraska*.[97] Yet during the years in which the laws had been in operation, English had gained a lasting foothold as the language of schooling. At the same time, the educational establishment and social psychologists sounded the alarm that bilingualism was not just anti-American. There was empirical evidence, they claimed, that it impaired cognitive ability and was thus harmful to children. What the reports failed to reveal was that the children from whom the data had been gathered were poor, as compared with the monolinguals studied, and that they were tested in English, their weaker language.[98] Meanwhile, other commentators and educators warned that compulsory English language measures were shortsighted and would prove counterproductive. They feared that forcing the foreigners to learn English would only provoke opposition, especially because in Europe one's language was considered almost as important as one's religion. The language "problem" would "solve itself, if left to its natural course."[99] Despite such warnings, the "harm" rationale remained a quiet undercurrent through the following decades as the schools continued to pressure the second generation to abandon their home language and culture.

Some communities undertook even more ambitious plans. In 1918, rebounding from wrenching strife among immigrant industrial workers, Lawrence, Massachusetts, organized an experimental elementary school entirely devoted to providing students, many of them English-speaking children of foreign-born parents, with intense training in American citizenship. The idea was to infuse all aspects of the school curriculum, as well as the life of the school, with the principles of democracy, teaching children "how to be a good citizen, by being a good citizen." The Lawrence approach was perhaps the most far-reaching in emphasizing specific ideals of citizenship, an approach not unlike today's character education programs. But it was not unique in its purposes. Public schools nationwide were implementing similar plans.[100] As the *Chicago Daily Tribune* noted in 1919, "Only an agile and determined immigrant, possessed of overmastering devotion to the land of his birth, can hope to escape Americanization."[101] No doubt a good number did manage to escape. All the same, by 1920 Americanization had become "a household term—among the native-born, a synonym of anxiety, dread, or duty; among the foreign-born one of misgiving, suspicion, or hope."[102]

Just one year later the Americanization project took a downturn. An economic depression dramatically curtailed contributions to private groups involved in the movement. Meanwhile, the more virulent strain of Americanization was giving many Americans pause. The term began to lose currency in favor of "citizenship" and "national unification." Yet opposition to continued immigration remained deeply imbedded, especially among those with muscle to exert in Washington.

In retrospect, many of the ideals espoused by some of the Americanizers were noble and well intentioned. One can even find a rational justification for the fears expressed. The country was at war. Some immigrants were returning to Europe to defend or recapture their homelands; others harbored anti-American and even anarchist views. The issue of conflicted loyalties was serious. At the same time, it was an era of intense nation building. The task of churning such huge numbers of immigrants into loyal and productive citizens was both compelling and overwhelming.

That being said, the inflammatory rhetoric, some of the remedies proposed, and the policies influenced by the more extreme elements in the movement were highly questionable. Their narrow concept of what it meant to be American, their insensitivity to the immigrants' language and culture, and the severity of their methods for transforming newcomers into idealized citizens of Anglo-Saxon "virtue" continue to provoke sharp criticism. But if Americanization, despite its promise of social mobility, was at times wrenching for those targeted, it proved far worse for those who were ignored. By casting the nation in an Anglo-Saxon image, the movement implicitly and effectively excluded Chinese Americans and Japanese Americans, while Mexican, African, and Native Americans were considered totally beyond the possibility of assimilation.

Just how effective the movement was in pursuing its objectives, and whether it caused more harm than good, remain disputable. In the immediate aftermath of the war, some commentators portrayed the experience as an object lesson on the dangers of absolutist policies aimed at quickly absorbing immigrants into mainstream society. The disintegration of Austria, and the realignment of national boundaries throughout Europe, further demonstrated the negative consequences for Germany and Austria for their having, out of nationalistic egotism, abolished all languages but German within their borders.[103] From that point on, the term *Americanization,* even in its generic sense of assimilation, elicited negative associations that remain to the present day.

Whatever the impact on the immigrants themselves, the Americanization movement left as its legacy a new political discourse wedding culture and politics. Culture became politicized, and diversity became trapped in the negative mindset of difference. The term *new immigrant* connoted not merely recent arrival but, more significantly, racial disparities in the sense of biology or "stock."[104] It was no longer sufficient for newcomers to demonstrate loyalty to America and its political principles. Seeming so fundamentally and almost ineradicably distinct from the mainstream, they had to prove they were loyal to the American way of life. The only way they could do that was to abandon their familial traditions, customs, and language and assume a new Anglo-Saxon identity.[105] "Loyalty" became essentially synonymous with "social conformity."[106] German immigrants learned this lesson the hard way. Amidst the hysteria of World War I, they could no longer remain partially German culturally yet politically and patriotically American. While that submissive view now seems harsh in our post-civil-rights society, which gives official lip service to diversity, it continues to permeate the ongoing debate over how best to integrate yet another wave of immigrants and their children into American society and the role that schooling should play in that effort.

Nativist Restrictions

The failure of Americanization education to quickly transform newcomers into Anglo-Saxons through and through, the arrival of a new influx of immigrants after the wartime hiatus, and related concerns that the country's prosperity and power depended on a more selective immigration policy, led Congress to relent and pass restrictive immigration laws. Americanization at least had implied that it was feasible to integrate the new immigrants. The new wave of restrictionist sentiment, in contrast, was grounded in nativist views that the newcomers were intrinsically inferior and therefore unwanted.

With strong lobbying efforts from organized labor, Congress passed the Literacy Test Act in 1917 over President Wilson's veto and despite strong opposition from social justice leaders like Jane Addams.[107] Aimed at immigrants from eastern and southern Europe, where there was a high rate of illiteracy, the test required immigrants over the age of sixteen to demonstrate reading and writing proficiency in some language. It made an exception for those fleeing religious or political persecution. The Act also excluded most Asians, although the Gentlemen's Agreement from 1908 had long before limited immigration from Japan. The literacy test led the way to the Quota Act of 1921, an emergency measure that was extended the following year.

Xenophobia ran high throughout the 1920s. The Ku Klux Klan, whose credo included a strong anti-immigrant strain, was a visibly active force in several states. Klan members verbalized what many old-line Protestants and assimilated "others" were thinking. In 1923, President Calvin Coolidge told Congress, "America must be kept American."[108] The response was the Johnson-Reed Act, commonly known as the National Origins Act of 1924, limiting the yearly number of new immigrants to 164,000 until 1927, and 150,000 thereafter. Thus ended an era in which immigration was relatively open except for Asians.

Under the new system, the narrow selection standards were again stacked against eastern and southern Europeans. Until 1927, 2 percent of the number of foreign-born residents from each country as of 1890 could enter the United States. After 1927, the total quota was allocated in proportion to the number of nationals of each country within the white population of the United States as of 1920 with certain exemptions. A stunning 70 percent of all immigrant slots were allotted to natives of the United Kingdom, Ireland, and Germany. The results were dramatic. In 1927 the quota for immigrants from Poland was 4,509; in 1921, 95,089 Poles had entered the United States. The Italian figures were even more striking, with a 1927 quota of 5,877, down from 222,270 Italians entering in 1921. In contrast, numbers for the United Kingdom rose from 79,577 to 91,110 over that same time period.[109]

Color was no longer the only ground for legally excluding individuals from the political community. Echoing racial assumptions grounded in social Darwinism, commentators of the day argued that the melting pot was pure myth, that it would "take centuries before the foreigners now become Americans."[110] Some, like Henry Platt Fairchild in his widely read book *The Melting-Pot Mistake,* warned that the "spheres" in which the native- and foreign-born were moving were "growing more and more distinct and irreconcilable." The book made four claims, some clearly reminiscent of today's anti-immigrant propaganda: that assimilation is a one-way street, demanding a total transformation and complete sacrifice of national traits on the part of the immigrant; that certain foreign groups exhibit characteristics that make them inherently unassimilable and unacceptable to the mainstream; that racial antipathy on the part of the native-born is simply a biological fact; and that "unrestricted" immigration was "slowly, insidiously, irresistibly eating away the very heart of the United States."[111]

Americanization "Lite"

Just a year following the adoption of national origin quotas, the commissioner of immigration at Ellis Island reported that "virtually all immigrants now look exactly like Americans," presumably meaning they were of Anglo-Saxon physical type.[112] Where the Americanizers had left off, the restrictionists had picked up and ultimately succeeded. By pulling in the gangplank, the Act effectively accelerated the acculturation of those already here, who, as the years passed, became progressively more detached linguistically and culturally from their families and their native roots. By the time America's doors again opened to immigrants on a wide scale, time and another world war had further acculturated what would become the "old" immigrants, their children, and their children's children. Whether they were fully assimilated or integrated in a more pluralistic way is a complicated question.

Without a steady stream of compatriots to reinforce their language and culture, foreigners began speaking English and adopting American customs and dress. Many first-generation immigrants, nonetheless, continued to carry on the ways of thought and accents of the Europe they had left behind and so remained "incomplete Americans."[113] Yet the gradual dilution of distinct cultural attitudes and behaviors became almost inevitable in their children as the second generation became at least visibly "Americanized" in what the historian Marcus Hansen called a "treaty of peace with society." As Hansen put it, "the problem of the immigrant was not solved, it disappeared."[114] It vanished from public consciousness and public discourse—from the news media, from congressional debates, from professional meetings, from government policies.

But it did not vanish from the public schools. Throughout the 1930s, although the pace of Americanization became less frenetic and its purposes less transparent, the schools continued to gently indoctrinate immigrant offspring in middle-class Protestant Anglo-Saxon republican ideals. Education of the day was a mix of Progressive child-centeredness combined with the political ideology of early common-school reformers. The entire curriculum, both overt and hidden, was consciously shaped toward that end. In schools from Maine to California, the day opened with Bible reading, prayers, the Pledge of Allegiance, and the national anthem. Weekly assembly programs and holiday celebrations were infused with patriotic songs and readings recalling significant actors and events in the nation's history. Children with surnames clustered with consonants or laden with vowels marched side by side, dressed in navy blue skirts or slacks and white shirts, sporting red bows or neckties, in celebrations marking the nation's founding and honoring its Founding Fathers. It was a time in which the country and its citizens, immigrants and native-born, set their collective sights inward.

In the interests of national unity, the public schools quietly continued in their mission to wash out ancestral ties, foreign loyalties, and signs of ethnic differences, ensuring that all schoolchildren spoke, dressed, acted, and felt like the idealized American. Many immigrant families feared that their children would become estranged, but they appreciated the economic benefits of assimilation and the need to converge toward the Anglo-Saxon norm. At the same time, they embraced the ideological dimensions of American identity, allowing them to be patriotic while remaining privately cognizant of their ancestral roots.[115] Among Roman Catholics, local parish churches were a significant force in getting immigrants to shed their ethnic rituals and blend into a broader American Catholicism. Labor unions instilled in workers a sense of solidarity based on class loyalties rather than ethnic attachments.[116] The emergence of mass media, initially radio and movies and later television, had a homogenizing cultural effect of a more voluntary but subliminal nature. Meanwhile the Depression invigorated a "democratic sense of commonality," while the threat of another war tempered the old "divisive stereotypes" and gave way to a call for "common heroes."[117]

There was a sense, nonetheless, that American society was still fragmented. Developments at home and abroad, including rising anti-Semitism, racial discrimination, and "unhealthy" forms of ethnic expression like the German-American Bund, caused social reformers to push for educational programs that promoted tolerance and harmony. A 1938 *New York Times* article titled "U.S. 'Melting Pot' Is Seen as Failure" described a seven-point program devised by New York University professor Francis J. Brown to "combat the rise of racial group intolerance" in the country and to avoid the "racial and religious strife" evidenced abroad.[118]

Liberal educational leaders espoused an early form of cultural pluralism that took its clearest form in the "intercultural education" movement. A driving force behind the movement was Rachel Davis DuBois, a Quaker and founder of the Service Bureau for Intercultural Education, the precursor to the Progressive Education Association's Commission on Intercultural Education. Joining DuBois were Progressive educators at Columbia University's Teachers College, leaders of ethnic organizations, and social scientists. DuBois was deeply influenced by Louis Adamic, a writer of Slovenian birth whose 1934 *Harper's* magazine article, "Thirty Million New Americans," described widespread feelings of alienation, inferiority, and disdain for their parents among the second generation. Traveling across the country, Adamic had grown increasingly troubled that immigrant parents were failing to impart to their children a sense of continuity, a feeling of being "part of something." He feared that immigrant offspring would become "neutral, unstirring citizens" without some action being taken on a national level.[119]

Like Adamic, DuBois promoted the idea that schools should recognize the traditions of immigrant parents in order to bridge the generation gap and help their children gain self-esteem and adjust to American society. Her view, not limited to Europeans, opened the curriculum to the culture and contributions of African and Asian Americans. Her strong support for ethnic identification provoked sharp disagreement from other school reformers, most notably the Progressive Education Association, leading the group in 1938 to sever its relationship with her.[120] Some of her detractors believed it would be retrogressive to revive ethnic pride among those who seemed assimilated. Others feared revitalizing allegiances to foreign countries. Still others warned that ethnic identification would forestall assimilation into the American mainstream and solidify ethnic and racial divisions.[121]

The interculturalists, and particularly the Progressives, had a certain discomfort with collective ethnic identity. They instead espoused an ideal whereby all would be incorporated as individuals into American society. Like their predecessors, they supported the right to culturally distinct identities and affiliations, though they also presumed that those distinctions and ethnic bonds would gradually weaken. For them, culture was a matter of past heritage and contributions and not something to be preserved for the future.[122] It was to be tolerated but not accepted. Driven largely by educational elites, the intercultural education movement never gained widespread support among local educators. Meanwhile, the tensions of the war abroad deepened concerns over the divisive potential of cultural differences, setting other assimilative forces in motion. By 1940 even Francis Brown, whose recommendations to combat racial intolerance had captured national attention and who had co-edited one of the leading intercultural studies textbooks, had second thoughts. He warned a gathering of the National Council on Naturalization and Citizenship that it was impossible to separate the "sense of cultural continuity" nurtured in the work of agencies like the Service Bureau from political loyalty to foreign governments. "We must no longer be hyphenated Americans . . . but wholly Americans," he said.[123]

World War II was a central event in shaping the national understanding of American identity for immigrant and native offspring alike. There was a feeling, reinforced by Hollywood and the news media, that Americans were all in this together. Upward of twelve million young men and women were serving in the armed forces. As military service transported them across the country and around the world, many for the first time left their immigrant enclaves and crossed cultural borders, uniting in a common enterprise under life-threatening conditions. The driving mission of the most ardent Americanizers had been accomplished, at least politically. The second and third generations were proving themselves to be loyal citizens. Many gave their lives for their families' adopted country. On the battlefield, hyphens vanished by necessity, at least for the moment. Everyone self-identified as American in contrast to "the other," whether ally or enemy. Many intermarried, transcending ethnic, religious, and even national boundaries as foreign "war brides" entered families that were barely gaining their own American bearings. The "melting pot" seemed to be working its magic, or at least that was the popular belief. And while the national origin quotas remained in place, the country opened its arms to cautiously embrace others previously considered outside the sphere of Americanization. In 1943 Congress repealed the 1892 Chinese Exclusion Act. Three years later, it granted citizenship to immigrants from the Philippines.

For those who returned home, the war rewarded immigrant offspring with the opportunity to share in the American dream. The 1944 GI Bill, along with federally subsidized low-interest home mortgages, expanded highway systems, and a postwar economic boom offered returning veterans unprecedented social and geographic mobility. The suburbs flourished, creating a new middle class. These institutional changes diminished the social and cultural distinctions once common among Europeans entering the labor market. They also dramatically transformed higher education, making college enrollment more the norm than the exception among second- and third-generation families.[124]

In the aftermath of the war, Americans of all backgrounds became more self-aware in affirming their democratic values in opposition to the atrocities and racial claims of Nazism and the threat of Communism abroad. And while the question of African Americans in particular was placed on the back burner, separate racial and color designations disappeared from the official lexicon describing European immigrants.[125] By the close of World War II, the less subjective notion of "nationality" had replaced "race" and its pseudo-scientific implications of cultural and cognitive determinism. The "second wave" immigrants, including Greeks, Italians, Jews, and Slavs, had officially shed their "probationary white" or "in-between" status. Concepts of race and color had been redefined. The dividing line between the socially acceptable and unacceptable had shifted. All European immigrants were presumably positioned to climb up the American ladder of social mobility as fast as their initiative would take them.

That, a least, is the European immigrant story as typically told in popular and scholarly accounts—a meteoric "up by the bootstraps" rise to what some sociologists have called "economic affluence," initially nurtured in the public schools, whether in factory-like classrooms of eastern cities or in rural schoolhouses of the Midwest.[126] Yet like Hansen's claim that the immigrant problem had disappeared, this romantic myth of a linear journey, though appealing and affirming, mistakenly suggests that the residue of "otherness" had faded from the immigrants' everyday lives as they easily discarded the outer signs of immigrant "difference." Strip away the gloss and it becomes clear how that passage, especially for the second generation, was often slow, gradual, and complicated. As Nancy Foner and Richard Alba remind us, many encountered "painful setbacks and difficulties" along the way.[127]

Just like today's immigrant offspring, their relative success depended on a number of factors, including government policies, the cultural and economic resources of their own ethnic community, and the receptivity of labor markets and social networks, what Alejandro Portes and Rubén Rumbaut call the "contexts of reception."[128] Immigration laws from the 1920s limited their numbers. In school they became subject to an elaborate sorting system driven by the frenzy of IQ testing, in the end irrevocably limiting the horizons of many within the second generation. Many faced prejudice and discrimination, sometimes unspoken but nevertheless discouraging, as they worked their way into the dominant society. For some groups, it took at least another generation to overcome those early rebuffs. To what extent official policies rejecting their home languages and cultures affected the second generation's sense of self remains immeasurable. In any case, the straight-line assimilation narrative was tinged with a sentimentality that distorted reality. As researchers and others summon up the past as a backdrop for examining current developments, it is tempting to legitimize the more negative side of those earlier efforts, particularly as they played out in the public schools. It also is easy to dismiss the important lessons learned from the experience as the United States once again struggles to resolve linguistic and cultural differences among a shifting population of immigrants and their children.

Though Americanization is no longer an organized movement and most Americans would reject its harsher elements, the ghost of those efforts and their inherent insensitivities lingers within the "deficit" rationale of current discourse and much of current practice on language and schooling. At the same time, while the story of "Americanization Past"

underscores the often overlooked commonalities between the "old" immigrant experience and the "new," there are equally significant differences that challenge popular attitudes regarding the assimilatory trajectory today's newcomers are expected to follow. Chapter 3 explores that
contemporary landscape and the distinct issues it raises.

CHAPTER THREE

The New Immigrants

THE NO. 7 subway train in New York City traverses an eight-mile route from Times Square through the borough of Queens. Nicknamed the "International Express" for the diverse communities it serves, in 2000 the White House officially designated the No. 7 line as one of sixteen "National Millennium Trails" for representing the immigrant experience. Built on the labor of European immigrants in the early twentieth century, the elevated train rumbles above the traffic as it punctuates, at regular intervals, sidewalk conversations in some 138 languages.[1]

Queens is one of the most multi-ethnic and multilingual counties in the nation. An estimated 46 percent of the 2.2 million residents are foreign-born, and 56 percent speak English less than "very well." More than half of those aged five and older speak a language other than English at home. In recent decades, old neighborhoods settled by Greeks, Italians, Irish, German, and Jewish immigrants have been repopulated by a flood of newcomers from Central and South America, the Caribbean, eastern Europe, and Asian countries, principally China, Korea, and India. Like the newcomers of the past, they cluster in ethnically defined neighborhoods, recreating their native countries in a public life of specialty and clothing shops, restaurants, food stores, and houses of worship. The bustling avenues and boulevards are dotted with doctor's offices, hair salons, money transmission shops, video stores, dry cleaners, and movie theaters. This is Manhattan's "lower eastside" of a hundred years ago, translated into a new mix of languages and cultures.

Queens even has its own official General Assembly, sort of a local

United Nations, made up of volunteers from community boards and organizations representing two dozen ethnic groups and an assortment of
religions and races. Among its activities, the Assembly publishes a Diversity Calendar listing major holidays of Christian, Jewish, Muslim, Sikh,
and Buddhist faiths along with civic observances.[2] A separate Immigrant
Task Force of community workers and advocates meets regularly to share
concerns and resources. Here is a world where diversity is celebrated and
used as a vehicle for civic participation.

Anyone who wants to see diversity in action can hop off the No.
7 train at 33rd Street, four stops beyond its East River crossing. Two
blocks west, through an old industrial neighborhood, sits the International High School at La Guardia Community College. Founded in 1985,
the school has served as a model for nine other schools in New York City
and two in California that form the Internationals Network for Public
Schools, now funded in part by the Bill and Melinda Gates Foundation.[3]
Housed in a no-frills industrial building like its offshoots, the Queens
school expressly offers a "multicultural alternative educational environment" for late-entry students who have lived in the country four years or
less. The overwhelming majority come from low-income families. Many
are refugees whose education has been interrupted by war and displacement. Past the heavy steel doors and a maze of college classrooms is a
small network of grey hallways that the high school calls its own, where
450 students from upward of fifty countries speak more than forty languages. In 2009, the school was one of three recipients of the Migration
Policy Institute's E Pluribus Unum Prize awarded to exceptional immigration initiatives.

Modest in resources but rich in camaraderie and commitment, the
school prides itself on its interdisciplinary program incorporating intern-
ships and community service, its extraordinarily low dropout rate, and
its phenomenal success in moving 90 percent of its graduates, all recent
arrivals, into college. But what is at least equally remarkable, and a key
part of the school's mission, is its commitment to maintaining the students' native languages and affirming their many cultures. As its own literature states, while it is essential for students to gain near-native abilities
in English in order to "realize their potential in an English-speaking society," the world has become "increasingly interdependent," and so fluency
in a language other than English should be considered a "resource for the
student, the school and the society." Language functions as both a medium of instruction and an object of analysis in various interdisciplinary
programs.[4]

This is a school where educators have figured out how to "create a community that values difference but that also values trust and support."[5] While it is not uncommon to see students clustering in the hallways by language, the school decidedly exudes a shared immigrant vision and purpose. In the classrooms the students eagerly and generously bridge the cultural gaps as they find common ground through English while alternately shifting into their native languages. The school clearly is America in the making. Cultural activities are threaded throughout the curriculum, and students must demonstrate native language proficiency to some degree as part of their graduation portfolio. Some take native language courses at the college. As the school's former principal, Burt Rosenberg, put it, "Language is so tied to who you are that to take that away diminishes your very sense of self."[6]

Just as International High School's student population is a microcosm of Queens, so too the school and the county are reminders that America is a continuous work in progress. Like the No. 7 train and the textured ethnic communities it crosses, each in its way gives a snapshot view of the most recent iteration of what it now means to be or to become "American." Much of that transformation flows out of the 1960s with dramatic changes in federal immigration laws. The revisions phased out the old and much vilified system of national origin quotas initiated in the 1920s. Those changes subsequently brought to the nation's shores yet another tidal wave of "new" immigrants whose numbers, diversity, and fluid identities now challenge the metaphorical "melting pot." A major point of scholarly debate is how successfully the children of those immigrants are integrating into the American economic and political mainstream.

New Faces, New Places

Becoming effective on July 1, 1968, the Hart-Cellar Immigration Act of 1965 eliminated national origin, race, or ancestry as a basis for immigration to the United States. It emphasized family reunification and needed skills, establishing a seven-category preference system for relatives of U.S. citizens and permanent-resident aliens, and for persons with special occupational skills, abilities, or training. In the end, it reversed decades of systematic exclusion and restrictive immigration policies, bringing in unprecedented numbers of immigrants from Asia, Mexico, Latin America, and Africa.

The law was a mix of moral imperative and political pragmatism with a strong dose of demographic shortsightedness. President Lyndon B. Johnson, placing his signature on the bill as he stood in the shadow of the Statue of Liberty, assailed the old quota restrictions. "This system," he

said, "has been un-American in the highest sense, because it has been un-
true to the faith that brought thousands to these shores even before we
were a country."[7] Johnson was not alone among his contemporaries in
holding that view. Just two years earlier, President John F. Kennedy had
called the old quotas an "anachronism" in an "age of interdependence
among nations."[8] Even worse, they were an embarrassment and a strategic liability. With the decolonization of Africa and Asia, coupled with the
former Soviet Union aggressively competing to capture the "hearts and
minds" of developing nations, the nationality quotas were posing a problem for U.S. foreign policy. For its architects in particular, the new law
was a sign of the times, extending beyond the nation's borders the same
ideals that animated the Civil Rights Act adopted the previous year. In
the same vein, it affirmed Supreme Court decisions, following on the
heels of *Brown v. Board of Education,* uprooting the remnants of legal
racism.[9]

The law's prime sponsors seemingly did not intend for it to change the
flow or face of immigration, despite warnings that it would. That fact is
somewhat perplexing, given how the population landscape subsequently
evolved. "The bill we sign today," President Johnson told the gathered
crowd, "is not a revolutionary bill. It does not affect the lives of millions.
It will not restructure the shape of our daily lives." Like other supporters, the president was trying to calm fears that the legislation might soon
become the engine for globalizing immigration on a massive scale. Senator Edward Kennedy (D-Mass.), who chaired the Senate immigration
subcommittee, likewise made express assurances, as did a number of
his colleagues, that "the bill [would] not flood our cities with immigrants. It [would] not upset the ethnic mix of our society."[10] Secretary of
State Dean Rusk struck a similar note, dismissing the possibility of "a
world situation where everybody is just straining to move to the United
States."[11]

History obviously has proved them wrong. The immigrant profile has
profoundly changed in terms of countries of origin, economic range, racial and religious makeup, and intensity. In 1970, foreign-born people
constituted 4.7 percent of the U.S. population. Today they constitute
nearly 13 percent—the highest share since 1890, when it reached a record high of 14.8 percent. More than half of these current newcomers entered the country after 1990.[12] The group includes close to twelve million
undocumented immigrants, roughly 30 percent of the foreign-born population.[13] Equally troubling is the fact that five million U.S. children live in
households in which at least one of the parents is unauthorized, and that
two million of these children are themselves unauthorized.[14] More than

three-quarters of the undocumented come from Mexico and other Latin American countries, including Central America.

Between 1990 and 2000 alone, the foreign-born population grew by more than 11 million. During that time, 9.1 million were admitted as legal immigrants, the largest number in any decade, exceeding even the 8.8 million admitted between 1900 and 1910 at the height of the "old" immigration.[15] These figures are indeed staggering. Projections for the future are equally so. By the year 2050, the foreign-born population will rise to 81 million, a growth of 129 percent, while the Hispanic presence will triple in size to 29 percent of the overall population. One in five Americans will be an immigrant, in contrast to one in eight today. The percentage of children who are immigrants, or who have a parent who is an immigrant, will rise from 23 percent to 34 percent. Only 47 percent of people residing in the United States will be non-Hispanic white, a significant drop from the current 67 percent.[16]

More than half of the current foreign-born population comes from Latin America, with about 30 percent from Mexico. Approximately another 20 percent come from various Asian countries, including China, the Philippines, India, Vietnam, and Korea. And so while Spanish remains the most common immigrant language spoken at home, the range of languages has become much broader.

One of the most interesting demographic stories of the time is not just the growth but the dispersion of the Hispanic population along with other groups, largely driven by job opportunities, affordable housing, and quality of life concerns. Although more than half of the foreign-born reside in California, New York, and Texas, migration patterns have shifted in recent years. The total number of Mexican immigrants, for example, roughly doubled between 1990 and 2000 to about 2.5 million, but the numbers of recent arrivals settling in California declined from 61 percent to 31 percent. Meanwhile, the largely Hispanic foreign-born population in states like Nevada, North Carolina, and Georgia more than tripled. Wake County, North Carolina, witnessed a 530 percent jump from 5,400 to 34,000. Similarly, a growing number of Southeast Asians, including Vietnamese, Hmong, Cambodians, and Laotians, now live in the Midwest and the South.[17] In the 1990s, the number of children of immigrants in pre-kindergarten through grade five increased by 206 percent in Nevada, 153 percent in North Carolina, and 148 percent in Georgia.[18] Cities like Las Vegas, Minneapolis, Charlotte, and Atlanta are now emerging "gateways" for the foreign-born. The impact on the schools continues to overwhelm school officials who are unprepared to address the needs these children bring with them.

A similar dispersal can be found in metropolitan areas where immigrants across the economic spectrum are moving directly to the suburbs and establishing thriving ethnic communities. High-tech, knowledge-based industries on the margins of cities are drawing educated and trained Asian immigrants in search of safe neighborhoods and good schools for their children. Typically less-advantaged Mexicans and Central Americans likewise find housing, made possible in part by laws eliminating exclusionary zoning. They also find ready work in low-level service industries like construction and landscaping. In 2005 the suburban growth rate was 15.7 percent, double the rate of 7.9 percent in 1990.[19] The New York metropolitan area is a clear example. Between 2000 and 2005 alone, the number of immigrants living on the outskirts of the city grew by about 225,000 as compared with a within-city increase of about 44,000.[20]

Aside from their numbers and changing patterns of density, the new immigrants have brought with them an almost unparalleled level of diversity. No longer predominantly European, white, and practicing in the Judeo-Christian traditions, an exceedingly high number are racial minorities. Many embrace beliefs, including Eastern faiths, that are unfamiliar to most Americans. Some hold religious values that radically depart from those of the U.S. mainstream. Forced marriages, for example, run counter to Western notions of individual autonomy and gender equality. Practices like female circumcision rouse immense outrage in most Americans and fly in the face of acceptable medical practice.

Today's newcomers run the socioeconomic gamut, from unskilled day laborers and migrant farm workers to highly educated computer scientists and health care professionals. Those who arrive with advanced schooling and middle-class standards of living understandably assimilate quickly. A growing number are drawn to the expanding knowledge-based economy. Many children of immigrants from Korea, India, and the former Soviet Union come from educated families where parents are professionals or small business owners. They live in single-family homes in comfortable, racially integrated suburban towns, often sprinkled with ethnic commercial areas. Many others live in urban ethnic neighborhoods close to more readily available low-paying jobs. The old Chinatowns of major cities, along with newer Koreatowns, as in Los Angeles, teem with newcomers struggling to forge a better life for themselves. At the far extreme are the children of undocumented Mexican and other Latin American families, living in overcrowded and temporary housing, working for below-scale wages in the shadows of the service industries or in seasonal agricultural work. In between are the black Caribbean immi-

grants. Often forced into crime-ridden inner-city neighborhoods by segregated housing patterns, they struggle mightily to maintain their strong
family and community values and save their children from the patholo-
gies of the street.

The children's educational achievement and social stability often reflect these differences. Some are high academic performers. Others are
more susceptible to alcohol and drug abuse, street gangs, and crime.
Some move on to elite universities. Others drop out of high school. In
urban schools in particular, among the foreign-born and children of
foreign-born parents there are as many Intel Science winners as there are
delinquents. Again, though the disparities in outcomes are particularly
noticeable between ethnic groups, there also are within-group differences
that often go unnoticed. Despite the conventional view of Asians as the
"model minority," many Asian immigrant children struggle at the bot-
tom of the academic curve. While 68 percent of Asian Indians hold at
least a four-year college degree, only 13 percent of Cambodian, Laotian,
and Hmong immigrants finish college. Many do not even finish high
school.[21]

Just as the immigrants of the past are today's ethnics, today's immigrants are forging the ethnic identities of the future. For most of them,
however, ethnicity is not something they can casually slip in and out of at
will. The ultimate role that it plays in their daily lives and decisions depends on society's attitudes toward their particular group. Skin color is a
critical determinant. Race and national origin definitively shape options
for the largely nonwhite population of "new" immigrants, for some more
than others, regardless of how much they choose to identify with either.[22]
For Miami's white middle-class Cuban community, for example, ethnicity has been both a source of economic opportunities within ethnic networks and an emotional bulwark against the negative forces of the surrounding culture. For others, like the Haitian and more recently arrived
black Cuban communities, ethnicity is a badge of subordination.

Race and economics largely determine where immigrant children live,
the quality of the schools they attend, and the friends they make. Not
unlike immigrant children of the past, many find themselves in poorly
financed schools and overcrowded classrooms, with inadequately trained
and credentialed teachers, outdated textbooks, limited technology, and
few enrichment programs. Many are tracked into unchallenging and
more typically vocational programs that limit their potential and, in
some cases, do not prepare them for real-world jobs. A disproportionately high percentage of males are placed in special education schools and
classes. Many drop out, limiting even further their chances for economic

advancement. It is thus not surprising that an increasing number, especially those at the lower socioeconomic rungs, are quickly disabused of the notion that simply speaking English is the key to becoming American.[23]

Transnational Lives

Today's immigrants maintain regular economic and political contacts with their homeland to a far greater extent than immigrants of times past. And so among the many criticisms leveled against them is the charge that they are not fully embracing the American way of life and may be torn in their political loyalties. This tendency toward what is now called *transnationalism* has broad implications for American identity, citizenship, and ultimately schooling.

A story from the world of sports puts a personal spin on this growing phenomenon. During the 2006 World Baseball Classic, superstar Alex Rodriguez found himself the subject of international scrutiny as he pondered whether to play for the United States, where he is a citizen, or for the Dominican Republic, where his parents reside. Ultimately he decided to play for the U.S. team but not without provoking some disappointment from fellow Dominicans, even in the United States, who had hoped he would choose otherwise.[24] Several decades ago, the decision would have been easy and evident. As an American citizen, Rodriguez unequivocally would have played for the American team. No one would have expected him not to.

Rodriguez was merely demonstrating a transnational or more fluid sense of national identity, one that has become more common among the "new" immigrants and their children. That reality suggests another dimension to consider in measuring integration beyond traditional markers like English fluency, intermarriage, education, or occupation status. All these situate the immigrant in the American present, as if a steel door had closed on the past. New immigrant lifestyles, supported by wider acceptance of cultural pluralism and changing conceptions of nationality and citizenship, now reveal a multidimensional pattern of integration.

A confluence of factors, including massive poverty in the global South and East, a demographic deficit in much of the North and West, and economic globalization worldwide are producing new migrations and refugee flows. As a borderless economy has opened up opportunities for workers with needed skills and training, both the highly educated and trained as well as the poor have streamed out of the Third World to fill jobs left vacant by a declining birthrate in developed countries. Though this free flow of human capital has created "inclusion and choice" for some, it also has created social displacement and affirmed inequalities for others."[25] In any case, an emerging viewpoint, at times promoted by sending countries themselves, is that immigrants should retain more connection with their homelands than the remote sentimental ethnicity maintained by American Euro-ethnics, and instead maintain ongoing economic and political interests in their native country.

This growing perspective defies the classic canons of citizenship and assimilation, which allowed little room, and no support, for looking back. For immigrants to retain their old customs was at most grudgingly considered acceptable as a transitional phase; for immigrants to remain politically loyal to their homelands was considered heresy. It remains to be seen what consequences this new perspective will have for American identity, and thus public schooling, the crucible within which future Americans are forged.

In the old days, when there was no accessible and inexpensive air travel to whisk us across the globe, no round-the-clock cable TV channels or closed-circuit radio stations or Internet service to update news or get a cultural "fix" from home, and no e-mail or videophone service to instantaneously correspond with family and friends at the touch of a button, migration was a more permanent and complete commitment. Today it is a far different experience. Aided by technological advances that virtually obliterate limitations of time and space, increasingly many immigrants are creating a new reality, maintaining "multi-stranded" ties linking their societies of settlement and of origin.[26] As these "transmigrants" traverse the globe and establish connections to their new country, they continue to develop and nurture social, economic, and political networks and obligations that extend back to their native land. They consequently defy to some extent the conventional image of the uprooted immigrant eagerly struggling to assimilate into the mythical mainstream culture.

Within this world, continuous streams of people, goods, money, and information flow across national borders, altering traditional patterns of integration and transforming cultural and political practices into an imagined single community that in reality exists in different places. For many immigrants, culture and community are grounded in more than one locality. No longer bound by geography, one's sense of being is "less anchored to a place than to a state of mind."[27] Meanwhile, modern-day civil and human rights movements have further weakened the exclusive claim on national identity and legitimized ethnic identities.

That is not to suggest that immigrants in the past did not move back and forth or maintain some identification with the home country. Yet the first pattern was qualitatively more tentative while the second was more typically symbolic. Some were sojourners, temporarily residing in the new country, at times intermittently or just long enough to earn sufficient income to support a better life back home. Still others initially intended to stay but had second thoughts and returned. Many affirmed their cultural roots by collectively maintaining various rituals and celebrations in their new country.

In contrast to the post-1965 immigrants, those of the past also had a looser sense of national identity to maintain or relinquish in the first place. Most had migrated from peasant societies intricately divided by language and culture where individuals felt a closer tie to their region or village than to the concept of the nation-state. Some were refugees fleeing political or religious persecution. Nationality and ethnicity rarely converged in Russia or Austria-Hungary for eastern European immigrants and especially for Jews, while for Italians a newly unified Italy remained torn by regional and class divisions. More pragmatically, the cost and difficulty of travel, limited means of communication, restrictive immigration laws, and widespread suspicion of cultural pluralism forced those immigrants who stayed in the United States to set their sights on becoming more exclusively American. For all these reasons inverted, the lure of transnationalism today is more widespread and more intense, and thus potentially more consequential than previous expressions. That reality has fanned the flames of hostility toward immigrants, not just in the United States but throughout the developed world, creating a political climate in which transnationalism is thought to forestall successful integration.

Commentators speak of transnationalism "from above" and "from below." Transnationalism "from above" is generally said to involve a global economy, aided by supranational institutions like the World Bank, the International Monetary Fund, and international nongovernmental organizations and corporations. Added to these forces are members of the professional middle class, the so-called "brain drain" immigrants, who form an important part of some migrant communities. However, although it is true that globalization has facilitated transnationalism, the two are technically distinguishable. Globalization is geographically broader and deterritorialized without relation to national boundaries; transnationalism is located in particular cross-national social spaces, typically linking two nation-states, within which migrants forge their identities, practices, and interests.

Transnationalism more commonly emerges "from below" in individual and collective ways. For many countries, diasporas or dispersed communities are a major source of tourism, political contributions, and flows of new ideas, attitudes, and cultural influence. The most typical manifestation comes in the form of remittances that fuel the economies of many less-industrialized countries. These immigrant exchanges are not new, but they are now more organized and particularly sustained by a broader spread of sending and receiving states than ever before. Immigrants return a portion of their earnings for a variety of familial and civic purposes. For some, sending money is a form of insurance against old age, preserving a place where they can retire in a society that respects and cares for the elderly. It also is a way for immigrants to enjoy a certain level of esteem back home in contrast to their relatively low status in the United States.[28] And for those left behind, "having someone who's doing well abroad brings confidence to the family. They can hold their heads high," says Dilip Ratha, the World Bank economist who is widely credited with putting remittances on the map.[29]

Immigrants cobble together funds, often collectively through hometown associations, to build bridges, roads, clinics, churches, schools, and soccer parks back home. Mexico alone has about three thousand associations of this sort.[30] Less commonly, they invest in both small and large business ventures and make charitable donations to philanthropic organizations raising funds for their city or region of origin. As a Somali refugee explained, at least prior to the global economic meltdown, the economy of his war-ravaged country had never been stronger, largely thanks to the financial commitment of those who had fled. Not only do these exchanges profoundly affect social and economic stability, national growth, and capital accumulation in developing nations, but they help reposition those nations in a newly emerging world order.

This phenomenon is playing itself out around the globe.[31] According to the World Bank, immigrants sent $300 billion back home in 2007. Those figures do not reflect the large sums sent through informal channels or hand-carried by travelers. India was the primary recipient, with China, Mexico, and the Philippines close behind. The Philippines received funds from emigrants spread throughout forty-six countries worldwide.[32] The United States, followed by Germany, Belgium, and Switzerland, is one of the top sending countries. In 2004 the United States recorded almost $39 billion in outward remittances.[33] Mexico and El Salvador captured the highest volume of U.S. funds, the latter receiving over $2.8 billion, just under 17 percent of its GDP, in 2005.[34] About 42 percent of adult immigrants from Latin America, some six million in number, regularly send remittances home. And although the longer they stay in the United States, the less money they send back, nearly a quarter of those who have been in the country for twenty to thirty years still send money to their families.

The majority of senders are women.[35] Monetary transfers of this kind have transformed political transnationalism into political clout, placing demands on local and national politicians abroad.

Like in the Somali experience, remittances have increased access to critical services like education and health and have significantly reduced poverty in underdeveloped countries. However, a weakened U.S. economy, growing anti-immigrant sentiments, increasingly strict immigration policies, and stepped-up border patrols are decreasing the number of Latin American migrants entering the country and hence decelerating the growth in remittances, especially to Mexico. Meanwhile, immigrants who are already here, fearful of losing their jobs or having already lost them, are sending less money home to support children, spouses, and parents.[36]

For many years, changes on the world scene created a political environment conducive to transnational lifestyles. Post-1965 immigrants were spared global pressures to quickly assimilate. There were no major world wars to spark the fires of patriotism and national demands for abandoning old allegiances. Neither the Cold War nor armed hostilities in Vietnam raised concerns regarding national disloyalty based on country of origin.[37] At the same time, American domestic policies legitimized ethnic pluralism through the allocation of resources based on racial and ethnic lines, most notably in the form of affirmative action programs that now have fallen into legal disfavor, while the prevailing rhetoric continued to promote America as a "land of immigrants."

That was the situation at least until the terrorist attacks of September 11, 2001, when the political landscape shifted. The subsequent "war on terrorism" and the escalation of military action in Afghanistan and especially Iraq, together with the horrors of suicide bombings abroad, have given more immediacy to already heightened concerns over immigration and divided loyalties. Not only are Muslim and Arab immigrants now treated with suspicion; even those immigrant populations whose value systems and religious practices are more compatible with those of mainstream America are experiencing a spillover of negative attitudes. Stimulated by open hostility toward undocumented Latin Americans entering the country, combined with fears of Islamic fundamentalism, the debate over immigration once again has reached a feverish pitch.

Transnational Citizens

Political transnationalism is driven in part by the nation-building policies and projects of sending countries eager to cultivate cross-border relations for political and economic advantage. Some nation-states, like France,

Italy, and Colombia, assign legislative seats to represent expatriate constituencies. An estimated one-half of the world's countries now recognize plural nationality, a change that seems to be gaining universal acceptance.[38] In 1991, four Latin American countries recognized dual nationality or citizenship. By 2000, the number acknowledging citizenship was ten—Brazil, Colombia, Costa Rica, the Dominican Republic, Ecuador, El Salvador, Mexico, Panama, Peru, and Uruguay. At least another ten countries in the Caribbean recognized dual nationality.[39] Although Mexico is by far the most active source of migrants to the United States, many of these other countries also produce significant numbers of newcomers.

Between 2001 and 2006 alone, the number of countries allowing individuals to simultaneously hold dual citizenship jumped from 100 to 151. Some of the most common countries of origin for immigrants to the United States, including Mexico, the Philippines, the Dominican Republic, Canada, and India, recognize as citizens children born to their nationals abroad. India's policy is somewhat selective by country but includes the United States in its orbit. Since 2006, an Overseas Citizen of India Card, offering American citizens of Indian origin visa-free entry for life, has spurred a back-migration of young people eager to reap the benefits of India's growing economy. China and Iran have no provisions for expatriation, and so persons born there maintain their primary citizenship even when they take up a second one elsewhere. The United States recognizes as citizens the children of foreigners born within its territories. And so a combination of the Anglo-American *jus soli* (law of the soil) rule, or citizenship by place of birth, and various *jus sanguinis* (law of the blood) rules in other countries have made dual citizenship more common among Americans. It is thus not surprising that Chicago has become a fixed campaign stop for Mexican politicians, while New York is now a critical state for elections in the Dominican Republic, which also permits its citizens to vote from abroad.[40]

The situation in the United States, which does not officially recognize dual citizenship, is less clear-cut. An American citizen is first and foremost just that. New citizens must swear under oath that they "absolutely and entirely renounce and abjure all allegiance and fidelity to any foreign prince, potentate, state, or sovereignty of whom or which [they] have heretofore been a subject or citizen." Yet, unlike Germany's naturalization law, for example, U.S. law does not require that the renunciation actually have that legal effect.[41] Practically speaking, the oath is simply not enforced, and U.S. law remains silent on dual nationality. Even though the American passport expressly prohibits American citizens from accepting

employment with foreign governments, enlisting in foreign armies, or becoming naturalized citizens of foreign states, some American citizens
continue to engage in these activities with no apparent consequences.

The immigrant experience, in fact, seems to have come full circle.
Third- and fourth-generation native-born Americans are now seeking al-
ternate citizenship in their ancestral lands. The requirements vary by
country. This recent interest should not be mistaken for the sentimental
or politically driven ethnic revival of the 1970s. Here the motives are
purely economic. Young people are looking to gain a foothold in the European Union's job market with its demand for workers who speak fluent
English. And so, on the one hand, the letter of the law continues to reflect
the old view of citizenship as an exclusive embrace of American ideals
and loyalties. Yet, on the other hand, the more inclusive spirit of diversity, including dual citizenship or nationality, suggests a different understanding of the role those ideals play, at least among some of today's immigrants and native-born Americans.

There is some evidence that increased opportunities for dual citizenship, combined with growing opposition toward unbridled immigration,
are hastening the desire of new immigrants to become American citizens,
as similar concerns did a century ago. In 2005 the proportion of legal
foreign-born residents who became naturalized rose to 52 percent, a 14
percent increase since 1990 and the highest level in a quarter of a century.
The number from the Middle East grew by 156 percent between 1995
and 2005. And while Mexicans were the least likely to become citizens,
during that same period the number of naturalized citizens from Mexico
rose by 144 percent, the sharpest rise among immigrants from any major
sending country.[42] Some of the increase was the result of several million
undocumented immigrants obtaining legal status under amnesty legislation in 1986. Yet some of it undoubtedly could be attributed to new dual
citizenship laws in a number of sending countries, freeing immigrants
from choosing between their native and adopted lands. These outward
manifestations of forging political attachments to the United States are
encouraging, yet they may be purely pragmatic with no deep significance.
The continued insecurities some immigrants experience in the face of
widespread animosity may merely reinforce their ties and loyalties to
their homeland regardless of whether they have American citizenship.

Since the early 1990s, the potential effects of these global and domestic
forces have engaged the intellectual energies of scholars across the disci-
plines. Talk of "transnationalism" permeates the pages of scholarly and
popular journals. Some consider transnationalism a crisis for the nation-
state as an independent entity. With the breakdown of national borders,

they warn, political loyalties will falter. Yet the evidence belies that claim. The dismantling of colonial empires and the collapse of multi-ethnic states like the Soviet Union and Yugoslavia have had a countervailing effect. And so the number of nation-states continues to rise.[43] Others celebrate transnationalism's emancipatory character and its resultant cultural and political hybridism, challenging historically limited visions of race, ethnicity, class, and nation. Still others argue that claims on both sides are overstated and that transnationalism has affected the lives of very small segments of immigrant populations.

Many Americans would be surprised to learn that transnational practices are not new. In the early 1900s, politicians from the home country similarly courted the immigrants. Irish nationalists made fund-raising visits to New York, not unlike Dominican political candidates and Irish nationalists today. The Italian government took even more aggressive steps to maintain ties with Italian migrants overseas. It established state agencies and funded private organizations for migrants, published and distributed a magazine describing the activities of Italians around the world, facilitated the reacquisition of Italian citizenship, and helped finance Italian schools overseas. It partially subsidized return trips home, and it even pressed for a separate bank to process remittances sent from abroad.[44]

Emigration that is temporary but long-term removes pressure from the labor market while improving the sending country's finances through expatriate remittances. Of course, the longer immigrants remain in the host country, the more deeply their children become assimilated and the more attachments they develop, making it less likely that they will be eager to return to their homeland. It therefore benefits sending countries to actively keep emigrants tied to the homeland so that they continue to send money, visit frequently for vacations and holidays, and finally return for retirement, bringing with them their capital and pensions.[45]

Mexico is a clear case and one that raises deep concerns in the United States for its potential impact on the political assimilation of Mexican immigrants, the largest and most examined group of newcomers. Mexican migration, at least initially, was more akin to labor migration than immigration. With long-term undocumented residents granted amnesty, and agricultural workers granted a special legalized status under the Immigration Reform and Control Act of 1986, heads of households began settling more permanently, bringing with them their parents, spouses, children, and siblings. Intended to stem the tide of illegal migration from Mexico, the law actually served as an incentive for more family and friends to relocate here, whether legally or not. What was largely a rural,

male, and temporary flow of migrant workers became a feminized, ur-
banized, and permanent population, many of them undocumented.[46]

The Mexican government's migration policy has primarily been aimed
at maintaining economic and social stability through a combination of
transnational ties, political rights, and collective and family remittances,
along with efforts to protect the human rights of the undocumented.[47] In
addition to American efforts under the now much derided Bracero Ac-
cord, which awarded a form of guest worker status to agricultural workers between 1942 and 1964 and effectively encouraged undocumented
immigration, the Mexican government itself has created structures that
foster transnational life among Mexicans living in the United States.
In 1990 the Ministry of Foreign Affairs established the Program for
Mexican Communities Abroad, which is largely responsible for organizing Mexican hometown associations in American localities. Through its
"Three for One" initiative, municipal, state, and local governments triple
migrants' collective contributions with matching grants.

Several years ago, the government converted that program into the Institute for Mexicans Abroad, aimed at strengthening immigrants' ties to
Mexico while promoting education and health programs. One of the Institute's most expansive initiatives is the Plazas Comunitarias, a program
offering online courses for young people and adults to help them complete elementary, middle, and high school in Spanish; it also offers literacy courses in Spanish and English and job training skills. The program,
overseen by Mexican consulates throughout the United States, provides
the curriculum, materials, and personnel training while American spon-
soring agencies provide the tutors and computer technology. At least 231
of these programs are now operating in thirty-two states, many co-
sponsored with local school districts, some in federal correction centers.
They clearly have transnational undertones. As the Consulate General of
Mexico in Atlanta has noted, "Considering the binational mobility of
Mexican migrants and the scale on which this population contributes to
economic and social development in both the U.S. and Mexico, the state
of their education and access to education should be considered as a bilateral responsibility."[48]

Other programs more overtly focus on preserving ties to Mexico. In
Spring 2007 the Institute sponsored a drawing contest, "Éste es mi Méx-
ico" (This Is My Mexico) for children aged seven to eleven who had some
Mexican connection in their background. The announcement invited
participants to consider what Mexico meant to them, offering such
prompts as: "What do you remember about Mexico? What do you know
about our national heroes? How do you perceive the colors, aromas, and

tastes of Mexico? How are these perceived in the country you live in?"[49] In 2009, Mexico's president Felipe Calderón signed a partnership agreement with Oregon state officials whereby the Mexican government would provide a pool of screened Spanish-speaking teachers to help meet the needs of the state's English learner population. Mexican officials previously had signed similar agreements with California, New Mexico, Utah, and Illinois.[50]

California's Proposition 187, denying public social services to anyone unlawfully present in the United States, spurred the Mexican government into more definitive political action. Adopted by California voters in 1994, Proposition 187 was followed by federal restrictions on receiving government benefits in the 1996 Immigration Reform Act. These measures taken together posed a threat to all Mexicans living in the United States, including those who had gained lawful residency through amnesty. The Mexican government formulated its own response. As of March 1998, in a dramatic turnaround on official policy, amendments to the Mexican Constitution introduced the legal concept of "indelible nationality," permitting Mexicans who naturalize abroad and the first generation born to them outside of Mexico to retain their Mexican nationality.[51] This enables them to hold Mexican passports, to own property and businesses in Mexico, and to vote in Mexican elections. Yet unlike Colombians and Peruvians, for example, who can cast absentee ballots for general elections, Mexicans technically cannot vote unless they return home. And unlike Dominican émigrés, they cannot hold high public office once they have assumed foreign citizenship.

The Mexican government has further nurtured relationships with Mexican American leaders in the United States, inviting them to visit and keeping them abreast of what is going on in the homeland.[52] The full reach of these developments crystallized during the presidency of Vicente Fox, who regularly met with migrant workers and Mexican business leaders in the United States, assuring them that he would "defend the rights of his constituents regardless of which side of the border they call home."[53] That the president of Mexico considered himself the leader of Mexicans living in the United States seems rather startling. Yet his declaration provoked little response from the U.S. media, though it undoubtedly represented a far looser view of political assimilation than would have been demanded a century ago.[54] Fox's successor, Felipe Calderon, in a 2008 tour of U.S. cities designed to counter opposition to immigration, likewise called on Mexican emigrants to help "transform Mexico" into an economic powerhouse, promising them new roads and jobs that would lure them back home.[55]

Mexico's leaders were not alone in invoking national solidarity across borders. In the aftermath of the 1992 Los Angeles riots, the South Korean government intervened politically and financially and South Korean politicians affirmed their view of Korean Americans as a "colony" of the homeland.[56] In her 1990 inaugural address, Ireland's former president Mary Robinson held herself out to be the leader of the extended Irish family worldwide, stating that she was "proud to represent them."[57] In a similar vein, the Portuguese government has embraced its emigrants and their descendants in a declared global nation with "both residents and non-residents, all treated equally."[58]

Transnationalism is a two-way street. Just as foreign politicians and governments take political and economic advantage of their émigrés, American-based diasporas become a major force in shaping American policy toward their homelands. Mexican and other groups are now able to promote the interests of their people on questions of immigration and trade in the United States while enjoying the full benefits and security of American citizenship. The influence of Cuban Americans in tightening American economic embargos on Cuba, the successful campaign by Haitian Americans in moving the Clinton administration to intervene in restoring the exiled president Jean-Bertrand Aristide to power in 1994, and the role played by Slovak American nationalists in garnering American support to dissolve the former Czechoslovakia into a separate Czech Republic and Slovakia, in 1993, are all examples of the political clout that immigrant groups effectively can wield.

It is not clear how long transnational tendencies survive in succeeding generations. This is not surprising, given the multidimensional nature of transnationalism and its varying effect on integration even among those who take an ethnic path within immigrant enclaves.[59] It is difficult to determine trends, even within the first generation, given the racial, economic, and geographic diversity among ethnic groups. Immigrants differ in their attitudes toward their home country versus the United States, and in their particular status back home. And it is difficult to precisely define what is "transnational," who is a "transmigrant," and even who is an "immigrant." For some, returning to the homeland is politically feasible and emotionally desirable; for others, particularly refugees and the undocumented, it simply is not an option.

In any case, transnational identities, practices, and interests, and the relationships among them, need to be more clearly defined. The same can be said for social versus economic and political manifestations. The frequency, scope, and spheres (public or private) of immigrant involvement are all significant. To be sure, an occasional remittance, annual visit, or monthly telephone or Internet contact back home, as compared with more regularized and institutionalized involvement, does not in itself create a transnational identity, nor does it seriously affect the pace of integration or the lives of children. Yet transnationalism in some sense can also exist in the heart and in the mind. Though only one-sixth of foreign-born Latin Americans participate in some form of political activism in their homeland, as measured by voting in home elections, about one-third still identify the home country as the "real homeland" after thirty years of residence in the United States.[60]

Transmigrant Children

In the transnational drama, children are key social actors and facilitators, roles that inevitably influence their academic participation and success. The scholarly literature, nonetheless, tends to treat immigrant children either as empty vessels into which their parents deposit attitudes toward both sending and receiving countries, or as "luggage" weighing down their otherwise mobile families. The first of these images ignores the reality of human agency and the inevitable and corrosive effect of American popular culture on intergenerational relationships within immigrant families. Despite the traditional values of most immigrant parents and their best efforts otherwise, their children are more than likely to acquire American outlooks and thus freely express their needs and wants. And while the second image evoked is real in the sense that children require a certain amount of care, depending on their age, it also belies the crucial part they play, often involuntarily and at their parents' behest, in maintaining essential ties within the transnational lives of their families.

Transmigrant children navigate between conflicting spheres of expectations, cultural values, and ways of social interaction.[61] Often they are the human link joining an extended family of relations dispersed between the old world and the new. Among Latin Americans and Afro-Caribbeans in particular, the geographic nearness and ease of travel have created a diverse configuration of family living arrangements. Some of these children are born and raised in the United States. Others are born in the United States after their parents have migrated but then sent home to be raised and educated by relatives. Still others are born abroad and migrate to the United States as children or teenagers. Even within certain Asian groups, children are likely to be the last to leave the home country, with one or both parents moving first to economically pave the way during a period of transition, which in some cases extends for years. In the meantime, e-mails and phone calls, along with videophone centers spread throughout ethnic neighborhoods, enable parents to talk with their children in real time—dispensing advice, checking up on school activities, sharing the details of their lives.

Once reunited with their children, parents sometimes use the threat of sending the children back to the homeland as a form of "transnational disciplining" and behavior control. They want to protect their children from the drugs, gangs, and violence that typify poor immigrant communities and from the sexual precociousness of American culture. For all these reasons, many families send their teenagers home for high school. Many working mothers send their small children back to the care of their grandparents. In school districts close to the Mexican border, officials even change the academic calendar to accommodate the Mexican tradition of spending the entire Christmas vacation in the home country.[62] And though transnational life is not an option for undocumented children living in the shadows, the threat of involuntary return is more constant, and the potential impact more permanent, making their daily lives in the United States tenuous and the incentive to maintain ties to the home country stronger.

Those children who do move back and forth sometimes labor in both worlds, whether in a small family-owned grocery in Los Angeles or on a farm in Guatemala. They also develop an identity shaped partially by experiences in their homeland. Language understandably plays an important part in sustaining transnational ties. Transmigrant children's schooling is often interrupted and fragmented while they struggle to carve a coherent identity out of two distinct linguistic and cultural worlds. At the same time, acting as language and cultural brokers, they ease the process of adaptation and community-building for their families, talking to teachers, doctors, landlords, and bill collectors on their behalf. This responsibility gives them more power than they traditionally would have enjoyed without the immigration experience. Transnational childhood and parenting can be as painful and disruptive as they are enriching.

Ethnographers warn against overstating the centrality of transnationalism in the sense of connection to the parents' homeland.[63] They note that only a small minority of the second generation remains embedded in transnational social structures and engaged in transnational practices, most significantly those residing along the Mexican border and who more commonly remain bilingual into adulthood. Even so, given the overall size of that population, the number of those involved might be quite substantial.[64] Other researchers have shifted the focus and examined the influence of transnational social fields on identity formation in transmigrant children and the countervailing effects of race, gender, and social class on the transnational activities that engage them. For Afro-Caribbeans, identification with the homeland is a mechanism for escaping racial barriers and restrictive economic opportunities in the United States. With parental encouragement, young people fiercely cling to the identity of their native islands. Studies of Haitian American college students reveal a sense of self shaped by personal, family, and organizational ties "back home" as well as an identity that looks to their race and homeland as part of a transnational political process.[65]

Some groups similarly stigmatized by labels seek strength in ethnic identity. Even where transnational practices are not part of their everyday lives, second-generation Asians have been shown to develop emotional ties to their ancestral land through transnational social spaces, including language and culture classes supported by their parents and communities, and the values they engender. The lure of travel to the home country awakens long-dormant attachments as well as a more instrumental understanding of enhanced job opportunities. Although they might not be living transnational lives in the present, they can imagine ties of more lasting significance in the future.[66] For young South Asians in particular, both the second generation and young immigrants who continue to join them are intensely transnational in their outlook. Beyond cultural and familial ties, they are keenly aware of what the Indian economy has come to offer in recent years. At least until the global economic downturn, the prospects for returning were far more positive than they had been for their parents' generation.[67]

Yet even setting aside transnational practices per se, the imagined cross-national community is a distinct immigrant reality. Immigrants across the economic spectrum often live in "ghettos" of ethnic shopping-malls, restaurants, groceries, newspapers, community banks, churches, and movie theaters, providing little contact with the integrated mainstream. As Chapter 4 will show, it is common practice for Asians in particular to send their children to after-school and Saturday language and culture classes. Instead of the "hyphenated American," commentators now speak of the "ampersand American," as in "Mexican & American" or "Korean & American."

Such identities can be "multiple and fluid" for immigrant children as they move from home and neighborhood to school and peers and eventually to the world of work.[68] For many these familial connections, whether reinforced here or abroad, are a source of strength and renewal that keeps their immigrant dreams alive. The effects of that common immigrant journey on identity and worldview are far more dramatic for transmigrant children, carrying them physically across national boundaries and imbedded cultures. Whether these affinities will survive into the generational future is yet to be known. Experts say that children of immigrants seem to have their feet firmly planted in the United States, notwithstanding regular trips back to their parent's homeland, but the intensity of these transnational ties, the question of whether they create a transnational identity, and their implications for schooling all need to be examined as time goes on.

The children of immigrants, whether first or second generation, cannot be studied as if seen in a snapshot. Migration is a dynamic experience, made all the more so in today's mass relocation of peoples across the globe. The continuous flow and replenishment of new immigrants into the United States from the same countries undoubtedly shapes both the evolving identities and the transnational interests of immigrant communities as they reconfigure themselves over time. As each succeeding second generation interacts with new arrivals, transnationalism and integration are likely to occur simultaneously among individuals of the same age. Even if the empirical evidence points to an American future for the second generation and beyond, a certain segment of each succeeding first generation of newcomers is likely to continue a pattern of transnational practices. The extended cumulative effect, particularly on the political dynamics here and abroad, is now only a matter of speculation. As seen in the Irish American community's material support for Sinn Fein and the IRA, even vague ethnic sentiments among the fourth and fifth generations can successfully be mobilized into transnational politics in the face of compelling circumstances.[69]

History has proved, moreover, that the present is not always an accurate predictor of the future. If the Americanization movement of the early twentieth century taught us anything, it was the dangers of overreacting to group differences or making long-term judgments based on present-day circumstances. No one could have foreseen the economic and educational success and the total political integration of today's fourth and fifth generations based on the very characteristics for which their ancestors were maligned and rejected. In like manner, today's immigrant youth may weave themselves into the American social and political fabric more easily and effectively than their parents' transnational tendencies might suggest. Yet even if they do, it remains to be seen to what extent they develop deep political understandings or undivided attachments, or shed their cultural identities.

CHAPTER FOUR

Language, Identity, and Belonging

L OOKING BACK OVER the past century from the "old" immigrants to the "new" underscores the deep divide between two competing visions of what it means to be American—one locked in the old assimilation ideal and the other embracing a more complex sense of self built on diversity and ethnic ties. A series of events in the summer of 2008 in a small Louisiana town poignantly illustrates these connections and contrasts. Once again language was at the center of the controversy.

Two cousins, daughters of immigrants from Vietnam and co-valedictorians at their high school commencement, each delivered part of her address in Vietnamese. One recited a maxim exhorting her classmates to "always be [their] own person." The other thanked her parents for the hardships they had faced in moving to the United States from their home country. "It's very important to my parents that I keep my culture,'" she later explained. "I felt if I expressed myself in Vietnamese it would be more heartfelt." Neither young woman anticipated the firestorm her well-intentioned remarks immediately ignited. Community members and the American Civil Liberties Union soon positioned themselves on either side of a school district proposal, later retracted, that henceforth all commencement speeches would be in English. One school board member matter-of-factly told the press, "I don't like them addressing in a foreign language."[1]

No doubt this story carried a sad contradiction. Rather than holding these students up as models of personal triumph, celebrating their mastery of two languages, school officials used them to convey a political message that had more to do with immigration and national identity than language. Equally startling was the fact that this was Louisiana, where bilingualism goes to the state's very founding, though perhaps only so long as the other language is French or at least nothing as exotic as Vietnamese. To be sure, the facts triggering the controversy would not have arisen a hundred years ago, when public schools forcibly stripped immigrant offspring of their ethnic trappings and particularly their home languages. With few exceptions, no immigrant student would have dared make a public school speech in a language other than English. But that was then and this is now, and cultural norms have changed.

As this brief story reveals, language differences evoke the inherent tensions that give language much of its real and symbolic force. For the United States, the conventional immigrant story has produced widespread misunderstandings about the importance of language in the lives of immigrant families and their children and the seemingly conflicting interests of the state. These social and political dimensions, from the abstract to the particular, demonstrate how the languages used in daily life construct and confirm personal identity, in ways subtle and profound, and how language ideologies within society shape a sense of national belonging.

The Personal Dimension

"Identity" refers to the pattern of meaning by which we structure our lives. In a social sense, it is a relative construct. It develops through recognizing a concept of self as both an individual and in contrast to others. It tells us "who we are, where we're coming from."[2] It also situates us as a member of a social group along with the values and emotional associations that come with that membership.[3] For immigrants and their children, the process of forging an identity is filled with contradictions.

More than a half century ago, psychologist Erik Erikson first presented identity as an organizing principle in discussions of what it means to be American. As Erikson saw it, "We begin to conceptualize matters of identity . . . in a country which attempts to make super-identity out of all the identities imported by its constituent immigrants."[4] He later suggested that the terms *identity* and *identity crisis* appeared to grow out of the experience of "emigration, immigration, and Americanization."[5] Himself an immigrant and thus understanding that experience firsthand, Erikson described emigration as a "hard and heartless matter, in terms of what is *abandoned* in the old country and what is *usurped* in the new one."[6] In the intervening years, identity has gained a more fluid, multidimensional, and self-defining understanding than Erikson had imagined.

Among other reference points, like race, religion, and gender, identity has become associated with ethnicity. Identity suggests one's sense of belonging to a group, within a larger culture, united by shared customs, values, behavioral roles, language, and rules of social interaction tied to a common ancestry.[7]

Many Americans, while maintaining a modicum of ethnic self-identification or awareness, are so many generations removed from the point of immigration that they have difficulty understanding the truth of Erikson's assertion. Only someone who has lived through it can fully appreciate what it takes to reinvent oneself in a new land with unfamiliar cultural norms and expectations, to face the constant pressure to let go and blend in despite the inner urge to resist, hold on, and remain distinct. It is what the Portuguese long ago named *saudade,* that "uprooted experience'" somewhere between the "memories of the past" and the "desire of the future."[8] These tensions are a familiar theme in contemporary fiction, much of it written by immigrant authors. The best-selling novel *The Namesake* comes to mind. There the Indian-born mother wistfully describes how "being foreign . . . is a perpetual wait, a considerable burden, a continuous feeling out of sorts . . . a parenthesis in what had once been an ordinary life, only to discover that that previous life has vanished, replaced by something more complicated and demanding."[9] Depending on the social context, language can play significantly in these feelings of "in-betweenness."

The anthropologist and linguist Edward Sapir was an early voice in drawing the link between language and identity. "Language," he explained, "is a great force of socialization. . . . The mere fact of a common speech serves as a peculiarly potent symbol of the social solidarity of those who speak the language . . . At the same time [it is] the most potent single factor for the growth of individuality."[10] As human rights historian Michael Ignatieff similarly points out, "It is language, more than land or history, that provides the essential form of belonging, which is to be understood." That understanding goes not only to the words per se but inextricably includes the "tacit codes" of family and community that form part of the deeper culture.[11] In the same way, adopting a new language with all its nuanced ways of expression is an essential part of the personal transformation inherent in migration. The processes of enculturation, acculturation, and deculturation are significant in shaping the bilingual's language skills and cultural identity. Especially where deculturation entails abandoning the first or mother tongue by coercion or expediency, as opposed to merely adding on the new, it makes the transformation all the more unsettling and uncertain.

The effects of language on the individual's sense of reality have long provoked lively debate. There was a time when linguists commonly believed that language predisposed us to a particular way of thinking about the world, popularly known as the Sapir-Whorf hypothesis (named after Edward Sapir and his student Benjamin Lee Whorf).[12] Strains of "neo-Whorfianism" continue to capture scholarly attention, though it is now suggested that even Whorf may not have ascribed to linguistic determinism as generally believed; he was merely making the case for the benefits of linguistic pluralism.[13] A weaker and more widely acknowledged version suggests that language influences the way we make sense of the human experience. Different ways of speaking both within and across languages can thus produce real effects on people, creating multiple expressions of the self that are partially a function of social context, and partially a function of available repertoires in each language and prevalent social and political attitudes toward each. This is especially so where bilinguals occupy two distinct "monolingual" worlds. Such is the case with many children who speak English in school and another language in their home and community.[14]

On the communal side, language is a mechanism of intra-group communication and representation. A shared language and the way it is used reflect shared patterns of thinking, including values, attitudes, and prejudices, and of behaving. It links individuals to the past and to each other through literary forms, oral traditions, history, myths, and rituals, anchoring their identities in a common "linguistic culture."[15] In today's technical vernacular, language is the "cultural software" through which group members attach and intuit meaning and give shape to their practices.[16] It thus characterizes the ways in which individuals position themselves in relation to others, often serving as a marker and symbol of ethnic group membership to both insiders and outsiders.[17] If you do not speak a given language, you do not have access to forming relationships with certain people, or sharing in the resources they control, or participating in certain activities.

What makes the link between language and identity particularly effective is that any given language elicits particular references that carry a certain emotive meaning or relate to a specific experiential setting, and vice versa. A clear manifestation is the way bilinguals switch languages depending on the person spoken to, the social context, or the topic. Such "code switching," even between social variants of the same language (for instance, between dialects and standard forms), not only signals various group memberships and identities, but also demonstrates how language serves definite social and communicative ends.[18]

It is not uncommon for immigrant families to converse in their first language when engaged in intimate or light conversation—for example, around the dinner table—and then switch unconsciously to English when talking about more distant or worldly matters. Often the switch to English reflects the "out of family" context in which certain subjects have been learned, especially for the second generation. For both speakers and listeners, each language can evoke different types of interactions and personas grounded in different linguistic inventories, cultural allusions, and autobiographic memories as well as levels of feeling and proficiency.[19] The first language learned retains strong emotional connotations, either positive or negative. Bilinguals often continue to pray (and swear) in their first language even after many years of using the second language on a daily basis. One plausible explanation offered is that the many neural connections established in early and middle childhood link the entire first language to systems for emotional arousal.[20]

Languages themselves vary in their ways of conceptualizing the self in relation to others. Asian languages, for example, utilize a system of honorifics that mark social relationships among the speaker, the listener, and the topic. These constitute an important aspect of socialization with no direct analogue in Western languages. Among some immigrants, like the Vietnamese and Koreans, ensuring the correct use of such forms as a sign of respect is an important incentive for maintaining the language among their children. In a similar way, cultural competence in French or Russian demands an ability to distinguish between the informal and formal "you" (*tu/vous* in French, *ty/vy* in Russian). The person who uses them inappropriately could appear either too "chummy" or overly polite or distant. These levels of intimacy are culturally conditioned and take some learning for speakers of languages that make no such distinctions. The fact that the French can know each other for years as colleagues or neighbors and still address each other in the formal *vous* completely baffles Americans, who at the same time admire the native French intuitive ease in using each form suitably. French formality, however, also baffles the Italians, who make a similar distinction but much more readily slip into the informal analog. Familiarity with these linguistic subtleties is invaluable for cross-cultural communication.

Research findings suggest that individuals who are not just bilingual but also bicultural may have distinct cognitive frameworks, associated with each of their cultures and languages, that evoke different worldviews and personalities. Two studies are particularly interesting on this point. In the first, Hispanic women who participated in both Anglo and Latino culture switched "frames" more quickly and easily than bilinguals who were monocultural. They classified themselves as more assertive when they spoke Spanish than when they spoke English, and they described women in ads in terms that expressed more self-sufficiency and extroversion when the ads were in Spanish versus English.[21] A study of Portuguese-descendant university students living in Paris proves similarly revealing. When they were asked to tell the same story in their two languages, in terms of verbal strategies and demeanor their French versions evoked the identity of aggressive and assertive (sub)urban Parisian youth speaking in colloquial and even vulgar French, whereas their Portuguese versions were far more reserved, as judged by other bilinguals. As these studies suggest, there seems to be a difference between what speakers can "do" and who they can "be" in each language. Language and identity essentially "summon each other up" at the deepest levels.[22]

Bilinguals often say that they simply "feel different" when they speak in their different languages. A personal anecdote from the writer/poet Jean Portante, born and raised in Luxembourg to an Italian-speaking family, movingly makes the point. Invited to present his recently translated book of poems at an Italian university, he began reading aloud in French as the book's Italian translator alternately read in Italian. Sensing a stir in the "magna aula," he looked up, at which point a student in the audience asked him whether he was Italian. At first the author shook his head "no" and then corrected himself and nodded "yes." The young man then asked him why he was not reading the Italian version. Taking the cue, Portante and the translator reversed roles. As he continued in Italian, he was overcome with sadness, he recalls, realizing that the Italian translation was the "genuine original" rendering of his poems. The text he had written in French sounded like a translation coming from the mouth of his translator. "Everything" he says, "had switched." As comfortable as he felt with French, his chosen literary language, he had regained his "inside" language, the one that "came from far away."[23] This is not to suggest that language is primordial in the sense of being essential to one's self-definition. It merely underscores an emotional or sentimental aspect to language that, while admittedly unquantifiable, is nonetheless evident through its various expressions.[24]

Language is the foundation for building a multimodal package that includes not just linguistic features, but facial expressions, movement, and other forms of "semiotic behavior." These make the speaker socially accepted within a particular context. Creating a bilingual identity entails a similar process. This range of modes and the cognitive frames revealed in the Hispanic bicultural and Portuguese studies, and not just language skills, make children who are born into foreign language communities potentially effective transnational agents as they move into adulthood. They implicitly share a set of pragmatic assumptions and values essential to communication and comprehension. On the downside, immigrants whose racial phenotype or overall physical appearance departs from the mainstream may still find themselves identified as "foreign" despite their success in acquiring the dominant language and all its multisensory accompaniments. Particularly if they continue to publicly use their native language as well as English, they never fully acquire what French sociologist Pierre Bourdieu calls the "symbolic" or "cultural capital" of being recognized as legitimate within the dominant culture.[25]

Language thus is not only a means for identifying and projecting our own sense of who we are and who we are not and the powers we assume for ourselves and others, but also a means through which others can impose their own assumptions about what they perceive we are or what we ought to be. Such differences and affinities again are a double-edged sword. They give coherence and positive identity to group members but at the same time engender prejudice and ethnic stereotyping.[26] Languages themselves bear testimony to that fact. The ancient Greeks identified non-Greeks or "the other" by their speech, which sounded like "barbar-bar" and hence the name *barbarians*.[27] The term comes down to mean those individuals who do not speak "our" language properly. Similarly the Welsh word for foreigner is *anghyfiaith,* meaning "not of the same language."

The value ascribed to a language is determined in part by the value ascribed to those who speak it. Studies have demonstrated that individuals assign positive or negative attributes to specific accents depending on the country or language group to which the speaker appears to belong.[28] Just consider the subtleties of upper- and lower-class or regional accents among Americans, and even more so among the British, and the visceral reactions they evoke. In a related way, language establishes a "text" from which others draw interpretative conclusions, sometimes producing "over-readings" that are even more robust than the text can support.[29] For some immigrant groups, like Hispanics, Afro-Caribbeans, and Asians, the racialization of language and accent can have a particularly profound effect on identity, creating a sense of marginalization. As Bourdieu tells us, when a person speaks, the individual wants not merely to be understood, but to be "believed, obeyed, respected, distinguished."[30]

The extent to which one uses the national language or the mother tongue serves as the standard for measuring attitudes in daily interactions. This is especially true in the context of the school. Schools expect students to conform to certain rules of social contact, whether implicit or explicit. By the same token, when schools adopt policies that effectively make minority languages invisible, they create an impression in the minds of minority children that their first language is backward, useless, of low status. That negative impression, indelibly carved into their identity, saps them of any desire to "invest" further in a language that carries no cultural capital. Such attitudes, in turn, reinforce negative representations of the language in the private sphere and in the media, which consequently influence educational policies. And so the ideology of implicit homogenization goes full circle.[31] Three decades ago, psychologist Wallace Lambert referred to this phenomenon as *subtractive* bilingualism, in contrast to *additive* bilingualism where the child's family and community equally valorize both languages.[32] Focusing on the cultural environment and the relative status of each language in the child's life adds much to our understanding of bilingual development.

Immigrants and their school-age children arguably are engaged in a more voluntary process as compared with other linguistic minorities like European regional speakers or even refugees and asylum seekers. Nonetheless, they still feel the push and pull of these competing forces as they struggle to integrate into the mainstream. As Joshua Fishman has described it, the dilemma for parents in particular is "either to remain loyal to their traditions and to remain socially disadvantaged (consigning their own children to such disadvantage as well), on the one hand; or, on the other hand, to relinquish their distinctive practices and traditions, at least in large part, and, thereby, to improve their own and their children's lots in life via cultural suicide."[33] One has to wonder whether the harshness of this choice is politically or socially necessary or worth the costs exacted. As I will soon discuss, especially for children, retaining their home language as they adopt the dominant language appears, in fact, to have an emotionally salutary effect, helping them keep one foot firmly planted in the security of their ethnic community.

Even beyond establishing our own identity and ethnicity, there is a dimension of mutuality that begs for consideration. Language is not only inward looking, but also outward looking. Languages other than our own can enrich our lives. The French novelist Stendhal tells us, "The first instrument of a people's genius is its language." It is the vehicle through which everything meaningful within a society travels and endures. Within that reality, language allows us to more completely access the history, art, politics, and literature of others, and with that the essence of their culture, complete with all the social and attitudinal subtleties often lost in translation. That being so, a reasonable conclusion is that those who are monolingual are culturally "disadvantaged" or "deficient" or "deprived." Many monolinguals, especially English speakers, would need time to absorb that point.[34] I suspect that many would immediately refute it.

The fact that language gives cultural access to diverse visions of the world has not been lost on forces within the European Union who are struggling to save national languages from the onslaught of English. In lieu of using a third language (presumptively English) between two speakers of different languages, they argue, mutual understanding will always be stronger, in both information and emotions, when each of the speakers knows the other's language. Rather than divide, linguistic and cultural diversity can bring people together.[35] The success of that project remains to be fully tested as English is fast becoming the second language of choice among the younger generation in Europe and throughout the world.

The Political Dimension

The link between language and identity goes well beyond the personal. It bears an equally important relationship to nationalism, having significant political and legal dimensions. The degree to which a nation enables, discourages, or absolutely prohibits minorities from using their mother tongues in the "public space" and the status that minority languages hold relevant to the national language speak volumes about the national self-perception. The dominant status of the French language in the French republican project, as compared with the status of "community languages" in the British "mosaic," are clear examples.[36]

From the perspective of the modern nation-state, language is an emblem of national identity, a tool in nation building, and a mechanism for social control and political dominance. As in the case of the ancient Greeks' "barbaros," it is a marker defining insiders and outsiders to the political community, and one that is most difficult to mask or shed. It can thus become a political weapon wielded against the less powerful. The state has a number of means at its disposal for forcing a language upon its citizens: defining an official, national, or common language by law; controlling the language used in the schools; setting the language used within the justice system; regulating the media. Language thus can be a way toward inclusion into the political community of the nation, as when children learn the official language in school. It also can be a mechanism of exclusion, as when children are forced to struggle through mainstream classes where they cannot understand the language spoken by the teacher and are, thereby, denied access to meaningful learning.

Central to developing and maintaining a common core of political principles and ideals, language policies and their institutional management support the state's efforts to incorporate foreigners into the wider society. Language makes an "imagined community" imaginable.[37] As political theorist Will Kymlicka tells us, along with a shared history, language makes citizens feel that they are "members of the same nation." "Citizens," he says, "share a sense of belonging to a particular historical society" in part because "they participate in common social and political institutions which are based on this shared language."[38] Looked at in the reverse, linguistic diversity in some sense defies the widespread assumption, within most democracies, that the sphere of public discourse should be monolingual. Granting linguistic rights, so the argument goes, can further lead regional minorities in particular to pursue autonomy and political independence and ultimately threaten the continued existence of the nation-state. Forging policies that both recognize the identity of linguistic groups and ensure these groups' participation in a shared public life poses a particular challenge for democratic government. As history has demonstrated, most often political cohesion wins out.

Strong cultural feelings and even biases associated with certain languages often evoke personal attachments guided more by the heart than by the head. Commonly used as a proxy for national origin or race, language serves as an acceptable rationale for the political majority to discriminate against or subordinate minority groups for whom language is a defining feature and marker. From the colonizing global exploits of European powers, to the carving and recarving of national boundaries among eastern European countries in the spoils of war, to attempts to suppress the language of Catalans and Basques in Spain, past events have shown that those in power can stifle expression and force the speaker to adopt a different linguistic code. We commonly speak of "language shift" in these situations. More accurately, we should speak of "language loss."

By mastering the dominant language by force or will, individuals give testimony to their loyalty to the nation and their motivation to integrate into a community that is based on a particular linguistic identity.[39] The opposite also is true. Speakers may use language to demonstrate not only social allegiance but also social resistance. Refusing to learn or to use the majority language, especially in the public sphere, which generally is considered especially and politically self defeating, undermines the government's efforts at integration. Storeowners, for instance, who post signs only in a foreign language, provoke criticism from other community members. Workers who insist on speaking a language other than English on the job invite suspicion and hostility from English-speaking coworkers and supervisors, and even sanctions from employers.

The depths of those feelings came to public light in 2007 when the Salvation Army fired two Spanish-speaking thrift shop clothing sorters for failing to comply with the organization's English Only policy. The federal Equal Employment Opportunity Commission took the organization to court, arguing discrimination on the basis of national origin in violation of EEOC rules and federal law. The situation touched off a tempest in Congress, with proposals to change the law and allow employers to require that workers speak only English on the job. "We have very few things that unify us as a country," Senator Lamar Alexander (D-Tenn.), a prime sponsor, told the press, "and one of them is our common language."[40] The case reveals how language differences can create insider/ outsider distinctions that prove unsettling and divisive within communities and institutional settings. The dispute ended in a consent decree whereby the Salvation Army agreed to adopt a new policy allowing non-English-speaking employees to speak their native language during work breaks and with customers who speak the same language.[41]

The idea that language is a core value of national identity initially took root at the end of the eighteenth century in Germany as both a response to Enlightenment rationalism and an expression of superiority over the French. The French were equally inclined to assert a similar belief in the reverse. It would take almost another century for this classical European discourse, joining language and nation, to fully realize itself as a mechanism for joining disparate peoples. Especially in cases like Germany, a country lacking a common religion or even a common ethnic identity, the idea of "one language–one nation" was markedly important.[42] And though the notion of a linguistically homogeneous nation-state has little grounding in reality, nationalistic movements typically invoke this view equalizing language and nation.[43]

In recent decades, transnational migration has made that connection all the more dynamic but also problematic, not only in the United States but particularly across Western Europe, where old regional languages continue to push for official recognition while they compete, at least in theory, with new immigrant minority languages for accommodation. As a matter of law, policy, and practice, there is a clear dichotomy between the two. Though regional languages bear some degree of "cultural capital," languages of migrant minorities bear none, seemingly running counter to the idea of the nation-state. As I discuss in Chapter 9, so-called "national" minorities in Europe have gained some language rights while immigrant languages are largely ignored and considered worthless despite their increasing presence especially in urban areas.

Rousseau, in his *Essay on the Origin of Language,* maintained that language precedes politics.[44] The view that language is the very foundation on which national identity is imagined and rests, though widely contested, is seemingly held by proponents of Official English in the United States who unswervingly push to make English the "official" language of individual states and of the nation.[45] On the international scene, the fact that language remains a volatile issue in countries formerly part of the Soviet Union, or that neither Belgium nor to a lesser extent Canada has forged a completely stable identity, with secessionist threats intermittently heard, also gives modern-day credence to that idea. Belgium seems to be "teetering on the edge" of dissolution between Flemish-speaking and Francophone regions. In any case, the situations in Belgium and Canada as well as the former Soviet countries merely suggest that national unity is better served by all citizens sharing a "common" language, a proposition that few Americans would dispute, without necessarily declaring an "official" language. They also suggest that the question is contextual.

There are, in fact, other examples pointing in the opposite direction. Just consider Switzerland, with four official languages (French, German, Italian, and Romansch), or India, with nineteen. While language problems have arisen in both cases, they have never posed a serious threat to national unity. Switzerland is probably one of the most politically stable countries in the world. Some attribute this to the fact that religion crosscuts language—Catholics and Protestants reside on both sides of the linguistic borders. Meanwhile, sporadic agitation for independence from India by Tamils and other groups seems to have settled down.[46]

What has held countries like Switzerland and India together in a union that transcends language differences is something almost "mystical," a "unique otherness." However defined, it draws from common customs, traditions, values, and political institutions that make the population different from the neighboring French, Germans, and Italians in the one case, and from the Pakistanis in the other. The United States similarly demonstrates a "unique otherness," albeit a somewhat more fluid one, that shapes its national identity and consequently how it integrates immigrant children into the mainstream. That identity bears the form of a national ideology incorporating today's American civic culture: individualism but also egalitarianism, nationalism but also tolerance for diversity. Attempts to transform those precepts into practice in the face of mass immigration have grown particularly contentious in recent years. Public debate on the issue typically turns on competing narratives, a common one using native language attrition and not just English fluency as a measure of immigrant integration into the American mainstream. The more developed the immigrants' native language skills and the more publicly they use them, the seemingly less integrated the speakers appear, regardless of their English language ability.

Yet again, language is here pressed into service merely as a surrogate channel for indirectly expressing concerns over politics, identity, and access to resources that cannot be directly expressed in a politically acceptable way. The emotional appeal is grounded in questions of status, harkening back to the nation's history of discrimination against people of Hispanic origin.[47] Immigration reform and the large numbers of undocumented immigrants, particularly from Mexico, fuel much of that discourse. What often gets lost in the political rancor is that this particular population presents a historically complicated case for integration into American society. Mexicans defy clear categorization within either of two commonly referenced typologies: sociologist John Ogbu's voluntary versus involuntary minorities or Will Kymlicka's analogous distinction between ethnic and national minorities. In each case, the first includes immigrants and the second covers those incorporated into the nation by slavery, conquest, or colonization. For Kymlicka in particular, the first are entitled to more limited "polyethnic" rights while the second are entitled to "self-government" rights, that is, to maintain themselves as a fully distinct society. He nevertheless agrees that conventional efforts to turn immigrants and their children into unilingual speakers of English is "deeply misguided policy," harmful to the individuals and depriving society of a valuable resource in a globalized economy.[48]

As noted, border states like Arizona and California, which are first points of settlement for many Mexicans, were wrested from Mexico by conquest. That historical fact partially explains the different and delayed pattern of Mexican American integration. Those Mexicans who have since migrated to the United States, like other immigrants who enter the country voluntarily, understand that they must overcome linguistic and cultural barriers to succeed. Yet as Ogbu suggests, the American majority has assigned them the same outsider status as those originally conquered and so they have adopted the same collective identity.[49] Similar to other groups, like the Basques in Spain, who historically have suffered subjugation or exploitation within a nation-state, Mexican immigrants have created to some extent a "secondary" linguistic and cultural system in which they view those differences in light of the past and in opposition to mainstream America.

This oppositional attitude undoubtedly operates subconsciously for many, although political rhetoric from community leaders at times suggests a more conscious awareness. The cultural system gains further reinforcement from a continuous flow of newcomers and from government policies that implicitly recognize Mexican Americans as more deserving or numerically needy of accommodations than other non-English-speaking groups. These factors also explain to some extent why Mexican Americans more typically retain their native language and thus transform into bilinguals rather than English monolinguals through succeeding generations. At the same time, the overwhelmingly high number and geographic concentration of Spanish speakers understandably poses an unprecedented threat to national identity, even one based largely on shared values and principles and only questionably on a shared language.

The United States is certainly not unique in using language as a proxy for deeper political concerns. France's Toubon Law, adopted in 1994, is a case on point. Among its requirements, the law mandated the use of French in all commercial advertisements and public announcements, or at least a French translation in a footnote. Commentators have ascribed various underlying purposes to the law: to insulate French from the onslaught of English, to help preserve France's international position in the face of transnationalism, to protect from further erosion its status as a nation-state within the European Union.[50] Yet underneath the Toubon Law lies an unshakable belief among the French that their language remains a symbol of political and cultural preeminence widely recognized in centuries past and that English in particular is imbued with features that threaten French values and norms.[51]

A particular language may be little more than a vehicle for binding people together, whether consciously or not, in opposition to countervailing forces. Just as national languages mark external group boundaries, so too minority languages mark internal group boundaries, even if the minority languages are not universally or regularly spoken. Gaelic and the rise of Irish nationalism provide a good example. Although the Constitution of the Republic of Ireland recognizes Gaelic as the "national" and "first official language," and although in 2006, 41.9 percent of the population claimed competence in Gaelic, only 1.3 percent spoke it daily outside the education system.[52] Beyond a few enclaves in western Ireland, few families speak the language on a regular basis.[53] The Official Languages Act of 2003 requires each public body to account for how it provides services in Gaelic and English. Gaelic is now mandatory in public elementary schools, while "Gaelscoileanna" schools, where the entire curriculum is taught in Gaelic, are gaining ground.[54] A similar transformation is occurring in Wales, where many Welsh are English monolinguals although the Welsh Language Act of 1993 has made employment contingent on bilingual competence. The teaching of Welsh in the schools is now preparing a new generation that can benefit more fully than their parents or grandparents from this cultural renaissance and autonomy. Both cases bear significant economic consequences for the speakers and political ramifications for each nation.

For all the reasons already stated, language policies are especially important to children, who most frequently are targeted by these policies through schooling. Language and education together play a central role in reconciling competing political claims of groups and individuals with those of the state. Both factors are essential to the establishment and preservation of modern nation-states. Schools are the primary arenas for integrating cultural and political differences into a national whole that is largely predefined. They operate on the "cutting edge" of society, both perpetuating a sense of continuity while integrating newcomers into the democratic project. Schools promote a shared sense of values and common destiny, helping to realize and legitimize the "artifact" of the standard language.[55] From this perspective, language is the most visible and palpable personal attribute over which schools have significant authority and control, and over which there remains unending controversy precisely for its cultural value and its political force. With the mission of schooling being so tied to socialization and nationalization, it is hardly surprising that the place of English vis-à-vis other languages in the schools has generated such heated debate and political maneuvering. The lack of consistent educational policies supporting the maintenance of immigrant languages raises a number of questions regarding language maintenance and identity formation among ethnic minority students.

Ties That Bind

Schools are not the only arena where children experience the forces of socialization. The family and the community play a prior and at least an equally effective role in that regard, though language policies rarely recognize either one in a positive way. Sociologists tell us that children need to be connected to, and not forcefully disengaged from, the nurture and support of their family and culture. They need what is referred to as the "social capital" embodied in relationships with their parents and other family members.[56] And while the evidence on academic achievement and school retention is compelling, the related and more fundamental emotional benefits are equally, if not more, significant. Children's primary bonds to family, as well as others' views of them, whether real or imagined, play a pivotal role in the process through which children define themselves. As philosopher Alasdair MacIntyre put it, "I can only answer the question, 'What am I to do [or 'what am I to think?'] if I can answer the prior question, 'Of what story or stories do I find myself a part?'"[57] For children of immigrant background, language symbolizes the continuous storyline joining the family with the country of origin.

Despite the intuitive appeal of this argument, much of the rationale underlying the education of English language learners appears implicitly to deny these truths. In most cases, from the time these children enter school, there is a decided attempt to erase their mother tongue from their minds. Working on the compensatory model, the starting premise is that these children suffer a cultural and linguistic deficit. Family background, including language, merely presents an obstacle to the child's educational development and social mobility. Many educators and policymakers simply assume that language can be isolated and that English acquisition is all that matters. Of course, that is not to deny the critical link between English fluency and literacy, on the one hand, and academic achievement, economic advancement, and civic participation, on the other. I only suggest that maintaining the home language is not necessarily a barrier to achieving those ends. In fact, it may be an asset. Herein rests the sociocultural argument for supporting native language development in the schools.

Needless to say, the upbringing of children itself depends on linguistic interaction. It is through language that young children learn the cultural beliefs and practices of parents and community, in essence what they value. Language represents the "emotional and behavioral texture" of their first and most formative intimate relationships. That association may very well explain why we affectionately refer to our first language as our "mother tongue," and why some individuals are willing to fight to the end to preserve it.[58] Abandoning the language represents, consciously or not, a break in those fundamental bonds, setting children adrift on a sea of cultural and emotional uncertainty. The force of these arguments has gained global recognition in worldwide events each year celebrating February 21 as International Mother Language Day. A UNESCO initiative dating from 1999, the day consciously reminds us of the important role the primary language plays in socializing children.

As I discuss in more detail in Chapter 8, among immigrants the second generation is typically English-dominant while the third generation, except for some Spanish speakers, generally speaks only English. Meanwhile, the first generation continues to communicate more effectively in the native language. Among foreign-born Hispanics, only 7 percent speak mainly or only English at home, giving rise to a potential linguistic and cultural disconnect between them and their "Americanizing" children.[59] In the United States, bilingualism is typically considered at most a temporary "intergenerational bridge" between competing states of monolingualism. Though that perspective presents the sociohistorical progression of linguistic assimilation, it overlooks the complex sociocultural processes essential to that development.

Commentators from the old immigration to the new have repeatedly noted the toll that schooling and its forced assimilation take on families. For many European children a century ago, shedding their ethnicity in favor of a new American identity was more coercive and alienating than liberating. Contacts with native-born children caused them feelings of inferiority and psychological distress.[60] In an 1897 address to the National Education Association, settlement house founder Jane Addams warned the membership that the contempt shown by some teachers to the immigrant child's background, "cutting into his family loyalty," was taking away "one of the most conspicuous and valuable traits" the child brought to school.[61] Addams later observed how in the process of wiping out differences, mass public schooling disengaged students from communities grounded in emotional bonds, religious beliefs, ethnic ties, and common expression.[62] A U.S. Immigration Commission Report in 1911 sounded a similar warning that Japanese children on the West Coast were learning English but losing their ability to communicate, particularly with their mothers, who had little knowledge of the language.[63] The immigrants were relinquishing the desirable aspects of their native cultures without receiving much of anything positive in return.

Writing in the 1930s on his own experience as a student in the New York public schools, noted educator Leonard Covello recalled that, with no recognition given to the home language or culture, "We were becoming American by learning how to be ashamed of our parents."[64] For Covello and his contemporaries, especially in the cities, the individualizing force of daily life drove a deep wedge between children and their families. Acculturation involved more than just learning a language. All the habits, rituals, and other expressions that gave meaning and value to their being, and the accepted roles of family members, lay open to challenge, rejection, and inversion. Parents, unable to communicate in English, had to rely heavily on their children to navigate them through the world outside the home and ethnic community. In doing so, they increasingly lost their emotional and disciplinary hold on them. Becoming acceptably American exacted a high price from the immigrant family both then and now.[65]

Children gain critical social capital from close-knit family and community interactions. As Robert Putnam has empirically demonstrated, those factors help children grow up healthier, safer, and better educated.[66] Immigrant parents initially are relieved to see their children quickly learning English, yet they soon realize that they no longer speak a common language.[67] The children, unable to fully express themselves in the language of the home, begin to mix languages as English progressively takes over. Scholars and advocates continue to lament how the loss of language and culture impairs parents' ability to preserve their values and guide their children through decisive phases of life. Researchers have explored how shifts in language dominance and cultural identity among immigrant children negatively affect family solidarity, creating "cultural dissonance," and, in the reverse, how a community's support system affects language maintenance.

Immigrant children are faced with an unpleasant choice. They can either adopt the language and cultural perspective of the school and risk developing a negative aspect to their identity, or they can resist these external pressures and risk becoming alienated from the dominant public environment and from themselves. In their zeal to become accepted into the mainstream culture, young people typically lose the ability to communicate in their ethnic language on a meaningful level and experience feelings of isolation and exclusion from the ethnic community.[68] As French linguist Louis-Jean Calvet tells us, children who no longer speak their mother tongue find themselves at the center of a linguistic conflict within the family that echoes similar conflicts within society.[69]

From their extensive studies of immigrant children over time, Carola and Marcelo Suárez-Orozco warn that even as such children build bridges to their new country, they need to continue "bonding with, talking to, and respecting their parents."[70] As they describe it, beyond basic everyday conversation, subtleties are often missed in complex conversations between immigrant parents and their children. "It is not uncommon to overhear discussion," they say, "in which parents and children switch back and forth between languages and completely miss one another's intent." In a deeper sense, they point out, in losing competency in the home language, children "often lose much of the sustenance that the culture of origin provides."[71]

Lily Wong-Fillmore likewise has underscored the importance of family language in teaching what she calls the "curriculum of the home": "a sense of belonging; knowledge of who one is and where one comes from; an understanding of how one is connected to the important others and events in one's life; the ability to deal with adversity; and knowing one's responsibility to self, family, and community."[72] She movingly describes the loss in parent-child communication, especially common in immigrant families:

> What is lost is no less than the means by which parents socialize their children. When parents are unable to talk to their children, they cannot easily convey to them their values, beliefs, understanding, or wisdom about how to cope with their experiences. They cannot teach them about the meaning of work, or about personal responsibility, or what it means to be a moral or ethical person in a world with too many choices and too few guideposts to follow . . . Talk is a crucial link between parents and children.[73]

Young second-generation Americans note how difficult it is to communicate thoughts and emotions to their parents, frequently resulting in arguments and family tension.[74] They describe how they rarely converse with their grandparents and how their inability to speak their native language has limited their relationships with members of their community.[75] As one bilingual educator explained, "Some families speak less and less Spanish at home and the whole family unit breaks down. You can't love or have powerful emotions in a language in which you're not comfortable."[76]

Researchers have documented these findings especially among second-generation Asian Americans. Contrary to conventional expectations and in contrast to other groups, the higher the concentration of Asian-origin students in a given school, the lower the students' knowledge of parental languages.[77] To the extent that Asian Americans present more visible racial differences and therefore invite more overt racial taunts from other children, they experience a stronger drive to shed their home language in their efforts to blend in. Perhaps more than others, they intensely struggle to reconcile conflicting forces and find a stable sense of who they are.

Young adults admit that they only later came to recognize the personal and career disadvantages of this lost opportunity. They too feel "somewhat uneasy," almost like "total strangers," in their own home, because their parents cannot completely understand them when they speak English. Their poor skills in their home language, they say, have invited criticism from relatives and family friends, and so they avoid social contacts with those who do not speak English. They regret how their inability to communicate has prevented them from effectively working within their communities or feeling welcome in their parents' native country.[78] The loss of their home language has exacted a dear price in family intimacy while creating in them feelings of shame and inadequacy whichever way they turn. It is not surprising that many prefer raising their own children bilingually. In one noted study, among a broad range of Hispanic and Asian American young people that figure stood at 68 percent in California and a stunning 82 percent in Miami.[79]

Perhaps no modern work more graphically reveals what a *Boston Globe* book reviewer called the "fathomless capacity of language to shape experience" than Richard Rodriguez's haunting 1982 autobiography, *Hunger of Memory*.[80] Though the author has positioned himself as a vocal and often-quoted critic of bilingual education, accepting the changes in his private life as the necessary price to be paid for the public gain of Americanization, he emerges from his life story as a deeply conflicted man in search of a coherent identity. The reader cannot help but sense his grief when his parents, at the urging of the nuns from his school, agreed to give up in an instant "the language (the sounds) that had revealed and accentuated [his] family's closeness." He describes how the loss of a commonly familiar language severed the "spiritual" bond between his parents, especially his father, and their children. "The silence at home," he tells us, "was finally more than a literal silence. Fewer sounds passed between parent and child, but more profound was the silence that resulted from my inattention to sounds." He confusingly admits that he would have been "happier" about his "public success" had he "sometimes recalled what it had been like earlier, when [his] family had conveyed its intimacy through a set of conveniently private sounds." And while he claims that "intimacy is not created by a particular language," he privately "broods over language and intimacy—the great themes of [his] past."[81] For Rodriguez, who came of age in the 1960s, identifying as an "American" was an all-or-nothing and indeed painful affair, as it was for many of his as well as previous generations.

Researchers now talk of the "immigrant paradox." It appears that although immigrants often do much better in society than would be expected, given their typical lack of financial resources and English language skills, their success diminishes with each succeeding generation, raising the question of whether becoming American is a "developmental risk." The paradox suggests that immigrant families have certain strengths, including language and culture, that often become lost in the process of assimilation.[82]

Recent studies, in fact, have shown that children who adopt the new language and culture without shedding the old, what has been called "selective acculturation," more successfully adapt to mainstream culture by effectively building an "intergenerational alliance" with their families. For them the process of integrating into American society is additive and not subtractive. Researchers have found within diverse groups, including Mexican American, Vietnamese, and Sikh students, a connection between academic achievement, on the one hand, and the level of native language use, and the transmission of cultural norms, values, and traditions within the family, on the other.[83] Findings among young adults have similarly shown a positive correlation between bilingualism and embeddedness within bilingual immigrant households and high school completion rates. Those least likely to drop out of school tend to have more native speakers in their home, helping them maintain their ethnicity while they master English.[84] A study of Hispanic parents and particularly their U.S.-born adolescent children drew similar conclusions. Those young people who had remained immersed in their cultural heritage, including its language, showed higher self-esteem and lower aggressive behavior over time.[85]

Data gathered from second-generation junior high school students of diverse immigrant backgrounds likewise reveal that those who had become fluent bilinguals reported lower levels of conflict and higher family cohesion, greater self-esteem, higher educational aspirations, and higher academic achievement. But it was not simply the open communication with parents or the attachment to the culture that made the difference. What was especially significant was the simultaneous mastery of both languages while preserving a "cultural anchor" in the family's own past.[86] These findings suggest that even though parents' learning of English is important to family economic mobility and their ability to help their children steer through the educational process, that effort alone may not necessarily achieve the same positive psychological and academic outcomes for the children, because the parents' English language skills are less significant than their children's. And while recent findings have linked second-generation English language skills to parental English language proficiency, the findings have no bearing on the emotional benefits of bilingualism per se.[87] There is far more to language than mere communication or English achievement test scores.

Families with sufficient economic means and community support keenly appreciate the importance of maintaining these ethnic ties. Determined to pass on their heritage, a growing number are now replicating a time-honored immigrant strategy in urban and particularly suburban communities nationwide. From Silicon Valley, California, to Montclair, New Jersey, they are enrolling their children in after-school and weekend language and culture classes as an adjunct to public schooling. Many of these parents are well educated. They typically speak their native language at home, watch Internet TV programs produced in their native countries, and regularly read native language newspapers. Yet much to their dismay, their children are increasingly answering them in English. Others speak their native language poorly but want to impart to their children what they regrettably have lost for themselves.

In cities and suburbs across the country, Presbyterian churches, the center of community life in Korean neighborhoods, offer weekend Korean language classes to ease the transition into American culture while preserving traditions and customs. Even among second- and third-generation Greek Americans, for whom the Greek Orthodox Church traditionally has provided a sense of community and ethnic affirmation, it is common for children to attend classes in Greek language, culture, and religious beliefs and rituals. Intensely proud of their ancient heritage and devoted to the language that "gave light to the world," Greek communities have long profited from an educational and emotional safety net that includes Sunday schools, afternoon schools, private schools, home tutoring, and summer camps.[88] The Armenian community, in the same way, sponsors church-based language classes beginning in preschool as well as regional social activities for young people into their twenties and even internship programs in Armenia to nurture future professionals.

Similar but secular-based practices can be found among a diverse group of immigrant families who widely support such programs for reasons that go deeper than language maintenance.[89] The Xilin Asian Community Center in Chicago is a clear example of this trend. In 1989 it started a program that eventually grew into eight independent schools offering Chinese classes to 2,000 students throughout the region. Many of the families work in high-tech industries. Thirty-six Polish schools likewise offer classes every Saturday in forty-five branches around the Chicago metropolitan region, providing language, religion, and cultural lessons to more than 16,500 students. Comparable programs are serving the children of Russian, Ukrainian, and South Asian immigrants.[90]

Refugee communities equally benefit from such initiatives. In St. Louis, the Bosnian American Education Center offers weekend classes in English and Bosnian to help bridge the language gap that many families face. As Sukrija Dzidzovic, the Center's co-founder and publisher of the Bosnian language newspaper *SabaH,* stated, "We have a conflict of two generations. Grandma is not able to talk to the grandchild. That's big. We have to figure out how to survive that."[91] For political refugees, whether from the Balkans, Southeast Asia, or Africa, the fact that they cannot return to their homeland makes their native culture and language even more precious and the will to preserve them even stronger.[92]

Now referred to as "heritage language" programs, these initiatives vary in their organization and staffing. Some rely on community volunteers and parents. Others hire paid staff. Some enjoy the benefit of national organizations like the National Council of Associations of Chinese Language Schools, the Islamic Society of North America, and the Korean Schools Association, which provide materials, training, and other support. Most are operated entirely by the ethnic community and housed in places of worship or community centers. Others lease space from local public or private schools. Some work in collaboration with embassies or consulates.[93]

For some families, the motivation rests as much in resistance as in retention. As eager as immigrant parents are for their children to learn the "instrumental" aspects of American culture, including English, many are equally ambivalent about their children's exposure to "expressive elements" that they find objectionable, including attitudes toward school, authority, violence, and sex.[94] Peter Kwong, who has studied Asian immigrants, notes that while programs across the Asian spectrum ostensibly aim to affirm the language and culture, they intentionally and even more effectively nurture closed social networks that foster positive attitudes toward academic achievement. In doing so, they insulate children from aspects of American popular youth culture that run contrary to Asian values.[95] From the children's perspective, they offer a safe and common space to express their frustrations and anxieties about growing up in an ethnic culture that places high expectations on them. They also afford them more leverage in negotiating parent-child relations, thus avoiding some of the alienation often found among immigrant offspring.[96]

A study of Chinese community schools in Britain bears proof to those claims. In that case, parents felt strongly that only through studying their home language, its history, and its literature could their children gain "a true understanding" of their family's "attitudes, standards and values." Weekend programs both eased conflicts between parents and children and contributed to their children's academic success.[97] Findings suggest that the personal and societal benefits such children in general derive from heritage language development not only are significant but increase with time. Armed with a strong ethnic identity, immigrant offspring experience greater ease in interacting with their ethnic community and sharing recreational experiences with their parents while learning from them linguistic nuances that prove useful in situations uncommon to English.[98]

Like the increasingly popular dual language immersion programs, including half English-dominant and half other-language dominant students, now found in both middle-class and low-income school districts, private heritage-language programs reveal how parents with the material resources and social awareness understand the importance of keeping the child linguistically and culturally tethered to the family and ethnic community. At the same time, the lure of globalization and transnationalism has afforded such community-based initiatives a more instrumental dimension. Just as native English-speaking families are pushing their children to learn "high need" languages, Chinese being the most popular, so too, immigrant families appreciate the economic and political gains to be had in acquiring the skills to function comfortably in multiple linguistic and cultural codes. What better place to start than within their own community? Meanwhile, as the economy improved in some of the traditional sending countries in the early to mid 2000s, other families began preparing for back-migration. In the Irish immigrant community in Yonkers, north of New York City, Irish-born residents planning to return home were enrolling their American-born children in Saturday morning Gaelic language classes. The idea was to help the children assimilate into an educational system where Gaelic is mandatory in public elementary schools. The subsequent global economic downturn, having hit Ireland especially hard, undoubtedly has put many of those plans on hold.[99]

Aside from ethnic community schools, heritage language programs are gaining increased interest among American educators. As commonly used in the United States, the term *heritage language* includes all non-English languages, including those spoken by Native Americans. In 1998 the National Foreign Language Center and the Center for Applied Linguistics launched the Heritage Languages Initiative to support such efforts in schools, community centers, and colleges. The aim is to build on the linguistic skills of learners who come from a home where a non-English language is spoken, who at least understand the language, and who share certain sociocultural beliefs that foreign language learners find difficult to acquire.[100]

Some public schools offer a "Spanish for Native Speakers" course that teaches literacy more than conversational skills. Not surprisingly there is a growing demand for such classes. Since 2000, the number of heritage speakers of Spanish who take the Advanced Placement Spanish Literature test has nearly tripled.[101] Though Spanish speakers are by far the most numerous, school districts are slowly responding to other markets. In Dearborn, Michigan, where 40 percent of public school students are of Arab descent, many of them fluent in a dialect, students can study

Modern Standard Arabic. In New York City, the French Heritage Language Program teaches French language, literature, and culture to public school students of Francophone background. Many immigrant parents and their children would welcome similar opportunities. The fact that public schools are not making them widely available to those with limited resources raises questions of equity and educational access.

Searching for Coherence

As researchers have found, it is not just "new" immigrant parents who feel the emotional pull toward their family's language and culture. Many of their children and grandchildren share these strong ties. They too nurture their dual identities and maintain or long to recapture their ancestral traditions. Teaching in an immigrant "Mecca" like New York, I have had the good fortune to interact with an ever-growing number of second-generation law students who fit that profile. Like the immigrant population of the city, their family roots are as far-reaching as China, India, Russia, the Philippines, Colombia, Israel, Yemen, and Haiti. Over the years, many of them have shared with me their thoughts on growing up in immigrant homes and the pains and joys of becoming American. And so I decided to more systematically tap into that rich resource for a firsthand understanding of language and cultural maintenance and loss. I put out several calls for student volunteers interested in talking about their experience growing up in an immigrant or bilingual family. Semi-structured interviews with thirty such students confirmed much of the research on ethnic minority development and language attitudes among immigrant offspring.[102] Strikingly common threads ran through discussions that lasted anywhere from fifteen minutes to over an hour.

Most of these young people, embarking on adulthood, talked about childhoods of longing to fit into the mainstream. Some had decidedly shunned their native culture and refused to speak the language through adolescence. They eventually discovered and came to appreciate their ethnic identity in college. That seemed to be the place where they started to redefine themselves, often through ethnic student associations. Most of them had traveled back to their parents' native country, many of them on their own or with friends, to discover their ancestral roots. Some had regularly spent childhood summers there. Some maintained online contact with cousins abroad by way of e-mail, instant messaging, Facebook, and video conferencing, effectively obliterating cultural and geographic distance. All of them were bicultural. Fewer of them were bilingual to any meaningful degree. Those who were not bilingual typically talked about "backtracking" to connect with their linguistic past.

One student who came to the United States as a young child regretted how she had spent so much of her life rejecting her identity, and now she was trying to "get it back." "It's different," she said. "It's hard and it's noticeable." As one Philippine American student told me, "I kind of feel that my culture got stolen away from me. Now I'd like to speak to my grandparents in Tagalog but it's difficult and I often finish in English." Another lamented how she could not communicate with her grandparents at all on their periodic visits to the United States and so she had no relationship with them. Having observed the interaction between her parents, who speak English, and their grandchildren, she felt like she was "completely deprived of the grandparent experience."

There also were those whose parents either insisted that they speak the native language at home or sent them to after-school or weekend classes, or both. And while they may have railed against the "added burden" when they were young, they admitted that it served them well both personally and professionally. Others, particularly Hispanics, had developed at least a modicum of Spanish fluency in high school or college. As one student whose family had migrated from Colombia said, "Even though I'm English dominant, I'm sometimes more expressive in Spanish." For him, with the Spanish population increasing, his language skills had become more important and helpful. Even so, he still wished he could have learned to write in Spanish at a younger age. His experience was not unique.

Even those who still spoke the language with their parents on a regular basis typically had never developed literacy skills or, I would guess, a speaking competency beyond the level of informal conversation. Some of them spoke only a nonstandard variant like Haitian Creole rather than French. Yet they appreciated the role that even the spoken language plays as a cultural symbol of in-group membership. As a student from an Italian immigrant family told me, language is the "key factor in your ethnicity." It's the "core of being who you are." "Language is a huge part of my identity," a woman of Taiwanese background likewise observed. "If you can't speak Chinese, then you're really not Chinese to those who can." She offered the example of going to Chinese restaurants where the waiters gave her a disapproving look when she tentatively spoke to them. "It puts up a wall," she explained, "between me and people whom I want to identify with. It makes me feel less Chinese, which is hard to admit." She continued to work at improving her fluency and hoped one day to be truly bilingual.

These linguistic gaps speak directly to curricular deficiencies and cultural insensitivities within the American educational system. As noted, heritage language programs designed specifically for such in-between speakers, while slowly increasing, are still rare. At the same time, conventional foreign language classes mistakenly assume that all students come to the task with no prior knowledge. They fail to take into account the range of competencies across speaking and literacy skills. Yet even among those of my students who were fully bilingual, some expressed difficulties reconciling their dual cultures. As one Korean American student observed, the best way to bridge the divide is to "embrace who you are but it's hard because the cultures clash." To support her point, she noted that, unlike her "white" friends, she could not have a lively political discussion with her parents, who would consider it rude. "The family dynamic," she said with a hint of resignation, was "just very different." That tension seemed most common among Asians, and it is beyond the ability of schools to resolve.

When asked what it means to be "American," my young and eager informants invariably talked of the United States as a place where you "can keep your own culture and customs," where you can "be an individual under all circumstances and not be ashamed of it," where you "don't need to distinguish between your two identities," where you "learn to tolerate differences," "where you have an open perspective." "There's no such thing as 'totally American.' The label is so flexible," I was told. One Chinese American woman admitted that when she was younger, she was certain that being American was being "as Caucasian as you could possibly be." But as she grew up, she realized how much she missed her family's culture. Now she understands that she can "be American while maintaining an identity with the past."

Some reveled in the opportunity to distinguish themselves from the masses and from an American identity that seems to defy clear definition. In response to their ethnicity, I heard comments like, "It makes me unique. It makes me stand out." "It gives me a sense of identity," explained an American-born student who speaks Armenian and remains active in Armenian youth organizations, a common practice within that community. "There's something more to me. I feel like I belong to something. It's a comfort zone," she said. Like others, she sensed that she had some advantage over her American counterparts. One Russian-born student, who had migrated as a young child and had a clearly American demeanor, observed how she found herself thinking differently from her non-Russian classmates, how she saw things from a "global perspective," from a "more general scheme," how she analyzed things "from a different angle." At the same time, she found it difficult to communicate with more traditional Russians of her generation. Yet, she said, "I'm just comfortable with the way I am. I no longer worry about people judging me."

Most had come to appreciate their family's values, having found a way to blend the old with the new. One young woman whose parents had migrated from Haiti said with great certainty, "I love the way my parents raised me. They valued education and respect. That's what I want to pass on to my children someday. I want them to speak Creole and to identify with our culture." When asked what she is, this native-born American unconsciously answered "Haitian," not "Haitian American" nor "Haitian and American." Her answer was not intended to slight the United States. It merely reflected pride in her home culture and perhaps a way that her family, like many Afro-Caribbeans, had consciously reinforced achievement and pride in their ethnic identity to distance themselves from American blacks, thus shielding their children from negative racial attitudes. For them, if you are nonwhite, "American" means someone of a particular lower status. Yet her answer was not exceptional. A number of white students either gave a similarly quick "ancestral roots" reply or hesitated before throwing in a hyphen or ampersand.

I could not help but mentally note the different responses the "identity" question would have elicited from earlier waves of immigrant offspring. My guess is that being "American" would have featured prominently in their stated aspirations. If nothing more, they at least would have known instinctively that a "hyphenated" response was more socially expected. To the contrary, in today's transnational world, the assimilation ideal seems to have given way to a more open sense of cultural pluralism with signs of continuing into the near future for at least some immigrant families. These discussions suggest how this transnational perspective provides a sense of narrative coherence that gives meaning to the immigrant experience. As the young Indian-born author Kiran Desai explained in reference to her book *The Inheritance of Loss,* "America might give me half a narrative, but I had to return to India for the other half of the story, for emotional depth, historical depth."[103] It is precisely for that coherence and depth that at least some of today's immigrant offspring are searching in selectively holding on to their family's culture and its language.

That being said, I also found other, less hopeful aspects that distinguished these "new" immigrant offspring from the "old." The Asian Americans were particularly sensitive to enduring racial differences. One Taiwanese-born student stated matter-of-factly, "I can't change how I look. I will always be perceived as an Asian. It took a while to acknowledge that fact and it happened in college." Another Korean American carried the thought into the next generation, certain that her children would have to learn the family language and culture so they could "un-

derstand why they look the way they do." As one Indian American student put it, "I will always see myself as Indian because people will always
see me that way. The stigma will always be there." Another remarked
how ethnic identity among South Asians had become intensified in the
wake of the September 2001 terrorist attacks, making them feel particularly "vulnerable."

Now feeling the sting of discrimination toward anyone who appears to
be Muslim, South Asians are reaffirming their identity while struggling to
integrate into a mainstream that at times proves unwelcoming. On the
one hand they are rooted in their parents' culture, but on the other hand
they are very different from their parents. They feel a need to straddle the
ethnic divide, and in their own way. As a young Indian American woman
explained to me, she could just as easily don an elegant silk sari to visit
relatives and family friends as wear fashionable J. Crew ensembles within
her own professional and social milieu. That continued embrace of traditional dress, used selectively as a form of ethnic identification, is particularly common among South Asian women.[104]

All planned for their children to acquire their ancestral language and
appreciate its culture, though some worried whether this was realistic as
the forces of assimilation, including the possibilities of intermarriage,
overtake their lives. "As American as I am," one student told me, "my
ethnicity is such a defining part of my personality. It would be a shame to
let it go. I'd like my kids to identify with my parents." A number of them
planned to give their children traditional ethnic names, a trend that demographers have noted among both the "new" first and second generations and the "old" third and fourth, so different from the past. Several
talked about taking their own children back to their parents' homeland.
As one student aptly summed it up, "You have to first know who you
are." A significant part of knowing who you are, is knowing where you
came from. And part of acquiring that understanding is knowing the language with all its emotive subtleties.

The heartfelt thoughts and feelings they expressed underscore the importance these young people placed on language in achieving an integrated sense of self for themselves and for their future children. They
recognized the value of difference and how it plays into the unique experience of what it now means to be American. College and the widespread
popularity of student ethnic organizations, the first far less available and
the second unknown to pre-1960s immigrant groups, had helped them
come to terms with their cultural background. They were still in the process of negotiating between past and present lives, internalizing as a
source of strength a self-defined hybrid identity, one unfamiliar to their

parents but also different from the mythical homogenized mainstream American of "melting pot" fame. Regrettably the public schools had squandered the potential bilingual skills and bicultural sensitivities these young people offered. Whatever these students gained along the way had come from their families and community or from their own initiative as young adults, but, for some, with a gnawing sense of time and relationships that could not be retrieved. And while some appeared lost in translation, many of them were making conscious efforts to find themselves through language and culture. Whether they can sustain such optimism amid cries for English Only and other policies that symbolize a misguided return to less tolerant times is a separate matter.

These very tentative findings admittedly pose the risk of overgeneralization. The sample was undeniably small and decidedly selective. All my informants were attending law school and living in New York City, where ethnic diversity is a common fact of life, reaffirmed and celebrated in many venues—from Bollywood movie houses in Queens to Russian nightclubs in Brooklyn and Latin and Creole dance clubs in Manhattan along with myriad ethnic parades that march up Fifth Avenue throughout the year. All were well educated, sufficiently self-aware, and deeply enough interested in their ethnicity to volunteer to discuss it. Their educational status and middle-class lifestyles had given them a sense of social acceptance that made them more comfortable affirming their ethnicity. Many of them expressly appreciated the opportunity to consciously reflect on the experience of growing up against the backdrop of language and cultural differences. They were far more generous with their time and open about their feelings than I had expected.

Given these factors, it is difficult to say whether their views and experiences fairly represent those of the current second generation, a heterogeneous group by any measure. Certainly some immigrant offspring, whether by chance or by choice, relinquish their family's language or cultural ties with little or no emotional residue. A broader and less self-selecting sample would shed more light on the subject. These findings, nonetheless, at least suggest that we now live in a society where it is more acceptable, feasible, and for some immigrants personally desirable to maintain linguistic and cultural differences. This fluid sense of American identity could well become more pervasive and even normalized as today's ethnic minority populations slowly grow into the majority through the coming decades. That point, important and consequential in itself, most often gets subsumed in seemingly disconnected, but in truth related, debates over immigration and educational policy.

CHAPTER FIVE

Rights, Ambivalence, and Ambiguities

F OR THE PAST four decades the issue of language and schooling has acquired a legal dimension with broad implications for policy and classroom practice. The arguments hark back to the 1960s when the momentum of the civil rights movement carried the education of English language learners into a dramatically new and unforeseen discourse of student rights, state and local duties, and federal mandates and proscriptions. In tune with the times, legal advocacy became the strategy for resolving the tension between the new diversity and the country's continuing need to maintain social and political stability. In the process, the notion of what it means to be American inevitably underwent reexamination and gradual evolution. From here an incongruous situation developed. As the nation struggled to establish national policies and legal norms that would make racial differences irrelevant to educational access, linguistic minorities breathed the spirit of *Brown v. Board of Education* into policies and practices that would effectively preserve language and cultural differences, all in the name of equal educational opportunity.[1]

Efforts to accommodate such differences reflect, in part, a more universal view supporting language rights as human rights. In the realm of education, that position rests on two related concerns: to learn the official language of the host country, in the interests of nationality, and to use and even develop one's mother tongue in the interests of self-identification.[2] These goals are not mutually exclusive, although developing the mother tongue in its fullest sense entails not merely toleration but affirmative steps on the part of the state to actively promote minority languages. On this score, Congress, the federal courts, and the executive branch have intermittently advanced and retreated in response to each other and to changing political and demographic forces. Regardless of direction, each implicitly has applied a deficit rationale marking the home language as a barrier while only occasionally, and then most tentatively, giving lip service to its place as a long-term resource to the child and to the nation.

The winding course of these events reveals a national ambivalence toward bilingualism and the uncertain role the home language might play in preparing first- and second-generation immigrant children to participate and thrive in an English-speaking society. The focus is on students, whether born in the United States or abroad, whose fluency and literacy in English is not commensurate with that of average native-born children of similar age. And while the debate over bilingual education ostensibly has centered on language, it is rooted in fundamental disagreements over culture, group identity, nationalism, and belonging that evoke deep passions on both sides.

A Judicial Nod to Pluralism

Legal and policy arguments on behalf of English language learners typically use language as a proxy for both race and national origin, characteristics that the Supreme Court historically has identified for special judicial protection under the Fourteenth Amendment equal protection clause.[3] Modern-day civil rights statutes likewise follow this pattern. Though the Court's landmark decision in *Brown v. Board of Education* is the most obvious point of departure for a discussion on educational rights, the Court first confronted the language question a quarter century earlier in a decision that turned not on equality but on the individual's right to liberty and the now fragile doctrine of substantive due process within the Fourteenth Amendment.

Meyer v. Nebraska is a case whose well-documented facts and surrounding events were freighted with the nativism, hysteria, and suspicion prevalent during and following World War I when German language schools, largely church-affiliated and common in the Midwest, became a target of hostility. These were the most numerous of the immigrant-based schools that reinforced native language and culture. With Germany as the enemy in the war, these schools became a symbol of national disloyalty and a perceived threat to national security. Inversely and for related reasons, education became a means of insulating immigrant children from what the nation's commissioner of education called the "demoralizing" effects of foreign languages.[4]

Like many other states, Nebraska enacted a law making it a criminal offense to teach a subject in a language other than English to any student attending a public or private school or to teach a language other than English to any student who had not completed the eighth grade. Robert Meyer, a teacher in the Zion Parochial School, was convicted of offering instruction from a German Bible to a ten-year-old child during a recess period. Echoing the sentiments of many native-born Americans of that day, the state maintained that the statute was merely part of a "general Americanization program" designed to counter the effects of isolated pockets of "little Germanys, little Italys and little Hungarys" that were springing up across the state, where parents were rearing children in a "foreign atmosphere and in a foreign language." Parents, the state argued, had no "inalienable right" to programs that were tantamount to "physical, moral and intellectual gloom." The Nebraska Supreme Court upheld the conviction, the judges noting that teaching students in a foreign mother tongue was "inimical to our own safety" and would "naturally inculcate in [students] the ideas and sentiments foreign to the best interests of this country."[5]

When the case reached the United States Supreme Court, the Nebraska attorney general similarly warned of the lesson, learned from the war, that "we must have a united people, united in ideals, language and patriotism."[6] A traditionally minded group, the justices recognized the legislature's desire "to foster a homogeneous people with American ideals."[7] Yet they also saw the need to protect individual freedom from state interference, a philosophy they were aggressively applying to strike down economic regulations.[8] And so they could find no rational justification for the state to prohibit the teaching of foreign languages. To their minds, "mere knowledge of the German language" could not reasonably be considered "harmful" but rather could be "helpful and desirable."[9]

The basis of Meyer's claim was his right to engage in his profession. But the Court did not stop there. In a stunning sweep, Justice James Clark McReynolds, writing for the Court, declared that the liberty interest within the Fourteenth Amendment due process clause included both the right of students to "acquire useful knowledge" and the right of parents to control their children's education, regardless of their native language. "The Constitution extends to all," Justice McReynolds stated, "to those who speak other languages as well as to those born with English on the tongue." And while it might be "highly advantageous if all had ready understanding of our ordinary speech," he said, the state could not "co-erce" that understanding "by methods which conflict with the Constitu-tion."[10]

Here was a conservative Court, in conservative and even xenophobic times, issuing an opinion written by an archconservative justice, uphold-ing individual liberty of the foreign-born. Apparently the majority could find no threat to the social or political order in the facts presented. There may have been, however, a more subtle undercurrent. To the extent that these schools promoted traditional values, the Court's conservatives may have seen them as a bulwark of stability against rising social and political radicalism in American society and beyond.[11] In any case, the decision was met with surprise and dismay throughout the educational establish-ment. From Stanford University to the University of Chicago, leading ed-ucators could not comprehend how "such an important nationalizing re-quirement" could possibly interfere with parental rights. Nor could they understand how the Court could reconcile its ruling with the deference traditionally afforded local and state officials on education matters, and overturn a policy followed by nearly one-fourth of the states.[12]

Though *Meyer* is unfamiliar to most Americans, it looms large in the history of American education. Homeschoolers, voucher proponents, and others most often invoke the decision to assert the right of parents to direct their child's education. Robert Meyer's attorney himself later re-marked how it was "purely adventitious" that the laws in question ad-dressed the teaching of foreign languages and not algebra or rhetoric, or any other subject.[13] The case was essentially a conflict over who would control education, parents or the state. That assessment seems plausible, considering the Court's ultimate disposition. Nevertheless, the arguments raised by state officials, and the language used by the Nebraska Supreme Court in particular, demonstrate the timelessness of the underlying fears and how issues of national unity, cultural conformity, and defined politi-cal commitments have remained a constant in debates over language rights, especially as they affect immigrants.

Two years after *Meyer*, in *Pierce v. Society of Sisters*, the Court took a similar turn, striking down an Oregon initiative requiring all children under the age of sixteen to attend public schools. Once again the Court swept beyond the property interests of the private school claimants, incorporat-ing within Fourteenth Amendment substantive due process "the liberty of parents and guardians to direct the upbringing and education of chil-dren under their control." In an oft-quoted statement with more rhetori-cal force than analytic value, the Court maintained that "the child is not the mere creature of the State; those who nurture and direct his destiny have the right, coupled with the high duty, to recognize and prepare him for additional obligations."[14]

The justices revisited *Meyer* and *Pierce* just two years later in a case that has all but vanished from the discussion on parental liberty rights but is particularly relevant here. In *Farrington v. Tokushige* the Court struck down as excessively burdensome under the Fifth Amendment due process clause a Hawaii statute and regulations imposing fees, daily hours of operation, teacher permit requirements, and other conditions on predominantly Japanese foreign language schools. The Court concluded that enforcement of the act would "deprive parents of fair opportunity to procure for their children instruction which they think is important and we cannot say is harmful."[15] Taken together, this trilogy of cases makes clear that parental decision-making and educational pluralism are substantive as well as structural.

The Court's expansive dicta, especially in *Meyer,* are indeed compelling. And while the facts are undeniably narrow, the ruling's modern-day relevance can best be assessed by weighing the facts against a series of more recent Court rulings. In *Meyer* the Court addressed the language laws only to the extent that they governed private and not public schools. And while the decision was an apparent nod to linguistic pluralism, it did not suggest in any way that students had an affirmative right to "foreign language" instruction provided by the state. It merely upheld a negative right to be free from state restrictions that barred such instruction within private schools.[16] The Court, in fact, ceded to the state the right to "prescribe a curriculum for public schools and . . . even mandate that all schools provide instruction in English,"[17] a point that has not been lost on modern-day opponents of bilingual education. Nor did the Court say anything about how preserving the language or culture of the home might benefit the student. Completely ignoring the fact that the case specifically concerned the child's home language, it simply banned the restrictions because it considered foreign languages in general "useful," but not necessarily "important" or "essential," to the child's academic and personal development. Commentators continue to peel away these layers to reveal the decision's nationalistic and traditional underpinnings shrouded in the language of personal liberty. It has even been suggested that *Meyer* was not really about liberty but about the child as property of the parent.[18]

Notwithstanding these limitations, the Court repeatedly has cited both *Meyer* and *Pierce* to support a private realm of family life that the Constitution protects from state interference. In case after case over the past four decades, the justices have built on the proposition that matters within the private sphere of family "involv[e] the most intimate choices a person may make in a lifetime, choices central to personal dignity and autonomy." In certain circumstances these matters may encompass fundamental rights entitled to some level of heightened judicial scrutiny beyond mere reasonableness.[19] The Court reaffirmed that holding most recently in *Troxel v. Granville,* a case addressing a parent's right to determine the scope of grandparent visitation. "In light of this extensive precedent," the justices noted, "it cannot be doubted that the Due Process Clause of the Fourteenth Amendment protects the fundamental right of parents to make decisions concerning the care, custody, and control of their children," an "enduring American tradition" and "perhaps the oldest of the fundamental liberty interests recognized by [the] Court."[20]

With the gloss of this subsequent history, *Meyer* holds a prominent place in the education of students whose dominant language is not English.[21] It speaks generally to linguistic diversity, to the fundamental right of parents to guide the education of their children, and to the constraints on state authority to enact legislation not even reasonably related to some legitimate state interest. The Court made clear that the child has a fundamental right to acquire knowledge that is "useful." And while this qualification is admittedly vague and subjective, as I discuss in Chapter 7, the Court's continued affirmations over the decades offer a potential avenue of legal relief, particularly to parents now operating under state initiatives, as in Arizona, California, and Massachusetts, that severely limit their freedom to choose bilingual instruction for their children.

The Carrot and the Stick

For more than a quarter century following *Meyer,* with immigration severely constrained, foreign language and culture moved off the political radar screen, not to return until the 1960s when the fervor of group rights took hold. At that point, *Brown v. Board of Education* set the tone and laid the foundation for a major revision in the nation's thinking on equality and schooling. In *Brown,* the Court made clear that equal educational opportunity means more than surface equality. True equality also considers intangible factors, like the "ability to study, [and] to engage in discussions and exchange views with other students," that form a crucial part of the educational experience.[22] The Court was recalling the harms that African American students suffered when legally separated or isolated from the mainstream.

At the very core of *Brown* was the right to equal dignity and respect, the right to be free from state action that implied inferiority or imposed a stigma on the individual based on group characteristics. For children in elementary and secondary school, said the Court, such feelings of "inferiority as to their status in the community may affect their hearts and minds in a way unlikely ever to be undone."[23] This vision of *Brown* has animated advocacy on behalf of English language learners, although in recent years the litigation has shifted from constitutional to statutory claims of increasingly narrow scope. Part of the rationale underlying dual language instruction, nevertheless, rests on the assumption that when schooling devalues children's language and culture, it devalues their identity with lasting damage to their self-esteem and their ability to succeed academically.[24]

But there is another aspect of *Brown* that has guided equality thinking and advocacy over the years. Aside from noting the harm that segregation inflicted specifically on black children, the Court more broadly recognized education itself as the "very foundation of good citizenship," as a "principal instrument in awakening the child to cultural values, . . . and in helping him to adjust normally to his environment."[25] The Court concededly was alluding to mainstream American values with a view toward cultural assimilation. Nonetheless, as some scholars and advocates have argued, the Court intended in *Brown* not solely to root out racial inequality, but to establish in the federal Constitution a fundamental right to education.[26] Though the Court ultimately rejected that argument two decades later in the interests of federalism, that thinking implicitly has animated legislation, agency interpretations, and court decisions promoting equal educational access beyond race and ethnicity, including the rights of English language learners to a "meaningful," "appropriate," and "effective" education.

In the years following *Brown*, the principle of equal dignity evolved into a principle of difference that recognized the potential for defining one's identity both as an individual and as a member of a cultural group. At the same time, language policy took a 180-degree turn from a negative and hostile focus on foreigners or immigrants, as evidenced in post–World War I state laws, to a positive and protective emphasis on racial and ethnic minorities. Suspicion and fear of linguistic and cultural differences gave way to celebration, at least within education circles. *Brown* was a case about racial exclusion. There was no legal grounding for addressing language as a right in itself without attaching it to national origin discrimination. Meanwhile, the constitutional underpinnings of *Meyer's* substantive liberty interest had fallen into disrepute, only tentatively resurfacing primarily in the context of privacy interests in contraception and reproductive choice, contentious issues far removed from language and education.[27] By that point *Meyer* itself had assumed historical significance as a case about family autonomy, and somewhat of a judicial aberration at that, totally divorced from the language question.

The spirit of *Brown* laid the groundwork for President Lyndon Johnson's War on Poverty and a spate of federal civil rights laws that harnessed the equality principle in the service of broad-scale social reform through public schooling. Equal treatment would no longer suffice. Addressing the 1965 graduating class at Howard University, Johnson stated, "We seek not just freedom of opportunity—not just legal equity but ability—not just equality as a right and a theory but equality as a fact and as a result."[28] In remarks made before Congress, Commissioner of Education Francis Keppel best captured the administration's ambitious goals: "The school must inspire hope, instill desire, and show all our children that they are free to develop their capabilities as far as their ability and ambition will take them."[29]

On that inspirational note, federal policy regarding non-English-dominant students soon set out on dual paths, conflating race with national origin discrimination. It held out the carrot of financial support while wielding the stick of civil rights enforcement. Where school districts were found to violate civil rights mandates, they would risk losing federal education funds. The approach ushered in a new role for the federal government, which historically had taken a back seat to the states on education policy. Particularly in the early days of federal intervention, no one knew for sure just how far federal officials might go in promoting and protecting national interests. As federal dollars flowed out of Washington and local school districts grew more dependent on them, the threat became troublesome, although perhaps more in theory than in fact. Despite much saber rattling and some close calls in the decades that followed, the government never pulled back funds from a school district for failing to comply with federal law. This two-pronged approach, nevertheless, ultimately drove national language policy. It also legitimized federal involvement in state and local matters, allowing Washington to do indirectly what the federal Constitution would not permit it to do directly. Funding and mandates were designed to work in unison. Yet in the years to come, the two strategies at times took uncertain and even conflicting directions as Congress, executive agency officials, and the courts wove in and out of the political maelstrom that language, schooling, and cultural pluralism progressively fomented.

Title VI of the Civil Rights Act of 1964 provided that "no person can be excluded from participation in, be denied the benefits of," or "be subjected to discrimination under any program or activity receiving Federal financial assistance" on account of race, color, or national origin. The language was purposefully vague as to whether Title VI prohibited only intentional acts of government discrimination or those that merely produced discriminatory effects. The House subcommittee members who drafted the bill were well aware that an *effects* standard would intrude on state and local autonomy, which could have mired the proposal in controversy. In fact, they suppressed any discussion on the question, effectively delegating it to the federal bureaucracy.[30] And so it went. Sacrificing clarity for political expediency, Congress set the measure on what would prove to be an uncertain course for the long term. The model regulations adopted the following year by the Justice Department specifically made reference to discriminatory effects.[31]

Title VI authorized federal agencies, including the former Department of Health, Education, and Welfare (HEW) (partially incorporated into the Department of Education in 1980), to adopt regulations (subject to presidential approval), to investigate complaints, to conduct compliance reviews, to commence enforcement proceedings, and to terminate a school district's federal funds in the case of noncompliance.[32] Rather than take direct action itself, the Department's Office for Civil Rights (OCR) could also refer claims to the Civil Rights Division of the Department of Justice. Title VI was designed primarily to prevent federal monies from being used to support racial segregation, OCR's overwhelming concern at that time. It thus paved the political way the following year for an unprecedented infusion of federal funds, which school districts would soon come to heavily rely on. The centerpiece of the Elementary and Secondary Education Act of 1965 was Title I, which provided funds for remedial instruction to educationally and economically deprived students. The 1964 Civil Rights Act and the 1965 funding legislation formed crucial pieces of the administration's plan for promoting equal educational opportunity. Together they became a major force in setting language policy in public schools nationwide.

A Confused Start

Within two years, Title I was supporting eighteen bilingual and English as a Second Language programs in the Southwest. The first approach combined English and native language instruction in a separate classroom apart from the mainstream. In some cases, students were taught literacy as well as subjects like math and science in their native language as they developed English language skills. In other cases, initial literacy was taught in English. The second approach, commonly used up to that point, combined English learners and English-speaking students in the same classroom with small-group intensive English language instruction for anywhere from one hour a week to several hours a day.

Though the Johnson administration endorsed bilingual education in concept, it did not actively support a separate law for that purpose. With the federal budget crumbling under an avalanche of Great Society initiatives piled on top of Vietnam War defense spending, administration officials feared the additional cost of yet another targeted program. But their restraint went deeper than just strained resources. In 1967, in response to pending federal legislation, Commissioner of Education Harold "Doc" Howe II cautioned Congress that there were "possible dangers" in the "spotlight" approach. "What suited the needs of one [ethnic] group would not necessarily suit the needs of others."[33] HEW secretary John Gardner was more direct. He warned congressional members that the bill was straying into the dangerous area of "ethnic entitlements."[34]

It deserves note that barely a decade had passed since Congress had broken the country's linguistic isolationism with the National Defense Education Act of 1958, which provided federal funds for foreign language instruction. Until that time, and then only in response to Sputnik and Cold War fear of the Soviet Union, the federal government apparently had little interest in the national benefits of promoting foreign language skills or cultural understandings. In retrospect, there was indeed an ironic twist. The country was dismissing the linguistic potential of Spanish-speaking children at an age when it was comparatively easy and inexpensive to maintain and develop their native language. At the same time, it was trying at great cost to meet the nation's need for adult citizens who could communicate in Russian but also in Spanish and other languages.

Congress soon began hearing conflicting voices. Bilingual advocates laid before federal lawmakers a grim picture of low achievement, high dropout rates, and poor self-image among Hispanic children in general and Mexican Americans in particular. They attributed the problem largely to the language barrier that Spanish-speaking children faced as they entered school. The data on educational deprivation was staggering. In the Southwest, the median years of schooling completed by Mexican Americans was 7.1 as compared with 12.1 for Anglos. In California, more than 50 percent of Spanish-speaking males and nearly 50 percent of females fourteen years of age and older had less than an eighth-grade education.[35]

A combination of forces in the early 1960s had dramatically increased the Hispanic population nationwide. Between 1959 and 1962, 275,000

Cuban refugees had poured into Miami following the Communist take-over in their country. With the elimination of national quotas from immigration laws in 1965, Mexican migrants were likewise crossing over the southwest borders in greater numbers in search of jobs. Meanwhile, similar economic motives were bringing a massive influx of Puerto Ricans, who were already American citizens, into northern cities like New York and Chicago. Yet it was the U.S. government's unusual efforts not to disperse and integrate the Cubans, as it had the Hungarian refugees who preceded them and the Vietnamese who followed, that ultimately laid the groundwork for new and historic federal policies on language and schooling.

Initially considering the Cubans as temporary asylum seekers, the federal government attempted to solidify them into a community that would spearhead a counterrevolution and return to Cuba. And so it provided the Dade County public schools with grants to hire bilingual teacher aides for programs using Spanish and English. The government withdrew those efforts when it became clear that Fidel Castro would not be overturned soon.[36] Many Cubans, nonetheless, still held hope that they would resettle in their homeland one day. The Cuban community in Dade County already had established a bilingual program in 1963 with seed money from the Ford Foundation. The population was largely well-educated and politically informed, and had their own core of trained native Spanish-speaking teachers. The program included both English- and Spanish-speaking children, who consequently showed significant gains in academic achievement and social interaction.

In the meantime, buoyed by the success of French-English language programs in Canada, university-based researchers in language and education were exploring the benefits of bilingualism in the Southwest, where demographics and history presented a markedly distinct profile and impetus for program development.[37] In Texas and New Mexico, they hoped to establish effective techniques to educate poor Mexican American students. Like the Cubans in Dade County, language advocates challenged the prevailing assimilation model and legitimized the reality that some ethnic groups, by force of will or circumstance, were maintaining their home language and cultural identity. The success of these early initiatives attracted widespread interest among educators and policy makers.

In November 1963, Lyndon Johnson, who was then vice president and chair of the President's Committee on Equal Educational Opportunity, convened a conference that forecast a dramatic turnaround on national language policy. The basic idea was that "the schools should capitalize on the bi-cultural situation in the Southwest rather than ignore it or even attempt to stamp it out." A discussion group moderated by HEW secretary Anthony J. Celebrezze concluded that "schools must provide acculturation for Mexican American children through bilingual instruction in Spanish and English, and must make use of the curriculum to reflect Spanish as well as American traditions, and should hire teachers in both cultures."[38]

The following June, the Conference for the Teacher of the Bilingual Child, sponsored by the University of Texas, presented an even more radical view that "the stigma . . . long . . . attached in our country to initial language learning in a tongue other than English has now the possibility of being converted into a mark of individual superiority."[39] These words were momentous not only in view of past Americanization efforts but in view of what was soon to come. The year was 1964 and Congress was about to embark on a crucial redefinition and expansion of the federal role in education while at the same time opening wide the country's borders through major immigration reform. These two redirections in national policy, seemingly unrelated at the time, would profoundly change education practice, the face of schooling, and the politics of language as they converged over the coming decades.

The momentum for bilingual-bicultural education was quickly building. The initiative that ultimately but qualifiedly pushed aspiration into action, and set the tone for future policy making, was what has come to be known as the "Tucson Survey," a 1965–66 yearlong study sponsored by the National Education Association. Conducted by a group of teachers in Tucson, Arizona, the survey examined "forward-looking" bilingual programs operating in the five-state area of the Southwest. The resulting report, *The Invisible Minority,* became a key point of reference in subsequent congressional hearings. It painted a portrait of schooling that was oblivious at best and insensitive at worst to the needs of Mexican American children.[40] Yet it also described specific "pioneering" efforts that were innovative and even inspiring, offering in the end a template on which educators could build future programmatic designs. It called for further federal legislation and "substantially increased appropriations." Unlike the culturally affirming reports of previous conferences, however, this one was threaded through with repeated references to the "handicaps" and "deficiencies" that Mexican American children had to overcome. The NEA sponsored a follow-up symposium in Tucson titled "The Spanish-Speaking Child in the Schools of the Southwest." The event effectively brought to life the bilingual education "movement."[41]

In one sense, the deficit rationale served Hispanics well in the expanding world of compensatory and remedial education. Along with other research and political mobilization efforts, the NEA report and conference presented a unified focal point and specific instructional approach through which Hispanics, ignored in existing poverty programs, could capture a portion of the federal dollars that were flowing largely to African Americans. In another sense, it limited the potential of these programs and of the children they were designed to serve.

Present at the Tucson meeting was Ralph Yarborough, a U.S. senator from Texas, who translated the report's findings into a legislative proposal supporting research on bilingual education and experimental projects in the schools. For the senator, the proposed program would "enable naturally bilingual children to grow up speaking both good Spanish and good English" and give them "a knowledge of and pride in their ancestral culture," an obvious show of support for his largely Hispanic constituents.[42] At the same time, he affirmed the importance of English literacy and assured his colleagues that the program was not intended to "create pockets of different languages throughout the country."[43] Beyond these benign declarations of legislative intent, Yarborough made a more profound and potentially consequential observation that went straight to the core of American identity. "If America stands for anything," he noted, "it is for the principle that we have something of relevance to say to so many of the nations on earth precisely because we are made up of immigrants from those nations."[44] The implications of that observation would gain sharper focus as the country became more linguistically and culturally diverse in the decades that followed.

Congressional hearings on the measure revealed the gap between the rhetoric of cultural affirmation, including language, and the reality of political compromise and policy implementation. While supporters, including parents and community representatives, shared a common goal to bring English language learners into the American mainstream, they sharply disagreed on how to get there. The nation's deep discomfort with language and cultural difference seemed to confront head-on a simmering disillusionment with the melting pot ideology and its perceived normativity. A new and less homogenizing metaphor was needed. Perhaps, as Commissioner Howe suggested to Congress, the "mosaic" would prove more appropriate. Despite his initial misgivings on a separate program, Howe looked toward students becoming "equally skilled in both languages."[45] At the same time, and like many others, he seemed locked into the remedial or compensatory mindset of existing federal intervention strategies. He too spoke in the language of linguistic and cultural deficiencies (not differences) impeding the academic success of Spanish-speaking students.

For many education officials, bilingual education was merely a transitional vehicle for developing English language skills, a means to an end and not an end in itself.[46] Other supporters, particularly university scholars and researchers, had a more expansive perspective. They viewed bilingualism and biculturalism as useful tools that could benefit all children as well as the whole nation. Notwithstanding this crucial disagreement, the bilingual concept, in the abstract, gathered amazing political steam as congressional members scurried to attach their names to the thirty-seven bilingual education bills introduced in 1967. If there was one overarching theme, however, that ran through the two volumes of testimony and supporting documentation, it was a push for cultural assimilation.

Not surprisingly, the Bilingual Education Act that emerged in 1968 presented an ambiguous commitment to bilingualism in any sense. The Act, often referred to as Title VII of the Elementary and Secondary Act of 1965, did not even define bilingual education. Although initially designed to address the needs of Spanish-speaking students, through negotiation and compromise it was extended to other groups to avoid both the appearance of inequity and the threat of legal challenges while garnering wider congressional support. As passed, its expressed goal was to meet the "special educational needs" of children between the ages of three and eighteen whose families fell within certain poverty guidelines and who were of "limited English-speaking ability" (LESA), defined as "children who come from environments where the dominant language is other than English."[47] This broad definition failed to distinguish between children who were English-dominant but primarily spoke another language at home, and those who demonstrated varying levels of speaking and literacy skills in English and their home language. Nor did the law require that students participate in racially integrated classrooms. It was a recipe for ethnic/racial segregation and local manipulation.

The Act expressly promoted "bilingual education programs" and "programs designed to impart to students a knowledge of the history and culture associated with their language."[48] In that light, the Act was historic. For the first time the federal government recognized that non-English languages and other cultures could help close the achievement gap for linguistic minority students. Yet it still hedged on whether the purpose was to promote assimilation or linguistic and cultural diversity. Was this the old Americanization project wrapped in a thin cloak of social sensitivity? Or was it an entirely new approach to integrating culturally and linguistically diverse groups into the American mosaic? And though the poverty factor may have made the case for federal intervention more compelling, it also cast a stigma from which the approach would never fully recover.

It should be understood that Title VII was not a statement of rights; the law did not mandate that school districts take any action on educating linguistic minority children. This was merely a modest experimental program primarily designed to provide short-term "seed money" for local initiatives. It would allow local officials to develop pilot and demonstration projects that could be replicated elsewhere. The funds would be discretionary and awarded among school districts on a competitive basis. Congressional ambivalence and executive opposition proved difficult to overcome. Although the original bill had authorized $85 million for a three-year period, the initial allocation for the first year was zero, largely the result of pressure from the Johnson White House, insufficient follow-up on the part of proponents, and the overwhelming costs of continuing the war in Vietnam.[49] When Congress revisited the program the following year in response to intense lobbying, it allocated a meager $7.5 million to seventy-six projects nationwide that served twenty-seven thousand students. Faced with such a small sum for such a politically controversial and unfamiliar program, few districts even applied for funds during the first several years.[50] Those that did apply faced conflicting legislative goals, a lack of trained bilingual personnel, and inadequate instructional materials and evaluation tools. They also met subtle and not so subtle resistance from Anglo teachers and administrators. In many cases, the assimilated offspring of earlier immigrants viewed these programs as a threat to American identity and to their job security.

The law provided no road map for promoting bilingualism or biculturalism. It was unclear whether schools should develop the child's native language skills or merely use the home language as an initial bridge to learning English. Congress, in fact, had discarded an earlier version that would have provided funds for teaching the native language in addition to English. Nor was it clear what emphasis should be placed on native culture. From the language of the law as passed, it was impossible to detect even a hint that the federal government was consciously setting a programmatic philosophy on language policy consistent with any broader aims of American society. Congress effectively had left the law wide open for interpretation by school districts and, more significantly, executive branch officials. The resulting inconsistencies and repeated turnarounds were soon evident.

A 1971 HEW manual reminded project applicants and grantees, with unfounded certainty, that "the ultimate goal of bilingual education" was a student "who functions well in two languages on any occasion."[51] Three years later, following congressional amendments to the Bilingual Education Act, the agency retracted in a memorandum stating that "the ultimate goal" of the federal program was for "children of limited English-speaking ability" to "achieve competence in the English language." It recognized using the child's native language and culture as a means to that end, but not as an end in itself. The memo made a similar retreat from biculturalism. In an apparent effort to clarify, or possibly dilute, legislative changes that year requiring instruction "with appreciation" for the child's "cultural heritage," the government asserted that although cultural pluralism was one of America's "greatest assets," it was a "private matter of local choice" and not "a proper responsibility of the federal government."[52] The memo cited congressional concerns that the ultimate goal of the program was not to establish a "bilingual society."[53] Meanwhile, the U.S. Commission on Civil Rights, in a major report describing the problems of segregation and educational inequality facing Mexican American children, unequivocally recommended that their language and culture should be "an integral part of the education process."[54]

Such disagreements would resurface repeatedly over the next fourteen years as the Bilingual Education Act underwent six congressional reauthorizations, each one redefining the law's purposes, the target population to be served, and the types of permissible programs and services covered. Despite all the compelling national implications, attempts to establish a stable language policy for the schools kept running into political roadblocks.

Throughout the 1970s, Congress continued to cast about on the question of language and culture. As bilingual education became caught up in ethnic and interest group politics, changes in immigration laws were bringing a renewed flow of immigrants from Europe and Asia. Congressional hearings in the spring of 1974 brought these realities to light. Between June 1970 and July 1971, more than thirty-four thousand Chinese had entered the country, mainly from Hong Kong and Taiwan.[55] Soon following were thousands of Vietnamese and Cambodian refugees. Upward of forty thousand Greeks were also migrating to the United States each year, most of them settling in New York City.[56] In response to lobbying from these and other non-Hispanic groups eager to get a piece of the "bilingual" pie, Congress in 1974 removed the poverty factor so that any limited-English-speaking student could participate. The policy providing "equal educational opportunity for all children" paved the way for additional programs targeting a wider immigrant base. For the 1974–75 school year, projects funded under Title VII covered forty-two languages, including twenty-three representing Native American tribes.

These changes were seismic. Former Puerto Rican–born congressman Herman Badillo (D-N.Y.), in his book *One Standard, One Nation*, recalls the political maneuvering it took to make them happen. Knowing that the amendments lacked sufficient support, he and his colleague Carl Perkins (D-Ken.), then chair of the House Education and Labor Committee, made an end run around a yes-no vote in the House. Rather than risk defeat, they took advantage of an obscure congressional rule whereby Badillo introduced the measure and immediately withdrew it. They then waited for the support of Ted Kennedy (D-Mass.) to carry a favorable vote in the Senate, as they knew it would, before submitting the matter to a House/Senate conference committee, which likewise gave it the go-ahead. Once incorporated into the total Elementary and Secondary Education Act amendments, separate sections could no longer be voted up or down. Cities like New York, Chicago, and Boston benefited handsomely from that maneuver.

And so the 1974 bilingual amendments became law without a direct vote in the House and largely through the political ingenuity of the man who has since become one of bilingual education's most vocal critics. Looking back at what he now considers a "complete distortion" of the law in the years that followed, Badillo insists that the measure was intended to have limited scope. "We all thought," he recollects, that "the purpose of bilingual education was to enable students to learn to speak English without missing out on course content. It was obvious to me and to all of us that the program would continue for a limited time only."[57] That may have been the consensus in the House, but there seemed to be other views emanating from the Senate.

Notwithstanding Badillo's memory to the contrary, statements made by Senator Alan Cranston (D-Calif.) in introducing the amendments implied an expansive vision of American schooling that gave some bilingual skeptics pause. Touting bilingual education as a "great force in fostering educational changes," Cranston praised the approach for "clearly reject[ing] the idea that the prime objective of the school is to wipe out all differences in style, heritage, and language background, delivering to society—at the end of 12 years—a nicely packaged, well rehearsed, automatic reciter of majority maxims." For him, this was the route that American education had "traveled historically," what he called the "assimilate or starve school or educational theory," and it "reflect[ed] an anti-minority tradition in American education" that was "beginning to change."[58]

In the end, the 1974 Act recognized that "a primary means by which a child learns is through the use of the child's language and cultural heritage" but only to the extent that it would "allow the child to progress effectively through the educational system."[59] It clarified the definition of eligible students, shifting the emphasis from the dominant home language to the child's ability to speak and understand English.[60] It further attempted to broaden the political base of support and, more significantly, to avoid the apparent dangers of racial or ethnic segregation in a provision that seems almost gratuitously inclusive. For the first time, programs could include English-speaking children on a voluntary basis, but only so they could better understand the target group's "cultural heritage" and "in no event" for the purpose of teaching them a foreign language.[61] That limitation, now widely considered counterintuitive, eliminated the possibility of dual immersion or dual language programs using federal funds.

Without a doubt, the size of the country's Spanish-speaking population (the fifth largest in the world), and the magnitude of the funds authorized for bilingual education (four times the amount appropriated the previous year) were staggering. One commentator speculated that making "not just bilingual, but genuinely bicultural education" available to an estimated five million children "could transform public education nearly as much as the Supreme Court's 1954 order outlawing segregated schools."[62]

Washington Post columnist Stephen Rosenfeld then hit a particularly sensitive nerve. With "practically no one paying heed," he noted, Congress had "radically altered the traditional way by which immigrants became Americanized" and the role that public schools had traditionally played as a "melting pot" for "assimilating foreigners to a common culture."[63] Senator Joseph Montoya (D.-Mex.), the co-sponsor of the original 1968 legislation, shot back. He contrasted the "melting pot myth" with the "American reality," saying that "the victims of this foolish attempt to create a bland uniformity in us have been the minority-language children of the poor, those who were the least able to fight for our respect." Montoya warned that "in a world that grows smaller every day, America should no longer ignore the language ability and cultural variety of its people or its heritage."[64]

American Federation of Teachers president Albert Shanker at least partially disagreed. In a commentary the following month, he pointedly stated, "The American taxpayer, while recognizing the existence of cultural diversity, still wants the schools to be the basis of an American melting pot . . . It is clear that what these children need is intensive instruction in English."[65] Though Shanker supported the idea of developing reading and writing skills in the child's native language, as he later made clear, he argued that bilingual programs were merely transitional and should "self destruct" as students were quickly integrated into the regular school program.[66] Shanker did not speak for the entire public school teaching force. The National Education Association held firm to its position that bilingual bicultural education was "inherently American" and "beneficial to all students."[67] Yet it was still unclear whether the leadership was merely supporting the use of the child's native language and culture as a means to an end or as an end in itself.

Both Cranston's and Montoya's words and, to some extent the fears the amendments provoked, seemed out of sync with HEW's memorandum later that year calling cultural pluralism a "private matter of local choice" and not a "proper responsibility of the federal government." They also contradicted Badillo's recollection that the outcome many early advocates had hoped to achieve was not only improved "educational opportunities for Hispanics," but "assimilation into mainstream America."[68] One really has to wonder what exactly was going on in Washington. Were some congressional members giving the amendments a political spin that the majority in Congress did not intend? Was the Republican White House pulling in the reins and taking advantage of legislative ambiguities? One thing was certain: the debate over bilingual-bicultural education was bringing to the fore thorny questions bearing on immigration, schooling, and what it means to be an American. It soon became even clearer that the *Washington Post* had shot the first salvo in the impending battle.

Given these conflicting messages from Washington, it is unsurprising that confusion and uncertainty reigned at the local level through the early years of federal funding. Added to that uncertainty were the novelty of the approach in the United States and wide disagreement in programmatic goals among the constituent groups. No one knew for sure what these programs should look like, how students should be selected, whether they should be grouped according to language ability or level of prior schooling, or how programs could avoid racial or ethnic segregation. Nor was it understood how the two languages should be worked into the instructional day, what the ultimate student outcomes should be, how they could be measured, or how long it would take to move students into mainstream classes. Some students could not even speak the standard form of their own language and lacked literacy skills when they entered school.

Programs were in dire need of instructional materials and adequately trained teachers fluent in both English and the increasing array of home languages and dialects. Many teachers and most school administrators had little understanding of the children's home cultures, often relying on bilingual paraprofessional staffers who lacked a college education to make the link between home and school. Even the selection of instructional materials became legally problematic. Before American publishers could meet the demand, books were ordered from foreign countries like Spain and Italy, and many of these contained references to Roman Catholicism that violated U.S. constitutional requirements for separation of church and state.

In school districts nationwide, well-intentioned but unprepared educators were intuitively writing the script, both individually and collectively. And they were acting out this drama against a racially and ethnically charged backdrop of interest group politics and community power struggles. Bilingual education was not merely a pedagogical approach. For some groups, Hispanics in particular, it was a vehicle for political mobilization and a symbol of ethnic solidarity and recognition. It also was a source of employment, in poor communities, for teachers and assistants who spoke the home languages, and thus created deep resentment especially from mainstream teachers whose ranks were brimming with outsiders. From these uncertain beginnings, rooted in the War on Poverty and education of the disadvantaged, both the Bilingual Education Act and similar state statutes worked on the premise that linguistic minority students had a "disability" that they needed to overcome. Wisconsin even placed its bilingual education statute in the same chapter of the state code as "handicapped children."[69]

Regulatory Entitlements

As Congress and HEW tugged to and fro over federal funding, agency officials embarked on a broader mission to establish legally enforceable obligations for local school districts. In 1968 HEW officially issued Title VI regulations and guidelines that laid the foundation for legal claims. Like the 1965 model regulations from the Justice Department, these banned the use of methods or criteria that had the "effect" of discriminating against individuals on the basis of race or national origin.[70] In other words, claimants did not have to prove that school officials intended to discriminate against them or had any invidious motive in establishing certain policies or practices. The guidelines stated that "school systems are responsible for assuring that students of a particular race, color, or national origin are not denied the opportunity to obtain the education generally obtained by other students in the system."[71]

In that year, 1968, the Office for Civil Rights was intensively engaged in uprooting racial segregation in the assignment of students and teachers to southern schools. The separate-and-different treatment afforded African American students as compared with whites was presumptive evidence of racial motivation on the part of school officials. The remedy was procedural. Local officials merely had to apply educational programs and practices of their own choosing evenhandedly to all students without regard to race. At that point, the direct implications for national origin discrimination and the more politically complex notion of equality as "difference" were still just below the federal radar screen. The shift from nondiscrimination to affirmative substantive entitlements sprang to life in a 1970 HEW policy guideline. This was the first official statement from Washington on the implications of Title VI for English language learners.[72] Despite silence in the Title VI statute and regulations, here the agency declared that Title VI applied to students whose dominant language was not English, conflating language with national origin. It also carried both the law and the regulations beyond an antidiscrimination principle and into the realm of affirmative government obligations.

HEW issued the policy in the form of a memorandum to school districts and not as a regulation per se. The implication was that the agency was not setting new policy, but merely interpreting existing policy. In taking this route, the government bypassed the procedural requirements of the federal Administrative Procedure Act, including the opportunity for the public to submit written comments before the policy could become legally enforceable, a process that could have provoked widespread debate. The memorandum stated that where students were excluded from "effective participation" in the education program because of their inability to speak or understand English, school districts had to take "affirmative steps" to rectify their language "deficiency." It was more than a mandate for equal treatment or inputs, though it did not endorse any particular teaching method.

The term *effective* suggested that the government would measure compliance in results or outcomes and that school districts had an obligation to act positively in that direction. Whatever was done had to "work." The memorandum specifically addressed two common but unspoken practices that historically had limited the opportunities of students with limited English ability. School districts could no longer use poor English language skills either as a basis for assigning students to classes for the mentally retarded or, at the other extreme, as grounds for denying students access to college preparatory courses. School officials also had to communicate with parents in a language the parents could comprehend.

The Nixon administration soon began monitoring compliance with the guidelines. HEW's Office for Civil Rights, focusing on the large numbers of Puerto Rican and Chicano students, cited fifty school systems for violations. According to an agency official, a "strong case" could be made that Spanish-speaking students in these districts were not receiving "an equal education" based on their "markedly lower" educational performance.[73] Yet the guidelines still spoke in the language of "deficiency." Some bilingual education advocates believed the term was politically and legally practical in pushing the needs of these students closer to those of racial minorities. Others considered it unnecessarily pejorative and factually inaccurate. Their concerns were well founded. The terminology of deficiency reflected a particular mode of thinking that indelibly stamped future discussion on educating linguistic minority students.

Lau v. Nichols

The HEW memorandum gained new legitimacy in 1974 in a Supreme Court decision that set in motion a national chain reaction. *Lau v. Nichols* remains the most substantive Court ruling to squarely address the meaning of equal educational opportunity for English language learners. At that time, the Court's prevailing concept of equality was still a response to racial discrimination. Equality under the equal protection clause required the state to treat similarly situated persons similarly. The discourse focused directly on the problems of segregation where both separation itself as well as different and unequal resources violated equality norms. *Lau* presented the Court with a distinct view, one that challenged the very notion of sameness. San Francisco school officials were in fact providing Chinese-speaking students with the same educational programs as the larger school population. Yet for the plaintiffs, therein lay the problem. The two groups were not the same and therefore the treatment had to be different, so the argument went. And while the inequalities were less palpable than in the case of racial segregation, they were equally invidious and harmful.

Like other cases striving to achieve social reform beyond the immediate facts, the *Lau* litigation operated on two levels. For the attorneys and activists, this was a test case with far-reaching potential. The circumstances in San Francisco were incidental to the larger plan. The choice of

Chinese-speaking children as the named plaintiffs indeed seemed odd, considering the overwhelmingly larger numbers of Hispanic students, in California and throughout the country, who had limited English language skills. But that choice was purely tactical. Far fewer Chinese students in the district were receiving special services, and so they presented a more compelling case of educational neglect. Moreover, the attorneys assumed that Chinese American children, widely considered the "model minority," might evoke more sympathy from the courts.[74]

Within the Chinese American community in San Francisco, the purpose of the lawsuit was much more immediate. In some measure, it was an act of desperation. For years the community had tried every known approach, from meetings to documented studies, proposals, peaceful demonstrations, and even violent protests, to convince school officials that their children's educational needs were not being adequately met, but to no avail. In the meantime, juvenile delinquency rates among Chinese American children were escalating, increasing 600 percent between 1964 and 1969.[75]

The fact that school officials were turning a deaf ear to these parents was not surprising, given California's appalling history. It was not until 1947 that the state repealed a constitutional provision, originally adopted in 1885 and amended in 1893, that allowed school districts to segregate children of Asian and Native American heritage.[76] For some administrators, that also included Mexican Americans.[77] Sentiments in San Francisco historically mirrored those of the state. As early as 1885, a report to the city's Board of Supervisors warned school officials to "guard well the doors of [the] public schools" and "defend [themselves] from this invasion of Mongolian barbarism."[78] A 1905 school board resolution calling for the segregation of Japanese and Chinese American children expressed similar fears. The document was painfully straightforward. The underlying intent was not solely to relieve "congestion" in the schools, but also "for the higher end that our children should not be placed in any position where their youthful impressions may be affected by association with pupils of the Mongolian race."[79]

Anti-Chinese policies of this sort did not stir much concern at the national level. China, at that point, did not present a serious political or military threat. Japan, on the other hand, emboldened from its recent victory over the Russians, proved otherwise. The school board's order the following year to transfer all ninety-three Japanese American children in the white schools to the segregated Chinese American school provoked an outcry from the Japanese government. It took a call to Washington and a promise from President Theodore Roosevelt that the government would limit Japanese immigration to convince city officials that reversing the policy would help ease growing tensions between the two countries.[80]

Set against this backdrop, the *Lau* litigation was long overdue. The prime force mobilizing the community was Ling-chi Wang, then a young graduate student in Semitic languages and literature at the University of California at Berkeley. Born in China and a native speaker of Minnan, one of the eight major Chinese dialects, Wang had come to the United States via Hong Kong, having acquired Mandarin, Cantonese, English, German, and Greek along the way. Like many of his classmates, he inevitably became swept up in the anti-war, civil rights, and counterculture mood that pervaded the Berkeley campus in the mid to late 1960s. Not surprisingly, he soon turned his activist energies to community organizing in San Francisco's Chinatown, where the immigrant population was booming.

With the abolition of the national origins quota system in 1965, thousands of Chinese had rejoined their long-separated families. Over the following decade, upward of two thousand Chinese immigrants settled in San Francisco each year. Most of them were from Hong Kong, and most were poorly educated. Many were of school age.[81] Although federal programs were providing job training and eventually language programs for the adults, little was being done to address the educational needs of their children. As Wang later recalled, he was particularly struck by the totally standardized, "Eurocentric," English-only curriculum and the inequitable distribution of resources among the various neighborhood schools. For him, there was something "inherently racist about assimilation," forcing children to accept certain cultural values and cast aside others. This approach, he feared, merely served to instill self-hate.[82] Though the NAACP had prevailed upon the district to racially integrate the schools through busing, the court order had done nothing to improve educational access for the thousands of non-English-speaking children.

Over the next three years, Ling-chi Wang organized the Chinese community in an attempt to change the system. He became involved in several studies undertaken by the school district to determine the extent of the language problems and how best to address them. He learned of the widely touted Coral Way School for Cuban Americans in Dade County, Florida, and the French-English program at the St. Lambert School in Montreal. He looked around the Bay Area and observed that some of the elite were choosing to educate their children in a highly regarded French-English school. He was convinced that bilingual education was the way to go, not only for its educational promise but also for its social benefits. For Chinese immigrant parents, it would address concerns that their children were losing their language and cultural identity, driving a wedge between generations. To his mind, the community had no choice but to demand bilingual education as a matter of right.[83]

Meanwhile, more than half the Chinese-speaking children continued to receive no special instruction in English while the services offered the remaining students were shamefully inadequate. The most the school district offered were some marginal programs in English as a Second Language for about a quarter of the students and two pilot bilingual programs for 260 others.[84] Barely one-third of the teachers involved were fluent in both Chinese and English. And so the community turned to litigation as a last resort.

Supporting the effort was Ed Steinman, a young legal services attorney.[85] At about the same time that Ling-chi Wang was rallying the Chinese community around the need for bilingual programs, Steinman fortuitously arrived at the Chinatown North Beach Office of the Legal Assistance Foundation. His mission was to work on test cases. Fresh out of Stanford Law School and armed with a fellowship jointly funded by the federal Office of Equal Opportunity and the Ford Foundation, Steinman initially focused on service cases. Many of them dealt with sweatshop wage problems. Not speaking Chinese, he communicated through interpreters. As he started asking his clients about their children, he learned of the educational neglect they were suffering at the hands of local school officials. When he confronted those officials, he hit a stone wall. As far as they were concerned, they were providing Chinese-speaking students with the same educational services they provided to other students, and that was all equality demanded of them. Realizing that these talks were futile, Steinman turned to community members, including Wang. They were primed to take legal action.

Steinman and Wang chose as their key named plaintiff Kinney Kinmon Lau, a six-year-old first-grader in Chinatown's Jean Parker Elementary School, where over 90 percent of the student population was Chinese-speaking. Unbeknownst to this young boy, his name would become memorialized in legal history. The boy's mother, Kam Wai Lau, was a sweatshop worker whom Wang knew. She had solicited the help of the Chinatown Neighborhood Legal Services office in a dispute with her landlord, and in the course of discussing her complaint, she mentioned that her son was struggling in school because instruction was carried on totally in English.

Kinney had come from Hong Kong at the age of five. Like many poor children from insular immigrant communities, he had little exposure to English and so his English skills were very limited. For Steinman, Kinney was the ideal plaintiff. Mistakenly believing the boy was American-born and that his mother was widowed, the true facts having been lost in translation, he thought the heart-wrenching details of Kinney's background were sure to attract media attention and, more importantly, sway the courts in his favor.[86] The boy also was young enough to still be in school while the litigation wound its way through the federal courts. The claim thus was not likely to become moot before reaching the United States Supreme Court.[87]

In July 1970, just months before HEW issued its Title VI policy statement on students with limited English ability, Kinney Kinmon Lau and twelve other similar children, more than half of them born in the United States, brought a class action suit in federal district court on behalf of nearly three thousand non-English-dominant Chinese-speaking students. By the time the case reached the Supreme Court, the class had been narrowed to eighteen hundred students, including those who were receiving nothing but regular English instruction without any special assistance. Remaining among the named plaintiffs were Kinney and seven others, five of them native-born American citizens, who would nominally carry the weight of the litigation. Named as defendants were the members of the San Francisco Board of Education, including Alan Nichols, the board president. Supporting the plaintiffs as amicus curiae were the Center for Law and Education, then based at Harvard University, and the Center's director, Marian Wright Edelman, who went on to found the Children's Defense Fund.

The children, suing through their parents, claimed that school officials were violating their rights under the Fourteenth Amendment equal protection clause and under Title VI of the Civil Rights Act of 1964. Drawing on the more subtle yet potentially more far-reaching "right to education" strand of *Brown v. Board of Education,* their attorney Ed Steinman argued that under *Brown,* equality must be measured "not only by what the school offers the child, but by the potential which the child brings to school."[88] The lower federal courts rejected both claims. As long as these students were receiving the same education on the same terms available to English-speaking students, school officials were meeting their statutory and constitutional obligations. Both courts gave only cursory attention to the plaintiffs' Title VI argument. Key to that argument was HEW's 1970 guidelines, issued just the day before the district court decision, making the federal government a crucial ally to the plaintiffs in the case.

From the appeals court's perspective, students came to school with "different advantages and disadvantages caused in part by social, economic and cultural background" that the court was not legally required to remedy. Absent any evidence of intentional discrimination, school officials had no affirmative duty to provide special remedial education programs to disadvantaged students, just as they had no affirmative duty to provide such students with better clothing or food so that they could more readily adjust to the school environment.[89] With an interesting twist on precedent, the court invoked *Meyer v. Nebraska* upholding the power of the state to impose "reasonable regulations" on schools, including instruction in English.[90] In language that rings shamefully heartless and factually wrong, the court concluded that the classification claimed to be invidious here was "not the result of laws enacted by the State, presently or historically, but the result of deficiencies created by the [children] themselves in failing to learn the English language."[91]

Though the majority opinion is indeed memorable, albeit for the wrong reasons, the more influential opinion came from Judge Shirley Hufstedler, who would later revisit these concerns as the first secretary of education in Washington. In a passionate dissent from the full court's refusal to rehear the case, Judge Hufstedler extracted from the plaintiffs' brief the concept of *constructive* or *functional* exclusion, which had originated in several early lower court decisions on special education.[92] In doing so, she laid out the rationale for what would later become the Supreme Court's opinion. As Steinman now recalls, "She did me a favor. She was one of the first women circuit court judges and her word carried a lot of weight."[93] Judge Hufstedler maintained that these children were "completely foreclosed" from educational access because they could not "comprehend any of it." They were "functionally deaf and mute," she said. "The language barrier, which the state helps to maintain, insulates [them] from their classmates as effectively as any physical bulwarks." From her perspective, these children were even "more isolated from equal educational opportunity" than the children who had suffered physical segregation in *Brown*.[94]

On its way to the Supreme Court, the case took on more national scope. Steinman solicited the help of others, parceling out the various arguments among prominent groups who submitted amicus curiae briefs on behalf of the Chinese-speaking students. Included among them were the National Education Association, the Puerto Rican Legal Defense and Education Fund, the Mexican-American Legal Defense and Educational Fund (MALDEF), the American Jewish Committee, and the Children and Government Project of the University of California at Berkeley's School of Law. The case held particular concern for MALDEF. Despite its active caseload pursuing bilingualism for Mexican American students, the group suddenly found itself on the outside of the first Court case to consider language rights under the Constitution. With Asian Americans popularly deemed a model assimilated minority, the plight of Chinese American students, they feared, could potentially minimize "the centrality of language to the racialization of Mexican Americans as non-White." And so, MALDEF structured its argument on the color implications of language discrimination.[95]

Meanwhile, the Court had granted the U.S. Department of Justice's request to appear as amicus curiae on the students' behalf. It was Justice's argument that ultimately shaped the Court's decision. Though the government raised the constitutional claims, it primarily rested its case on the Title VI regulations and guidelines, and on HEW's 1970 interpretative memorandum calling for "effective participation" and "affirmative steps." Perhaps surprising at first glance, it was perfectly reasonable that the Justice Department under Gerald Ford had entered the case. It was the government's regulation, after all, that the appeals court had blithely dismissed.

Arguing on the government's behalf was J. Stanley Pottinger, former director of the Office for Civil Rights and then an assistant attorney general. Pottinger asked the Court to affirm his own 1970 memorandum. The government's brief drew from prior school desegregation cases where the Court had explicitly determined that "equality of educational opportunity [could not] be measured solely in terms of 'buildings, curricula, qualifications and salaries of teachers, and other 'tangible' factors.'" In a statement that now seems self-evident, the brief argued that "one intangible but indispensable element of an effective education is the student's ability to comprehend the language of instruction."[96] As much as the Justice Department wanted to make a political statement, it avoided using the word *bilingual* for fear of antagonizing supporters.

Ed Steinman now frankly admits that the government's argument saved the case. Just two months after the Ninth Circuit opinion, and a month before the deadline for the plaintiffs to file their certiorari brief in the Supreme Court, the Court had decided *San Antonio Independent School District v. Rodriguez,* placing Steinman's constitutional claim in serious doubt.[97] In that landmark suit challenging the system of financing public schools in the State of Texas, the Court had rejected the argument that education was implicitly a fundamental constitutional right, which would have demanded the Court's most rigorous level of scrutiny. The *Rodriguez* plaintiffs had based their claim on the essential connection between education and the effective exercise of rights, like free speech and voting, expressly guaranteed in the Constitution. The Court concluded that even accepting the plaintiffs' argument as a matter of law, there was no factual proof that Texas was not affording children the "opportunity to acquire the basic minimal skills necessary for the enjoyment of rights to speech and to fully participate in the political process."[98]

With the ink on that ruling barely dry, Steinman realized he had a rough road to travel in pursuing his equal protection claim. And so he pushed the argument a step further, echoing Judge Hufstedler's astute and powerful observation that not only were the Chinese-speaking children denied minimally "adequate" education, they were totally foreclosed from "any education." They existed in an "academic vacuum." It was as if the pages were "blank, the print conveying nothing."[99] At oral argument, both Steinman and Pottinger repeatedly used the term *effectively excluded* to describe the harm suffered by these children, a graphic contrast to the "effective participation" required by the 1970 Title VI guidelines. Their reasoning gave greater weight to the constitutional claim in light of the Court's suggestion in *Rodriguez* that the result there may have been different if the state's financing system had "occasioned an absolute [and not merely relative] denial of educational opportunities."[100] Yet arguing in the shadow of the decision's deference to local autonomy, neither Steinman nor Pottinger mentioned a specific remedy. Steinman, in fact, conceded that school officials should take "whatever steps" they believed "reasonable" in their expert judgment.[101]

In a tightly worded opinion, written by Justice William Douglas, the justices implicitly embraced the spirit of effective exclusion while setting aside the letter of the constitutional claim. Any minor disagreements were left for concurring opinions. In correspondence and conference debate following oral argument, all had agreed on a narrow statutory ruling to avoid the hard questions that an equal protection approach would have raised.[102] What effect would it have on *Rodriguez,* decided just the previous term? Would it eliminate the distinction between de facto and de jure discrimination in school segregation, also affirmed in the previous term?[103] What bearing would it have on the various right-to-treatment disability cases percolating up through the lower courts? Would it expand services to students who were otherwise handicapped, such as the blind and the deaf, or those who were deficient in reading skills? Where would the constitutional right to education end? Even the Title VI route was not trouble-free. Would a decision for these numerous Chinese American students demand similar rights for the individual Portuguese- or Italian-speaking child? As Justice Lewis Powell warned his colleagues, it could "open [the] door to every fragment of the student population."[104] The politics of difference were indeed complicated.

The Court's collective wisdom was that a narrowly crafted Title VI ruling, focused on the specific facts and free of dicta, was the prudent course to take. It would respect federal-state relations and the strongly held tradition of local control over education. It also would avoid a threat to the legislative or executive branches. If the justices were wrong in their interpretation of Title VI, Congress could always go back to the drawing board and remedy the error. As Steinman later noted, the justices were still feeling the sting of criticism from the *Rodriguez* decision the previous year. And so they spoke in a singular voice to demonstrate that they were holding true to *Brown*'s promise of equal educational opportunity without undermining recent precedent or opening the Pandora's box of a fundamental constitutional right to education.[105]

In going the statutory route, the Court quoted from the Title VI regulations prohibiting actions that have a discriminatory "effect" on "individuals of a particular race, color, or national origin" even where "no purposeful design is present."[106] The justices specifically referenced HEW's 1970 guidelines calling for "effective participation" for students and "affirmative steps" to be taken by school districts, despite the appeals court's inattention to this significant detail. At the same time, they tacitly transposed on to the statute the constitutional reasoning of "constructive exclusion" and "intangible considerations" from *Brown* and earlier desegregation cases, the student's "ability to study, to engage in discussion and exchange views with other students."[107] In other words, equal educational opportunity demanded that students be able to fully participate in the educational experience. And full participation required the ability to communicate. Not only was education compulsory in California, but English proficiency was a requirement for high school graduation. And so they concluded:

> Under these state-imposed standards there is no equality of treatment merely by providing students with the same facilities, textbooks, teachers, and curriculum; for students who do not understand English are *effectively foreclosed* from any *meaningful* education.
>
> Basic English skills are at the core of what these public schools teach. Imposition of a requirement that, before a child can *effectively participate* in the educational program, he must already have acquired those basic skills is to make a mockery of public education. We know that those who do not understand English are certain to find the classroom experiences wholly *incomprehensible* and in no way *meaningful*.[108]

Title VI prohibits discrimination on the basis of race and national origin, not language. So while the Court spoke in terms of "language deficiency," it was using language as a surrogate for those other factors while shifting the burden from the students to the school district. School officials had agreed to comply with Title VI of the Civil Rights Act of 1964 and "all requirements" as a condition to receiving federal funds. Quoting Senator Hubert Humphrey during congressional debate on the Act, the Court noted, "Simple justice requires that public funds, to which all taxpayers of all races contribute, not be spent in any fashion which encourages, entrenches, subsidizes, or results in racial discrimination."[109] And so, within the limitations of the law, what essentially was a case about language was inextricably tied to race.

The Court glided over significant empirical points. There was no discussion as to whether the school district's arguably neutral English-only instructional program adversely affected Chinese students more than the majority or whether the language of instruction was actually the direct cause of their lower academic performance. The Court merely assumed that HEW had already considered the adverse effects generally and mandated an "affirmative" and "unconditional" response—something other than a neutral program.[110] The Court, in fact, interpreted the "effects" standard in such a way that it would deny district officials any possible defense once the plaintiffs proved disparities in educational performance. To the extent that the 1970 guidelines gave no attention to causation, they spared the plaintiffs the burden of proving any such effects in the first instance. The Chinese community, lost in the elation of what appeared to be a sweeping victory, failed to see that this was a fragile standard waiting to be undone as the consequences played out in subsequent Title VI cases and as federal intrusion into local decision making became more burdensome and unpopular. Nor could they foresee the decades of noncompliance that lay ahead.

In the end the Court framed the legal right in terms of inputs or equal treatment, but negatively—"not the same" textbooks, facilities, and so forth—implying that at least in this case, "equal" meant "different." At the same time, it suggested a vague measure of outputs in that the education provided had to be "effective." The justices expressed no preference for bilingual education although they seemed open on the language question. "Teaching English to the students of Chinese ancestry is one choice. Giving instruction to this group in Chinese is another. There may be others."[111] The suggestion was that the school district could use the native language as a tool for developing competence in English. The justices were clearly aware of the cultural ramifications and made every effort not to touch on them. The rationale and the ruling were totally consistent with the "deficit" rationale underlying the Bilingual Education Act. Noticeably absent from the decision were any lofty dicta, common in constitutionally based education opinions, about the role of schooling in meeting the needs of society.

The Court remanded the case to U.S. District Court judge Lloyd Burke in San Francisco, the same judge who had originally ruled against the plaintiffs in 1970. This was the typical course followed in school desegregation cases from *Brown* on forward.[112] The approach made practical sense. District court judges were closer to the community and arguably more aware of and sensitive to competing local concerns. They presumably could negotiate a politically acceptable and flexible remedy that would garner widespread compliance. Even so, putting the details into a "comprehensible" or "meaningful" education was no easy task under the most favorable conditions, which these were not. The school administration was looking for a minimal effort with no community input. Community members, on the other hand, long alienated by an unresponsive school bureaucracy, wanted some level of control over their children's education.

In the months that followed, schools officials dragged their heels. Meanwhile a district survey taken that April revealed a total of 2,422 students who spoke little or no English but were not receiving services. The largest numbers by far were Chinese and Spanish speakers and Filipinos. There also were smaller numbers of students whose dominant language was Samoan, Japanese, Arabic, Korean, Burmese, French, German, Hindi, Portuguese, Russian, or Vietnamese. District administrators insisted that they could not extend bilingual education to these "handfuls." For community leaders, that argument was nothing more than a "red herring."[113] Along with like-minded parents, they formed a coalition demanding that the school board appoint a task force to develop a master plan meeting the needs of the district's diverse limited English-speaking students. For the first time in the city's history, Hispanic, African American, various Asian, and white parents united in a common cause, using the Supreme Court's decision as a rallying point.

HEW officials appreciated what was at stake, that the outcome could hold national implications for all children whose first language was not English. They also had to take steps to make certain that the court's remedy was consistent with the agency's perspective. The Department of Justice requested leave to intervene in the case as a party plaintiff.[114] Bilingual advocates both within and outside California also kept careful watch. A strong bilingual-bicultural plan would be a "psychological boost" for their cause; a weak one could be a setback.[115] Meanwhile, back in San Francisco, school officials continued to resist significant change, although in time they realized they had little choice. They were facing down a doggedly determined and broadly representative community with backing from the federal government. They finally conceded and approved the task force's seven-hundred-page report. Developed with the assistance of the Center for Applied Linguistics in Washington and with input from the Justice Department, the plan would be implemented in September 1975.

The plan was a spectacular win for the Chinatown community and its supporters. It went even further than the transitional remedy originally sought but later tactically abandoned in the course of the litigation. It called for maintenance bilingual-bicultural instruction that would develop the students' primary language while ensuring that they acquired English language skills. The goal was for students to become "fully bilingual and biliterate." And although a shortage of qualified teachers initially delayed implementation, for the long run the litigation and its aftermath had sufficiently mobilized the community to elect a school board that proved sympathetic to bilingual instruction.[116] The community groups seemed to have every reason to celebrate.

For Kinney Kinmon Lau and his parents, nonetheless, it was a bittersweet moment. While the litigation was running its course, the boy had lost five years of "meaningful" and "effective" education that could have made a critical difference in his life. By the time the school district initiated dual-language instruction, he was too old for any of the programs. He and his family had moved from Chinatown and avoided publicity. He had difficulties with math and science. He struggled with English throughout high school but eventually mastered it, graduating from San Francisco City College with a major in computer programming. For him as for many others, assimilation had its price. Having Anglicized his name to Kenny, and finally Ken, as an adult he spoke English without a trace of accent but could no longer read or write Chinese. In a 2002 interview with the *Boston Globe,* he regretted how his lack of Chinese literacy skills prevented him from working in foreign countries like his native Hong Kong. What ultimately happened to the remaining plaintiffs in the case remains a mystery. One can only speculate on their missed opportunities. But for Ken Lau, the final assessment was sobering. "People risk so much to come here," he said, "and I think they should be able to retain their language and their culture." Yet he also added, "I don't know if bilingual education is better—I'm still trying to work it out."[117]

As typically occurs in long-standing litigation, the bigger picture over time has been mixed for two generations of English language learners in the San Francisco schools. From just 1,050 in 1970, the number of Chinese-speaking students enrolled in the city's bilingual programs has jumped to nearly 25,000 today. The federal district court still maintains jurisdiction over their education. The school district continues to file annual reports pursuant to the 1976 consent decree though Judge Burke has since retired. In the wake of Proposition 227, the 1998 California voter initiative aimed at dismantling bilingual education, the *Lau* decision has taken on particular importance. Linguistic minority parents in San Francisco, unlike those in other California school districts, are exempt from the stressful and indeterminate process of requesting waivers to enroll their children in bilingual programs. For them it is still a legal entitlement protected by the now thirty-five-year-old court order. Meanwhile, the school district has been spared the political turmoil that Proposition 227 has wrought in other communities. As Ling-chi Wang more recently noted, "*Lau* prevails," at least in San Francisco and at least for the time being.[118]

That being said, serious systemic shortcomings remain. When the district court threatened to terminate the consent decree in 2006 because it had become little more than mechanical reporting, advocates jumped to its defense. Ed Steinman joined with the U.S. Department of Justice as intervenor in filing an affidavit that successfully opposed termination, arguing that *Lau*'s goals were yet to be fulfilled. Despite the passage of more than three decades and vigilant oversight by the Bilingual Community Council established under the decree, the district had still not established a comprehensive bilingual program with adequate student assessment, staff development, monitoring, bilingual staff, Chinese language materials, or parent involvement.[119] Apparently the measured compromise reached in *Lau,* a broad federal statutory right with deference to state and local authorities in fashioning a remedy, had fallen short of its original promise. But then again, local change was only part of its intended legacy.

The *Lau* Remedies

The initial *Lau* decision, "big news" within the small but growing advocacy network, scarcely attracted any immediate mention in the press outside of California. That apparent indifference subsequently proved short-lived. In the months and years that followed, as the various actors in the *Lau* drama wrangled over operationalizing the Court's decision, *Lau* served as the engine driving a rash of activity at the federal, state, and local levels. Advocates used the decision to push Congress, HEW, state legislatures, and the courts to more clearly define the right to a "meaningful" education and the obligations of school officials in meeting that mandate. Pottinger and Wang themselves testified before Congress. Wang deliberated with federal civil rights officials on enforcement guidelines and later helped draft California's Bilingual-Bicultural Act in 1976.[120] Within months of the decision, Alaska, Michigan, New York, and Rhode Island joined the ranks of sixteen states that had adopted laws mandating transitional bilingual education since Congress had passed the Bilingual Education Act in 1968. By the end of 1977, ten additional states had followed suit.[121] Several lower court decisions likewise drew on *Lau* to support a legal right to bilingual education, in some cases as a component of a desegregation plan.[122]

Lau instantly started tugging at the political machinery in Washington. Congress held hearings to revisit the Bilingual Education Act, which was up for reauthorization. The annual amount appropriated for bilingual programs had jumped from $7.5 million in 1969 to $45 million in 1973 covering 209 projects and 129,500 students representing twenty-four languages. Over the next two years, under the pressure of *Lau* compliance, that dollar amount nearly doubled, as did the number of students participating in Title VII programs.

Meanwhile, HEW set about formulating a set of guidelines to assist school districts in complying with the implications of the 1970 memorandum and the Court's ruling. The agency convened a task force composed largely of linguistic minority group representatives, lawyers, and educators, all of whom were sympathetic to an approach that would include instruction in the home language. Terrel Bell, then U.S. commissioner of education, issued the task force recommendations in the summer of 1975 through a memorandum sent to school districts. The proposals came on the heels of a U.S. Civil Rights Commission report concluding that bilingual education was the most effective means of teaching large numbers of non-English-speaking students.[123] Six years later, as secretary of education under a different president and in a different political climate, Bell would do a complete turnaround and pull back a similar proposal in the face of widespread opposition from both sides in the debate. It was the mid-1970s. Multiculturalism was at its peak, and the backlash against bilingual instruction, sparked in some measure by these very guidelines, was yet to appear. The recommendations quickly took on a life of their own. The Office for Civil Rights established nine "Lau Centers" throughout the country to provide technical assistance to school districts in helping them abide by the guidelines. Meanwhile, the agency aggressively threatened to withhold federal funds from districts that failed to comply.

The "*Lau* Remedies," as they are commonly known, were far more specific than the Court's ruling. For the elementary and intermediate grades, they qualifiedly mandated one approach, bilingual education. That mandate was somewhat confusing in view of an official HEW statement to the contrary just the previous December. At that time, Under Secretary for Education Frank Carlucci had made clear that "no single program is appropriate for the individual circumstances of all [school districts] subject to the requirements of Title VI . . . as reinforced by *Lau*."[124] Despite that caveat, the guidelines required school districts to provide bilingual instruction where there were twenty or more elementary school students, from any one non-English language group, whose sole or predominant language was other than English. Similar instruction had to be provided to intermediate school students who did not speak English. No mention was made as to whether students were literate in their native language.

The guidelines offered local officials the choice of either a transitional bilingual education program using the home language until the student developed adequate English language skills, a bilingual-bicultural education program, or a multilingual-multicultural education program. In the latter two cases, the home language would continue throughout the student's education to develop skills in two languages.[125] School officials had the option of choosing none of these approaches provided they could demonstrate that an alternative was at least as effective. From the local perspective, that choice would come up empty. How could school districts prove that something was as good as something else whose merits had not yet been proved? Essentially they would have to prove the unprovable.[126] In any event, the guidelines implicitly permitted maintenance programs to satisfy Title VI requirements, as a matter of law, even though Congress would not provide federal funds to support such programs under the Bilingual Education Act's 1974 amendments. It seemed that as congressional skepticism toward preserving linguistic and cultural differences was sharpening, the concept maintained support within the ranks of the executive branch.

The federal position grew even murkier the following April when HEW issued a memorandum to its regional offices stating that bilingual education was not required for non-English-speaking students. The "*Lau* Remedies" were not "exclusive" but merely "guidelines" that investigators from the Office for Civil Rights would use to determine if a school district's plan was acceptable once a Title VI violation had been found. In practice, agency officials were using them as a benchmark for judging Title VI compliance in the first instance.[127] The agency seemed to be backpedaling in the face of political opposition. The federal and national ambivalence toward bilingualism and biculturalism could not have been more apparent. And the resulting confusion at the local level could not have been more pervasive or disruptive.

Martin Gerry, then acting director of OCR and chief architect of the agency's bilingual policy under President Ford, believed that bilingual programs were the only ones that "were working." Gerry based that conclusion on his experience as a court-appointed monitor overseeing a 1971 Texas court order. Years later, he noted that if he had given school districts the choice, they would have opted for English as a Second Language because it was "cheaper and [more] politically popular with a lot of people" than bilingual instruction. Yet he also admitted, in hindsight, that the *Lau* Remedies were too rigid. "It would have been better," he said, "to develop an individual plan for each student along the line of the special-education model. Bilingual instruction is not right for every kid."[128]

The *Lau* Remedies evoked the same fears that have since resurfaced in debates over immigration and the status of English. Civil rights leader Bayard Rustin warned against the "proponents of cultural isolation" who were advocating bilingual education as a means of "creating a separatist, alternative culture" where English would not play "a pivotal role," producing "bilingual illiteracy on a massive scale."[129] But the remedies were more than just a challenge to the assimilation project. Teachers rightly foresaw in them a need for bilingual staffers. School districts would favor Hispanics in hiring and possibly would try to upend tenure and seniority rights in the case of layoffs. That threat soon became all the more real as the country found itself in the worst economic recession since the 1930s, with school districts facing severe revenue shortfalls. The seniority issue became especially critical in New York City, where city officials were facing impending bankruptcy while trying to comply with a federal court consent decree that put the force of law behind bilingual instruction for Spanish-dominant students.[130] At the same time, school officials nationwide railed against this unprecedented intrusion on local decision making in both personnel and curricular matters. Several districts, including Seattle and the State of Alaska, threatened to sue HEW.[131]

The agency was especially vulnerable to attack. Once again it had sidestepped the regulatory process, failing to give the public the opportunity to comment on proposed policy changes before they became final. Unlike the July 25, 1970, memorandum at issue in *Lau*, the *Lau* Remedies had never even appeared in the *Federal Register* as required by law, despite repeated assertions by federal officials that publication was imminent.[132] These technical slights ultimately proved fatal when Eskimo-run school districts in Alaska did, in fact, take HEW to court. Under the resulting

consent decree, HEW agreed to withdraw the guidelines, publish a regulatory policy in the *Federal Register*, and make it available for public
comment.[133] By that time, the *Lau* Remedies had been in force for three
years and HEW regional offices had used them to negotiate over 350
"Lau" plans or consent agreements requiring native language instruction. Transitional bilingual education was fast becoming the dominant
approach.

It took another two years for the newly created Department of Education, under its first secretary, Shirley Hufstedler, to finally publish proposed regulations in the closing months of the Carter administration. By
that time, the number of *Lau* plans had grown to nearly five hundred.
Hufstedler was the former dissenting Ninth Circuit judge who had developed the legal framework for the Court's decision in *Lau*. The proposals, eliciting a record forty-six hundred public comments, mostly critical,
seemed to please no one. Public hearings nationwide could not save
them. Close to 450 individuals testified. Groups like the National Association for Bilingual Education, La Raza, and the Mexican American Legal
Defense and Educational Fund argued that the regulations lacked adequate detail to preserve bilingual education as a mandate. The American
Federation of Teachers and even the National Education Association, as
well as others, believed that the proposal was overly detailed and vigor-
ously lobbied to bury it. Opponents of bilingual education argued that it
infringed on local decision making and undermined the American tradition of decentralized education. They questioned how Washington could
mandate an approach that was still experimental, with no conclusive evidence that it was more effective than others. They invoked Congress's understanding that the newly formed Department of Education would not
dictate curriculum to local school districts. They warned that federal programs could lead the United States to become another Quebec with all its
political conflicts.[134]

As opposition grew, Congress passed an amendment to an Education
Department appropriations bill that prohibited the Department from implementing the proposals until June 1981. They were effectively dead.
The Reagan administration seized the political moment and, having been
in office just one month, announced with great fanfare that it was with-
drawing the proposed regulations. Calling them "harsh, inflexible, burdensome, unworkable and incredibly costly," the newly appointed secretary of education, Terrell Bell, told the press, "Nothing in the law or the
Constitution anoints the Department of Education to be national school
teacher, national school superintendent or national school board."[135]
That statement coming from Bell was indeed surprising. Remember it

was he who had issued the 1975 *Lau* Remedies when he was commissioner of education in the Ford administration. Why the change of heart? The political climate in Washington and in the nation had changed dramatically. The new administration had come into office on a broad-based mandate for deregulation. The new secretary's marching orders were to dismantle the very agency he had been appointed to lead, a mission he seemed doggedly determined not to accomplish. In the end, OCR reverted to the 1970 HEW guidelines requiring school districts to take "affirmative steps" without prescribing a particular method of instruction.

Codifying *Lau*

Before opposing forces undid both the *Lau* Remedies and the proposed Title VI language regulations, Congress codified and extended *Lau*'s central holding in a separate statute that ultimately proved more enduring. Intended primarily to rein in court-ordered busing and as a remedy for racial segregation in the schools, the Equal Educational Opportunities Act (EEOA) of 1974 also prohibited the state from denying "equal educational opportunity" based on national origin.[136] The law specifically required states to take "appropriate action to overcome language barriers" that "impede" students from "equal participation" in the instructional program.[137] This provision was not part of the original bill but instead was proposed from the floor of the House following weeks of heated controversy over the busing provisions.

Nothing in the legislative findings or the stated purpose of the Act indicated any congressional intent other than to restrict busing as a mechanism for achieving racial balance in the schools. The only legislative reference appeared indirectly in an identical bill proposed by President Richard Nixon in his March 1972 address to the nation. The proposal called for "an educational bill of rights for . . . [those] who start their education under language handicaps." Though approved by the House Committee on Education and Labor later that year, it was never passed by Congress.[138] A Committee report on that bill quoted President Nixon as stating that children with limited English proficiency would not have "true equality of educational opportunity until [their] language and cultural barriers [were] removed."[139] The Court's findings and conclusion in *Lau* implicitly resurrected Nixon's 1972 proposal.

The law as adopted drew on the deficiency model of earlier policies under Title VI. Nonetheless, it presented subtle linguistic shifts with a decidedly different tone and implications. On the one hand, it seemed to offer a more modest approach than HEW's 1970 memorandum. There the agency's call for "affirmative steps" and "effective participation" suggested that school officials were obligated to produce results. The Act seemed to retreat from *Lau*'s more definitive call for a "meaningful" education, one with a substantive language element implicitly different from mainstream instruction. The term *appropriate* implied that some amount of education judgment should play into the calculus on a case-by-case basis.

In other ways, Congress gave the legislation broader scope than Title VI. Where the 1970 HEW memorandum spoke in terms of the "inability to speak and understand the English language" as the trigger for official action, the EEOA spoke more generally of "language barriers," which might include reading and writing skills, reflecting intervening amendments to the Bilingual Education Act. The legislation applied to all public school districts, not just those that received federal funding, although all school districts, in fact, receive some federal funds. It also applied to the states. More significantly, plaintiffs did not have to prove that school officials acted with any intent to deny them an "appropriate" education. The law also explicitly granted them a private right to sue officials in federal court. Unlike Title VI, it authorized the Justice Department to take direct enforcement action without waiting for the Office for Civil Rights to refer the case.

As the scope of the *Lau* decision and Title VI coverage became increasingly uncertain, as I discuss in Chapter 7, and as the *Lau* Remedies fell under attack, the EEOA became the preferred line of litigation for protecting the rights of English language learners. The most definitive and influential interpretation came in 1981 from the Fifth Circuit Court of Appeals, a court active in shaping the rights of racial minorities in school desegregation cases. In *Castaneda v. Pickard*, the appeals court laid out a science-based framework. Courts would apply three criteria to assess whether school officials were taking "appropriate action" to ensure equal educational opportunity.[140] The program must be informed by an educational theory recognized as sound by at least some experts in the field or "deemed a legitimate experimental strategy." It must be reasonably designed to effectively implement the educational theory by providing the "practices, resources and personnel necessary to transform the theory into reality." And it must produce positive results in overcoming language barriers after a sufficiently long trial period. In other words, students must actually be learning English and to some extent subject matter. The court noted congressional concerns that "schools make a genuine and good faith effort" to remedy language deficiencies while taking into consideration "local circumstances and resources." It made clear that Congress did not intend to mandate bilingual education but rather deferred to the "educational values" and "political decisions" of state and local authorities.[141]

According to the court, special programs had to be "reasonably calculated" to move students toward "parity of participation in the standard instructional program within a reasonable length of time." The goal was twofold—to develop English language skills, and to overcome academic deficiencies—leaving the precise sequence and manner to school officials. For the *Castaneda* court, like the Supreme Court in *Lau*, special language programs were not a permanent track but merely a temporary stop on the road to a typical, equal, mainstream education. They were a way to level the playing field.

The decision no doubt provided clearly articulated criteria to hold state and local school officials accountable for improving learning outcomes. Deferring to local discretion and using a "reasonableness" standard, it also set the stage for a new discourse on educating an increasingly diverse population of students, some whose parents would more single-mindedly press for English language instruction. In that sense, it held promise for promoting both equal educational access and administrative flexibility. Yet in another sense, the decision gave legal weight to an anti-bilingual, anti-immigrant backlash that was rapidly gaining momentum. It remained to be seen how aggressively and effectively other federal courts and executive branch officials might use the *Castaneda* standards to effectively support or push back on those forces.

CHAPTER SIX

Backlash

A S THE 1970s wore on, the idea that schools should accommodate linguistic differences attracted mounting criticism and open hostility. Critics pounded the media with tales of excesses nationwide, laying blame on the federal government for funding a project with neither a research-based rationale nor wide support within the educational establishment. Anxieties especially over the mounting number of Spanish speakers gave force and direction to an organized movement ostensibly promoting Official English and more directly English Only in the schools. The continued onslaught of ambivalent, ambiguous, and conflicting directives from Washington prevented local educators from establishing a coherent set of best practices, further fueling the opposition and galvanizing into action various stakeholders, including parent groups, teachers' unions, and advocacy organizations. Proponents found themselves on the defensive while the federal government incrementally pulled back on rights and programs that had barely found their grounding. In the following decades, the state accountability movement and high-stakes testing, along with state voter initiatives and ultimately the federal No Child Left Behind Act, placed constraints, some more obvious than others, on efforts to develop dual language skills among immigrant children.

Seeds of Opposition

The Court's decision in *Lau v. Nichols* had given political force to the 1974 amendments to the Bilingual Education Act. By the time the Act again came up for reauthorization in 1978, however, the political sands had started shifting and the seeds of opposition to bilingual and bicultural education began to bear fruit. Two studies played a pivotal role in shaping the debate on language policy in the schools.

In April 1977, just as debate on the Title VII reauthorization was about to begin, the American Institutes for Research (AIR) issued a scathing critique of thirty-eight Spanish bilingual projects in their fourth or fifth year of funding. Commissioned by the U.S. Office of Education, the $1.3 million study included approximately twelve thousand students. The interim report concluded that, when compared with students not instructed bilingually, Title VII students performed better in math but worse in English vocabulary and reading on standardized achievement tests.[1] The study also found that bilingual programs were highly segregated, retaining students in separate classes beyond the point where they were proficient in English. Bilingual proponents believed the initial findings were strategically released to weaken support for Title VII, which was up for reauthorization the following year.[2] If so, the strategy was effective. The 1978 amendments to the Bilingual Education Act subsequently placed greater emphasis on English language acquisition and included measures to limit segregation.

As quickly as the naysayers seized upon the report, educational researchers were equally quick to point out its methodological flaws, which were numerous. The study measured student progress after only five months into the programs, hardly sufficient time to measure effects. It failed to account for cross-program differences, including purposes, staffing, materials, teaching methodologies, student socioeconomic background, and years of prior schooling. It ignored the fact that some Title VII classrooms may have included English proficient slow learners placed there for more individualized instruction and not to overcome language barriers. Meanwhile, at least two-thirds of the students in the comparison all-English classrooms had previously been enrolled in bilingual education. One might reasonably attribute their superior performance, at least in part, to the success of bilingual instruction and not to its failure.[3]

Notwithstanding these serious shortcomings, the AIR study made for good press and fed the growing hostility toward bilingual instruction. The hostility gained added force later that year from a monograph written by Noel Epstein, then the education editor for the *Washington Post*. With a pre-publication boost in the *Post*, this searing criticism of the federal program, its implementation, and its underlying philosophy was like red meat to the hungry pack of oppositionist wolves. Epstein took the federal government to task for failing to demonstrate, "after nearly nine years and more than half a billion dollars in federal funds," whether transitional bilingual education made a significant difference in student achievement, English acquisition, or attitudes toward school.[4] That point had educational merit. His attack, however, was much deeper and more ideological, striking at disagreements over assimilation, American identity, and the government's role. He challenged the appropriateness of federal programs supporting "affirmative ethnicity." More directly he questioned the government's responsibility, in the first place, to finance and promote "student attachments to their ethnic languages and cultures," what he considered the "jobs long left to families, religious groups, ethnic organizations, private schools, ethnic publications, and others."[5] For certain groups, he suggested, perhaps poverty and discrimination rather than language were at the heart of academic failure. In the end, he called for the federal government to consider redirecting its funding from bilingual education to English immersion.

Epstein provoked a sharp rebuke from bilingual education proponents. Noted sociolinguist Joshua Fishman called the study "an ignorant critique . . . [heap]ing bias upon bias, suspicion upon suspicion, misinterpretation upon misinterpretation."[6] And while Fishman admitted that bilingual education was only a "partial solution to all encompassing problems," he still believed that the approach was "here to stay."[7] Little did he or other advocates realize how Epstein's proposal was on the cutting edge of a national movement that would soon take off with unrelenting speed.

The AIR and Epstein reviews effectively stripped bilingual education of its pedagogical underpinnings. All that seemingly remained was a political agenda to maintain the Spanish language and the Hispanic culture. Critics claimed that agenda would soon erode national unity and so they demanded that Americans consciously commit themselves to English as their common bond.[8] No longer was the debate simply about the instructional value of bilingual education; it also was about the evils of ethnocentrism. Both were topics of intense questioning in the 1977 Title VII reauthorization hearings. Even longtime civil rights supporters like Gary Orfield justifiably raised the dangers of ethnic segregation and called for alternative approaches.[9] Many bilingual programs undeniably were separating students in classrooms on the basis of national origin. Advocates for bilingual-bicultural programs were put on the defensive.

Other factors also set the tone for the 1977 hearings, diluting whatever congressional enthusiasm remained for preserving the child's native language and culture. Though less restrictive immigration laws had broadened the potential constituent group for bilingual education, newcomers from Asia and Europe, including Chinese, Russians, and smaller numbers of Greeks, Italians, and Portuguese, as well as Haitians, were eager to assimilate into the American mainstream like migrants of the past. They differed from Mexican or Puerto Rican immigrants, whose proximity to their homelands supported dual identities and attachments. They also had little, if any, interest in the ideology of ethnicity as political leverage, though some of their leaders seemed to espouse such views. For these immigrants, the home language and culture were private matters, leaving the public arena of schooling for English, the key to success in their adopted homeland. These groups supported, at the very most, a transitional approach with a speedy exit into the education mainstream. For some, English language classes from day one with supplemental instruction in English as a Second Language were even more preferable.

Hispanic advocates continued to press for maintenance or developmental bilingual programs that would affirm native culture and develop native language skills. Language rights had become a key issue distinguishing Hispanics from other minority groups while Spanish had become a prime political pillar in the emerging Chicano movement.[10] By that point, the arguments supporting bilingual education had taken on several casts, from promoting justice for groups that historically had suffered discrimination, to enhancing academic achievement among disadvantaged students, to preserving ethnic languages and cultures as a national resource. Regardless of the rationale, the ideological divide regarding means-ends and the home language and culture would continue to provoke passionate debate as migration spread from across the globe.

The 1978 amendments to the Bilingual Education Act reflected rising anti-immigrant sentiments and a clearer stress on assimilation. They expanded the definition of eligible children from those with "limited English-speaking ability"(LESA) to those who were "limited English-proficient"(LEP), thus recognizing reading, writing, and listening skills as important aspects of language development.[11] They explicitly incorporated HEW's position that the goal of federal bilingual programs was English language competency. Schools could use native language instruction only "to the extent necessary" for children to become competent in English.[12] The focus was on transition and remediation and not maintenance or enrichment. The amendments also removed the ban on foreign language learning, but limited the inclusion of English-speaking children to 40 percent and only for the purpose of helping LEP children improve their English language skills.[13] That provision, admittedly faint-hearted, met with little interest from state or local school officials, despite Americans' "scandalous" incompetence in foreign languages, as a presidential commission noted the following year.[14] A declining economy and mounting political opposition to bilingual education pushed all the weight onto transitioning English language learners into mainstream classrooms.

At that time, some school districts were under pressure to employ bilingual teachers to comply with legal mandates under the *Lau* Remedies or federal court orders. Some of those hired were not fully proficient in English, and had little or no experience in U.S. schools. In many communities, Title VII projects had brought into the mix a cadre of bilingual support personnel—resource teachers, guidance counselors, family workers, paraprofessionals. While regular programs were crumbling under the strain of large class sizes, limited materials, decreased guidance services, and cutbacks in enrichment classes like music and art, bilingual programs appeared to be riding a wave of federal largesse. The situation provoked resentment among rank-and-file teachers and within organized labor.

The Winds of Change

As the decade drew to a close, one thing was unmistakable: Congress had lost the political will to legislate national education policy affirmatively endorsing bilingualism or biculturalism. A new administration in Washington would soon give that message even greater force. Just months after taking office in 1981, President Ronald Reagan told the National League of Cities that it was "absolutely wrong and against the American concept to have a bilingual education program that is now openly, admittedly dedicated to preserving [students'] native language and never getting them adequate in English so they can go out into the job market and participate."[15]

That same year, the Department of Education released a report that proved a significant setback for bilingual instruction. Based on a meta-analysis of thirty-nine studies, the authors Keith Baker and Adriana de Kanter concluded that there was insufficient empirical evidence to support continued funding for transitional bilingual education to the exclusion of other approaches.[16] They particularly recommended structured English immersion. The report drew heavily on the success of Canadian French immersion programs.[17] Yet it failed to acknowledge obvious differences between English language learners in the United States, who did not speak the dominant language and often lived in poverty, and Canadian English-speaking students immersed in French instruction by their middle-class parents. In fact, the Canadian researchers who had studied these programs had cautioned against transferring their findings to the United States.[18] Despite severe criticism for its faulty research methodology and inadequately supported conclusions, the Baker and de Kanter study was widely cited, especially during the Reagan years, as bilingual education fell under a barrage of attacks.[19]

The Reagan administration had galloped into Washington on the horse of "New Federalism," with a sweeping mandate to return decision making to state and local governments. The mood of the country had decidedly changed in reaction to more than two decades of intense federal involvement and regulation. The federal courts, along with much of the education community, likewise were endorsing greater flexibility at the state and local levels. Even bilingual education supporters, like the National Education Association, were expressly rejecting maintenance and even late-exit transitional programs. As one former staffer in the Carter administration put it, it was "like people in the District of Columbia rooting for the [Los Angeles] Raiders."[20] The handwriting was clearly on the wall, and even the most stalwart advocates knew it was time to compromise.

After much wrangling, the 1984 Title VII amendments authorized a funding "set aside" of between 4 and 10 percent for "special alternative instructional programs," that did not use the native language.[21] Though a seemingly small concession from bilingual advocates, this was a major symbolic victory for the opposing forces. It was the first time in sixteen years of legislative authorizations that supporters felt compelled to recognize the legitimacy of other approaches. In signing the bill into law, President Reagan assured the American public that he would "work with Congress to further expand this much needed flexibility."[22]

The most prominent and forceful advocate for this position was Reagan's secretary of education, William Bennett. In a speech in New York in September 1985, Bennett attacked the federal Bilingual Education Act as a "failed path," a "bankrupt course." "After seventeen years of federal involvement and after $1.7 billion in federal funding," he declared, "we have no evidence that the children we sought to help—that the children who deserve our help—have benefited." Educators, he said, had "lost sight of the goal of learning English as the key to equal educational opportunity." "As fellow citizens," he urged, we need a "common language," the language in which our "common history is written" and in which our "common forefathers speak to us, through the ages." His words were hauntingly reminiscent of Theodore Roosevelt's famous "Children of the Crucible" speech back in 1917 hailing the "language and culture" inherited from the "builders of the Republic."[23]

Bilingual education activist James Crawford, now president of the Institute for Language and Education Policy and then a reporter for *Education Week,* reviewed the voluminous mail the Department received in reply to Bennett's speech. What he found were letters running five to one in favor of the secretary's views. But to his surprise, they had less to do with educating linguistic minority children and far more to do with, as Crawford put it, "illegal aliens on welfare, communities being 'overrun' by Asians and Hispanics, 'macho-oriented' foreigners trying to impose their culture on Americans, and—a special concern—the out-of-control birthrates of linguistic minorities."[24]

Bennett's "bilingual education initiative" was essentially a pitch for structured English immersion, though few if any such programs then existed. A congressionally mandated study of 191 school districts in nineteen states had recently confirmed local support for a traditional English Only approach. While programs for predominantly Spanish-speaking students typically offered instruction in both Spanish and English, 91 percent of the programs for non-Spanish speakers still used all-English instruction.[25] In any case, the winds of change were blowing over Washington and across the nation. The 1988 amendments to the Act increased funding for alternative approaches to 25 percent. The remaining funds were set aside for transitional bilingual education. The amendments set a three-year limit for students to remain in federally funded programs.[26] Arguments to maintain the native language and culture had lost political currency.

Through the early to mid-1990s, bilingual education unexpectedly got a brief reprieve. If neither the first Bush administration nor the Clinton administration appeared enthusiastically supportive, neither was it hostile toward the concept. Nor was Congress. The 1994 Title VII amendments recognized the benefits of bilingualism and biculturalism not only to LEP children, but also to the smaller numbers of English-proficient students participating in these programs and to the entire country. In words that were on the cusp of things to come, the law recognized that "as the world becomes increasingly interdependent and as international communication becomes a daily occurrence in government, business, commerce, and family life, multilingual skills constitute an important national resource which deserves protection and development."[27] It was a way to promote the nation's "competitiveness in the global economy."[28]

Notwithstanding such expansive rhetoric, the law made clear that its purpose was "to help insure that limited English proficient students master English" and "meet the same rigorous standards for academic performance expected of all children and youth."[29] It seemed that after a quar-

ter of a decade of wavering on language policy in the schools, Congress
had reached a compromise. The amendments allowed some discretion at
the local level while expressly recognizing, for the first time in the nation's history, that immigrant languages were not a problem to be remedied but an asset to the nation and one that the federal government was
cautiously willing to fund.

That compromise proved fragile and short-lived. As academic achievement, especially among Hispanic children, continued to lag and immigration reform became a hot-button issue, the backlash against bilingual education became more strident.[30] The 1994 Republican sweep in Congress
once again turned the political tide. Though proposals to totally end federal funding for bilingual programs failed, others aimed at continuing
Title VII's slow but steady shift to English immersion gained support.
The debate was not just an "inside-the-Beltway" battle of ideologues. In
pockets across the country, Hispanic parents who historically had been
bilingual education's strongest supporters began to publicly voice outrage that their children were coming out of the schools with poor reading
skills in both Spanish and English. Most were not looking to abolish the
approach, but merely wanted better and shorter programs. As sociologist
Rubén Rumbaut noted at the time, bilingual programs ran the "spectrum
from excellent to truly lousy ones that become a political, bureaucratic
trap for immigrant children . . . Parents don't want to be part of an 'experiment' where maybe their kids will come out having learned English in
six years."[31]

Language in the Crossfire

To best understand the course of events through the 1980s and 1990s,
one has to look at the wider political landscape against which they were
unfolding. At that point, bilingual education became caught in the crossfire of immigration reform and related demands to declare English the official language of the country. The individual most identified with turning
those demands into action was the late Samuel I. Hayakawa, a Canadian-
born semanticist, former college president, and then Republican senator
from California. In 1981 Hayakawa introduced in Congress the English
Language Amendment, the first federal proposal to declare English the
nation's official language.

At first glance, the amendment appeared merely symbolic. After all,
Americans and others had long recognized English as the de facto language of the country. But the proposal had considerable substance with
far-reaching consequences. It expressly prohibited state laws, ordinances,

orders, programs, and policies that would require the use of other languages. It also prohibited both federal and state governments, including the courts, from mandating any program, policy, or documents that would use a language other than English. The implications for voting, government services, and education were staggering. The proposal specifically would have repealed the Bilingual Education Act of 1968 and subsequent amendments. It also would have annulled the 1975 amendments to the Voting Rights Act requiring bilingual ballots in areas with high concentrations of certain non-English speakers.[32] Those amendments and the accommodations they demanded were as much a driving force behind the federal Official English proposal as was bilingual programming. Though the joint resolution died, it set a pattern for similar proposals repeatedly put before Congress in the years to come. None has ever gone to a full congressional vote, but supporters of the concept remain resolute.

In 1983 Hayakawa went on to form a group called "U.S. English" along with Dr. John H. Tanton, an ophthalmologist from Petoskey, Michigan, a small resort town on the shores of Lake Michigan. Still active in the movement, Tanton has defied conventional political categorization. So has the group's advisory board, whose members over the years have included Jacques Barzun, Dinesh Desai, Nathan Glazer, Norman Podhoretz, Arnold Schwarzenegger, and the late Senator Eugene McCarthy. Tanton, a former head of the Sierra Club's population committee, former president of Zero Population Growth, harsh critic of neoclassical economics, and self-described progressive, had founded the Federation for American Immigration Reform (FAIR) in 1979 with the goal of ending illegal immigration and reducing legal immigration.

In a 1984 fact sheet, U.S. English laid out the broad scope of its mission and its position on educating children whose dominant language was not English: bilingual education should be replaced with English language acquisition classes, bicultural education should be eliminated from the public schools, and a two-year limit should be imposed on special English instruction. Much of that agenda has since become reality to some degree. U.S. English now boasts 1.8 million members nationwide.[33]

As it turned out, Tanton's connection to U.S. English came to a crashing end. In 1986 he wrote a provocative memo on the impact of immigration in California. Published two years later in the *Arizona Republic*, the memo barely gave language, presumably the prime interest of the organization, a passing mention. It was all about culture and numbers. Intended for an internal discussion group, it warned of the "Latin onslaught," their "low educability," and their unwanted traits like the "morbida" (bribe). It implicitly portrayed Hispanics as overactive breeders, asking, "Can homo contraceptivus compete with homo progentiva [*sic*] if borders aren't controlled?"[34] The memo shook U.S. English to its very roots. The organization's executive director, Linda Chavez, as well several prominent board members, including veteran journalist Walter Cronkite, resigned over the incident. Tanton later broke ties with the organization. Yet despite the internal turmoil, U.S. English was still getting its message across at least to some Americans. That same year, an 84 percent to 16 percent victory in Florida made the English language amendment the most popular ballot initiative in the nation.

Two new groups also appeared on the scene in 1986. Larry Pratt, a former Virginia state representative and president of Gun Owners of America, founded a group called "English First," which has a mission similar to that of U.S. English and a current membership of over one hundred fifty thousand. English First initially defined for itself three goals: to make English the nation's official language, to offer "every child the chance to learn English," and to "eliminate costly and ineffective multilingual policies." The group prides itself on being the only pro-English organization to "testify against bilingual ballots in 1992" and to "lead the fight against bilingual education in 1994."[35]

In the meantime, John Tanton, along with several former U.S. English associates, moved on to found ProEnglish. The driving objective was to defend the Official English initiative adopted by Arizona voters in 1988. The Arizona Supreme Court overturned the amendment in 1998, but voters reinstated a revised version in 2006.[36] "Ending bilingual education (e.g., foreign language immersion) programs in public schools" remains high on the ProEnglish action agenda. So does declaring English the official language of the nation. The group makes clear that Official English does not mean "English only," expressly rejecting the term as "loaded" and "divisive." It recognizes the use of other languages to the extent that there is a "compelling" purpose, such as protecting health and safety, ensuring equality before the law, promoting tourism, or teaching foreign languages.[37] Noticeably absent from the list is any mention of using the home language to educate language-minority students, even as a bridge to learning English. A four-month investigation by the Southern Poverty Law Center's *Intelligence Report* following the 9/11 terrorist attacks placed Tanton at the helm of the country's growing anti-immigration movement. With a cover depicting him as "The Puppeteer," the report revealed how his network of connected organizations, allegedly linked to racist groups, was wielding significant influence in Congress.[38]

Though Tanton rails against the racist label his detractors have pinned on him, his inflammatory rhetoric suggests he justifiably may have earned it. A lead article in the summer 1998 issue of *The Social Contract,* published by Tanton, argued that "multiculturalism" was replacing "successful Euro-American culture" with "dysfunctional Third World cultures."[39] In a more recent interview with the *Washington Post,* Tanton questioned whether the United States could survive the "invasion" of people from Latin and Central America, Korea, and China; he expressed concern that the American culture and the economy would "irreparably erode" with continued waves of legal and illegal "interlopers."[40]

Tanton's anti-immigrant diatribes were indeed vexing, even more so because they echoed proposals emanating from Washington as reflected in the 1985 speech by William Bennett, then secretary of education, attacking the federal Bilingual Education Act. U.S. English had effectively found an ally in the Reagan administration while John Tanton's "over-the-top" remarks would soon resonate among many Americans. Bennett's speech did not go unnoticed in the Hispanic community. The Spanish-American League Against Discrimination (SALAD), a Miami-based civil rights and educational group, fired off what later became a blueprint for an alternative to proposals restricting native language instruction. The statement was unequivocal: "We won't accept English Only for our children. We want English plus. English plus math. Plus science. Plus social studies. Plus equal educational opportunities. English plus competence in the home language."[41] Along with the League of Latin American Citizens, SALAD launched a campaign known as "English Plus."

Two years later, the English Plus Information Clearinghouse (EPIC), a coalition of more than fifty civil rights and education organizations opposed to Official English, came to life as a joint project of the National Immigration, Refugee, and Citizenship Forum and the Joint National Committee for Languages. Included among the founding members were numerous ethnic advocacy groups along with the American Civil Liberties Union; the American Jewish Committee; the American Jewish Congress; the Center for Applied Linguistics; and Multi-cultural Education, Training, and Advocacy, Inc. (META), a group actively involved over the years in litigation supporting the rights of linguistic minority students. The intent was to provide a counterweight to the Official English/English Only movement by centrally gathering information on language rights and by developing policy alternatives. The group's "Statement of Purpose" recognized English as the dominant language and its importance to "national life, individual accomplishment, and personal enrichment." It also recognized the need to "foster multiple language skills among all of our people in order to promote our position in the world marketplace and to strengthen the conduct of foreign relations."[42]

That carefully crafted wording gently shifted the discourse from "language as a problem" to "language as a resource," offering a counterattack that was reasonable and broadly appealing. Implicitly assailing the ideology of monolingualism, it leveled the linguistic status of English and non-English speakers by noting that each had language skills from which the other could benefit. The subtlety of the message, however, proved not just a benefit but also a burden. Some members of the public confused English Plus with English Only, setting the group's mission on its head. Some language-minority activists believed English Plus was overly assimilationist, lacking a serious commitment to maintaining non-English languages and cultures. Defenders, on the other hand, understood that compromise was the price to be paid for building a broad coalition of support essential to defeating English Only.[43]

By the time EPIC fell victim to an unsteady funding stream in the mid-1990s, the coalition's message had made a small mark. Thanks to its efforts, the states of New Mexico, Oregon, Washington, and Rhode Island, in addition to numerous cities, including Atlanta, Cleveland, Dallas, San Antonio, Tucson, and Washington, D.C., had adopted English Plus laws or resolutions declaring themselves officially multilingual and multicultural. Oregon's Senate Joint Resolution 16 resolved "to welcome, encourage and protect diverse cultures and use of diverse languages in business, government and private affairs." New Mexico's House Joint Memorial warned that an English Only policy would threaten the state's multicultural tradition of "diversity with harmony."[44] These measures were largely hortatory with no legal enforcement power. Yet at least in those states, they seemed to hold at bay the Official English movement for the time being. Congressional sponsors have repeatedly introduced a similar "English Plus Resolution," most recently in January 2009, "recognizing the importance of multilingualism to vital American interests and individual rights." None has made it out of committee.[45]

To be sure, EPIC's driving philosophy promoting "language as a resource" continues to inspire language diversity while "English Plus" remains a rallying cry for opposing English Only and the anti-immigrant sentiments of Official English proponents. But practically speaking, without a well-funded and centralized organization backing it, that cry remains a whisper in countering the heavily endowed, organized, and much publicized efforts within the Official English/English Only movement and the anti-immigrant mood that has enhanced its base of support and maintained its momentum. Though in its short life, EPIC mobilized the forces of English Plus, it was less successful at stopping the forces of U.S. English, which already was making inroads beyond the federal level.

In 1986, by nearly a three to one margin, voters in California had adopted Proposition 63 amending the state constitution. The measure included a provision allowing anyone living or doing business in the state to sue state or local governments for actions that diminished or ignored "the role of English as the common language of the State of California." U.S English seized on the referendum's success to draft model language for similar voter initiatives in other states. That same year the Georgia legislature passed a nonbinding resolution declaring English the state language. Hispanic leaders and public officials denounced these initiatives as divisive, exclusionary, and racist. Yet the group's leadership remained steadfast in its position. Gerda Bikales, then U.S. English executive director, heatedly warned: "Government should not stand idly and let the core culture, the shared culture formed by generations of earlier immigrants, slip away. The government should not allow its own citizens to feel like strangers in their own land. If anyone has to feel strange, it's got to be the immigrant, until he learns the language."[46]

Her words were indeed telling. Bikales's fears had little, if anything, to do with language but all to do with the cultural and political changes that Spanish, with its vast numbers of speakers, portended. This clearly was a battle between "us," primarily the offspring of the old European migrations, struggling mightily to hold on to the heart of America, and "them," the new immigrants, seemingly threatening to hijack it. Language with its legal uncertainty, seeming neutrality, and deep symbolism provided the most socially acceptable and available point on which to focus the fight. The following year, similar voter referenda passed in Colorado, Florida, and Arizona. Those early state-level victories bred even more success in the years that followed. In 2009, twenty-six states had operating Official English measures in some form, up from only six just a decade previously. In 2007 alone, similar legislation was introduced in more than twenty-one states, fifteen seeking to establish a new English law and six merely strengthening existing law.

Meanwhile, proponents continue to pursue federal legislation making English the official language of the nation. In 2009 the English Language Unity Act was once again introduced into the U.S. House of Representatives with more than a hundred bipartisan co-sponsors. If adopted, it would require the federal government to conduct all official business in English while giving government agencies commonsense flexibility to protect public health, safety, and the criminal justice system. Hailing the proposal, U.S. English board chairman Mauro Mujica made clear, "Making English the official language is not a partisan issue, it is an American issue," and, he said, one intimately tied to "immigration and assimilation."[47]

The closest the country has come to an official pronouncement occurred in May 2006 when the Senate passed two separate amendments to a comprehensive immigration bill declaring English the "national" language or the "common and unifying" language of the United States. In June 2007 the Senate passed by a 63–34 vote the S. I. Hayakawa National Language Amendment Act declaring that there is no affirmative right to receive services in languages other than English, except where required by federal law. The amendment failed as part of a larger immigration reform proposal.

Some Americans view English Only and particularly Official English laws as simply a symbolic and benign gesture, sort of like naming the official state flower or bird, or perhaps a long overdue correction of a historical oversight. For others these initiatives may be nothing more than expressions of patriotism, or a means for reaffirming one's value system, or a nostalgic return to the mythological melting pot. A mere vague declaration that "English shall be the official/national language of the state/country" seems on its face rather innocuous. Yet, as the opponents argue, tied to calls for limits on immigration, these proposals can be veiled expressions of racism and xenophobia. Even where they include the necessary exceptions to protect public health, safety, and national security, the mere symbolism of a "national" or "official" language, given the political context, can prove divisive. In the long run, it can reshape the nation's sense of what it means to be American, though that is precisely what the proponents believe they are avoiding. Obviously the concept of change depends on where you start and how you see the status quo on American identity. Such was the case in the early decades of the twentieth century when national origin quotas all but closed the nation's borders to certain groups considered unassimilable. As Joshua Fishman put it, "politically speaking" this is a "stampeder," an issue "whose importance far transcends its own limits."[48]

Proposition 227 and Its Aftermath

Perhaps nowhere is the connection between immigration and language more evident than in state voter initiatives, most notably California's Proposition 277, aimed at undoing bilingual education. The genesis of the California measure goes back to November 1994 when the state's

voters adopted Proposition 187 denying undocumented immigrants social services, medical care, and public schooling. On this last count, supporters were pushing for the Supreme Court to revisit *Plyler v. Doe,* a
1982 decision striking down a similar education law in Texas.[49] The
strategy failed. In March 1998 a federal district court issued a ruling that
declared Proposition 187 unconstitutional, preempted by federal law.
The newly elected governor, Gray Davis, dropped the state's appeal.[50] But
that was not the end.

The movement assumed new life in a more refined version directly targeting bilingual education, thus giving direction to forces that were already poised to take off. California's Proposition 227, the "English for
the Children Initiative," adopted by 61 percent of the state's voters the
following November, was intended to officially replace bilingual education with structured English immersion. Support for the initiative built
largely on fears that transitional programs were causing low English
reading and math scores and high dropout rates, particularly among Hispanic students, denying them the tools they needed to succeed in the
American economy. "Therefore," stated the text of Proposition 227, "all
children in California public schools shall be taught English as rapidly
and effectively as possible, . . . by being taught in English."[51] Little did
the voting public realize that less than half of the state's kindergarten-
through-grade-twelve Hispanic students were even classified as limited
English proficient. Only about 30 percent of them were enrolled in bilingual programs and less than 20 percent of that number was receiving instruction from a certified bilingual teacher.[52]

Barely beneath the surface of the surrounding debate lay intense anti-
immigrant feelings. Those feelings were best reflected in the views of the
initiative's prime mover, Silicon Valley entrepreneur and sometime political aspirant Ron Unz, though surprisingly he had been a vocal opponent
of Proposition 187. Spending $1.2 million—more than half from his own
money—Unz parlayed his personal philosophy promoting immigrant assimilation into an organized attack on bilingual education and multiculturalism.[53] Fired up by his California victory, he took his initiative on the
road, meeting success with similar measures adopted with 63 percent of
voters supporting Arizona's Proposition 203 in 2000 and 68 percent in
favor of Question 2 in Massachusetts in 2002. His only loss came that
same year when Colorado voters rejected by a 56 to 44 percent vote
Amendment 31 to the state constitution.[54] A fifth initiative, not directly
related to Unz, met defeat in Oregon in 2008.

Proponents of the California measure still roundly deny that its mandates undermine the native language and culture of English language

learners.[55] Though it is true that the law does not expressly address cultural issues and literacy, it implicitly and undeniably devalues both, as far as the student's home language is concerned. The facts prove the case. Proposition 227 requires schools to place English language learners in English language classrooms using a prescribed methodology, "structured English immersion," where instruction must be "nearly all" (undefined in the law) in English but with a "curriculum and presentation designed for children who are learning the language." Students can remain in these classrooms generally for a period not to exceed one year. Parents may request a waiver, in person and on an annual basis, to place their child in a bilingual program under three circumstances: if the student already knows English; if the student is at least ten years old and the school agrees that an alternative curriculum would better serve the student's English education; or if the student has tried the immersion program for at least thirty days, and school officials agree that the child has "special physical, emotional, psychological, or educational needs," and an alternative curriculum would better support the student's educational development. A finding of "special needs" does not guarantee the right to a waiver. Schools are required to offer a class in which students are taught English and other subjects through bilingual and other alternative educational techniques only when at least twenty students speaking a given language in a given grade receive a waiver.

Despite all these constraints, Proposition 227 apparently afforded parents too much choice, and school officials too much discretion, for Unz's liking. And so he drafted even more details and restrictions into the Arizona initiative that followed. Proposition 203 expressly prohibits any subject matter instruction in a foreign language and makes clear that "children must learn to read and write solely in English." It requires written documentation, of no fewer than 250 words and placed in the child's record, explaining the child's "special and individual physical or psychological needs" that justify placement in a bilingual program. It authorizes teachers and local school districts to "reject waiver requests without explanation or legal consequence."

Again, a student under the age of ten in either state cannot obtain a waiver to enter a bilingual program unless the child is no longer an ELL, a situation that directly defies the conventional purpose of bilingual instruction. The alternative is where the school principal and educational staff determine that the child has special needs after the child has remained for at least thirty days in an English language classroom, where the language used by the teacher is "overwhelmingly" English. As one Arizona teacher aptly noted, "The ones that really need it the most . . .

that come in from Mexico and do not understand English at all, are put into this classroom where the teacher is talking to them only in English, and the teacher cannot help them at all, so they go home frustrated."[56]

Neither the California nor the Arizona initiative guarantees all parents equal access to information. This has proved problematic for linguistic minority families, many of whom lack the educational resources and language skills to acquire the information on their own. Whether the waiver is granted depends to a significant degree on the school district's commitment to bilingual education. In some California districts, the school board or the superintendent has directed school staff not to grant waivers. In some cases the policy is unspoken or principals have their own agenda and simply do not bother implementing the waiver provision.[57] In the wake of Proposition 227, parents of California's immigrant children descended upon the state capitol in Sacramento. School administrators, they charged, had not informed them of their rights to request an alternative program. Even when they were informed, they had to make the request by appointment during the workday. In some cases, school districts simply had refused to offer bilingual instruction.[58]

It is not merely implementation, but the law itself, that has stymied the right to waivers. The fact that, under Proposition 227, parents can sue for damages if school personnel, including teachers, fail to provide the required type of English instruction has chilled the ardor of even school personnel who support bilingual education, despite the teachers associations' having agreed to indemnify them. They fear they might appear to be unduly pressuring parents to request a waiver. Similar constraints now operate in Arizona and Massachusetts, although the Arizona law again goes even further, prohibiting any public or private third party from indemnifying school board members or other officials or administrators who willfully refuse to implement the terms of the law. Though the Massachusetts law contains many of the same provisions, including waiver eligibility requirements, a subsequent legislative amendment added a loophole for dual immersion programs serving both ELLs and English-speaking students. The change effectively countered Question 2's intent to limit bilingual education to older students.[59]

There are cases, nonetheless, in which district policies have worked to the parents' benefit. In some California districts, the staff has more assertively encouraged parents to request waivers. In some instances, school officials have allowed parents to mail in their waiver requests though Proposition 227 requires a personal visit. Some districts have ignored the required detailed documentation of need for bilingual instruction, or have interpreted the one-year English immersion mandate as a minimum rather than a maximum, or require a thirty-day period of English immersion only when students first enroll in the school and not each year. Schools also differ widely in how they define eligibility for bilingual instruction.[60] With all these deviations and circumventions, it is not surprising that the number of students in bilingual programs differs widely from one locality to another.

In any case, state bilingual initiatives have a degree of political permanence untypical of other educational policies. Proposition 227 can be repealed or amended only by a statute either passed by a simple majority of the legislature and submitted to the voters for approval, or passed by two-thirds of the legislature and signed by the governor. Arizona's Proposition 203 requires a vote of at least three-fourths of the members in each legislative house and the governor's signature.[61] Faced with a challenge to such arduous procedures, the Ninth Circuit Court of Appeals upheld the constitutionality of Proposition 227.[62] The plaintiffs had charged that in mandating statewide action before any change could be made in how English might be taught to ELL students, the measure restructured the "political process" in violation of the equal protection clause of the Fourteenth Amendment.

Though the U.S. Supreme Court had struck down similar state laws addressing housing discrimination and school busing based on racial discrimination, and the legal system had recognized language as a proxy for race or national origin, the court concluded that the initiative was not about race but about education. "While bilingual education has obvious racial implications," the court noted," the record established "neither that racial discrimination was the impetus of bilingual education, nor that racial animus motivated the passage of Proposition 227." It was purely a matter of deciding the most effective approach for these children to "function as American citizens," a decision not for the courts to make.[63] The fact that the appeals court accepted structured English immersion as the "best" available approach without sufficient supporting evidence was revealing. Equally telling was the court's functionally linking instruction to American citizenship while giving no regard to the diverse abilities and needs of the children or the aspirations of their parents. It was no accident that immigration and national origin discrimination had formed the backdrop to Proposition 227, as the dissenting opinion from the court's refusal to rehear the case pointed out. The court itself acknowledged that nearly every ELL student in the state was either Hispanic or Asian/Pacific Islander.[64] The word *immigrant*, in fact, repeatedly appeared in the Proposition. So was this primarily a case about education, or more clearly about national origin? Or perhaps both, inter-twined?

In the end, the appeals court's reasoning reveals how far the courts have withdrawn from the rights recognized three decades ago in *Lau*. It also underscores the fragility of recognizing language as a proxy for national origin. That rationale supported early administrative interpretations of Title VI and particularly the 1970 memorandum that still forms a basis for the Office for Civil Rights' enforcement policies. Overall, one would have expected the court to be more sympathetic to the claims of the parents, given the power inequities in the initiative process and the direct impact that resources generally have on the outcome of these measures, Proposition 227 being no exception.

No Child Left Behind

It was only a matter of time before the Unz philosophy coalesced with the state accountability movement, gaining a firm foothold in Washington with the election of George W. Bush. Assuming the presidency in 2001, over the following year his administration worked hand in hand with Congress to revamp federal spending for education. Though generally supportive of bilingual programs as governor of Texas, as president Bush made no attempt to keep the Bilingual Education Act intact. The result was the No Child Left Behind Act (NCLB), a controversial overhaul of federal education legislation enacted with broad bipartisan support and the endorsement of liberal Democrats, including Sen. Edward Kennedy (D.-Mass.), its co-sponsor. Title III of the NCLB effectively dismantled the 1968 Act. Unlike its predecessor, noticeably absent from the law were any legislative findings addressing the benefits of bilingual education or bilingualism to the child or to society. Nor did the law take note of conditions that negatively affect the education of English language learners.

The law removed from the federal glossary all references to bilingualism or bilingual education—from its title, the "English Language Acquisition Act," to the renamed Office of English Language Acquisition, Language Enhancement, and Academic Achievement for Limited-English-Proficient Students (formerly the Office of Bilingual Education and Minority Language Affairs), and the National Clearinghouse for English Language Acquisition and Language Instruction Educational Programs (formerly the National Clearinghouse for Bilingual Education).[65] More fundamentally, it shifted the terminology from offering "equal educational opportunity" and "equal access" to closing the "academic achievement gap," a term increasingly favored in education circles. Rather than focus on instructional "inputs" in the equality mode, the law would hold school systems accountable for producing student "outputs" as measured by standardized tests.

Title III distributes funds by formula to each state depending on enrollments of LEP (limited English-proficient) students, including "immigrant children and youth." The law has two main goals: English language acquisition and accountability, that is, helping students develop English proficiency while at the same time meeting state academic content and achievement standards.[66] Local school districts and state education departments must demonstrate in their plans how the language curriculum chosen is tied to "scientifically based research" and "demonstrated to be effective." Silent on what types of programs might meet the standard, the law neither mandates nor precludes any particular teaching approach. It only requires that schools place LEP students in "language instruction educational programs," loosely defined and with some qualifications.

Any efforts to develop and maintain native language skills are implicitly limited to dual language programs that include students whose dominant language is English, an obvious concession to middle-class mainstream parents. In that case, participating students are expected to "to become proficient in English and a second language" (more correctly the "first" language for LEP students).[67] Yet the law presents strong deterrents against establishing such programs. The fact that schools are judged by the percentage of LEPs reclassified as fluent in English each year creates a built-in incentive to set aside native language instruction in the interest of quickly developing English language skills. Threaded throughout the law are repeated references to "attain[ing] English proficiency" and developing "high levels of academic attainment in English."

A highly contested system of standards-based accountability further induces schools to focus on English language instruction. In order to receive federal funds, states must demonstrate that students have made "adequate yearly progress" (AYP) on state standardized tests annually administered in math and reading/language arts in grades three through eight and once in high school, in addition to science tests in three grades. A school that fails to meet the mark risks being "restructured." Department of Education regulations from 2006 exempt English language learners from taking the state English reading/language arts content assessment on the first administration after they enroll in U.S. schools. Beyond the first year, they must take both tests and their scores are counted in the school's accountability rating.[68] In addition, states must annually assess ELLs in English language skills, covering reading, writing, speaking, and listening. Every two years, any school district that receives Title III funds must submit, to its state education department, data documenting the percentage of ELL students who have achieved English proficiency, transitioned into mainstream English classes, and met the same academic achievement standards required of other students.

The law permits states to administer the reading/language arts and math content assessments in the student's native language, or to use accommodations on the English assessments for the first three years the student has been in U.S. schools, with up to two additional years depending on individual circumstances. Accommodations include small-group administration, extra time or flexible scheduling, simplified instructions, bilingual dictionaries, and recorded native language instructions.

Put into practice, these requirements have raised serious concerns. Critics note that ELLs differ widely across language skills in both English and their home language. Those who enter U.S. schools from abroad also differ in years and quality of prior schooling. To classify them into one group for accountability purposes, and to impose the same time frame for all to achieve English language proficiency, they argue, defies sound pedagogy and fundamental notions of fairness. Indeed, research findings indicate that it can take from one to six years, although more typically two to four years, for ELLs to become proficient in *conversational* English. Acquiring proficiency in *academic* English is a longer process, taking from five to eight years to catch up with native speakers scoring at the 50th percentile on tests of English reading comprehension. Data from California underscore these discrepancies. Whereas 49 percent of seventh-grade ELL students in 2007 scored at the level of "early advanced" or "advanced" on the California English Language Development Test (CELDT), the state's English proficiency test, only 9 percent scored at a similar level of proficiency on the ELA, the state's English language arts test.[69] It is unsurprising that children who appear deceptively fluent in English fare poorly when transitioned too quickly into mainstream English classrooms. It also stands to reason that if students are tested prematurely, their low scores are not signs of failure, but of the normal progression of language learning.

Some states have set the 36th or even 40th percentiles for reclassifying ELLs as "fluent English proficient." James Crawford and Stephen Krashen point out that about 30 percent of ELLs reach that point after five years.[70] The ELL group, moreover, is constantly in a state of flux. New students speaking limited English enter while those who arguably have gained proficiency leave for the mainstream, both events pulling down average scores. This creates a "treadmill effect" where ELLs' average performance is unable to progress very far. It provides no accurate reading of either overall student improvement or program success.[71]

Though the high-stakes testing movement preceded the NCLB, the law energized and nationalized it. Not surprisingly, arguments supporting and opposing this trend abound. From the standpoint of ELLs, the debate has become particularly contentious and complicated. Since 2002, all fifty states have adopted standardized testing schemes that measure student academic achievement in English reading/language arts and math. Nineteen states, including New York, use statewide tests as a graduation requirement. The negative consequences for students are profound. Dropout rates have increased, leading students to enroll in Graduate Equivalency Diploma (GED) programs, often with the encouragement of school officials. The GED provides a way for over-age ELLs to circumvent testing and for schools to boost their graduation rates. It also offers far fewer economic advantages and life opportunities. Data from New York City support the connection between testing and the GED. Between 2002 and 2003, when the NCLB testing took effect, GED enrollment rose from 24,466 to 37,010.[72]

Critics argue that current ELL testing practices overall do not produce valid measures of academic achievement because they are based on categorical views of language and erroneous assumptions about the capacity of the tests to effectively communicate with ELL students. The tests are created and normed on monolingual, English-speaking student populations and are related to grade level. The structure of the test items favors communication styles that are not culturally universal—multiple-choice questions, open-ended questions. States are required to develop and administer native-language assessments only "to the extent practicable." At least ten states do so for at least some grades.

Even there, native language assessments are meaningful only for students who have received content-area instruction in their native language and who have a high level of literacy and content-specific vocabulary in that language. Most English language learners fall outside that profile. And though it is true that an estimated two-thirds of those classified as ELLs are not immigrants but native-born Americans, there are still many older students who enter U.S. schools with limited or interrupted formal education. Many lack literacy skills in any language. Some speak indigenous languages, like Mixtec and Zapotec from Mexico or a nonstandard dialect or patois, like Haitian Creole rather than French. Even among the native-born, many lack the vocabulary and syntax they need to test in their native language or in English.[73] Besides, translated items may function differently across language groups. For any and all of these reasons, critics maintain, native language assessments are especially inappropriate for students enrolled in structured English immersion classes where all instruction is in English.

Another option, providing students with bilingual dictionaries, assumes they have word-searching skills. As an alternative, some educators believe that simplifying the English wording of test questions is a more effective way to assess English language learners. Yet it is difficult to simplify language without simplifying constructs and some content. As in translation, the tests' validity and reliability are seriously compromised.[74] Aside from the limitations of the accommodations themselves, few states provide sufficient guidance to school staff in matching the accommodations to individual student characteristics, including English proficiency, literacy in English and the home language, age, continuous years of formal schooling, languages of instruction, and type of language support program used.[75]

The testing question has driven a deep divide within the community of advocates promoting the rights of ELL students. Some have employed the tests as a shield, and others as a sword. There is merit to be found in both arguments. Groups like the Institute for Language and Education Policy and the National Association for Bilingual Education maintain that English language tests are intrinsically unfair to students whose native language is not English. Schools are making "high-stakes" decisions regarding the education of these students based on test results that are considered to be inaccurate, they argue. In the meantime, students are "fed a steady diet of [math and reading] test-prep, worksheets, and other 'skill-building' exercises" while their language-learning needs are marginalized.[76]

As Jim Cummins, a key researcher on bilingual development, says, English learners are now part of the accountability map. "That's the good news . . . That's the end of the good news." To underscore the absurdity of the situation, he cites a Maryland English as a Second Language teacher who calculated that in the 2004–2005 school year, English language learners in a fifth-grade class had missed thirty-three days of ESL classes, or about 18 percent of their English instruction, due to standardized testing. For Cummins and other critics of the NCLB, federal and state policies impose a "pedagogical divide" in which "poor kids get behaviorism and rich kids get social constructionism," in other words, "skills for the poor and knowledge for the rich."[77] While ELL students are limited to basic skills in English and math via "teaching to the test," more privileged students receive a well-rounded education including arts enrichment and the critical thinking and higher order analytic skills essential for college admission and the workplace.

On the other side of the debate stand the Mexican American Legal Defense and Educational Fund and the National Council of La Raza, longtime advocates of bilingual instruction. These groups resolutely defend the NCLB and oppose any proposals to exempt ELL students from standardized tests for more than the one year now allowed. For them, test results hold school officials' feet to the fire to successfully move students toward meeting state standards. At the same time, these groups continue to press for valid and reliable state assessments, preferably in the student's native language. They also call for "universal implementation of the best research-based instructional practices" for ELLs, including native language instruction.[78] Needless to say, the testing issue has become a topic of lively debate as the NCLB has moved beyond its designated 2008 reauthorization date and a new administration has taken charge in Washington.

In the end, no one can state with certainty that the achievement of ELLs has improved as a result of the NCLB. Based on tests administered to about seven hundred thousand students nationwide, data released in 2007 from the National Assessment of Educational Progress reveal that educational improvement had slowed since the law was put into effect in 2003. Mathematics gains were not as large as those found in earlier periods, and the average eighth-grade reading score remained below the level of achievement shown in 2002.[79] Findings and anecdotal reports further suggest that high-stakes testing demands like those of the NCLB may worsen the plight of ELL students, reinforcing inadequate preparation and increasing dropout rates.[80]

The law as it stands clearly marks a dramatic reversal from the letter and spirit of the original 1968 Act, yet this turn was not unforeseen in a stormy history spanning four decades.[81] Without expressly banning bilingual education, the NCLB and its implementing regulations implicitly establish national policy that merely gives perfunctory recognition, at most, to the child's native language while overlooking the native culture, inevitably moving the nation toward English immersion programs. Though experience has shown that it may take a number of years for students to perform at or above grade level in English and the native language, the Act pushes schools to demonstrate English test results in the lower grades.

Educators across the country admit that they have either discontinued bilingual programs or foresee discontinuing them under pressure from the NCLB. Even in states and localities that remain more supportive, the NCLB has "corrupted" or at least distorted bilingual instruction. "Teaching to the test" has affected these programs in a uniquely disquieting way. Teachers are known to increase the amount of time spent in English instruction in the weeks preceding the statewide test and afterward return to language instruction that is more balanced between English and the native language. In some cases, schools are transitioning students into mainstream classes before they have acquired sufficient mastery of English.[82]

Anecdotally there is a sense that the NCLB's testing requirements have effectively decreased the number of bilingual programs nationwide. The real effect is less clear-cut, even among states that still require the approach as a matter of law. Since the NCLB was enacted, the proportion of ELLs in bilingual education has increased slightly in Texas, remained static in Illinois, and decreased slightly in New Jersey. One of the most critical factors determining these effects is whether the state has developed tests in the students' native languages, which hinges on both state attitudes toward native language instruction and the numbers and diversity of languages represented among the ELL population. As a result, bilingual programs have fared better in states, like Colorado, New York, and Texas, that provide some native language tests. In California and Arizona, the combination of state anti-bilingual initiatives and federal law has produced a dramatic drop-off in bilingual programs. Statewide, only 6 percent of California's 1.6 million ELLs, most of them Spanish-speaking, were in bilingual programs in 2007, down from 29 percent when Proposition 227 was adopted. In the Santa Ana School District, the number of ELLs in bilingual programs plummeted from six thousand in 2002–03 to eight hundred in 2006–07. In Nevada, where state tests must also be given in English, the Clark County School District has phased out transitional programs in which children learned to read first in Spanish and then transitioned into English, and expanded their dual language immersion programs.[83]

Federal requirements are not the only force driving down enrollments in bilingual education. Those numbers started dropping long before the NCLB even appeared on the Washington radar screen. Between 1993 and 2003, the proportion of ELLs receiving "some" or "significant" native language instruction had declined from 53 percent to 29 percent nationwide. The NCLB was merely symptomatic of broader political shifts and organized opposition that slowly had been taking shape over the previous two decades.[84] Some of those pressures were coming not only from the mainstream but from within the Hispanic community itself.

Throughout the NCLB's authorization process, despite the change in focus and the elimination of any "bilingual" references in the law, Title III surprisingly provoked no organized opposition from the Congressional Hispanic Caucus. Meanwhile, few individual Hispanics raised concerns calling for native language testing and parental notification in the case of students placed in English Only programs.[85] While bilingual education had been an important rallying cry for ethnic mobilization and the right to self-determination, especially among Hispanics back in the 1960s and 1970s, it seemed to have lost political steam. What appeared to matter most in 2002 was the NCLB's promise to close the persistent achievement gap between Hispanic and non-Hispanic white students by holding schools accountable to parents and to the American public.

Congressional silence may have reflected a changed mood not merely among Hispanic leaders but within the Hispanic community itself. Survey data, admittedly sensitive to how the questions are framed, cautiously confirm a swing away from bilingual education over the previous decade. Back in 1989–90, the National Latino Political Survey reported that approximately 80 percent of Puerto Rican, Mexican, and Cuban American respondents "support" bilingual education, although less than 10 percent of any group based their support specifically on the desire to "maintain Spanish language and culture."[86] A 1996 survey of Hispanics in Texas and California had similar findings. Jump to 2002, the year the NCLB was passed, and except perhaps for Mexican Americans, the numbers had almost reversed themselves. A Public Agenda survey that year found that 51 percent of Mexican Americans, 62 percent of non-Mexican Hispanics, 63 percent of mixed immigrant groups, and 69 percent of East Asian Americans agreed that "all courses should be taught in English."[87] Yet a more recent February 2008 poll of five hundred registered voters in Texas, presumably including large numbers of Mexican Americans, found that 78 percent supported bilingual education programs to assist students in public schools.[88] Those numbers may reflect both consistent official support in Texas, where bilingual programs are offered throughout the elementary grades, and a relatively high concentration of newly arrived Mexicans eager to maintain their language and culture.

If non-Mexican Hispanics seemed to be losing enthusiasm for their children receiving instruction in their native language, at least some of that change of heart could be attributed to two factors: the intense public campaigns waged against bilingual education in the heat of state English Only voter initiatives, and the equally intense pressure from the high-stakes testing movement that gained ground in the years leading up to the No Child Left Behind Act. Many immigrant parents understandably feared that native language instruction would "leave their children behind." Meanwhile, the group most actively maintaining their native language and culture, Mexican Americans, continued to support bilingual instruction for their children. None of the groups surveyed directly opposed maintaining or developing their children's home language skills as a heritage language outside of a bilingual education program. The fact that pollsters did not ask that question as an adjunct to English language instruction says much about the debate over language and schooling and the systemic failure to recognize the value of languages other than English.

CHAPTER SEVEN

More Wrongs than Rights

THE TESTING mandates of the federal No Child Left Behind Act have come to dominate discussion and debate over the education of English language learners. It is easy to forget that the law is merely a funding measure that neither grants nor technically denies English language learners a legally enforceable right to a particular education. Yet as a practical matter, its built-in incentives toward English instruction, largely tied to student testing and school accountability, are powerful and effective. There is indeed an ironic twist to all this. Though the testing question has provoked sharp criticism, at the same time it has created a national database demonstrating the enduring achievement gap between ELL students and others. Those comparisons have been useful in litigation challenging state and local educational practices and policies. And so, undaunted by the backlash of the past three decades, bilingual education advocates continue to plow their way through a dizzying maze of federal statutes, administrative regulations, agency memoranda, and court decisions. Grounded in vaguely worded rights to a "meaningful," "appropriate," or "effective" education, these government pronouncements are of mixed utility in defining the scope of educational rights for English language learners.

Administrative Enforcement

One avenue of legal recourse is federal administrative enforcement and the threat that Washington will deny federal funds where a school district is found to be violating the law. Claimants can file a complaint, or the Office for Civil Rights can initiate an investigation on its own. The problem lies in determining exactly what the law requires and what must be proved to make the case for noncompliance. For English language learners, any affirmative right to specialized educational services, and corresponding obligations on the part of school officials, now rest precariously on three Office for Civil Rights documents: the May 1970 memorandum to school districts (requiring "affirmative steps" and "effective participation"); a December 1985 guidance document outlining procedures applying the 1970 memorandum and the standard laid out in *Lau v. Nichols* (calling for a "meaningful" and "effective" education); and a September 1991 memorandum updating the policy.[1] This last document explicitly incorporates the *Castaneda v. Pickard* guidelines (mandating "appropriate action" and "equal participation"), noting the similarity between the Equal Educational Opportunities Act and the 1970 OCR policy under Title VI.[2]

The 1991 memorandum takes a neutral position on bilingual education. It makes clear that OCR does not "require or advocate a particular program of instruction" nor does federal law "require one form of instruction over another." Tracking the appeals court ruling in *Castaneda,* programs must be: based on a sound educational theory; adequately supported so they have a "realistic chance" of success; and evaluated and revised periodically. The memorandum essentially takes a "what works" position, stating that "any educational approach that ensures the effective participation of language minority students in the district's educational program" is "acceptable" under Title VI. As for *Lau*'s "meaningful access," students must remain in programs until they can "read, write, and comprehend English well enough to participate meaningfully" in the alternative program provided. Once students are mainstreamed, they must receive whatever assistance they need to overcome any academic deficits they may have suffered in other subjects while intensively learning English.

Though the memorandum defers to school officials on instructional methods, it requires that teachers of bilingual classes must speak, read, and write both languages and have received training in the methods of bilingual education. The guidelines go no further in recognizing the child's native language, nor do they mention the child's native culture. And so, rather than acknowledging a substantive right to native language instruction, any affirmative entitlements are limited to certain procedural rights that focus on developing English language skills and mainstreaming. How rigorously OCR enforces these mandates depends on the prevailing administration's view toward native language instruction and linguistic diversity. In recent years, enforcement has been weak at best.

Federal Litigation

Aside from federal agency enforcement, parents and advocacy groups may pursue their claims in the federal courts under statutory and constitutional guarantees. Specifically, they can sue under Title VI of the Civil Rights Act of 1964, the Equal Educational Opportunities Act of 1974, or the Fourteenth Amendment, in addition to whatever rights state law might provide. Court decisions have placed constraints on each of these.

Statutory Rights

Advocates at first believed that *Lau v. Nichols* would realize their greatest hopes and dreams for rights recognized in the courts. Much to their dismay, it has since become evident that *Lau* initially promised more than it could ultimately deliver from a Supreme Court whose changed membership has progressively whittled away at the Title VI statute and regulations. In the intervening years, the Court has limited the statute to instances where it is obvious that the wrong is purposeful or intentional, that is, where school officials have chosen a course of action because of, and not in spite of, its discriminatory effects on racial or ethnic groups. Merely proving that an educational program offered evenhandedly to all students has a disproportionately negative effect on English language learners, as was the case in *Lau*, no longer suffices under the statute itself, though agency regulations, like those adopted by the Department of Education, may still recognize a claim on mere adverse effects.[3] Practically speaking, unless a school district is completely ignoring the educational needs of students, it is near impossible to marshal evidence of discriminatory intent while the federal courts, in any case, typically defer to state and local officials on instructional approaches.

Even where individuals make a claim under agency regulations, the Court has held that they do not have a private right to take their Title VI case to court.[4] If all that exists is proof that their children have underperformed academically compared with other students (discriminatory effect), the only course for parents is to file a complaint with the Office for Civil Rights and hope that federal officials either conduct a speedy investigation, and perhaps threaten to withhold the school district's federal funds, or refer the case to the Department of Justice, which may or may not take the district to court. Neither option is truly substantive. Limited government resources, combined with the political vagaries of enforcement policies, leave parents and students to the will or whim of agency officials. The one hope is for Congress to take corrective action. Legislation proposed in both congressional houses in the spring of 2008 essentially would have dispensed with the regulatory approach, expressly adding to the Title VI statute a subsection prohibiting any practice "that causes a disparate impact on the basis of race, color, or national origin." Both bills expired without congressional action.

In the meantime, all that remains of *Lau* is its core finding of fact that an English-only program constructively excludes, from equal educational access, public school students who do not speak the language.[5] Merely offering such students the same educational services as the larger school population forecloses them from a "meaningful" and "effective" education. And so when advocates now invoke the *Lau* decision, it is more in the sense of policy than law, for the political message it conveys and for its continuing symbolic force.

With *Lau* and its Title VI underpinnings effectively unraveled, what has kept *Lau*'s legacy alive is the Equal Educational Opportunities Act of 1974, arguably adopted to codify the decision. The burning question here is: What is the right to an "appropriate" education for English language learners? We know at least from the appeals court decision in *Castaneda* that the Act may not guarantee education in the child's native language or culture. Subsequent decisions have placed even more limits on the law.

Some federal courts have given school districts an easy pass, removing any scientific rigor from the court's inquiry into the soundness of the theory on which a program is based or the program's relationship to it.[6] For the district court in *Valeria v. Wilson*, the case challenging California's Proposition 227, it was enough that structured immersion was the "predominant method" for teaching immigrant children in Canada, Israel, and many western European countries and used by numerous school districts in the United States.[7] Yet, as I discuss in Chapter 9, western European countries have been slow to respond to the linguistic needs of immigrant children, and so they are hardly an example to follow. Some federal courts have placed the burden on claimants to demonstrate that the school district's program was not based on sound educational theory in the first instance. Others have accepted, without question, that the school district possessed sufficient expertise to make a sound judgment.[8]

In the extreme, these decisions suggest that a program might be acceptable so long as even one expert can testify that the program's underlying theory is sound, or at least legitimate in an experimental sense, and that it supports an effective educational program.[9] Carrying these interpretations to their logical conclusion, an "appropriate" education under the EEOA could be whatever works in the eyes of local school officials. Such a loose standard could leave programs hostage to radical political theories and ideologies that may have little support in the wider scientific community, presenting plaintiffs with difficult hurdles to overcome.[10]

The EEOA expressly adopts an effects standard for defining wrongful discrimination. Claimants need not prove that school officials intended to deny them an "appropriate" education. Yet, similar to Title VI, Congress based its authority to enact the EEOA on section 5 of the Fourteenth Amendment, which authorizes Congress to enact laws that enforce the equal protection clause. As the Court has stated, the clause prohibits only intentional discrimination, while statutes adopted pursuant to Section 5 must provide a remedy that is "congruent and proportional" to the injury that Congress intended to address.[11] And so the justices in a future case conceivably could limit claims under the EEOA (and under the Title VI regulations, for that matter) to those where intent can be proved, placing yet another barrier to challenging instructional programs for ELLs. So far, the federal courts have not gone down that road.

Despite these potential drawbacks, advocates still consider the EEOA to be the "last living cause of action" for claims brought on behalf of ELLs.[12] So long as the law stays free of further erosion in the courts, its measure of "appropriate" and "effective" education and the standards set out in *Castaneda v. Pickard* provide the best available roadmap for litigators to follow. Those standards have also remained a key fixture in federal civil rights enforcement for more than two decades. At the most basic level, schools must make a genuine and good faith effort to remedy language "deficiencies." Programs must be adequately supported to have a realistic chance of success. That factor at least invites the court to examine not only the instructional approach being used, but such programmatic details as the language skills of the teaching staff, the student-teacher ratio, and the achievement gains of students. And though the Act does not require bilingual education, it provides a vehicle for implementing and assessing bilingual programs in states, like Illinois and Texas, that still require them. Even in the case of structured English immersion, measures like dropout rates, test scores, and graduation rates are fair indicators of compliance with the law. Of course, the basis for measuring "equal participation" under the EEOA could be decisive, and so it demands close attention. To what group are ELL students being compared? Is it other students in the school district, who may be low performers themselves? Or is it English-speaking students in the state or across the nation, a more valid benchmark for comparison?

As litigator Roger Rice pragmatically sums it up, "There won't be another *Lau* to stand for any great proposition. On the other hand, so long as we have §1703, together with state court 'adequacy' cases, we can say that school districts have an obligation to educate LEP kids and make these programs work."[13] Rice is referring to a litigation approach that has been used with increasing success in state courts over the past two decades. Such suits, brought on behalf of students residing in property-poor school districts, challenge the state's system of funding public schools, basing the claim in variously worded education guarantees in state constitutions. The argument is that the state has failed to provide certain students with an adequate education, one that enables them to meet state academic standards.[14]

The funding question took center stage in the Supreme Court's 2009 decision in *Horne v. Flores,* the most significant case involving English language learners since *Lau,* with potential for even greater consequences.[15] In a series of decisions dating from 2000, the Arizona state legislature has been embroiled in a seemingly endless tug-of-war with the federal judiciary over resources for educating ELLs. In this class action suit brought in 1992 by families in the border city of Nogales, the court initially held that the state's failure to provide "adequate" funding for the education of ELL students violated the "appropriate action" mandate of the EEOA.[16] Though the state had adopted a valid theory for educating ELL students, it had failed to establish "programs and practices . . . reasonably calculated" to implement the theory. Working through *Castaneda*'s "what works" analysis, the court considered a range of factors including class size, teacher qualifications, and the adequacy of the tutorial program and teaching materials. The court concluded that the level of state funding was "arbitrary and capricious" and bore "no relation" to the actual funds needed to ensure that students mastered specified "essential skills."[17] In 2001 the legislature increased additional funding from $150 to $340 per English language learner. A cost study ordered by the court concluded that $1,200 per student was needed. That same year, the court applied the order statewide. This continuing drama, popularized in the press, brought the court in 2006 to impose on the state $21 million in fines, later lifted on appeal.

In an interesting twist on the very mandates that some bilingual advocates have roundly criticized, the district court in 2007 invoked the NCLB in directing the state to "effectively educate non-English-speaking students."[18] The appeals court upheld that ruling, agreeing that the state's two-year additional funding for ELL students, adopted in 2006, was irrational and could not adequately meet their needs. Those needs had become "even greater" under Proposition 203, the court said, when "Arizona moved away from bilingual education and required most classes to be taught in English, regardless of students' language abilities." As the court noted, "A tenth grader . . . who speaks no English but must pass a biology course in English will require considerable assistance."[19] Under threat of fines, in April 2008 the legislature approved an additional $40.6 million for ELL education. As in the past, the former Democratic governor, Janet Napolitano, let the bill become law without her signature. The State Board of Education agreed that the state remained out of compliance with the 2000 court order.

The Republican-dominated state legislature retained former U.S. solicitor general and independent counsel Kenneth Starr to take its appeal to the U.S Supreme Court. The legislators argued that the decision violated the federal court's traditional deference to state and local governments on educational matters.[20] The more far-reaching and controversial claim was that the NCLB's Title III requirements should serve as the benchmark for "appropriate action" under the Equal Educational Opportunities Act.[21] The court of appeals had expressly rejected that proposition, drawing a distinction between the EEOA's "equality-based framework" and the "gradual remedial framework" of the NCLB. While the EEOA looks toward equalizing educational opportunities for individual students, the court had noted, the NCLB addresses accountability among schools.[22]

The Supreme Court largely agreed with the Ninth Circuit on that score. In a 5–4 ruling that turned heavily on federalism concerns, Justice Samuel Alito writing for the majority in *Horne v. Flores* stated, "Compliance with the NCLB will not necessarily constitute 'appropriate action' under the EEOA." That did not mean, however, that the NCLB was "not relevant" to the state's argument that circumstances had changed since the district court's initial ruling in 2000. The NCLB, the Court noted, had "prompted the State to institute significant structural and programming changes" and had "significantly increased federal funding for . . . ELL programming in particular," while the law's "assessment and reporting" requirements "provide evidence" of the "current effectiveness of Nogales's ELL programming."[23]

Though that portion of the ruling gave plaintiffs and their attorneys some comfort, the overall disposition was far less favorable. The majority remanded the case to the lower courts to reconsider four changes that had occurred since 1992: the implementation of English immersion in lieu of bilingual education to teach English; the increases in overall funding for ELLs; the structural, curricular, and accountability reforms in Nogales; and the implementation of the NCLB. The Court questioned the lower courts' undue reliance on funding as the sole measure of EEOA compliance and the implicit suggestion that the EEOA demands "equal results" between ELLs and other students.[24] The "ultimate focus" of the Act, the Court noted, is on the "quality of educational programming and services provided to students, not the amount of money spent on them."[25] To that end, quoting *Castaneda v. Picard*, the majority emphasized that the EEOA allows state and local education authorities "a substantial amount of latitude" in deciding the contours of an "appropriate" education.[26] At the same time, however, the justices were unwilling to state whether the *Castaneda* three-part test provides "much concrete guidance regarding the meaning of appropriate action."[27] The Court also left open for another day the question as to whether the EEOA validly abrogates the state's sovereign immunity from suit in federal court in the first instance.[28]

What is especially surprising about the decision is the apparent willingness of the majority to stake a position in the charged debates over instructional methods and the arguable connection between funding and student achievement. Citing to a brief submitted by the American Unity Legal Defense Fund, the Court made a sweeping assertion upholding "documented, academic support for the view that SEI [structured English immersion] is significantly more effective than bilingual education."[29] In a lengthy dissent read partially from the bench, Justice Stephen Breyer rightly implied that the majority was selectively relying on evidence to reach a foregone conclusion. For him, the Nogales English immersion program was still "a work in progress." Moreover, there was countervailing evidence that the state had "considerably overstated" the "optimistic improvement in the number of students completing the English-learning program." In fact, even the state's own witnesses were unable to firmly draw that conclusion.[30]

Educators, policy makers, and advocates are watching carefully to see how the case unfolds as the lower courts consider the factors laid out by the majority. In the least it is now clear that proof of inadequate funding alone is not enough to succeed under the EEOA. Yet it also is clear, and no one in the case has denied, that English language learners do in fact require additional funding for textbooks and instructional materials, teacher training, special assessments, tutoring, and other individualized instruction.[31]

Meanwhile, the legislature has adopted a policy whereby all ELLs, with few exceptions, receive four hours of intensive English language instruction each day in specialized classrooms until they pass the state's language exam, a goal that, according to state education officials, most students can accomplish in just one year. Critics argue that the policy is based on "flawed interpretations of research," is "related to immigration, and anxiety about the predominance of other languages in our society," and is "ripe" for more litigation.[32] Not only does the program effectively segregate ELLs who are mostly Hispanic, in violation of Title VI, but with only six instructional hours allotted to the school day, it leaves little time for learning in the content areas that students need for high school graduation.

This inevitable tension between developing English language skills and acquiring knowledge in the content areas similarly arose in long-running litigation in Texas, pushing the EEOA in the direction of educational factors beyond funding. In *United States v. Texas,* Judge William Wayne Justice, the same judge who had ruled on behalf of undocumented immigrant children a quarter of a century earlier in *Plyler v. Doe,*[33] issued a 95-page opinion overturning his contrary ruling from the previous year. In a lawyering tour de force, MALDEF and META attorneys had persuaded the judge to revisit the case based on the Ninth Circuit's intervening decision in *Flores v. Arizona* and on a mountain of damaging data. Adopting the Ninth Circuit's conclusions of law, the judge ordered Texas officials to revamp the state's programs for ELLs in grades seven to twelve and to improve the system for monitoring ELLs throughout the grades.[34]

Carefully examining achievement scores, dropout rates, graduation rates, retention rates, and exclusion from advanced academic achievement, the judge found that the state had failed under *Castaneda* to provide secondary students with "compensatory and supplemental" education to remedy academic deficiencies incurred while they were learning English. The state also had failed to adequately monitor and evaluate the programs offered. The judge concluded that, given the number of limited English-proficient secondary school students, many of them in Texas schools for three or four years, "the primary culprit" was the change from bilingual instruction in the elementary grades to English as a Second Language instruction in the secondary grades. He gave the state six months to develop a plan.

As researchers publicly responded to the court's decision, it became clear that the state's focus on English language skills, even in the elementary grades, was catching up to students as they reached middle school, where the focus was on content literacy. Students could "decode language," experts maintained, but they could not "comprehend" it. They lacked background knowledge in academic English, the language needed to succeed in the higher grades. Meanwhile, the English they did learn was "at the expense of their education" in the content areas.[35] It remains to be seen how broadly the court's rationale and the detailed evidence on which it relied influence national views on education programming, especially for middle and high school ELL students. As Justice Stephen Breyer pointedly stated in his dissenting opinion in *Horne v. Flores*, "It is important to ensure that [English language learners], without the cultural heritage embodied in the language of their birth, nonetheless receive the English language tools they need in a society where that second language 'serves as the fundamental medium of social interaction' and democratic participation."[36]

Constitutional Rights

Aside from statutory claims under Title VI and the EEOA, litigators still have available the federal Constitution. As already discussed, in a string of modern-day cases drawing on the Court's 1923 decision in *Meyer v. Nebraska*, the Court has recognized a substantive component to the Fourteenth Amendment's due process clause. There the Court has suggested a heightened level of scrutiny for laws and policies that infringe on the right of parents to direct the education of their children.[37] To the extent that a significant number of parents request native language instruction, this line of reasoning conceivably could invite the court to question school district policies that categorically deny those requests. More specifically, it could be argued that constraints within state voter initiatives like California's Proposition 227, and the substantial obstacles to changing them, place an "undue burden" on parents' rights to determine an important aspect of their child's education.

The prospects for claims under the Fourteenth Amendment's equal protection clause seem less promising. As the *Lau* attorneys learned at the eleventh hour in the wake of the Court's decision in *San Antonio Independent School District v. Rodriguez*, the Supreme Court is unwilling to recognize education as a fundamental right under the equal protection clause, which would trigger more demanding judicial scrutiny.[38] And so the Court generally upholds education programs so long as the state can offer some reasonable justification, including the preservation of local control. And though national origin is considered a suspect classification entitled to the Court's most careful scrutiny, it demands that claimants prove that school officials adopted certain policies or practices specifically with the intent to discriminate against them on those grounds.

One particular equal protection case, nonetheless, deserves mention here, not for the rights it directly grants to language education, but for its indirect connection to litigation arguing for additional funds for ELLs under the Equal Educational Opportunities Act. In *Plyler v. Doe,* a 1982 landmark ruling, the Court held that for the state to deny undocumented immigrant children free public schooling would condemn them irreparably to second-class citizenship.[39] Less well-known than many Supreme Court decisions, *Plyler* remains a moral guide and an effective bulwark against proposals, like California's ill-fated Proposition 187, that deny rights to undocumented immigrants and particularly education to their children.

What triggered the litigation was a 1975 Texas statute that withheld from local school districts any state funds for the education of children who were not legally admitted into the country. Some school districts continued to openly admit them, some charged tuition, and some refused to admit them under any conditions. The issue came to a head in July 1977 when the trustees of the Tyler Independent School District decided to charge undocumented children a $1,000 tuition fee to attend the district's schools. On the first day of school, Tyler officials "targeted" those children who could not speak English. As a community worker later recalled, "It was a complete and total chaotic situation. If you looked poor, you were out of school."[40]

MALDEF stepped in. As legal scholar Michael Olivas recounts, for the group's attorneys *Plyler* was the "Mexican American *Brown v. Board of Education:* a vehicle for consolidating attention to the various strands of social exclusions that kept Mexican-origin persons in subordinate status."[41] With four Mexican families agreeing to risk deportation and sue Superintendent Jim Plyler and the school board, they brought a class action suit in federal court challenging the tuition policy on the grounds that it violated the Fourteenth Amendment equal protection clause.

On its way to the Supreme Court, *Plyler* was consolidated with other similar cases naming as defendants the State of Texas and its commissioner of education, along with other school districts. In language reminiscent of *Brown,* Justice William Brennan, speaking for the majority, underscored the important socializing function of the public schools, how they impart a shared sense of values, and the role that education plays in raising the "level of esteem" in which the group is held by the majority. In view of the costs to the individual and to society, including the "stigma of illiteracy," he declared, the discrimination contained in the Texas law could "hardly be considered rational unless it furthers some substantial state interest." Preserving state funds for educating children legally in the country, without further justification for targeting those here illegally, was unacceptable. Refusing to provide education to the children of undocumented immigrants, he warned, would result in a "subclass of illiterates within our boundaries, surely adding to the problems and costs of unemployment, welfare, and crime." The state's grounds for discrimination, the child's undocumented status, he noted, rested on a characteristic that, like race, was effectively immutable, at least given the child's inability to change it.[42]

The state's true motives were not lost on the Court. At the end of the day, it was even more apparent that the children were mere pawns in a larger battle over immigration run amok. In response to the Court's ruling, state officials vented outrage that Washington was forcing them to bear the cost of fixing a problem that resulted from the federal government's own failure to enforce the law. Yet at the same time, they could not deny that undocumented children amounted to merely 1 percent of the total school population. The governor himself admitted that education funding was only "peripheral" to what was really at issue: illegal immigration and undocumented workers. "I don't think there is any question at all," he told the press, "that once again we have created a situation here that makes immigration, primarily from Mexico, attractive."[43]

As a *New York Times* editorial summed it up, "State obligations are plain; the nation's duty to control its borders and educate all within them is plainer still."[44] Those words, written over a quarter of a century ago, hold true today, yet the underlying problem has only worsened. And although the superintendent, Jim Plyler, since retired, then called the children a "burden," he now acknowledges that denying them schooling would have been "one of the worst things to happen to education— they'd cost more not being educated." For District Court Judge William Wayne Justice, *Plyler* became "the most important case [he] ever decided."[45]

The politics here were and still are "tricky," intricately bound up in cries for immigration reform. There are anti-immigrant forces that want to relitigate *Plyler*. Lawsuits, like the Arizona litigation, that rely on resource inequalities provide the needed ammunition. Groups like the Federation for American Immigration Reform (FAIR) turn such arguments on their head. They argue that the added costs of educating English language learners are burdensome and siphon off resources from students who legally reside in the country. FAIR estimates that Texans spend more than $4 billion annually on education for undocumented immigrant children and for their U.S.-born siblings. In California, the figure is

$7.7 billion.[46] The critical flaw in these arguments is that they mistakenly conflate undocumented children with ELLs. Most ELLs are native-born Americans.

That is not to overlook the added costs of educating English language learners. Even immigrant advocates like Roger Rice acknowledge that fact. The city of Houston, he says, pays a $4,000 extra stipend to each bilingual teacher. To train a bilingual paraprofessional in San Antonio costs about $8,000. The range in additional cost, Rice notes, is "phenomenal. Some say five percent, others double."[47] A 2008 report commissioned by the New York Immigration Coalition found that ELL education requires an extra funding weight of approximately twice that of regular education.[48] But cost alone, advocates argue, should not be the deciding factor regarding the right to free public schooling. To reverse *Plyler* would prevent a significant population of undocumented immigrant children, many presumably English language learners, from even getting into the schoolhouse door. That possibility puts ELL litigators in a "Catch 22." Taking cases to court under the EEOA based on inequitable resources, now a risky strategy in view of *Horne v. Flores,* may ultimately produce even greater harms if *Plyler* were the price to be paid.

A Modest Proposal

As longtime litigator Peter Roos sees it, "It all goes back now to *Castaneda* and its limits and states' rights. There's certainly still a role for the court, but not for native language instruction."[49] That is undeniably so. Yet it should not be forgotten that *Castaneda*'s limited jurisdiction merely translates the decision into a set of guidelines that courts in other areas of the country can follow or reject at their discretion. The same holds for the federal court's decision in the Texas case that gave more bite to the vague wording of the law itself yet still took no position on native language learning. And so it is worth exploring how a stronger version of the EEOA, one that builds on contemporary understandings of bilingualism and transnationalism, might incorporate native language instruction within a judiciously fluid definition of *appropriate* and *effective* education.

More that two decades ago, Martin Gerry, the former OCR director responsible for the *Lau* Remedies, suggested that rights for linguistic minority students might better fit the individualized procedural model developed under federal law protecting students with disabilities.[50] Perhaps he was right. English language learners certainly do not suffer from an innate disability, but like those who do, they demand different educational services to ideally prepare them to function effectively in the mainstream. Gerry's suggestion makes even more sense today when the knowledge base and research findings on language and schooling are more developed, their connection to identity and personal well-being more apparent, and the instructional options broader than the transitional bilingual and English as a Second Language programs of the 1970s and 1980s.

Looking in that direction, we might consider a federal English Language Learners Act, along with Department of Education regulations, that in combination would require school officials to develop for each ELL student an individualized education plan (IEP), with parental input, outlining clearly articulated linguistic and academic goals, and requiring annual assessments and testing accommodations, similar to the IEP mandated under federal law for students with disabilities. Such a procedurally based law would guarantee the right to an education that permits the child to proceed from grade to grade or some similar substantive standard, with the inclusion of dual language instruction within a range of approaches, where deemed appropriate and desirable in consultation with the child's parent, and where administratively feasible.[51] Meanwhile, parents could challenge the child's placement through an administrative process. As in the case of disabilities, the law would only provide a federal floor of educational guarantees below which state law and local practices could not fall but which they could exceed.

This model accounts for the wide diversity among English language learners, providing a formal mechanism for considering on an individual basis their age at entry into U.S. schools, their fluency and literacy in the home language, the years and quality of previous schooling in their native country and in the United States, and their cognitive abilities. It removes their education from the "one size fits all" model of structured English immersion implicit in much of today's policy and discourse. It further builds on what educators and researchers have learned over the past four decades in addressing the needs of these students through various approaches that go beyond late-exit transitional programs that segregate ELLs for the long term. It also provides schools with a profile of information needed to determine what types of testing accommodations, if any, might be appropriate for each student, based on language and other academic and personal factors.

What especially distinguishes this model from current practice is its evenhandedness, implicitly rejecting the deficit/remedial/subtractive rationale and the current presumption, whether in law or fact, against native language instruction. It implicitly recognizes that the cultural and demographic settings, as well as national interests, have changed dramatically in recent decades. It suggests more clearly defined procedures for school officials to follow in assigning students to a particular instructional program, preventing perfunctory decisions based purely on financial expediency or political ideology. It also permits parents a voice in their child's education without the restrictions of "waiver" provisions that now exist in Arizona and California and to a qualified extent in Massachusetts. At the same time, it allows a constrained measure of administrative flexibility, a factor the Court most recently underscored in *Horne v. Flores*. It takes into account situations in which the number of speakers of a given language is small, or where teachers of less commonly spoken languages cannot be found, or where school officials can demonstrate that another instructional model is more appropriate for the student.

This approach is indeed reasonable and would prove far less costly to implement and enforce than federal law protecting the rights of students with disabilities. Yet it is not surprising that Martin Gerry's words fell on deaf ears and have remained unexplored. The reason is political and lies largely in differences that have little to do with education. Students with disabilities garner support from a broad political spectrum that cuts across racial, social, and economic lines while provoking no ideological opposition. They require services that, although costly, pose no threat to American identity. English language learners, in contrast, are children whose parents remain remote from the American mainstream, often poor immigrants who lack the political awareness, financial resources, and basic language skills to make their voices heard and whose presence in this country has met increasing hostility. Some of them reside in the United States without proper documentation, and so they consciously remain outside the view of the law. Unable to engage in self-help, they rely on others to advance their interests while protecting their anonymity.

Even beyond these differences, given the nation's checkered history on language policy, professional disagreement over instructional approaches, and widespread anti-immigrant sentiments, it is doubtful that Congress would adopt such a statute, at least in the near future. Legislative sponsors would have to forge, for the first time, an enduring consensus on underlying philosophy and ultimate goals for educating ELLs. That simply will not occur without a broadening in the constituency for native language instruction and a dramatic change in national attitudes toward the place of languages other than English in today's world.

That constituency undeniably is growing, slowly but steadily, among educated native-born Americans who enthusiastically pursue dual language immersion programs for their children as research evidence stacks up on the side of bilingualism and as new instructional models emerge. The more difficult task is to convince policy makers and the general public, fearful of the immigrant "onslaught," that bilingualism is good for the children of immigrants, and that linguistic and cultural diversity are good for the nation. Until such time, ELL advocates are left to nibble at the edges of current law and be content with smaller victories.

CHAPTER EIGHT

Setting the Record Straight

THE "WHAT WORKS" standard, now apparently endorsed by the Supreme Court, implicitly raises the question of whether dual language instruction for English language learners is good educational policy. The response necessarily confronts several contrasting arguments resting on facts and assumptions that beg for closer scrutiny than the Court itself seems willing to apply.

Some critics, including many proponents of English Only, suggest that bilingualism is potentially harmful to ELLs' cognition and learning, a theory once widely embraced and now increasingly discredited. They and others more forcefully maintain that developing native language proficiency inevitably prevents students from gaining the English skills and content knowledge needed to succeed in an English-speaking society. They also argue that, unlike immigrants of the past, Spanish-speaking children in particular, regardless of instructional approaches, are failing to learn English while the adults are simply unmotivated to do so.

Leading psychologists, linguists, and educational researchers have examined both the cognitive and the instructional questions and, in recent decades, have presented persuasive results to the contrary. Demographers and linguists likewise have refuted the "resistance to learning English" argument with encouraging findings on the shift to English dominance among second- and third-generation immigrant offspring. A look at these developments, while not intended to be exhaustive, helps clarify important yet misunderstood factors that bear on both legal rights and language policy in the schools.

Bilingualism and Cognition

For nearly a century, psychologists have debated the connection between bilingualism and cognitive development. Repeated studies have dissected the way bilingual children mentally organize their two languages and the effects of that organization on other aspects of cognitive functioning. Looked at historically, the methods used and the consequent findings often reflect prevailing attitudes toward immigration and preconceived notions of language and its role in preserving national identity.

Until the 1960s the professional and popular consensus was that learning two languages was intellectually burdensome. Bilingual children were thought to suffer academic retardation, lower IQs, mental confusion, and even social maladjustment.[1] Early studies were built on two assumptions: that the child's cognitive system is constructed to cope with only one language, and that monolingualism is the cognitive-linguistic norm.[2] Both beliefs gained considerable support during the early twentieth century when IQ testing held sway among psychologists. Many of these studies, as Margaret Mead noted at the time, failed to control for social class, education, and the influence of different attitudes and "habits of thought."[3] Nor did they describe what language skills were being used to classify students as bilingual. Was it solely their speaking ability and listening comprehension, or did it also involve literacy? Was it just informal conversational, or more formal academic fluency?

Researchers often selected their subjects not on their linguistic abilities, but rather on their belonging to an immigrant family, speaking a foreign language at home, or bearing a foreign surname. Meanwhile, they tested non-English-dominant children in English, a language they had not yet mastered. Equally questionable was the use of standardized "intelligence" tests, given the inherent difficulties in objectively defining intelligence across cultures and the social and linguistic incompatibility between the norming and testing populations. The practice of measuring intelligence by means of a paper and pencil test was likewise of dubious validity. Needless to say, immigrant children were consistently marked as intellectually inferior.

Though perplexing by today's understandings, these modes of inquiry undeniably were connected to the larger sociopolitical environment. Much of this research was carried out between the two world wars at the height of American isolationism, when educators discouraged bilingualism as an undesirable trait associated with foreigners. Left ignored were contrasting studies. Several biographies, in particular, suggested that bilingualism carried no negative effects but rather produced advantages in the verbal flexibility that comes with having more than one referent for each concrete object.[4] These findings were limited to middle-class children raised from birth in bilingual homes.

The debate over language and cognition took a dramatic turn in the early 1960s with Elizabeth Peal and Wallace Lambert's research showing bilingual Canadian students outperforming monolinguals on almost all tests of cognition.[5] The two groups studied were matched on age, sex, and socioeconomic background. The bilingual sample of ten-year-olds living in Montreal was made up of middle-class children with "balanced" or equal ability in French and English. Within this group, the child's first language (English) was the more socially prestigious and dominant and therefore not likely to be replaced by the second (French). Several dozen subsequent studies have drawn similar conclusions. They too have confirmed that bilinguals do not suffer from "mental overload" as formerly thought and that many bilinguals, especially those who are equally proficient in both languages, may enjoy cognitive advantages on certain dimensions like divergent thinking and creativity. Research findings suggest that particularly immigrant students who actively serve as "language brokers" for their parents may gain an advantage on math and reading achievement test scores.[6]

More recent studies have looked at processes. A leading voice in this debate is that of Jim Cummins, whose theory of interdependence between the bilingual's two languages has significantly influenced educational policy. According to this line of thought, the level of competence a child achieves in the second language is partly a function of the competence achieved in the first language at the time the child initially is exposed to the second. The more the two languages are linguistically congruent—for instance, English and Spanish versus English and Chinese—the stronger the interdependence effect.

Cummins maintains that bilingualism creates in children a more analytic orientation toward language, a higher sense of "metalinguistic awareness," what Courtney Cazden has called "the ability to make language forms opaque and attend to them in and of themselves." Instruction in first-language literacy develops not merely those skills, but also a deeper conceptual and linguistic processing competence, the capacity to reflect on the nature and functions of language, that affects the acquisition of general literacy and academic learning. And so, even in the case of English and Chinese, children who have developed some literacy in the first language transfer to the second certain concepts, such as the idea that the printed word represents the spoken word or that the purpose of writing is to communicate one's thoughts to an audience that is not now present.[7] By the same token, bilingualism is thought to promote the learning of even more than two languages.[8] The interdependence hypothesis has been at the center of disputes over bilingual education, typically assailed by critics who argue that "time on task" or maximum exposure to English is what really matters in developing English language skills and improving academic achievement.[9]

Psychologist Ellen Bialystock's research on bilingualism and cognition merits particular note. She too has identified a connection between bilingualism and children's metalinguistic awareness, which gives them a "more refined cognitive process" for approaching skills like reading.[10] She also has found that children raised bilingually have higher levels of selective attention. This ability to screen out irrelevant information may offer them an early advantage in tasks like problem solving.[11] Bialystock suggests that bilingualism may lead to more "fluid intelligence," manifested in what earlier Canadian researchers had identified as creative thinking and flexibility of thought.[12] Her more recent work on adults has found that these same processes carry benefits at the far end of the life cycle, protecting bilinguals from cognitive decline as they age.[13] Subsequent research supports this proposition. It appears that the more languages individuals speak, the better their cognitive state into their nineties, even for those with no formal education.[14] As Bialystock and fellow psychologist Kenji Hakuta describe, "Knowing two languages is much more than simply knowing two ways of speaking . . . It seems evident that the mind of a speaker who has in some way attached two sets of linguistic details to a conceptual representation, whether in a unified or discretely arranged system, has entertained possibilities that the monolingual speaker has no need to entertain."[15]

Psychologists now think of intelligence as a multidimensional construct. What we currently understand as "emotional" intelligence may bear on traits intuitively related to multilingualism, like adaptability and social competence.[16] There thus may be a link between cognition and interpersonal relationships. Speaking more than one language may bring with it greater communicative sensitivity. To successfully interact on a social level, bilinguals need to be aware of cues that trigger when to use one language or the other. That awareness, and experience in making the necessary computations, may afford them increased understanding of the social nature of language and its communicative function. The implication is that bilinguals may be particularly adept in situations that require reading the abstract mental states of others and predicting their behaviors, a highly useful trait in a culturally diverse and transnational world.[17]

It would be misleading to suggest that research findings on bilingualism have been universally positive. Though the results are overwhelmingly so, a far smaller number of studies have found negative cognitive effects.[18] Several theories have attempted to explain why bilingualism succeeds in some circumstances and not in others. Jim Cummins maintains that children must first cross a threshold competence in their first language to avoid cognitive deficit and then pass a second threshold in their second language to reap the cognitive benefits of bilingualism.[19] Others suggest that the greatest cognitive effects come at the early stages of second-language learning. Yet they too support the proposition that bilingual children show an unusually high "objective awareness" of language that may lead to an increased reliance on verbal mediation in cognitive tasks.[20]

Still others, in particular Wallace Lambert, have offered a sociocultural interdependence hypothesis, that the critical element in successfully gaining access to more than one linguistic code is the relative social status of the two languages and its internalization. That view may explain why the cognitive benefits of bilingualism are typically found either among families that are mixed-bilingual, or in situations like the Canadian studies where children receive their education through the medium of a lower-status language, in that case French. The fact that both languages are valued in the community and in the home results in *additive* bilingualism. That situation stands in stark contrast to the *subtractive* bilingualism generally associated with the underprivileged and viewed as a cause of academic failure among many immigrant children in the United States and in Europe.

These findings, while persuasive, suggest a measure of caution in drawing broad conclusions on the cognitive and other advantages of bilingualism. The causal order between bilingualism and cognition remains uncertain.[21] In other words, it is unknown whether bilingualism leads to greater cognitive ability or whether, instead, individuals with higher intellect, or greater visual memory, or more acute phonological sensitivity are more adept at developing skills in more than one language.[22] Researchers need to examine whether the benefits of knowing two languages accrue only where the individual is equally or at least adequately proficient in both languages; and whether the order of learning the two languages, simultaneously as in bilingual homes, or sequentially as in school, makes a significant difference. They need to explain to what extent cognitive development is dependent on sociocultural context, especially the dominant/nondominant relationship of the bilingual's two languages. They further need to explore whether all children, including those with learning deficits, gain from bilingualism, although research findings indicate that even below-average children may share those cognitive advantages.[23]

Jim Cummins himself has underscored the educational limits of his interdependence and threshold hypotheses. Neither one, he notes, says anything about whether reading should be introduced in one language or the other, how much instructional time should be spent through each language in the early grades, or when English should be introduced. A variety of models, he maintains, seem to work under varying conditions. For him, the more central factors concern whether and to what extent the school makes a "serious attempt" to promote students' native language literacy, to "affirm" their "academic and cultural identities," and to establish "partnerships" with their parents.[24]

These reservations and caveats are indeed worthy of attention. That being said, however, there is still no evidence that the ability to communicate in more than one language inevitably causes harm, and it appears to carry cognitive and social benefits of some order for many individuals. As Ellen Bialystock concludes, "Even if these advantages prove to be more transient or more fragile than some of the more optimistic data suggest, their role in discarding old fears that bilingualism confuses children and retards their intellectual growth has been a worthy outcome."[25] Bialystock is not off the mark. Her conclusions, in fact, make intuitive good sense. Half the human species is known to function bilingually, some even trilingually—a goal that the European Union has set for its younger population. The human brain obviously has the capacity to process more than one language. That fact alone suggests that multilingualism is a natural human condition, a mind-boggling assertion, especially from the American point of view.[26]

What Works?

Beyond the relationship between bilingualism and learning, the merits of various instructional approaches have led to similarly widespread misunderstandings. After years of debating the "what works" question, and with the federal "right" to education for ELLs precariously now resting on that standard, it seems there should be a ready answer. A fundamental problem is that the question itself is both overly simplistic, given the multivariate nature of the issues and the vast diversity among ELL students, and also crucial in view of their frequently low academic achievement. How well students perform in school is influenced by a host of complex mediating and interacting variables located in the classroom, the community, and the home—from the educational level of parents, to the experience of the teacher and the values and social capital of the community—that have nothing to do with the particular educational approach used, or even resources, for that matter. So many ELLs are born into poverty that it is difficult to sort out the academic from the social causes of their failure to achieve.

Frequently in play is a constellation of disadvantages associated with low socioeconomic status, including poor nutrition and a lack of linguistic/cognitive stimulation and emotional support for learning in the home that make the causative connection between inputs and outputs murky at best. Most bilingual programs have been transitional, aimed at moving students into the mainstream after three years. Many of these programs still suffer from inadequate materials, inadequately trained teachers who are not truly bilingual, and unclear objectives. Nor is it clear to what extent teachers use each language for purposes of teaching, explanation, or reinforcement.

Much, in fact, depends on the goals to be met, most directly literacy in English only or in two languages. There lies one of the most contentious points in the "what works" debate. To be sure, high-stakes testing has placed heavy weight on standardized test scores as learning "indicators," especially on English reading, ignoring equally valid "outcome" measures for the long or the short term. Grade retention and dropout rates, high school graduation, and college attendance are all important. Comparing dual language achievement among ELLs further presents problems specifically related to language, including differences in student attitudes and motivation to learn or retain the language, literacy in the home language, the length of time students have been instructed in English, and the language abilities of their teachers.

There also is the problem of distinguishing among the various bilingual methodologies. What proves successful for the student ideally entering U.S. schools in kindergarten can be dramatically different from what works for the student entering in the ninth grade with large gaps in schooling and poor native-language literacy skills. The kindergartner would likely reap enormous benefits from the dual immersion approach. The high school "student with interrupted formal education" (SIFE) has far less time to develop English language skills while learning in the content areas. In that case, the more advisable alternative might be a "newcomer" or an international school where the goal is to accelerate English language acquisition in order to facilitate academic skills and quickly orient the student to the United States.

Though initially learning to read in the home language might benefit Spanish-speaking students whose first language is easier to decode than

English, the same may not hold where the home language has a totally different orthography, as with Chinese or Japanese, or is only marginally related to a standard language, as with Haitian Creole. A very basic issue in testing English reading ability is at what point it is fair to test children who are learning to read in two languages. In fact, the distributive characteristic of vocabulary and syntactic structures across languages, depending on the context in which they are learned (such as home versus school), suggests that children instructed in two languages should be tested in both to give a full picture of their bilingual development as it proceeds. Research studies typically fail to address that point.

The literature comparing various approaches is indeed vast. Much of it suffers from the same methodological weaknesses generally found in education research. Samples tend to be small, effects are measured over a short period of time, and random sampling—the gold standard of scientific research—is seldom used. As noted, numerous factors can influence achievement, a whole spectrum of instructional possibilities fall beneath the bilingual umbrella, and the extraordinarily high mobility within the ELL population makes it difficult to track student progress over time. It thus is not surprising that the number of high-quality studies examining program effectiveness for ELLs has been estimated to be as few as five and at most fifty.[27] Of course it is easy to just throw up our hands and say that the evidence supporting English-only or dual language approaches is not conclusive. That fact in itself suggests that no one method should hold favor as a matter of law or policy but should be left to the judgment of local educators in consultation with parents.

But the stakes here are high, and so the findings are worth examination. Though it may seem counterintuitive from the perspective of the principle of "time on task" (the more time initially spent on English, the better it is learned), a growing body of research now indicates that instructing students in their native language while developing their English language skills leads to higher test scores and academic achievement. A number of research reviews or meta-analyses published in recent years suggest that bilingual development is a win-win situation. Specifically, children instructed in their native language as well as in English tend to outperform similar children in all-English classes on tests of English reading proficiency. This is the case from elementary through high school.[28] These findings go back to arguments made by Jim Cummins and others that there is a cross-lingual dimension to language proficiency, that in learning English, ELLs rely on a host of metalinguistic and metacognitive resources drawn in part from their first language.

One analysis is particularly noteworthy. The National Literacy Panel on Language Minority Children and Youth study, funded by the U.S. Department of Education, found that the most rigorous research designs using random assignment of students showed the largest advantage for bilingual education. Though the findings across these studies were small, they all consistently favored bilingual instruction for its positive effect on developing English reading skills. The text of this story is indeed interesting, yet perhaps less so than the political footnote. Despite having chosen the members of the panel and having spent $1.8 million on the study, the Department of Education decided, even before the report was finally edited, not to release it, claiming that it was "too long and inaccessible to be useful to practitioners." The decision raised serious questions regarding the Department's motives, provoking speculation that it was specifically the panel's conclusions, which cautiously supported bilingual instruction, that proved troublesome to the Bush administration.[29] Federal officials ultimately agreed to surrender the copyright and allow the panel to publish its findings privately.[30]

The findings corroborate those of a frequently cited five-year study conducted in five urban and rural school districts across the country. Here dual language immersion and late-exit bilingual programs were the only ones that helped students reach the full 50th percentile in both languages across the curriculum—math, science, social studies, and literature and to maintain that level of high achievement through the end of schooling. They also produced the fewest dropouts. The 50–50 dual language programs (half instructional time in English and half in the native language) were the most effective, achieving the highest results after only four years.[31] These results, in turn, confirm those of a large-scale study comparing dual language and English immersion programs in Miami, where by the fifth grade there was no between-group gap in English language performance while the dual language students had gained proficiency in two languages.[32]

Such positive outcomes, while encouraging, are neither definitive nor flawless. There are wide variations in programs labeled "bilingual" as well as those labeled "English Only." Some of the former teach the content areas through the native language more than others. Of the English Only programs, some permit a minimal amount of assistance in the child's native language while others completely immerse students in English. Many of the studies available for meta-analysis lasted but one year, too short a period for bilingual programs to fully demonstrate their positive effects. Beyond concluding that reading instruction in the child's primary language promoted English reading achievement, they left numerous questions unanswered. It remains unclear whether primary language instruction is more beneficial for some ELLs than for others—for instance, those with weaker or stronger native language skills. Nor is it clear how much emphasis should be placed on developing knowledge and skills in each of the languages or how long students should receive instruction in their primary language.[33] Needless to say, more carefully controlled longitudinal studies are needed.

Notwithstanding these limitations, dual language immersion is by far the fastest growing bilingual model, proving once again how politics shapes educational practice, especially on the language question. This model has proved particularly appealing to educated native-born American families looking for the social and economic benefits of early bilingualism. It also has gained favor among immigrant families who live transmigrant lives and want their children to develop native language skills for trips to the home country.[34] As of June 2009, there were 346 such public school programs scattered among twenty-seven states and the District of Columbia, from a French-Haitian program in New York City to Spanish in Omaha, Cantonese in San Francisco, and Japanese in Atlanta, although Spanish clearly dominates the field. Even under the constraints of Proposition 227 in California, dual language immersion programs grew from just 25 in 1990 to 201 in 2007.[35] One of the earliest and most nationally acclaimed models is the Oyster-Adams Bilingual Elementary School in Washington, D.C., a Spanish-English program with a student body balanced between native English and native Spanish speakers. Founded in 1971 as a grassroots effort, the school has defied the historical failures of D.C. public schools and has won numerous awards for its sustained and outstanding achievement record. Key to its success is a strong parental base of support combined with high academic standards and ongoing professional development.[36]

These programs all share essential features: they integrate language-minority and language-majority students for at least 50 percent of instructional time at all grade levels; they provide content and literacy instruction in English and the partner language to all students, the latter for at least 50 percent of the day; they use only one language in the classroom at any given time; and they maintain a student balance, each group making up between one-third and two-thirds of the total population. A variation, the 90/10 model, starts in kindergarten with a curriculum that is 90 percent in the native language and 10 percent in the second language with a gradual increase in the second language until it reaches 50 percent in the upper elementary grades. Many programs include students with learning disabilities. Many have waiting lists. Spanish-English programs commonly include English-dominant Hispanic students within the native-born English-speaking group.

A unique aspect of dual language immersion is that it optimizes the abilities of all students while avoiding the segregation of English language learners, a decided weakness in older bilingual models. It ensures that the minority language is given equal status with English in an environment of strong school and parent commitment. Parents typically must agree to keep their children in the program for a certain number of years and to remain actively involved in the school.[37] Initially modeled after early Canadian French-English immersion programs, the theoretical assumptions on which these programs are based draw from the research on linguistic interdependence and bilingualism already discussed.[38] The possibilities for implementation depend on a number of factors, including the relative sizes of the linguistic minority and majority populations in the school, the availability of financial resources, and the "prestige" of the foreign language as a "world" language. It is far easier to interest native English-speaking parents in a Spanish or Chinese program than one focusing on Hmong or Serbian, for example. It also takes a core of majority-language parents willing and eager to send their children to the same schools and place them in the same classrooms as English language learners.

In recent years, much attention has been given to voter initiatives in California, Arizona, and Massachusetts that have significantly curtailed bilingual programs in favor of structured English immersion. Contrary to popular belief, there is no direct evidence to suggest that these initiatives have increased academic achievement or helped ELLs learn English faster. In Massachusetts, ELL students continue to lag academically behind others. In 2006, three years after the state had ended statewide bilingual instruction, 83 percent of children in grades three through twelve could not read, write, speak, or understand English well enough for mainstream classes after one year in Massachusetts schools. Of those who had been in school for at least three years, more than half were not fluent in English.[39] In 2007, only 53 percent of ELL students in the state graduated from high school, as compared with 86 percent of non-Hispanic white students. The dropout rates, similarly, were 25 percent versus 7 percent.[40]

Findings from California are equally troubling. Despite claims by Proposition 227 supporters that ELL test scores have increased since the measure took effect, several independent analyses of the data suggest that improved scores are not attributable directly to the breakdown in bilingual programs, nor has the focus on English Only instruction caused

ELLs to learn English more quickly. The additional time devoted to English appears to be inconsequential. Family factors, such as the presence of books in the home, have had a greater effect on ELL achievement than specific school or state policies, including the language used for instruction.[41] In Arizona, reading and math scores on state tests for third-graders actually declined between 2003 and 2004 following the adoption of Proposition 2003. The overall percentage of ELLs passing state tests in language, reading, and math trailed behind percentages for other students.[42] Meanwhile, 60 percent of English language learners in English Only programs in grades one through five showed no gains in English proficiency, while 7 percent lost ground, contrary to the expectations of the measure's proponents. "The theory underlying the model," researchers concluded, was "false."[43]

In all three states the achievement gap between English learners and non-English learners in reading and mathematics on the National Assessment of Educational Progress further widened in the fourth grade as compared with scores from Texas and New Mexico, where bilingual education is still required. As Russell Rumberger, one of the key researchers, sums it up, structured English immersion "clearly is not a panacea" for ELLs.[44] In fact, it may not be worth the loss in potential bilingualism and biliteracy. These findings again beg for more detailed studies, tracking individual students and not groups, comparing the effects of clearly defined instructional approaches, not just on English or math achievement but on native language skills and on longer-term factors like graduation rates, college attendance, and career success.

In the end, one problem cannot be ignored. If federal and state policies continue to move programs for English language learners toward structured English immersion and away from models incorporating native or dual language instruction, the basis for comparing approaches for different populations and bringing more definitive clarity to the "what works" question inevitably will be lost. We can only hope that the research community has the resources needed to win this race against the forces of English Only.

Bilingualism and Language Shift

Aside from concerns over academic achievement, Official English/English Only proponents fear that a growing population of newcomers who speak, think, and dream in another language are endangering the country's very soul. To them English is both a mark of, and a gateway to, assimilation. It is the common bond, the glue that keeps us together, they argue, and so it needs to be spoken by all Americans. Some, like former House speaker Newt Gingrich, warn that without a common language, "the civilization will decay and the culture will collapse." Like many others, Gingrich sees bilingual education as part of the problem. At a ProEnglish press conference in 2007, he unequivocally called the nation's "30 year experiment with bilingual education" a "disaster." To his mind, bilingual schools should be converted into English "immersion centers."[45]

There is no doubt that English is the key to academic success and economic mobility in the United States and increasingly elsewhere. Nor can it be denied that some bilingual programs have been poorly implemented and have failed to move ELL students into the mainstream. But many others have proved successful, as the data on literacy and achievement demonstrate. Gingrich's inflammatory rhetoric is representative of a widely held view that immigrants today are not interested in learning English, unlike the "old" immigrants of days gone by. Such beliefs, forcefully expressed nationwide in letters to the editor, editorials, and blogs, embody assumptions about both groups that drive efforts to dismantle bilingual education and to declare English the nation's official language. On closer look, that conventional wisdom may just have it backward.

First of all, some of the "old" European immigrants from a century ago were not as quick to learn English as is now commonly believed. Many lived and worked in ethnic enclaves where they functioned day-to-day in their native language. Census data from 1910 show that even some second- and third-generation immigrants, whose ancestors had arrived in the mid-1800s, were still speaking only German.[46] More immediately, today's immigrants fully understand how their life chances and especially those of their children are tied to mainstream institutions that operate in English. Their children, in fact, are learning English at the same rate as earlier groups, and more quickly than the Germans noted.[47]

For first-generation adults, the problem often arises from circumstances beyond their control. Federally funded English as a Second Language programs now serve only 1.1 million adults, far short of the 12.5 million permanent resident and undocumented immigrants living in the country.[48] A 2006 survey of 184 ESL providers in twenty-two cities nationwide found that 57 percent maintained waiting lists ranging from a few weeks to more than three years. In New York City, most adult programs, overwhelmed by the demand, had shifted to a lottery system, turning away at least three out of four applicants.[49] In Arizona, where legal and undocumented immigrants represented 14.5 percent of the population, more than 4,000 people were waiting to get into government funded English classes as of June 2007. More than 1,400 had been rejected because they had no proof of legal residence as required under the ballot initiative adopted by voters the previous November.[50]

Even immigrants lucky enough to gain entry into ESL programs face overcrowded classrooms, inexperienced teachers, and inadequate materials. Yet no Official English bill to date has included a provision addressing these shortages. Coercion, not empowerment, seems to be the "operative principle."[51] Other immigrants are precluded from attending classes by their struggle to meet work and family obligations. This is especially true for many women. Immigrants, both documented and undocumented, often have little choice but to work long days and on weekends. Classes in English, whether day or evening, are a luxury they cannot afford in money or time. Some are seasonal workers and migrate from region to region throughout the year. Still others are elderly or disabled and face physical challenges in acquiring English language skills.

Many immigrants remain trapped in jobs forged by ethnic networks where the native language maintains a sense of solidarity and a source of protection, and where using English could be risky for them economically and socially. These jobs offer little or no opportunity to learn English. Meanwhile, other kinds of jobs remain closed to these workers because of their lack of English language skills. A case study of Portuguese women working on the assembly lines of a Canadian factory illustrates this point. The line workers depended on other Portuguese speakers to help them meet efficiency standards, and they could not risk losing these friendships by speaking English.[52] This scenario is not unique to the setting, but is representative of the immigrant experience, especially for many poor women.

Despite all these obstacles confronting the first generation, the failure to learn English is still erroneously perceived as a willful act, and therefore a measure of national apathy and even disloyalty. Those who "refuse" to learn English presumably have no interest in participating in the American project, or so the argument goes. Most of the concern is directed toward Spanish speakers. Yet Hispanics themselves affirm the importance of learning English. In 2006 a national survey asked Hispanic adults which of five factors was the "greatest barrier that keeps Latinos from succeeding in the United States," and the largest number (24.5 percent) of respondents chose "learning English."[53] Polling data reveal that a clear majority of Hispanics (57 percent), regardless of income or education level, agree that immigrants have to speak English to be part of American society. Upward of 46 percent believe that language is the prime source of discrimination against them, even more than immigration status, income/education, or skin color. A vast majority (92 percent) expressly recognize that teaching English to the children of immigrant families is an important goal. Yet an almost equally large number (88 percent) believe it is important for public schools to help students maintain their native tongue.[54]

Attitudes among broader populations of immigrants follow similar trends, at least regarding English. Eighty-seven percent believe it is "extremely important" for immigrants to speak and understand English, while more than half note that English is a far greater challenge for them than discrimination.[55] Arguably, part of the problem is that many mainstream Americans do not understand how difficult it can be for immigrants to learn English, and many react negatively to accented or less than perfectly grammatical English. When people criticize first-generation immigrants in particular for not learning the language, what they really mean is that "they don't sound like us."

Meanwhile, the second generation typically is fluent in English by adolescence, and by the third generation many have lost their native language altogether. With the range of technology, including television and the Internet, available to today's newcomers, and the broad access to preschool programs, there are far more opportunities to learn English than immigrant children enjoyed in the past. And so, despite common beliefs to the contrary, the process of shifting to English dominance is proceeding faster than ever. Researchers note that immigrant children quickly show a preference for English. Unlike their parents and the voting public, young people understand that language, particularly English, is more than a measure of achievement; it is a way for them to establish themselves socially. Speaking English without a foreign accent is critical to their blending into the mainstream and gaining acceptance from their American peers.

Of course, immigrant children do not all learn English with the same ease or at the same pace. Though time living in the United States is a significant factor, family income and educational background are just as important for the benefits they carry. Students from higher-income and more educated families are more likely to have attended school in their native country, developed literacy in their native language, and built a substantial knowledge base in academic subjects, all of which equip them to "hit the ground running" and learn English more quickly when they enter U.S. schools. They tend to come from homes with educational resources like books, reference materials, and computers that further develop both pre-reading and literacy skills and promote academic performance. They are more likely to live in ethnically diverse communities and thus have opportunities to interact with English speakers.[56] Students who lack these advantages face formidable challenges in learning not just conversational but academic English, which affects overall achievement. That fact explains in part why some students have been found to languish in transitional bilingual programs for years while others have quickly moved into the mainstream, why some have succeeded while others have failed. Schools are equally challenged in trying to level the playing field for a growing population of students who suffer from exactly those disadvantages.

English fluency or dominance, however, should not be confused with English monolingualism. On the question of whether immigrants and their offspring are shifting totally to English, the findings are mixed. The language spoken in the home is the clearest indicator. Census data from 1990 indicate that the move toward English monolingualism among third-generation Asians was proceeding at roughly the same pace as it had among European immigrant families from the early twentieth century. Among Hispanics the pace appeared slower depending on a number of factors, including geography. Cuban children growing up in or near Miami and Mexican children living near the U.S.-Mexican border were more likely than others to speak Spanish.[57]

A 1999 poll of Hispanics nationwide found that 40 percent of the second generation spoke only English at home while 43 percent spoke both English and Spanish equally. For the third generation, those figures rose to 78 percent for English and 21 percent for both languages. As for their TV viewing habits, 68 percent of the second generation watched only programs in English while 26 percent watched programs in English and Spanish. Again the numbers jumped to 88 percent for English and 11 percent for both languages among the third generation. More current data show that although for most Hispanic immigrants English is not the primary language used at home or at work, it is for their grown children. Only half of the adult children of Hispanic immigrants, and only one-fourth of the third and higher generations, speak even some Spanish at home.

But home language is different from language proficiency, which for Spanish speakers in particular is a measure of language retention. About two-thirds of second-generation and one-half of third- and higher generation Hispanics are comfortable speaking both English and Spanish. The most highly educated are the most likely to speak both languages, having refined their skills in school. The suggestion, in reverse, is that an increasing number of less-educated Hispanics are losing their Spanish language proficiency or never fully developing it.[58] Findings from California and Florida, areas of high immigrant concentration, indicate that among a broad group of Hispanic and Asian American young people within the second generation, the majority preferred to speak English only, although a significant number also endorsed a bilingual alternative. The two categories combined (English only and English plus another language) exceeded 95 percent, with only 3 percent preferring to speak solely a foreign language.[59]

Among Hispanics in particular, the third generation's uniquely visible native language retention, albeit reduced, is still striking. Equally striking is the decided pull of English as reflected in movie viewing habits. Within a five-year period in the late 1990s, despite exponential growth in the Hispanic population, one major theater company in southern California cut its number of movie houses catering to Spanish speakers from twenty to nine.[60] Apparently the market was shrinking among the younger population that forms the bulk of movie theater audiences. A similar picture presents itself in southern Florida, the home of nearly twelve hundred multinational corporations, including a number of European banks that do business with Latin America. Despite a vibrant Cuban community, business leaders face severe shortages of workers with adequate Spanish skills. Many of the second- and third-generation Hispanics merely speak what they call "kitchen Spanish," that is, "good enough to ask *abuela* (grandma) for a *galleta* (cookie) but not to conduct business."[61]

Religious practices among Hispanics likewise reveal an assimilatory trajectory. At a time when churches of every denomination imaginable are adding Spanish services to accommodate newcomers, an increasing number of ethnic congregations are moving in the opposite direction— adding English services to meet the demands of the second and third generations while maintaining a sense of community.[62] Though 77 percent of first-generation Hispanics attend churches with Hispanic clergy, Spanish language services, and a mostly Hispanic congregation, that figure drops to 53 percent among the second generation and 47 percent among the third.[63] The decline undeniably is slower than would have been found among European immigrant families in the last century, when the second generation worshipped overwhelmingly in English. The difference can be attributed in part to the lower Hispanic rate of ethnic intermarriage, which was a potent force for native language loss and mainstream assimilation among early twentieth-century immigrant families. The current pattern among Hispanics might also merely reflect a transitional bilingualism. That fact in itself is not bad, but rather something that should be nurtured for the long term.

Despite all this compelling data, the Official English/English Only forces seem oddly impervious to the facts on language assimilation among today's immigrants and their offspring. The movement to make English the nation's official language seems to be nothing more than a solution in search of a problem, and a divisive solution at that. One has to question why numbers have proved so useless on the language question whereas they loom so large in the wider immigration debate. To some extent, it depends on who has the resources to control the media spin and what makes for good press. The steady shift to English is also hidden from public view by the equally steady flow of new immigrants who reinforce their language among those already here, creating layers of linguistic assimilation.

Overall, despite fears and public cries to the contrary, the data demonstrate that today's immigrants in general, and Spanish speakers in particular, are still learning English through a typical intergenerational progression and, like immigrants of the past, absorbing not only politics but much of "American" culture through both mainstream and ethnic media. Together with contemporary findings on the benefits of bilingualism and dual language instruction, that basic fact goes a long way toward discrediting the unremittingly alarmist and unfounded arguments we continue to hear from those who ignore, or simply do not understand, the subtleties of language teaching and learning, and the rich resources that immigrant offspring bring to the school setting. Those resources bear both national and transnational importance as the following chapter points out.

CHAPTER NINE

Looking Both Ways

ABOVE the corner doorway of a residential building in Berlin's Kreuzberg neighborhood, home to the city's Turkish community, rests a captivating sculpture molded to the façade. Entitled "Looking Both Ways," it depicts a colorful androgynous figure, marionette-like and seemingly dangling in midair. Tugging at the figure in opposite directions are two men in Western laborer's clothes on one side, and a man accompanied by a woman in a long skirt on the other. Its Janus-like face gives the illusion of movement looking back and forth, hence the title. Here is the abstract rootless immigrant caught between two worlds. Fifty years ago the artistic symbolism, now quite evident, would have baffled most Europeans. Today it resonates deeply, as millions of immigrants from all parts of the globe, but mostly from the East and the South, now live in a borderless Europe.

The metaphor of "looking both ways" is indeed striking for its personal message of immigrant angst. I propose, however, appropriating it for a different purpose, one that helps tie together themes intimately related to this book. The idea of a dual vision with its inherent tensions suggests a comparative lens for exploring the impact of migration on language and schooling. Current developments in western Europe, where the conversation appears to be moving on a different plane, provide an especially pointed contrast with the United States.

At first glance this suggestion might seem tangential to the American discussion, given how matters of language are shaped by each nation's distinct history, politics, and cultural values. It might also seem inverted, as we intuitively believe that Europe has much to learn from America's long experience in educating immigrant children, rather than vice versa. There is even an arguably overstated American belief that we are more open and perhaps more "enlightened" on these issues than the Europeans. Yet many of the concerns and fears now voiced in Europe, the policies advanced, and the surrounding discourses offer deeper perspective and new insights for moving the American discussion, perpetually looking inward, in directions not yet considered.

Some European policies admittedly call for a measure of caution. Others in practice seem to defy their own rhetoric. Nonetheless, taken together they provide a reference point, terminology, and frame of both similar and contrasting norms for defining and understanding our national sense of self, where we linguistically stand on the global scene, and the changing role of schools in engaging immigrant children to meet the demands of today's world order. More immediately, they offer policy makers and educators a context for examining how the stream of European reports on immigration and multiliingualism, now making their way across the Atlantic via the Internet, may be relevant to the American experience. I especially focus on France and Germany as two distinct models of citizenship, immigrant integration, and school governance, without suggesting that they represent policies and practices throughout Europe. But before going there, we need first to examine the demographic and political backdrop against which these issues continue to crystallize.

The Strains of Immigration

Throughout western Europe, the competing forces of diversity and cohesion are tugging at every national boundary. Nations are now struggling to maintain their identity in the face of mass migration, a perceived resistance toward integration, and pressure to forge a united Europe. Postcolonialism, geographic access, the collapse of the former Soviet empire, political asylum, and the recent expansion of the European Union all pose challenges to national identity.[1]

The movement of peoples across borders is not new to Europe. The concept of independent nation-states, with sovereignty to determine citizenship entitlements, has produced scores of migrants over time. In the twentieth century alone, millions of individuals were displaced after each world war and especially after World War II. Countries like France and Germany have a long history of labor in-migration, dating back to the late 1800s, though prior to that time many Germans, in particular, had migrated out to America. In the twentieth century, France became a haven for refugees and exiles, including Italian anti-Fascists, Spanish Republicans, and Jews fleeing Nazism. Through the 1960s and early 1970s, West Germany actively recruited *gastarbeiter* (guest workers), primarily from Greece, Italy, Yugoslavia, and Turkey, to meet the demands of postwar industrial growth. Initially invited as sojourners, many of them were later joined by their families and ultimately stayed. The Turkish population remains the largest by far. During the same period, scores of Algerians and Moroccans from an area in North Africa known as the Maghreb settled in France. In both cases, these events produced second and even third generations that now claim German or French identity despite popular resistance to the contrary.

More recently, an unanticipated European pattern has emerged. Countries like Italy, Spain, and Ireland have transformed from historically fertile sources of out-migration into points of destination. Many of the migrants come from eastern Europe, the former Yugoslavia, the Middle East, Asia, and North Africa, and still others from Latin America. Those from European Union member states can freely travel across national boundaries and work within the EU, with some legal constraints; others arrive as refugees or asylum seekers, some without documentation or marketable skills. Meanwhile, countries like France, Great Britain, the Netherlands, and Portugal are straining to absorb a stream of former subjects fleeing social and political unrest in the aftermath of decolonization. Spreading throughout western Europe, these migratory flows have created widespread economic and social upheaval across continents and hemispheres.

It has been estimated that nearly 9 percent of the European Union's population was born in another country.[2] They represent at least one hundred seventy-five nationalities.[3] All the western European nations currently record at least one major immigrant city. Germany and France as well as the United Kingdom have several. Thirty cities in Europe are each home to more than a hundred thousand foreign-born, who, in many cases, account for at least 10 percent of the population.[4] Upward of fifteen to twenty million of these newcomers are Muslims, whose numbers have tripled over the past thirty years and are expected to double again by 2025.[5]

Immigration is transforming western Europe in profound and apparently unwelcome ways. Countries that unrealistically considered themselves as homogeneous—culturally, linguistically, and religiously—now face increasing diversity combined with a declining native birth rate, the clear makings of a demographic crisis. The responses to this immigration have run the gamut from obligatory assimilation with no accommodation for ethnic, linguistic, or religious differences, as in France, to the

multicultural but not multilingual approach taken in the United Kingdom and until recently in the Netherlands, to apparent denial and inevitable social isolation, as in Germany. Whatever the official posture, the
long-term effects and inevitable alienation among immigrants, especially
those from Third World countries, are becoming more visible and troubling.

The politics of immigration is incontestably tied to national self-
understanding. Since the codification of citizenship two centuries ago,
nationality in most of western Europe has derived from the traditional
German concept of *jus sanguinis* (ethnic descent or "right of blood").
The French idea of citizenship, based largely on *jus soli* (territoriality or
"birthright citizenship"), runs closer to the U.S. model of shared principles and values. Changes in German nationality law in 2000 introduced a
modified version of *jus soli*. Yet tradition runs deep, and so the strong
pull toward assimilation evident in French identity, at least in theory, is
decidedly absent in the German. Though attitudes are slowly changing,
the idea of North Africans identifying and being accepted as French, albeit nominally and grudgingly and related to French colonial ties, is perhaps more thinkable than the idea of Turkish immigrants identifying or
being accepted as Germans.[6]

The task of integrating outsiders is not easy. Individual countries may
officially promote or merely tolerate pluralism to some degree but in a
carefully circumscribed way, as the political firestorm over the wearing
of the Muslim veil in French schools strikingly revealed.[7] As many will
recall, France caused an international flap in 2004 when the French parliament modified the Education Code in a move that was said to have
targeted Muslim girls wearing the Islamic *hijab* or headscarf.[8] Just a year
previously, President Jacques Chirac had told a group of secondary
school students in Tunis that "most French people saw 'something aggressive' in the veil and that the secular state could not tolerate 'ostenta-
tious signs of religious proselytism.'"[9] As a nation built on republican
values, egalitarianism, and a myth of national homogeneity, France has
fervently pushed back against the forces of multiculturalism. And while
that concept is gaining some legitimacy under the sheer pressure of immigration, Muslim integration remains a hotly contested issue. Muslims
now comprise four to five million, or 8 percent, of the French population,
the largest concentration on the continent. Many of them are second or
third generation and hold French citizenship. In reality, given the nation's
history of discrimination and broken promises, many of them feel much
bitterness and disaffection.

Civic incorporation does not necessarily translate into social and economic integration—a lesson the French have learned in recent years. The deplorable and separate existence of North Africans, many of them Muslims living on the periphery of cities like Paris, gives testimony to that fact.[10] Tragic car burnings and fires in housing projects in the autumn of 2005, along with violent unrest and public expressions of disenfranchisement, have brought the reality of immigrant marginalization to the world's attention.[11] As a member of the French parliament remarked, "We've combined the failure of our integration model with the worst effects of ghettoization, without the social ladder for people to climb."[12] These demographic shifts have generated provocative existential questions for the French state: What is "authentic French culture?" Who is truly French?[13] And in a resolutely secular country, can one be both French and Muslim?

The French are not alone in resisting immigration. The Germans, and even the traditionally tolerant Dutch, have become openly critical of immigrants who refuse to adopt the cultural values of their new country.[14] Much of the criticism lies in the growing fear of terrorism and of Muslim fundamentalism. The involvement of Muslims, some of them European-born, in terrorist activities has given credibility to those fears. The 2004 attacks in Madrid by Islamic extremists, similar bombings in London by British-born Pakistanis the following year, the murder of anti-Islamic Dutch filmmaker Theo Van Gogh, the discovery of the "Hamburg cell" instrumental in the 9/11 attacks on the United States, and the 2007 arrest of a Turkish man living in Germany in a foiled plot to bomb major German and American targets have all put Europe's much prided diversity and tolerance to the acid test.

Events in spring 2006 surrounding the Somalian refugee Ayaan Hirsi Ali's resignation of her seat in the Dutch parliament presented yet another spin on the immigration problem in Europe. A screenwriter on director Theo Van Gogh's fatal film, and a vocal critic of Islam, Ali found her citizenship put into question by her own political party following charges that she had falsified significant details in her 1992 asylum application, a fact that she had publicly admitted. The position taken by Dutch officials echoed rumblings across the continent from the top levels of governments, suggesting strains in Europe's vaunted post–World War II status as a haven for those seeking work or political asylum. Such incidents have fueled growing suspicion that immigrants settle in western Europe to exploit its social benefits, only then to challenge its fundamental values.[15]

The Netherlands, where almost 20 percent of the 16.4 million inhabitants are persons of foreign background, has taken a lead in implementing strict assimilation measures, some of which begin while migrants are still in their country of origin. The government has upped the age and income requirements for certain immigrant groups in what some believe is an effort to stem the tide of Muslim women headed for arranged marriages. As of March 2006, under the Integration Abroad Act, foreigners interested in joining spouses or family members in the Netherlands must pass an entrance examination to prove that they can speak some Dutch and that they are at least familiar with the country's permissive values even if they disagree with them.

Included in a study package is a two-hour film, *To the Netherlands,* showing scenes of nude sunbathers, gay men kissing in public, and run-down neighborhoods populated by immigrants, hardly an enticing travelogue for the average Muslim. The film presents a stinging rebuke of female circumcision, "honor" killing, and spousal abuse, all punishable crimes, and underscores the importance of learning Dutch. As the video puts it, "You have to start all over again. You have to realize what this means before you decide to come here."[16] Citizens of the European Union and European Economic Area (EEA) countries as well as the United States, Canada, Australia, Switzerland, New Zealand, Japan, and South Korea are exempt from the exam. As government documents make clear, the law targets Moroccans and Turks, two of the largest migrant communities in the Netherlands. Human Rights Watch in particular has sharply criticized the discriminatory intent and practical effect of the law's blanket exemptions for certain nationalities. As of 2007 the Dutch also introduced an integration exam for most migrants already resident in the country.[17]

Germany has approached its immigration dilemmas in an equally exclusive way. Whereas France and Great Britain, for example, at least theoretically have accepted immigration as part of their national colonial and imperial histories, similar recognition would be completely unknown to the Germans.[18] When France closed its borders following the 1973 oil crisis, it offered foreigners already employed there the option of remaining and being joined by their families. Some became naturalized and many of their children gained citizenship by virtue of being born on French soil. In contrast, prior to 2000 those born in Germany of foreign parents could not become citizens. Now granted citizenship, they are demanding equal rights as their parents take part in a wave of naturalizations. A Turk born and raised in the country and fluent in German still faces hurdles in becoming a citizen, whereas an individual born and raised of German parents in Siberia, who has never stepped foot in Germany and speaks not a word of German, is automatically entitled to

citizenship and even settlement support. To be eligible for a German passport, a foreigner must at minimum demonstrate a "satisfactory knowledge" of German.

The system by all objective measures seems fundamentally unfair,
though the German government is taking steps to facilitate the integration process. A 2005 law entitling immigrants to German language lessons in "everyday life" is but one example.[19] For migrants without EU
citizenship, both language classes and integration classes on the country's
justice system, culture, and history are not just available but obligatory.
Those who refuse to participate risk losing their residence permits and
social benefits.[20]

Government officials view the new immigration law, which also re-
laxes rules for skilled workers and asylum seekers, as a step forward in
establishing Germany's place in a global world. As the former interior
minister Otto Schily observed, "There is a broad social consensus that
Germany is a country of immigration . . . [It] serves the economic and demographic interests of our country."[21] Set against the past four decades,
that is indeed a stunning concession. There are those who ask if this is
"too little, too late." To some extent, that may be so. Over 30 percent of
the 7.2 million foreigners now living in Germany, upward of 2.6 million
of them Turkish, have been there for at least twenty years. Many are eager to fully integrate into the social and political life of the country. Yet a
good number of others remain content with living lives separate and
apart from mainstream German society—a fact that often limits them to
second-class citizen status but also raises serious questions as to their
willingness to identify as Germans.

Disconnected Discourses

Immigration in western Europe understandably has placed new and
pressing demands on the schools. Academic achievement, dropout rates,
and future economic mobility loom large in the debate over social and
political integration. Questions of language and culture in this context
are particularly complex, riddled with contradictions, and far more so
than most Americans realize. As European states individually address immigration's effects on national identity, they also experience collective
pressure from within the European Union to establish a European identity with all the burdens and benefits of individuals moving freely across
open borders. Meanwhile, deeply rooted Europeans as well as newcomers, some with worldviews starkly different from the mainstream, increasingly embrace transnational and multiple identities that require

and support linguistic and cultural competencies. At the same time, the business community most directly feels the need to promote language skills, particularly English, to maintain a competitive place in the global economy.

The European Commission; the forty-one-member Council of Europe; the United Nations Educational, Scientific, and Cultural Organization (UNESCO); and the Organization for Security and Cooperation in Europe (OSCE) all repeatedly affirm multilingualism and linguistic diversity. The economic and political value of specific languages, like Chinese, Arabic, and particularly English, continues to gain ground. All the same, small regional groups, like the Basques and Catalans in Spain and France, the Welsh in Great Britain, and German and French speakers in northern regions of Italy are slowly gaining official recognition and affirmative educational policies for their distinct languages. With conflicting forces operating on so many fronts, it is not surprising to find clear differences between American and European discourses on language, schooling, and immigration. Those differences fall along several distinct fault lines of varying clarity and depth.

Monolingualism, Bilingualism, and Multilingualism

In the United States, the debate over language and immigrant schooling has revolved around bilingualism, but only in a limited way. Although the issue of whether public schools should foster proficiency in two languages intermittently emerges from the shadows, for the past forty years the spotlight has largely rested on whether the home language, most typically Spanish, should be used merely as a bridge toward learning English. Among some Americans, as proposals promoting English Only and Official English demonstrate, immigrant bilingualism is a force to be feared. And even where bilingualism within the native English-speaking population is considered an asset, any thought of promoting proficiency in more than two languages seems beyond the national imagination. With English fast becoming the common language of science, diplomacy, and commerce, many Americans cling to the false belief that developing competency in other languages is a luxury at best and an unnecessary burden at worst. The country is but slowly coming to realize that language skills carry benefits critical to preserving national security and useful for promoting economic growth.

The European Union, on the other hand, has placed particular emphasis on multilingualism and has done so largely as a matter of necessity. The EU now recognizes twenty-three official languages among its twenty-seven members. In addition, 60 regional or minority languages and more than 175 migrant languages are spread throughout member states. Beginning in 1992 with the Maastricht Treaty, support for language learning and individual multilingualism became a "cornerstone" of EU education policy. Over time, that policy, at least rhetorically, has become more inclusive. The underlying philosophy supporting language education lends itself to two interpretations. The first looks to linguistic diversity in the sense of equality. The second recognizes, more pragmatically, that the free movement of workers requires multiple linguistic competencies.[22]

Meeting in Barcelona back in 2002, European Commission members endorsed teaching at least two foreign languages beginning in the early grades. The idea was to promote both a healthy economy and a linguistically diverse society.[23] The Commission was not alone. The director general of UNESCO, Koichiro Matsura, struck a similar, though obviously less consequential, note announcing 2008 as the International Year of Languages. He too hailed multilingualism as a critical factor in promoting mutual respect, intercultural dialogue, and peace.[24] The facts support these aspirations. Many educated citizens of EU member countries are already able to hold a conversation in a second language, and 38 percent reportedly have sufficient skills to converse in English.[25]

In 2003 the European Commission's Working Group on Languages issued its first report, including an "action plan" that promoted the teaching of "regional, minority, migrant, and neighboring languages."[26] In 2006 the European Parliament identified "communication in foreign languages" as one of eight competencies "necessary for personal fulfillment, active citizenship, social cohesion and employability in a knowledgeable society."[27] The push toward a comprehensive European language policy gained momentum with the appointment in 2007 of Leonard Orban, the first EU commissioner with multilingualism as a separate portfolio. The appointment responded to several factors, including a single economic market, increased mobility within the European Union, unprecedented migration, and advances in communication and globalization.

A final report issued in 2007 by the Commission of the European Communities' High Level Group on Multilingualism likewise affirmed the Commission's ambitious goal, first articulated in a 1995 *Whitebook*, for every citizen to develop "practical skills" in at least two languages in addition to his or her mother tongue. While recognizing the widespread appeal of English, it laid out a number of personal benefits in knowing still other languages, from career opportunities, to communication skills across the range of cultures, to increased cognitive flexibility and functioning. In a sweeping and eye-opening nod to a more culturally diverse

Europe, the report declared that promoting heritage language literacy among young second- and third-generation immigrants would allow them to establish economic contacts in their countries of origin, to engage in intercultural dialogue, and to assist in the integration of newly arrived immigrants.[28]

A July 2008 report of the European Commission's Business Forum on Multilingualism echoed these connections. The report warned that Europe is "running the risk of losing competitiveness" as emerging Asian and African economies are speeding ahead in developing language skills. It stressed the importance of multilingualism to integration and the value of migrant workers as "cultural mediators and sales resources." While noting that English is now considered more as a "basic skill" than a foreign language, the report urged that other high-demand languages like German, French, Russian, and Chinese not be overlooked.[29] The report complemented a more socially driven document prepared for the Commission by a multinational group of intellectuals, chaired by the Lebanese author Amin Maalouf. The Maalouf Report, as it is popularly known, urged all EU citizens to learn a second "personal adoptive" language in addition to one for professional purposes. The overall vision was to create a network of interlingual speakers across Europe. The implicit motive was to eliminate the need for a *lingua franca* like English. The report also recognized immigrant languages and cultures, while encouraging immigrants to adopt the language and culture of their host country.[30]

In a 2008 "communication" entitled *Multilingualism: An Asset for Europe and a Shared Commitment,* EU Commissioner Leonard Orban laid out a blueprint for member states to meet the "challenges of a larger and more diverse EU."[31] Though Orban acknowledged the rapid spread of English, he declared it to be inadequate in itself, as the demand for studying other languages continued to grow. Multilingualism, according to Orban, "is in the genetic code of the European project . . . It is not just the ethos, but [a] concept and philosophy as well."[32] The Commission plans to publish in 2012 the findings of a major survey on the success of its multilingual strategy, evaluating the proficiency of European schoolchildren in two foreign languages by the end of lower secondary education. In almost all European countries, compulsory learning of a foreign language now begins in primary education, in Spain as early as the age of three.[33]

These proposals are indeed compelling. Yet one striking feature is that they typically and pragmatically emphasize multilingualism for purposes of business competitiveness and intercultural dialogue while scarcely addressing the link between language and identity, the personal benefits to maintaining one's mother tongue, or the cognitive advantages of speaking more than one language. Apparently lost is the human element. As one European Commission official, whose children attend the European School in Brussels, noted in response to the September 2008 communication, "Diversity of language skills for young children is great but which language is your mother tongue? Which one is in your heart?"[34]

One also has to wonder how open-ended or practically effective the implementation of multilingualism at the national level may be, considering the official monolingual reality of many western European countries and the fact that they tend not to afford all minority languages equal respect. Whereas using different languages for international communication is important for purposes of an integrated Europe, societal multilingualism within one state is often seen as a threat to social cohesion. A 2008 report prepared for the European Parliament, in fact, noted that multilingualism and linguistic diversity within the European Union are sometimes conflicting policy agendas, the first influenced by "harder" priorities like "economic competitiveness and labor market mobility" and the second by "softer" issues like "inclusion and human rights." In terms of concrete actions, the report concluded, multilingualism has clearly won out.[35] That reality raises serious concerns as to where immigrants and other linguistic minorities stand in the whole language debate.

Looking back specifically at the Maalouf Report, there appear to be other forces within the European Union promoting multilingualism with a different agenda. For some Europeans, it is a defense against the onrush of English, the de facto lingua franca that is diluting the importance of national languages. The *Charte européenne du plurilinguisme* lends credence to these suspicions. Endorsed by policy makers, researchers, and members of civil society, it argues that "there cannot be a sole language for Europe. Europe must find its completeness in refusing to think or to work according to the language biases of superpowers today or in the future, especially when these languages are in the minority in Europe." Extolling the benefits of multilingualism for mutual understanding without the limits of translation, the document conveys a decided message. A European citizenry that relies less on English and more on its own languages is good for both national and European identity.[36] The Council of Europe's 2003 guide to language education policy, although not specifically tied to immigrant education, goes even further in promoting plurilingual competence as "a condition and a constituent of democratic citizenship in Europe."[37]

These concerns may be well founded. Most Europeans consider English and one or two other "prestige" languages as foreign languages to learn at school for their practical economic and political value and not for purposes of creating a multilingual society, though that conceivably could be the end result of the rise of English.[38] More than 90 percent of European schoolchildren learn English, and the percentage is growing. In Germany it has reached 96 percent among secondary school students, and in France, 97.5 percent. In thirteen EU countries, including Germany, Greece, Italy, and the Netherlands, English is the mandatory first foreign language.[39] This trend unfortunately has reinforced the thinking of many Americans and British that it is adequate for them to be monolingual in English.

Assimilation versus Integration

For three-quarters of a century, the theme of *assimilation*—dissected, repudiated, and resurrected in various incarnations—has largely shaped the national creed on the process of becoming American. The word *assimilate,* meaning "to integrate somebody into a larger group, so that differences are minimized or eliminated," suggests a loss of any originally distinct properties or characteristics and a degree of natural compatibility between the two entities.[40] In a descriptive sense, it points to the various adjustments that immigrants make and the extent to which immigrants become incorporated into the host society. This popular understanding carries a normative expectation that newcomers should shed their native culture and adopt the language, attitudes, behavior, and political loyalties of the dominant group. Whether based in Anglo-Saxon conformity or the metaphorical melting pot, the assumption for many years has been that the evolution from foreigner to 100 percent American is direct, inevitable, and in a short time complete. Europeans, on the other hand, almost uniformly use the term *integration,* although with wide variations in interpretation among and even within nations.

The draft *Universal Declaration of Linguistic Rights,* though of no official status, provides useful distinctions between the two terms. Among the signatories in 1996 were over a hundred nongovernmental organizations, PEN centers, and experts in linguistic legislation under the leadership of International PEN and CIEMEN, a Barcelona-based language rights organization. The still unfulfilled hope was that the *Declaration* would lead to a legally binding United Nations convention. Article 4.1 defines integration in terms of mutual obligations. It allows persons who settle in a language community the "right and the duty to maintain an attitude of integration," that is, "an *additional* socialization." In this way, they may "preserve their original cultural characteristics while sharing with the society in which they have settled sufficient references, values and forms of behaviour to enable them to function socially without greater difficulties than those experienced by members of the host communities." Article 4.2 makes clear that *assimilation,* that is, *replacing* one's culture with the "references, values and forms of behaviour of the host society," must be an "entirely free decision."[41] The implication is that nations must offer immigrants a choice between these two modes of adaptation.

In a similar way, the *Hague Recommendations Regarding the Education Rights of National Minorities,* developed by a group of international experts under the sponsorship of the OSCE, affirm the additive nature of integration. Intended merely as a framework to assist the fifty-six member states, including the United States, in developing policy on minority education, the *Recommendations* interpret international instruments to grant minorities the right to "maintain their identity through the medium of their mother tongue" and the right to "integrate into and participate in the wider national society by learning the State language."[42] Expressly limited to "national" minorities (ethnic groups that "constitute the numerical majority in one State but the numerical minority in another"), and not legally binding, the *Recommendations* nonetheless are recognized as an "important pillar for peace and stability." According to legal experts like Fernand de Varennes, they in fact have proved more politically and legally persuasive than the 1996 *Declaration.*[43] *The Common Basic Principles on Integration,* adopted by the European Union Council in 2004, provides a more binding definition of integration as a "dynamic two-way process of mutual accommodation" that respects immigrant languages and cultures.[44]

As a practical matter, the term *integration* in various European countries has covered the conceptual spectrum from assimilation to multiculturalism and everything in between. As the *Declaration* suggests, assimilation demands action only on the part of newcomers. It assumes that they will shed their cultural differences and blend into a homogeneous landscape. Multiculturalism, on the other hand, incorporates those same differences as an asset to diversity, demanding a mutuality of accommodations on the part of all the members of a society in flux. Given that range of understandings, the difference in actual practice between integration and assimilation may be more symbolic than real, depending on a given country's history and culture or the political posture of the particular speakers. For the political Left in France, for example, the term *integration* has been used interchangeably with *insertion,* largely in the sense of "socioeconomic enablement," while implicitly rejecting the term *assimilation* for its association with colonial policies that degraded non-European cultures.[45] The implication is that those "inserted" into the social fabric of France can still retain their cultural identity. For those on the Right, the term *integration* has been little more than a euphemism for state-imposed assimilation, which has been the traditional French position.[46] Put into operation, the term has functioned in a mechanistic way without adequately addressing the social characteristics or the larger value issues. As noted, in the Netherlands racist events of recent years have generated intense debate over the "failure of integration," causing a breakdown in the Dutch "multicultural consensus."[47]

Integration can also show a dark side. While in its fullest form it appears more respectful of cultural differences than assimilation, it may lend itself to isolating immigrant groups and preventing them from becoming active members of the political community. The underlying assumption is that newcomers are so fundamentally different that they are incapable of blending into the mainstream even if they choose to. A clear example is the Turkish population in Germany. In the past, the German state promoted policies designed for Turkish immigrants and their children to maintain their distinct language and culture and to remain apart from the German mainstream. The official expectation was that they would return to Turkey. Now two generations later, the German government has had to shift gears. Recent trends in other western European countries toward stricter limitations on immigration and citizenship further demonstrate how the rhetoric of integration can belie the intent or the effect. Yet the discussion in Europe in the least provides a context for teasing out these fine conceptual points and their implications for public policy, whereas the American fixation on the language of assimilation precludes the broader possibilities that integration offers in theory and in fact.

Immigrant versus Regional Languages

For the past four decades, discussion of language and schooling in the United States has centered on immigrant children, save for the periodic call for more speakers of whatever the "critical" language of the day happens to be. As for indigenous populations of Native Americans and Hawaiians, while federal law has provided certain accommodations for their languages, their rights and interests have been eclipsed by the more vocal and visible debate over educating the growing numbers of children from immigrant homes, and the high concentration of speakers of one particular language, Spanish. In western Europe, just the opposite prevails. There, regional/territorial languages, depending on the context, arguably carry "covert prestige" or "cultural capital" not typically attached to immigrant languages. This distinction raises issues related to the production of "otherness" that overlap but also differ from reactions simply to linguistic difference.

Language rights in Europe flow directly from an evolving conceptualization of minorities over the centuries, from religious to national to linguistic group members. The linguistic turn in the 1990s was in part a strategy to use language, in the sense of individual human rights, as a more politically palatable and less threatening base for minority policy than claims to self-determination or collective group entitlements.[48] Yet regional groups, in fact, consider language an essential aspect of their collective identity. The primary threat is the loss of intergenerational transmission, and so minority rights are now essentially a matter of language preservation and revitalization. Those same groups have come to play an increasingly important role in the politics of both specific countries and the European Union.

EU member states have used a variety of approaches—constitutional, legislative, decentralized, and centralized—for protecting regional cultures and languages. Ireland gives constitutional recognition to the Irish language, declaring it the "first official language" of the country.[49] Article 6 of the Italian constitution provides for the "protect[ion] [of] linguistic minorities by special laws." Legislation adopted in 1999 pursuant to Article 6 covers eleven languages, including French, Provençal, Friulian, and Sardinian. It permits kindergarten instruction in those languages as well as teaching the respective cultures and traditions in elementary and secondary schools.[50] Article 3 of the Spanish constitution establishes Castilian as the "official Spanish language of the state," but further declares that the "other languages of Spain (Catalan, Basque, Valencian, and Galician) will also be official in the respective autonomous communities, in accordance with their Statutes."[51] In other cases, like the Welsh Language Act of 1993 and Scotland's Gaelic Language Act of 2005, protected status has come directly from the central government of the United Kingdom.[52]

This distinction between regional and immigrant languages is also evident at the supranational level. Despite all the recent "talk" of multilingualism, including references to immigrant languages, policy initiatives and especially rights protections lag far behind. Whereas the European Community has not given official status to any linguistic minorities within the workings of the European Union itself, EC institutions have taken a number of steps that clearly favor regional minorities. International instruments and declarations, primarily from the European Commission and the Council of Europe, addressing language rights with varying degrees of detail, largely ignore the immigrant question. A study of regional and minority languages, sponsored by the European Commission in 1992 and completed in 2004, exclusively addressed languages of European origin. Though the purpose of the study was to examine the European Union's potential for sustaining its linguistic and cultural diversity, the mandate excluded the languages of immigrants, like those from the Middle East, Central Asia, and Africa.[53] By the same token, within the European scholarly community of linguists and language advocates, regional languages dominate the discussion and the literature. In one sense, regional accommodations may be intended to weaken the power of individual countries in the interest of European integration. In another sense, they may reflect a concern for preserving the status quo of a Europe with common and traditional religious and social values that some speakers of immigrant languages may not share.

Even when immigrant rights may be implied, the scope of those rights is vague and enforcement is weak at best. For example, the European Commission's directive of July 25, 1977, expressly "obliges Member States, in cooperation with States of origin and in coordination with mainstream education, to promote teaching of the mother tongue and culture in the country of origin."[54] The precise meaning of "promote" is, of course, open to wide interpretation. European countries also are signatories to the United Nations Convention on the Rights of the Child, adopted by the UN General Assembly in November 1989. Article 8 of that agreement respects the child's right to "his or her identity," while Article 30 expressly grants the ethnic and linguistic minority child the right to "enjoy his or her own culture" and to "use his or her own language."[55] None of these rights, however, is specifically framed in the context of education. The United States, by the way, is the only country besides Somalia that has not ratified the Convention.

Article 8 of the *European Charter for Regional or Minority Languages,* opened for signature in 1992 and now ratified by twenty-four member-states within the Council of Europe (fifteen of them EU members), is unambiguous on the immigrant language question. It promotes and protects the "historical regional or minority languages of Europe" from preschool to adult education but expressly excludes the "languages of migrants." In a less definitive way, Article 14 of the Council's *Framework Convention for the Protection of National Minorities,* opened in 1995 and signed by thirty-five states, grants "every person belonging to a national minority" the right to "learn his or her minority language." It offers no definition of "national minority," although most signatories have interpreted the *Framework* to include groups lacking territorial identity, like the Roma and speakers of Yiddish.[56] In any case, it does not cover migrants as conventionally defined. The United Kingdom, nonetheless, has taken an uncommon interpretive approach, including immigrant ethnic groups in line with the definition of "racial groups" under the Race Relations Act of 1976.[57]

As for regional minorities, the *European Charter* and the *Framework Convention* are the clearest expressions of interest in learning one's mother tongue and being educated in it. The *Charter*'s purpose is to protect and promote languages themselves, as part of Europe's "cultural heritage," and not to protect individuals. The *Charter* technically grants no rights but rather recognizes certain state obligations in an á la carte selection of provisions.[58] Signatories can choose the articles to which they may subscribe ("according to the situation of each language"). They can also choose which regional minority languages they want to include. Enforcement is weak, at best, if states fail to live up to their commitment. Only eleven member states have fully complied with the *Charter* monitoring process.[59] Both the *European Charter* and the *Framework Convention* further contain "escape" or "clawback" clauses that effectively undercut the substance of the obligation. Each qualifies rights by what is "appropriate," "reasonable," or "practical," where the numbers of students or the demand are "sufficient" or "substantial," with the obligation to enforce "as far as possible" and "within the framework of their educational systems."[60] This "sliding scale" model is typical of minority provisions in human rights treaties.

Unlike the United States, where similarly vague terminology in laws, regulations, and court decisions is often strengthened with administrative agency oversight, threats of federal fund termination, and/or rights to judicial review, the European model provides no judicial or quasi-judicial body with authority not merely to investigate and judge individual claims, but to impose palpable sanctions and hold school officials to even a "good faith" standard. Countries simply must file reports every three years on the *European Charter* and periodically on the *Framework Convention,* while a committee of experts keeps watch over compliance. Final oversight rests in the hands of the Council of Europe's Committee of Ministers, which can exert pressure on recalcitrant states, but again merely in the form of recommendations. Unlike the European Commission, the Council of Europe lacks any legal standing within its member-states.[61]

A report prepared for the Council in 2003 found that although the Advisory Committee had at times extended rights, its recommendations in general were uncommonly weak and inconsistent across groups and countries.[62] Earlier assessments had similarly found that recommendations lacked clarity on specific steps that states should take in moving toward compliance.[63] As language advocate Tove Skutnabb-Kangas points out, "If experts on minority protection show vacillation and uncertainty and confusion, how are educational decision-makers supposed to know what to do?"[64] More importantly, the express exclusion of immigrant languages in the *European Charter* defies the notion of equal human rights for everyone. These points have invited widespread criticism.[65]

Not all countries share the views expressed in these documents. Some, consciously or not, remember the threat to national cohesion that language minorities presented long ago in the formation of nation-states.[66] There is a lingering fear that accommodations for regional languages would inevitably provoke claims to political autonomy and even separatism. France, for example, is one of the few European states that has ratified neither the *European Charter,* though it signed the document in 1999, nor the *Framework Convention.* Events surrounding the *Charter's* failure were especially telling. Concerns within the Constitutional Council that any departure from linguistic homogeneity would run counter to the French constitution initially gained wide support from the French media and among the public. The French people were not merely a "community of citizens" but a "community of Francophones."[67]

A uniform language policy goes back to 1789 and the *Declaration of the Rights of Man and Citizen,* the founding document of the modern French state. In their zeal to firmly establish French as the "langue nationale," French revolutionaries subordinated feudal idioms and rural dialects to the national interest, promoting a particular type of "civisme" or good citizenship that included a linguistic aspect.[68] As the French empire fanned out across hemispheres, the language came to be viewed as an instrument of conquest and as having a clear cultural mission.[69] For the French, the concept of a national language is not a threat to human rights but a condition of equal citizenship embodied in Article 1 of the French constitution, which guarantees equality before the law for all citizens without distinctions of origin, race, or religion. Rather than refuse rights, the French thus reject the very concept of defining any groups lest it fragment and destabilize the French population.

In an interesting turn of events, the debate in France surrounding the *European Charter* and the public spotlight it cast on the language question served as a catalyst for gradually shifting national opinion. In May

2008 the UN Committee on Economic, Cultural and Social Rights once again publicly deplored France's "lack of official recognition of minorities."[70] The following week, the French National Assembly approved a constitutional amendment declaring that "regional languages are part of [France's] heritage." The near-unanimous vote ignited a firestorm in the press. An overwhelming majority of the French people (68 percent) and especially those under the age of thirty (80 percent) supported the proposed amendment.[71] The Académie française, the institution that has defended the purity of French since 1635, thought otherwise, issuing a vitriolic warning that recognizing regional languages in the constitution would be "an attack on French national identity." Representatives of regional groups in turn took the Académie to task for refusing to recognize the country's diverse citizenship. "All we ask for is to speak our languages in public, to have services in our language, for parents to have the right for their children to be taught in the language of their choice," they urged.[72] It should not be forgotten that it was not until 1951, with the passage of the Deixonne Law, that regional languages were even allowed in the classroom, and then only for one hour per week with an additional hour for culture and literature.[73]

The French senate initially rejected the proposal by a vote of two to one, but later approved it with minor modification. The language of the amendment, promoting regional languages as a common cultural heritage and not as the heritage of any distinct region or group, was significant.[74] Given those carefully crafted limits, along with all the surrounding controversy, it is of little surprise that the languages spoken by immigrants with no historical ties to the country have received such meager protection or even attention, particularly in France.

Rhetoric versus Reality

In the context of schooling, language is a means for eliminating diversity, hence the primacy of the official or national language.[75] But it also is a means for sustaining diversity. Well-organized groups in Europe have campaigned for regional language schools, some more successfully than others. The Bretons in France, the Irish in Northern Ireland, and the Hungarians in Slovakia are all cases in point. Some countries now offer bilingual or immersion classes. Some limit the use of minority languages to preschool and/or primary education. Some use two languages as media of instruction. Others gradually replace the home language with the national language at higher levels. Still others teach the national language as a second language. Some offer mother tongue instruction for only several hours each week. Few recognize minority languages across the broad range of education.[76] Except where provided by treaties following each of the two world wars, schools in which the minority language is the exclusive language of instruction, administration, and interaction are relatively rare; the most numerous are found in Spain as well as Finland, the latter offering Swedish-medium schools for Swedish speakers. In cases where the regional language is used on a limited basis, the aim is often to preserve the particular cultural group by saving a dying language that younger generations no longer speak.

The nationalistic ideology of one nation/one language historically has prevailed with even greater force in the case of immigrant languages. Though certainly not new to Europe, only in recent years has the question emerged on a broad scale representing language groups—Turkish, Chinese, and various North African languages—outside the western European family. More recent arrivals from eastern European countries like Poland, Russia, and Romania are further changing that pattern. The near invisibility of these languages within mainstream education has led their speakers to understand that their language is useless, a belief that inevitably becomes internalized into their identity construction. That representation consequently dampens interest in minority languages among immigrant children, a vicious cycle indeed.[77] Unlike the U.S. situation, no one immigrant language dominates any European country, with few exceptions, Turkish in Germany and North African Arabic and Berber in France being the most widely noted. In both instances, most speakers are now in the second and approaching the third generations and proficient in the national language.[78] Along with negative racial and religious attitudes toward outsiders who "don't look or think like us," in some countries the very diversity of foreign tongues may explain in part why immigrant groups have failed to mobilize sufficient political support for language programs in the schools.

Throughout Europe, guidelines or directives on developing proficiency in immigrant languages are "scant and outdated." At the national level, schools rarely afford children of immigrants, guest workers, or refugees direct attention to developing their own language and inadequate attention to learning the official language as a second language. Public discourse and legislation often speak of them in exclusive terms as "foreigners" *(étrangers, Ausländer),* dismissing their languages as obstacles to integration while referring to their languages as "nonterritorial," "nonregional," and "nonautochthonous."[79] The conceptual exclusion affirms restrictive notions of citizenship and nationality based on bloodline, particularly in countries like Germany. And though children of immigrants are now the topic of intense study among sociologists, the focus remains on the achievement gap and social and economic mobility; the language question is sidestepped.[80] To some extent, these priorities are understandable, especially in countries like France and Germany where, again, second- and third-generation immigrants speak the national language. Even many first-generation immigrants to France come from French-speaking former colonies. They continue, however, to raise other social concerns related to non-mainstream cultural and religious differences combined with widespread poverty. And so their rights to heritage language instruction are of less educational immediacy or interest than their economic and political integration.

In some European countries, 10 percent or more of the student population comes from an immigrant background. In Germany that figure in 2005 was 44.8 percent for young people between the ages of six and eighteen.[81] Yet, with few exceptions, there is limited evidence that individual countries have responded to the collective call promoting multilingualism among immigrant children beyond teaching them English. A study of fourteen immigrant-receiving countries, all in western Europe except for Australia and Canada, found that bilingual programs played only a minor role in most school systems. More than 50 percent of children in primary grades who were not fluent in the language of instruction were attending regular classes, with supplemental support to improve those skills. Fewer than half of those programs had an explicit curriculum. At most they commonly offered additional native language classes; they rarely used the native language as the medium of instruction in academic subjects.[82] Practices varied, in part as a function of local priorities and demographics. Equally in play were other factors related to each state's history, political environment, and goals for immigrant integration. In some cases, policies were a matter of conscious planning and official designation. In others, they evolved over time, whether by happenstance or in response to new political pressures.

Another study, of thirty-three European countries or regions ("regions" referring to the distinct makeup of Belgium and the United Kingdom), similarly found that placement in mainstream classrooms with additional in-class support was the most common approach. Separate classes for a transitional period, ranging from merely a few weeks to one or two school years, ranked second. Only Italy used direct mainstreaming as the sole strategy, a striking throwback to the "sink or swim" approach long abandoned in the United States. In any case, the aim was for students to master the national language.[83]

Some countries now offer native language instruction as a subject on an optional basis for several hours each week, typically in primary rather than secondary schools. Several, including France and Germany, have provided such programs in certain languages and cultures within the school curriculum. Yet even here the goal, at least originally, was to facilitate the expected reintegration of children into their parents' countries of origin without considering the benefits the children or the state might gain from instruction in two languages. In 2004 this practice was completely abandoned in the Netherlands, which has shifted its policies toward assimilating immigrants into Dutch society. Sweden and Finland remain among the few countries where immigrant students are entitled to mother tongue instruction if they wish it. Elsewhere the decision is more practically tied to the presence of a minimum number of students or the availability of qualified teachers.[84] While this approach speaks to the "breathing room" left in European international instruments, the potential danger is that it can be used to mask local authorities' lack of interest in, or even hostility toward, instruction in students' mother tongues.

Language programs for immigrant students in western Europe have encountered obstacles, including unwritten mother tongue languages, shortages of appropriate materials and trained teachers, and resistance from students, parents, and school staff, not unlike in the United States.[85] Yet the problems run even deeper. Teacher education does not commonly cover bilingualism, bilingual education, or second-language learning. Many immigrant families see no value in their children maintaining a language that carries low social and economic capital in relation to either the official language or English. In some cases, mother tongue education as a subject and not as the medium of instruction depends on bilateral agreements between the host country and the country of origin, with each sharing the costs, to varying degrees, under what is called the ELCO (enseignement de langue et culture d'origine) program. This strategy is most prevalent in countries, like Germany and France, that have more long-standing and sizable communities of immigrant workers.

In Germany, where education is decentralized among sixteen federal states (Länder), each with its own minister of education, and where the federal government plays only a minor role, there is no national policy on language. Depending on the numbers, some states place immigrant children in a mixed multinational preparatory class, at times with students of different ages spread over several classes, and where communication is predominantly in German.[86] Instruction in the immigrants' mother tongue is offered primarily in the western states and to children from Turkey and the former Yugoslavia.[87] Under the European Convention on the Legal Status of Migrant Workers, opened for signature in 1977, children of parents who came as guest workers from one of the official "sending countries" have the right to "special courses" for teaching the mother tongue "so far as practicable" to "facilitate their return to the State of origin."[88] Either the Ministry of Education assumes full responsibility or the embassies and consulates of the countries of origin operate the programs. In the latter case, the Ministry provides classrooms and assistance for the salaries of teachers, who remain employees of the home country.[89] Though remigration was the primary goal in the past, the view has broadened slowly to include the familial and professional benefits of bilingualism.

Bilingual instruction, that is, instruction through the medium of two languages, still remains spotty and uncoordinated at best. In Berlin, where approximately one-fifth of schoolchildren speak a first language other than German, there were only eighteen primary schools offering some form of bilingual instruction as of 2006. Besides German, the most common language was English, although other languages, including Turkish, Portuguese, and Greek, were offered.[90] In the case of immigrant children, German educators tend to reject the approach not for its linguistic consequences but largely based on the imperatives of social integration and fears of separating migrant students from the mainstream.[91] The depths of those feelings became evident several years ago when school officials in a multilingual suburb of Berlin, having consulted with parents, banned the use of languages other than German on school grounds and on school trips, in the interest of integration. Berlin's center-left and center-right parties both endorsed the policy while the federal prime minister for integration, Maria Böhmer, praised it as a model for all German schools. In a startling affront to human rights, the school even received a special prize for its efforts.[92] The National Integration Plan adopted by the sixteen federal states in 2007 implicitly confirms that view. Though the Plan recommends remedial courses in German for immigrant students, depending on their linguistic ability at the time they enter school, it makes no mention of native language instruction.[93]

Immigrant leaders see the issue otherwise. In recent years, secondary schools have offered immigrant languages, including Turkish, within the foreign language curriculum. A December 2008 proposal from Cem Özdemir, co-chairman of Germany's Green Party, to offer additional Turkish language courses specifically designed for Turkish students met with overwhelming support from the Turkish community but mixed reactions from German politicians. Proponents maintained that such programs help integration. If Turkish students seemed disinterested in learning the language, they argued, perhaps grouping them with German students who have no knowledge of the language could be the cause. "Germans say multilingualism is important but they change their attitude when it comes to Turkish," remarked the head of the Turkish Federation in Berlin.[94]

The situation in France is only marginally different. Non-Francophone children arriving in the country between the ages of seven and eleven may be placed in a *classe d'initiation* (CLIN), and after the age of eleven in a *classe d'accueil* (CLAD). The maximum time allowed for each has been two years. The goal is to totally assimilate the child as quickly as possible.[95] Like many countries in western Europe, nevertheless, France has made a decided push in recent years to develop strategies for incorporating languages into the general education program. Curricula adopted in 2002 for primary schools expressly acknowledge that "plurilingualism" is not a handicap per se. Here, as elsewhere, the emphasis has been on regional and major European languages while the languages commonly spoken by immigrants have remained on the margins.[96] Though primary school dual language programs exist for certain regional groups, they are all but nonexistent for immigrant languages. The French, in fact, never officially use the term *bilingual,* which has positive connotations in French society, to refer to immigrant children or even native-born French who speak English at home. They rather reserve it for mainstream European languages and immersion programs in regional languages.[97] Migrant languages are called *langues d'origine* (languages of origin), implying lower status than regional languages like Breton, Corsican, and Basque, or foreign languages like English, Spanish, and German. The term *langues d'origine* notably contrasts with "heritage" or "community" or "patrimonial" languages, designations commonly used in other countries.

The categorization itself is somewhat arbitrary. For example, Arabic has appeared on the primary school foreign language list since 1995 when the policy was first implemented. Originally taught within the "languages of origin" provision, it is now included along with Chinese and Portuguese in the category of "foreign languages." The change suggests equal standing with dominant European languages. Even so, like the situation of the Turks in Germany, it fails to recognize that many students come from homes where Arabic is spoken and therefore require a different instructional approach from students who are beginners in Arabic.[98] It is therefore not surprising that, despite the large numbers of Arabic speakers in France, as of 2006 only 20 percent of students studied any variety of Arabic at the primary school level.[99]

Since 1973 French primary public schools have offered courses under the ELCO model in languages and cultures of origin on an optional basis for three hours per week either during the school day *(cours intégrés)* or more typically after school hours *(cours différés)*. The program grew out of diplomatic negotiations progressively made in the 1970s and 1980s with Portugal, Italy, Tunisia, Morocco, Spain, the former Yugoslavia, Turkey, and Algeria. The initial idea was to hire and pay teachers under contract to the French National Education System. The aim was to mediate between the family and the school and to maintain linguistic and cultural ties with the home country in the expectation that immigration was only temporary. That expectation, of course, was not born out. Today many French-born children of immigrant background will remain in France and maintain only limited contacts with their family's country of origin. The program is no longer restricted to students of a particular national origin.

French teachers have looked unfavorably upon these classes, suspecting that the cultural element veers toward religion, especially in the case of Arabic and Turkish.[100] Countries that fund the programs, particularly Morocco, as well as the parents themselves appear to have both cultural and religious motives. The French Ministry of Education, on the other hand, sees these classes as offering students a better understanding of their community language and culture, thus facilitating their integration.[101] More numerous in the 1980s, these classes have since fallen off. While some parents have found them appealing, students more often have found them burdensome.[102] The spread of English and the consequent pressure on all students to develop proficiency in the language may be contributing to the decline in interest in native languages. Besides, for the sizable number of Maghrebi students whose parents are Berbers, standard Arabic is a completely foreign language. The same holds for Kurdish speakers from Turkey. Yet it is also reasonable to assume that students who have some family familiarity with even an Arabic dialect or other language would enroll in native language classes if they were offered alongside English and incorporated into the regular school curriculum.[103] Even so, among educators the dominant aim again is for children to shift as quickly as possible to French. Where a migrant language is spoken in the home, educators encourage parents to enroll their children in school as early as two years of age. And though French schools promote "intercultural education," it is solely within the context of European values with no attention to cultural diversity.[104]

Despite the scarcity of these programs, the concept of bilingual or multilingual education itself is not new to Europe. Since 1958 the governments of European Union member-states have jointly operated a system of "European Schools" specifically designed for the children of civil servants working for one of the supranational European institutions. Now numbering fourteen, these schools serve approximately twenty thousand students, including everyone from the offspring of cabinet ministers to those of cleaning staff and porters. Where space is available, they admit a small number of non-civil-servant children who pay a nominal fee. They are all tuition-free and are legally considered public institutions.

Known for their high scholastic achievement, language equity, and success in developing multilingual proficiency, the schools aim to develop the child's first language and cultural identity as well as a European identity. Combining elements of maintenance, enrichment, and transitional approaches, these programs use the first language as the foundation for learning throughout the years while gradually increasing instruction in the second language. Students also learn a third language, with a fourth as an added option.[105] Since 1981 the French government has authorized similar "International Sections" in state schools where 25 to 50 percent of the student population is made up of foreigners. These too largely serve students from privileged backgrounds. Plans are under way to more equitably expand these programs. In Germany, some states have established European Schools that incorporate a European dimension and a language component, though immigrant minority languages are only marginally covered. One need not think too hard to understand why EU member-states have not adapted this successful model, or at least its basic philosophy, to educating immigrant, refugee, or other linguistic minority children. The implicit message of elitism and "us/them" mentality is clear.

Learning Both Ways

For Europeans, opposition to immigration is not merely about jobs, linguistic and cultural dissonance, or the public costs of providing language accommodations. The large Arab and Turkish populations in countries like France and Germany, together with the "otherness" of Islam and the feared dangers of Islamic fundamentalism, are perceived to be a more serious threat to national identity, cultural integrity, and security than Spanish speakers in the United States, who largely share mainstream American values and religious practices. That, of course, is not to suggest that Muslims are monolithic in their religious beliefs or practices, or that Islam is inherently radical or definitively irreconcilable with democracy, or that its followers tend toward terrorist activities. Nor does it deny that many Muslims in Europe strive mightily to integrate into mainstream society. In fact, a 2008 Gallup poll found that French and German Muslims were at least as likely as the general public to identify with the countries where they reside.[106]

Equally important is the fact that immigration historically is not a dominant component of the European national narrative as it is in the United States, where it has continued to shape the family histories of most Americans as well as the nation's collective identity. At the same time, the moral stain of institutionalized slavery and the rights-based laws and regulations adopted to overcome its consequences have shaped the American perspective on equality. Those measures form the foundation for much of modern-day advocacy on behalf of language rights in the United States while legitimizing ethnic identification and cultural diversity. Diversity itself is a value recognized in the law. On the other hand, unlike Europe, the United States has not been torn over the centuries by regional language differences, repeated wars, and shifting national and linguistic boundaries. And while English is our de facto common language, it does not consciously bear the same intimate symbolic ties to the nation or the same constitutional status as the official languages of most European countries. We do not speak "American" as the French speak French and the Germans speak German.

The French particularly distrust ethnic and religious characteristics as divisive and anti-egalitarian. They consider diversity to be a threat to social cohesion rather than an integral part of citizenship, regardless of what EU leaders might say. In contrast to the elaborate system of data gathering established by the United States government, French law prohibits identifying citizens on the basis of national origin, race, or religion, though critics argue that egalitarianism too often becomes a "pretext for inflexibility" and a "cover for ignoring inequalities."[107] This resolve, that all French citizens have a single identity, has profoundly influenced policies toward linguistic minority children and their parents. The school is not simply a vehicle for transmitting republican ideals. It is the very embodiment of those ideals. The French system of schooling, therefore, is distrustful of private backgrounds and their potential for inhibiting equality, effectively turning the American argument for language accommodations on its head. For the French, the values and social capital associated with civil society are superior to those existing within ethnic or national cultures. The only way to achieve civic equality, the French believe, is to leave cultural differences, including the mother tongue, at the schoolhouse door and to achieve a complete command of the French language. Refraining from speaking an immigrant language denotes alignment with the French republican project and thus lifts one above the status of immigrant.[108]

The Germans, mindful of the atrocities of Nazism, likewise steer clear of racial or ethnic classifications while historically fusing national identity with the German language and a set of monolithic values. Like France, despite at least four decades of intense immigration, Germany still lacks a sense of self-understanding as a nation made up of diverse peoples and cultures.[109] Any reference to ethnic diversity within German schools typically is limited to regional minorities.[110] At the same time, and unlike the French, reacting to the Nazi preoccupation with playing children off their parents, German schools are especially wary of "leveling down" family backgrounds and stress parental participation as essential to the child's educational success.[111] Other countries similarly bring their own distinct histories and priorities to the discussion of language, identity, and schooling.

Bearing in mind these differences, there are still a number of lessons for the United States to learn from the European discussion on immigration and language while recognizing the apparent gaps between supranational verbal exhortations on diversity and the reality of meager policy initiatives at the national level. In the same way, European nations can gain insights particularly from the evolution of American civil rights protections and education practices over the past forty years, despite further work to be done on both counts.

To be sure, it is easier to recognize injustices when committed by others. As the rights of regional minorities have overshadowed those of immigrants in western Europe, so the immigrant question in the United States has obscured the rights of Native Americans. The particular histories of these two groups admittedly differ, but the state's obligation to help revitalize and maintain their languages and cultures should be of equal importance. Similarly, the growing European interest in preserving regional languages and operating bilingual programs in Breton in France and Basque and Catalan in Spain, for example, could further add to the discussion of purposes and methods for promoting heritage languages in the United States.

On a separate but related point, the European conversation on promoting multilingualism as a practical necessity for EU unification and economic integration should alert the United States that the mindset of monolingualism is shortsighted and rapidly becoming obsolete. Monolingualism could soon put the United States at an economic and diplomatic disadvantage. Though English is now becoming a common language across the globe, mastery of more than two languages is gaining ground at least among educated Europeans, notwithstanding weak policy enforcement at the EU level. In the not too distant future, communication on a globally meaningful scale will demand more robust linguistic skills and cross-cultural understandings than Americans now seem willing to fully acknowledge.

The United States, moreover, has something to learn from the discourse on integration and its pluralistic ideal reflected in international documents, despite national practices and popular sentiments to the contrary. It could likewise learn from the failed policies of countries like France, Germany, and the Netherlands, notwithstanding the rhetoric of integration. Up to now those nations have either demanded complete assimilation, or until recent years denied any responsibility toward immigrants, or unrealistically believed that a multicultural society would simply develop naturally without government intervention.

That being said, signs of change or at least more open discussion are now afoot in the United States and most notably in Washington, where the terminology of *integration* seems to be acquiring new political currency. Legislation introduced in Congress in July 2009 to support English literacy and civics education for immigrants calls for an "office of citizenship and immigrant integration" to be established in the federal Department of Homeland Security.[112] A Task Force on New Americans, established in the Department two years earlier, subsequently issued a report that used the term *integration* interchangeably with the phrase *political assimilation* to describe a process of "embracing shared political principles" that "exemplify democratic traditions" and "build a sense of community and common identity as Americans." The report recognized that while integration "cannot simply imply accommodation and multiculturalism without a unifying component," assimilation in the sense of a group's adopting another's values "cannot imply a one-way street."[113] The suggestion was that the incorporation of newcomers involves an element of mutuality on the part of both the immigrant and the larger society.

How deeply this new terminology, along with its suggestively more inclusive philosophy, is filtering into the mainstream, or whether it will prove more symbolic than real in reshaping public discourse and policy, remain unclear. Initiatives, like the Migration Policy Institute's National Center on Immigrant Integration Policy, offer hope in that direction. The Center has adopted a progressive view of immigrant integration as a "two-way process by which immigrants and their children come to feel—and be—American and by which American identity and culture expand to reflect each new generation of immigrants."[114] Yet reports from more conservative-leaning groups still seem locked in the language and mindset of assimilation.[115]

Other developments in Europe present lessons of a more cautionary but highly relevant nature. Unending controversies in France over regional languages vis-à-vis the revered constitutional status of French should give pause to the forces of English Only and Official English. Even recognizing the historic differences, ideological ties to one language as the very symbol of national unity and identity, inscribed into the constitution, can become a recipe for social conflict, especially in a society as linguistically diverse as the United States. And though international documents may appear useful as an alternative source of language rights, the reality of European experience has shown otherwise. Though the inspirational force of "language rights as human rights" has helped create a more accommodating climate for minority and particularly regional languages, any practical effect has been seriously undercut by the lack of effective enforcement mechanisms, vague terminology, and a reasonable deference to individual states and local conditions. Language rights, in fact, get far less favorable treatment in human rights instruments, even in education clauses, than other human attributes like sex, race, or religion.[116]

This last point suggests that Europe has something to gain from the United States on the question of language rights and policies for immigrant children in particular. Most fundamentally, certain countries need to abandon lingering views of the child's native language as a tool for reintegrating into the home country and see it instead as a means of communication and identity formation in the "here and now."[117] Individual states might take a more assertive role in providing resources and clearly articulated policy directives on language education for immigrant children. The U.S. model, a combination of carrots and sticks, funding and sanctions, while admittedly in need of strengthening and a more cohesive focus, is a helpful point of departure. This type of centralized regulation is closer to the norm of educational governance in countries like France and the Netherlands than in the United States, where education traditionally has been a matter of states' responsibility and local control with only minimal federal involvement. Of course, it could pose some difficulties for decentralized education models like that of Germany, where policies emanate from individual state systems.

Immigrant groups in Europe are exceedingly diverse and often lack the language skills, political know-how, and effective organized advocacy to mediate their concerns, particularly at the level of international policy. Unlike immigrants to the United States, and most notably Hispanics, they also lack a politically mobilized and integrated group of second-, third-, and even fourth-generation members to push for language programs, admittedly with mixed success. It is thus left to individual countries to affirmatively include them within the European multilingual project. And even though the United States has still not resolved the question of "best" instruction or assessment strategies, beneath the layers of politics there is much to extract from four decades of lawmaking, research, public debate, and practice. As those experiences continue to demonstrate, though the pressure to teach immigrant children the national language and culture is understandable and justified, it need not preclude nurturing their mother tongue.

On that count, in lieu of relying on tenuous agreements with countries of origin, as has often been the case, schools in Europe might offer immigrant languages as part of the primary school curriculum, with student progress noted in regular school reports. At the same time, there should be a national commitment and support for developing curricula, teaching methods, and teacher training programs aimed at dual language instruction. Similar structures could be put in place at the secondary school level where learning a second language is a more common practice. Meanwhile, English could be offered for purposes of international communication. These efforts would go a long way toward legitimizing minority languages in the minds of the majority and of the speakers themselves.[118]

The Council of Europe has documented that some immigrants in Europe, like those in the United States, engage in transnational activities. By the same token, some immigrant children live transmigrant lives.[119] Even for those who do not, the effects of globalization still allow receiving countries to benefit economically and politically from the language skills and cultural understandings these students could offer if they were given proper attention. Whether responding to developments in the Middle East, or the possibility of Turkey entering the European Union, or the expanded opportunities for international trade, European countries would be wise to tap the resources of their Arab, Turkish, Chinese, Hispanic, and other students from immigrant backgrounds.

More immediately, recognizing the home languages and cultures of immigrant and second-generation youth in Europe might ease these young people's feelings of social exclusion and defuse some of the tension and hostility they feel toward their adopted countries. Despite all the official gestures promoting individual "multilingualism" (national languages) as a way to unite Europe politically and economically, that project is a "hard sell" for those who oppose any practice that suggests "multiculturalism" or linguistic diversity at the national level, or is perceived to threaten social cohesion, as does the dominant Muslim question. Paradoxically, in the United States, despite policies and laws suggesting support for linguistic diversity and multiculturalism grounded in the legacy of civil rights, the norm of English monolingualism still holds enormous power on the individual level.

Overall, these differences demonstrate how language policies and educational practices are tied to notions of citizenship and identity, which in turn are steeped in history and tradition. Yet they also reveal that societies are not static, nor are they isolated, and that new developments demand more relevant and perhaps even global approaches. There is much to be gained from sharing experiences and exploring inclusive solutions to educating and integrating the scores of migrant offspring who challenge but also enrich schools on both sides of the Atlantic, defining the national identities of their parents' adopted lands. Most fundamentally, by highlighting our strengths and our shortcomings, these comparisons help us understand who we are as a nation and where our best efforts on behalf of immigrant children can take us.

CHAPTER TEN

A Meaningful Education

THE RELATIONSHIP between language and national identity in the United States is indeed a web of paradoxes. The nation has never established an official language by law, yet English has become a symbol of what it means to be "American." Though we pride ourselves on our racial, ethnic, and religious diversity, we pull back when it comes to language. While as a nation we emphasize pluralism, whether from guilt over slavery or satisfaction in the success of our "oneness from many," we deemphasize linguistic differences based on an American pretense that culture is separate from language. We admire multilingual skills in other peoples, at least in theory, yet we cling to English monolingualism in practice. And while we give lip service to supporting foreign language learning among native-born Americans, learning English is a subtractive process for the foreign-born and their children. For them, the road to integration is paved not just with the struggle to attain English fluency but with having to abandon the home language, or at least maintain it as only a private language that they should use in public and only in conditions of extreme necessity. Though elite circles highly value being fluent in many languages, immigrants who are "true bilinguals" are presumed to harbor social indifference and civic ambivalence. For them, bilingualism is portrayed as a badge of economic doom for the individual and political doom for the nation.

Even as record numbers of college students enroll in study-abroad programs to sharpen their language skills and cultural understanding, and education-minded English-speaking parents rush to enroll their children in Chinese "immersion" preschool programs, mainstream attitudes toward immigrant offspring and their languages remain skeptical at best and hostile at worst. Those attitudes are deeply rooted in historical ambivalence, misapplied fears of language and its cultural associations, unspoken racial categorization, and unfounded claims regarding language maintenance and language shift. Despite the rich linguistic and cultural resources that immigrants bring to the country, we do everything to undermine those skills and sensitivities in their children. As the late Samuel Huntington told us, "There is no Americano dream. There is only the American dream created by an Anglo-Protestant society. Mexican Americans will share in that dream and in that society only if they dream in English."[1] For Huntington and Official English/English Only proponents, there is no dreaming bilingually, at least not at the American taxpayer's expense. Yet especially in times of national crisis when we need adults who can understand and speak other languages, we hastily put together legislation and program initiatives to repair the damage done. And when the crisis abates, we return to "business as usual." In a post-9/11 world wracked by terrorism and uncontrolled migration, we see language as both a bridge to international diplomacy and a menace to societal security.

Nowhere have these contradictions crystallized more vividly and repeatedly than in public schooling. And nowhere has the attempt to confront these same contradictions been more contentious than in modern-day disputes over the broad terrain commonly called "bilingual education." For more than four decades, educators, policy makers, advocates, and critics have engaged in pitched debate over how best to educate children, whether native- or foreign-born, whose dominant or home language is other than English. In an equally disquieting way, the federal courts, Congress, and the Office for Civil Rights have wavered on language policy in the schools, struggling to define a legal right to education that still leaves some discretion in the hands of state and local school officials. Reflecting obvious ambivalence about "difference" and fear of unraveling a mythical consensus on what being "American" really means, the conflicting messages coming from Washington have set the education of English language learners on a winding path from which it still searches to find its way. Vague legal standards have kept the key actors in this drama on an unending quest to define what is a "meaningful," "appropriate," and "effective" education. But the ground is shifting. And those shifts demand a fresh look at how to put these terms to use in the best interests of the children they originally were intended to serve.

From its inception the United States has been an evolving project, a grand experiment, reconstituting itself with each successive wave of immigration, and reexamining itself with each epic moment—from civil war to world wars to an elusive war on terrorism. Through all these upheavals, tradition has been a key force in shaping the national consciousness regarding newcomers and the languages they speak. As in the past, change is now producing anxieties. Much of the current opposition to linguistic diversity masks deep concerns that the post-1965 immigrants, with their visible though not universal tendency toward bilingualism and transnational lifestyles, are threatening American identity in irreversible ways. Old notions of assimilation in which immigrants completely blend into the mainstream no longer hold. The mainstream itself, more pointedly than ever, seems to defy definition.

These developments present a dilemma to a nation reluctant to move beyond the "melting pot" metaphor or face up to the unspoken failings of past Americanization efforts. But they also present opportunities to embrace a more expansive collective identity in ways that were politically inconceivable and socially destabilizing to past generations, and that are now less imaginable to contemporaries abroad for a number of historical and political reasons. In contrast to western Europe, where immigration and the pull of European unity are chipping away at national identities seemingly carved into stone, the United States is more securely positioned to draw on its long immigrant experience, mining its rich linguistic and cultural resources and its post-ethnic comfort with diversity while avoiding the mistakes of the past. Despite resistant forces, there is concededly more room in the American paradigm, compared to the European, for embracing plural identities. At the same time, by way of comparison we have much to learn about ourselves from the complex issues surrounding European integration policies and instructional practices and their enduring ties to nationhood.

Both the drive toward multilingualism supporting European unity and the current unmet demands for speakers of "critical" languages worldwide affirm the importance of language on the international and diplomatic fronts. The United States has lamented its foreign language shortfalls during other national crises—from the Cold War to Vietnam, Desert Storm, and Bosnia and Kosovo—but this time the need is recognized as permanent. As former Senator Paul Simon (D-Ill.) warned in the wake of the September 11, 2001, terrorist attacks, returning to "business as usual" is no longer an "acceptable option."[2] Soon afterward, the National Security Education Program sponsored a briefing to underscore the country's vital need for specialists with an understanding of language nuance, able to read between the lines and discern meaning in situations that threaten U.S. security.[3] Most recently, a congressional committee report affirmed a "roadmap" prepared by the Department of Defense back in 2005. The report outlined a strategy for developing "robust foreign language and foreign area expertise" to help service members communicate with foreign partners and avoid the misunderstandings that surround language barriers. It roundly assailed American education for failing to address these needs.[4]

A 2006 report issued by the country's business and educational leaders posed similar warnings. We must maintain the ability, the report said, to "compete successfully with countries that boast multilingual, multicultural, and highly skilled workforces" while "explain[ing] America's identity and values more effectively."[5] The recent economic crisis is a shocking reminder of how crucial these skills are in a world where America remains a prime moving force, at least for the near future. It is a wake-up call to how the "rise of the rest"—countries like China, India, Brazil, and Russia—along with a multilingual Europe, are economic phenomena with political and cultural consequences.[6] To function successfully in shifting global markets, individuals need a working knowledge of local languages, appropriate discourse styles, and cultural values and practices. Simply relying on English as the sole language of global communication, we risk the world "talking" over our heads as we become ever more culturally trapped. Though Americans, like the British, take great satisfaction in the fact that English is fast becoming the lingua franca worldwide, we fail to realize that this opens the door to other nations' understanding our idiosyncrasies, and each other's, far better than we understand theirs. Policy makers and education leaders might consider using the various pronouncements supporting multilingualism in Europe as a model for initiating a similar national conversation in the United States. Repeated messages and financial support, from the highest government offices, establishing national priorities and goals could prove effective in changing the monolingual status quo. The National Security Language Initiative is but a modest and much too quiet step in that direction.

For decades, linguists and bilingual education advocates have been preaching the gospel of "language as a resource, not a deficit." After many years falling on deaf ears, that message is slowly gaining currency. Evidence from a variety of sources, both empirical and ethnographic, now supports a more open view toward bilingualism and dual language education. Many English language learners live transmigrant or at least transcultural lives. Some repeatedly return to their native country. Even more maintain close relations, by phone and Internet, with family members left behind. Either way, they require dual language skills in their daily lives. Meanwhile, the diversity within this population, together with the pedagogical insights and experience time has afforded, have broadened our understanding of their cognitive needs and linguistic potential.

Commentators throughout the decades, from the old immigration to the new, have drawn the connection between language and individual identity along with the value in keeping children tied to their home language and culture. Sociologists and psychologists point out how immigrant offspring gain emotionally and academically from close-knit families and communities. Many young adults themselves affirm the significance of these relationships. Their positive intergenerational bilingualism is often misconstrued, especially within anti-immigrant circles, as a sign of resistance to learning English. Psychologists further tell us that bilingualism is not burdensome to the brain, as once thought, but instead enhances mental flexibility and the ability to read social cues. Education researchers likewise have gathered evidence that dual language instruction may improve English literacy and academic achievement, provided that schools are willing to take a long-term view of learning. These promising findings beg for programmatic flexibility, stepped-up initiatives, and national commitment to inform more detailed, carefully controlled, and replicated longitudinal studies.

That brings us to the realm of instruction, where the decades-long bipolar debate between bilingual education (most typically transitional programs) and initially English as a Second Language (ESL), but more currently structured English immersion, has become pedagogically obsolete. In recent years we have witnessed the birth of educational approaches reflecting the realities of changing demographics, student profiles, and parental preferences: dual language immersion, international high schools, newcomer schools, heritage language preservation. These newer models are achieving positive academic results in an integrative environment. They avoid both the ethnic and racial segregation of older bilingual approaches and the fragmentation and loss of content instruction typical of ESL pull-out programs. They also provide alternatives in the pacing and sequencing of native language versus English literacy skills, depending on the needs of individual students. At the same time, they offer parents options for deciding whether and to what extent the schools should maintain their child's home language and culture. Many Asian Americans, for instance, consider native language learning to be a private matter. Many Hispanic parents, on the other hand, especially those living near the Mexican border, are more eager for the schools to assume that responsibility.

Dual language immersion programs for English language learners recently have gained increased appeal across ethnic groups. Heritage language programs now recognize the prospects for developing fluency and literacy among students who are proficient in English but come from homes where another language is regularly spoken. Nearly half to two-thirds of children of immigrant origin fit that profile. These students, long ignored in debates over language and schooling, are an untapped resource for mediating across linguistic and cultural bounds, especially in regions like Latin America, East Asia, and the Middle East, where the United States has important economic and "geopolitical" interests.[7]

As for the legal right to education for English language learners, limiting court interpretations of Title VI and the Equal Educational Opportunities Act, along with anti-bilingual state initiatives, have created less ambitious expectations of what the law reasonably can deliver. Whatever remains of the Supreme Court's 1974 decision in *Lau v. Nichols* does not encompass the child's legally enforceable right to learning in the home language. In fact, it never did acknowledge such a right, despite the widespread belief that it had. When advocates lament the loss of language "rights" and the "undoing" of *Lau,* they essentially grieve over the sea change in educational philosophy and the obstacles parents and litigators must overcome to rebut a political and, in some states, a legal presumption in favor of English Only instruction despite a lack of supporting evidence. The Court's recent ruling in *Horne v. Flores* appears to support that presumption.

In the effort to determine what is "appropriate" and "effective," driven by federally fueled high-stakes testing and school accountability mandates, education has lost a sense of what is "meaningful" to the individual child and to the nation. That standard takes on more depth than even the justices envisioned in *Lau* when we consider the importance of language in shaping an individual's sense of self, as well as the pressing demands of globalization and transnationalism. Viewed in that light, a "meaningful" education is one that builds on the linguistic and cultural identities that children bring to school. It prepares children academically and socializes them for the world of tomorrow, and not for the world of a hundred years ago at the time of the "old" migration, or forty years ago when the Bilingual Education Act was first passed, or even thirty-five years ago when *Lau* was decided.

It therefore seems reasonable for national policy to support native language learning in some form and to afford parents greater voice in choosing among approaches within the bounds of administrative possibilities and each student's circumstances. In the best of worlds, a flexible procedural model, a trimmed-down and less adversarial or litigation-prone version of federal law protecting the rights of students with disabilities, would address some of these concerns. Not only would it provide important information for more accurate student assessment, but it also would allow for more individualized program design and student placement. Legal advocates might further pursue claims that categorical constraints on native language instruction, as found in California's Proposition 227, for example, deny parents a constitutionally protected liberty interest in directing the education of their children. Meanwhile, lawmakers in Washington should take the lead in promoting *additive* bilingualism, placing dual language instruction and research at the forefront of federal reform while revamping testing requirements for English language learners. In the very least, Congress should expressly include the *Castaneda v. Picard* standards in whatever legislative and regulatory initiatives ultimately emerge from political wrangling over the No Child Left Behind Act.

On a final but important note, insofar as the debate over language and schooling focuses on academic achievement and test scores, it misses the connections among linguistic and cultural diversity, political integration, and civic participation. Lost in standoffs over English Only proposals, testing, and funding, the rising incidence of transnational affinities and dual identities presents educators and policy makers with inevitable challenges but also with transformative opportunities.

On the challenge side, immigrant education has a dimension of mutuality that needs to be incorporated into both the national discussion and local policies on language and schooling. Leaving behind the old Americanization extremes, schools that serve students whose immigrant backgrounds and worldviews set them apart from the mainstream have a compelling interest in creating for those students a community of meaning and a sense of shared destiny.[8] Especially for children who live transnational lives or whose families have little or no experience with democratic governance, public schools serve a vital role in cultivating the knowledge, values and attitudes that make "good citizens"—citizens who embrace common political principles, a shared allegiance, and a common historical memory while leaving room for differences at the margins. At the same time, and without here delving into the merits of "global citizenship," a thorny subject indeed, schools must also recognize the inner conflicts that students from immigrant families experience, in their beliefs and affiliations, for conceptualizing citizenship in a global context.

That being said, those very conflicts, along with the life experiences that give rise to them and the multiple civic identities they create, also offer wide opportunities for immigrant offspring to enrich classroom discussion and to promote both national and local interests. Here is the point where language, civic engagement, and the global aspect of integration all converge. These students bring to the school setting the linguistic and cultural capital to function effectively within and across national borders. And so rather than push them to block out the past, as traditionally is done, schools should incorporate into classroom discussion their diverse political backgrounds, examining whether and how their native countries have tackled similar questions, helping them explore the workings of American democracy as compared to other systems, drawing on original documents and texts in their respective languages.

And just as immigrant offspring serve as language brokers between their families and the larger society, they can also bridge the political gap by affirming within their home and community an appreciation for representative government and social commitment. Bilingual and bicultural competencies enable secondary students in particular to develop a sense of active citizenship and political attachment, serving as tutors, camp counselors, assistants at food pantries, and interpreters at local hospitals, churches, and community meetings. With all the talk of civic education and service learning among educators and policy makers, these positive attributes and potential contributions largely remain unspoken and unrealized outside of specialized schools and scattered private initiatives.

This vision of American identity and schooling demands not mere tolerance of, but respect for, linguistic and cultural differences. It neither denies the truth of today's immigrant politics, nor falls prey to the potential but avoidable excesses of transnationalism or cosmopolitanism feared by conservative commentators. At its core, it recognizes the distinction between *citizenship*, which is essentially about status, rights, and responsibilities, and *belonging*, which is about feeling "accepted" and "welcome." Schools can do much to facilitate both of these ends for children without "sealing them off" in "miniature replicas" of the societies their parents left behind.[9] The pointed message is that we can be politically equal, equally engaged, and culturally compatible without being culturally identical or monolingual.[10]

As Robert Putnam wisely suggests, the challenge immigration poses can best be met not "by making 'them' like 'us,'" but rather by creating a new more capacious sense of 'we,'" not by "bleach[ing] out ethnic identities" but by creating "overarching identities."[11] Public schools, traditionally the crucible for molding newcomers into "true Americans," are key to redefining what this concept means within a more current and inclusive American narrative and a view of schooling that looks beyond national borders. Linguistic skills and transcultural sensitivities are essential to this project as the nation pushes the bounds of another frontier, this time with global dimensions.

NOTES / INDEX

Notes

1. The Symbolic and the Salient

1. Jim Rutenberg, "Bush Enters Anthem Fight on Language," *New York Times*, April 29, 2006, A1.
2. Daniel Pipes, "On New York's Khalil Gibran International Academy," March 7, 2007, www.danielpipes.org.
3. Daniel Pipes, "A Madrassa Grows in Brooklyn," *New York Sun*, April 24, 2007, 5.
4. Kim Landers, "Arabic Public School in NYC Sparks Outcry," *ABC News* (Australian Broadcasting Corporation), September 5, 2007, www.abc.net.au.
5. "Protest Greets the Opening of an Arabic School in New York," *ABC News*, September 4, 2007, www.abcnews.go.com.
6. Elissa Gootman, "City Names New Principal for English-Arabic School," *New York Times*, January 9, 2008, B3.
7. Ole Waever, Morten Kelstrup, and Pierre Lemaitre, *Identity, Migration and the New Security Agenda in Europe* (London: Pinter, 1993), 23.
8. John Higham, "Cultural Reponses to Immigration," in *Diversity and Its Discontents: Cultural Conflict and Common Ground in Contemporary American Society*, ed. Neil J. Smelser and Jeffrey C. Alexander (Princeton, N.J.: Princeton University Press, 1999), 56.
9. Samuel P. Huntington, *Who Are We? The Challenges to America's National Identity* (New York: Simon and Schuster, 2004).
10. *The Civic Mission of Schools: Report from Carnegie Corporation of New York and CIRCLE* (New York, 2003), 11.
11. *Bethel School District No. 403 v. Fraser*, 478 U.S. 675, 681 (1986); *Ambach*

v. Norwick, 441 U.S. 68, 76–77 (1979); *Edwards v. Aguillard,* 482 U.S. 578, 584 (1987); Rosemary C. Salomone, "Education for Democratic Citizenship," *Education Week,* March 22, 2000, 48.

12. *Abington v. Schempp,* 374 U.S. 203, 230 (1963).

13. Rosemary C. Salomone, *Visions of Schooling: Conscience, Community, and Common Education* (New Haven, Conn.: Yale University Press, 2000), 38–41.

14. David Lopez and Vanesa Estrada, "Language," in *The New Americans: A Guide to Immigration since 1965,* ed. Mary C. Waters and Reed Ueda (Cambridge, Mass.: Harvard University Press, 2007), 231.

15. Harold F. Schiffman, *Linguistic Culture and Language Policy* (New York: Routledge, 1996), 13; Joshua Fishman, "Language Policy: Past, Present, and Future," in *Language in the USA,* ed. Charles A. Ferguson and Shirley Brice Heath (Cambridge: Cambridge University Press, 1981), 517.

16. Marshall to Webster, January 14, 1831, Noah Webster MSS., New York Public Library; American Academy of Language and Belles Lettres, Circulars I-III, cited in Shirley Brice Heath, "Language and Politics in the United States," in *Georgetown Roundtable on Languages and Linguistics: Linguistics and Anthropology,* ed. Muriel Saville-Troika (Washington, D.C.: Georgetown University Press, 1977), 270.

17. Noah Webster, *Dissertations on the English Language* (1798; Gainesville, Fla.: Scholars' Facsimiles and Reprints, 1951).

18. Noah Webster, preface to *An American Dictionary of the English Language* (New York: Foundation for American Christian Education, 1828), n.p.

19. John Howe, *Language and Political Meaning in Revolutionary America* (Amherst: University of Massachusetts Press, 2004), 84.

20. Richard Alba and Roxane Silberman, "The Children of Immigrants and Host Society Educational Systems: Mexicans in the United States and North Africans in France," *Teachers College Record* (2009), www.tcrecord.org.

21. *Lau v. Nichols,* 414 U.S. 563, 566 (1974).

22. *Children That Speak a Language Other Than English at Home: Percent 2007,* Annie E. Casey Foundation, Kids Count Data Center, www.kidscount.org.

23. National Clearinghouse for English Language Acquisition and Language Instruction Educational Programs (NCELA), *How Many School-Aged English Language Learners (ELLs) Are There in the United States?* www.ncela.gwu.edu; *Survey of the States' Limited English Proficient Students and Available Educational Programs and Services 2000–2001, Summary Report* (Washington, D.C.: U.S. Department of Education 2002), 3, 6; Randy Capps et al., *The New Demography of America's Schools: Immigration and the No Child Left Behind Act* (Washington, D.C.: Urban Institute, 2005), 5.

24. Richard Fry, *The Role of Schools in the English Language Learner Achievement Gap* (Washington, D.C.: Pew Hispanic Center, June 2008), 2.

25. Richard Fry and Felisa Gonzales, *One-in-Five and Growing Fast: A Profile*

of Hispanic Public School Students (Washington, D.C.: Pew Hispanic Center, August 2008), 16.

26. Kate Menken and Tatyana Kleyn, "The Difficult Road for Long-Term English," *Educational Leadership* 66, no. 7 (April 2009), www.ascd.org/el.

27. P. J. Hopstock and T. G. Stephenson, *Descriptive Study of Services to LEP Students and LEP Students with Disabilities, Special Topic Report #2: Analysis of Office of Civil Rights Data Related to LEP Students* (Washington, D.C.: Department of Education OELA, 2006).

28. U.S. Department of Education, *National Assessment of Educational Progress in Reading and Mathematics, 2007* (Washington, D.C.: U.S. Department of Education, 2008).

29. Huntington, *Who Are We?*, 365.

30. Lorraine Ali, "Speech Impediment," *Newsweek* (Periscope), October 1, 2007, 14.

2. Americanization Past

1. Letter from P. P. Claxton, Commissioner of Education, to Franklin K. Lane, Secretary of the Interior, November 1, 1913, reprinted in U.S. Bureau of Education, *Bulletin No. 51* (Washington, D.C., U.S. Government Printing Office, 1913), 5.

2. Harold F. Schiffman, *Linguistic Culture and Language Policy* (New York: Routledge, 1996), 220.

3. Edwin H. Zeydel, "The Teaching of German in the United States from Colonial Times to the Present," *German Quarterly* 37 (1964): 344–345.

4. Gary Gerstle, "Liberty, Coercion, and the Making of Americans," *Journal of American History* 84, no. 2 (September 1997): 549.

5. *Debates and Proceedings of the Constitutional Convention of the State of California, 1878–1879*, vol. 2 (Sacramento, 1880–1881), 801–802, reprinted in *Language Loyalties: A Source Book on the Official English Controversy*, ed. James Crawford (Chicago: University of Chicago Press, 1992), 53.

6. Schiffman, *Linguistic Culture*, 224. *Nativism* is a term generally used to describe opposition to immigration based on a belief in the moral or racial superiority of the dominant stock as exemplars of values associated with the nation-state. The underlying fear is that immigrants are intrinsically inferior, will distort those values, and are not capable of becoming assimilated into mainstream society. See Peter Schuck, "The Treatment of Aliens in the United States," in *Paths to Inclusion: The Integration of Migrants into the United States and Germany*, ed. Peter Schuck and Rainer Münz (Oxford: Berghahn Books, 1998), 207.

7. Edward George Hartmann, *The Movement to Americanize the Immigrant* (New York: Columbia University Press, 1948), 15.

8. Mark Wyman, *Round-Trip to America: The Immigrants Return to Europe, 1880–1930* (Ithaca, N.Y.: Cornell University Press, 1993), 40.

9. Gary Gerstle, "Liberty, Coercion," 535.

10. Wyman, *Round-Trip to America*, 77–79.
11. Woodrow Wilson, *A History of the American People* (New York: Harper and Bros. 1902), 5:212.
12. "The High Tide of Immigration—A National Menace," *Judge*, August 22, 1903.
13. Hartmann, *Movement to Americanize*, 21.
14. U.S. Immigration Commission, *Abstracts of the Immigration Commission with Conclusions and Recommendations and Views of the Minority* (Washington, D.C.: U.S. Government Printing Office, 1911), 1:14.
15. Matthew Frye Jacobson, *Whiteness of a Different Color* (Cambridge, Mass.: Harvard University Press, 1998), 79.
16. Oscar Handlin, *The Uprooted* (Philadelphia: University of Pennsylvania Press, 1951), 247.
17. David A. J. Richards, *Italian American: The Racializing of an Ethnic Identity* (New York: New York University Press, 1999), 226–227.
18. U.S Immigration Commission, *Abstracts*, 1:48.
19. Elwood P. Cubberley, *Changing Conceptions of Education* (Boston: Houghton Mifflin, 1909), 15–16.
20. Lawrence A. Cremin, *The Transformation of the School* (New York: Vintage Books, 1964), 67–68.
21. Israel Zangwill, *The Melting Pot* (New York: Macmillan, 1909), 37.
22. J. Hector St. John de Crèvecoeur, *Letters from an American Farmer* (New York: Dutton, 1957), 39.
23. Frederick Jackson Turner, *The Frontier in American History* (New York: Henry Holt, 1928), 1–38.
24. Zangwill, *The Melting Pot*, 37.
25. John Higham, "Integration vs. Pluralism: Another American Dilemma," *Center Magazine*, July/August 1974, 70–71.
26. "Roosevelt Bars the Hyphenated," *New York Times*, October 13, 1915, 1.
27. "Abolish Hyphen, Roosevelt's Last Words to Public," *Chicago Daily Tribune*, January 7, 1919, 4.
28. See, e.g., Edward L. Godkin, "The Harm of Immigration," *Nation*, January 19, 1893, 42–43; Paul Joseph Repp, "Why America Is Better," *Independent*, February 24, 1910, 409–410; W. F. Wilcox, "Popular Delusions about Immigration," *Independent*, February 8, 1912, 304–307; Percy Stickney Grant, "American Ideals and Race Mixture," *North American Review* 195, no. 677 (April 1912): 513–525.
29. Isaac B. Berkson, *Theories of Americanization: A Critical Study* (New York: Teachers College, Columbia University, 1920), 62–63, 67–68.
30. Horace Kallen, "Democracy versus the Melting Pot," *Nation*, February 18, 1915, 190–194, and February 25, 1915, 217–220; Stephen J. Whitfield, introduction to Horace M. Kallen, *Culture and Democracy in the United States* (New Brunswick, N.J.: Transaction, 1998), xix.
31. Randolph S. Bourne, "Trans-National America," *Atlantic Monthly*, July 1916, 86–97.

32. For a critique of Kallen's and Bourne's arguments, see Werner Sollors, *Beyond Ethnicity: Consent and Descent in Ethnic America* (New York: Oxford University Press, 1986), 181–186.

33. Berkson, *Theories of Americanization*, 123–131.

34. Julius Draschler, *Democracy and Assimilation: The Blending of Immigrant Heritages in America* (New York: Macmillan, 1920), 178.

35. U.S. Immigration Commission, *Abstract of the Report on the Children of Immigrants* (Washington, D.C., 1911), cited in Cremin, *Transformation of the School*, 72.

36. David B. Tyack, *The One Best System: A History of American Urban Education* (Cambridge, Mass.: Harvard University Press, 1974), 230.

37. Adele Marie Shaw, "The True Character of New York Public Schools," *World's Work* 7, no. 2 (December 1903): 4206.

38. N. C. Dougherty, "Recent Legislation upon Compulsory Education in Illinois and Wisconsin," *National Education Association Journal of Proceedings and Addresses* (1891): 400.

39. David Tyack, "Preserving the Republic by Educating Republicans," in *Diversity and Its Discontents: Cultural Conflict and Common Ground in Contemporary American Society*, ed. Neil J. Smelser and Jeffrey C. Alexander (Princeton, N.J.: Princeton University Press, 1999), 72.

40. Shaw, "The True Character," 4209.

41. Diane Ravitch, *The Great School Wars: A History of the New York City Public Schools* (Baltimore: Johns Hopkins University Press, 1974), 244.

42. Frank V. Thompson, *Schooling of the Immigrant* (New York: Harper and Bros., 1920), 35.

43. Selma Cantor Berrol, *Immigrants at School, New York City, 1898–1914* (New York: Arno Press, 1978), 224.

44. See *Education of the Immigrant: Abstracts of Papers Read at Conference under the Auspices of the New York–New Jersey Committee of the North American Civic League for Immigrants, New York City, May 16 and 17, 1913*, reprinted in U.S. Bureau of Education, *Bulletin No. 51*, 18–24.

45. U.S. Immigration Commission, *Abstracts* 2:37.

46. *Constitution of 1879 as Amended 1943, Statutes*, 55th Legislature, 1943, 470, reprinted in *Education in the United States: A Documentary History*, vol. 5, ed. Sol Cohen (New York: Random House, 1974), 2978; State of California Statutes, 59th Legislature, 1947, 1792, reprinted in Cohen, *Education in the United States*, 5: 2979; *Report of the Special Committee of the Board of Supervisors of San Francisco*, reprinted in Cohen, *Education in the United States*, 3:1769; *Report of the San Francisco School Board*, reprinted in Cohen, *Education in the United States*, 4:2971; *Senate Document no. 147*, 59th Cong. 2nd sess., 1906, 1–2, reprinted in Cohen, *Education in the United States*, 5:2973.

47. *Mendez v. Westminster School Dist. of Orange County*, 64 F. Supp. 544 (S.D. Cal. 1946), aff'd, 161 F. 2nd 774 (9th Cir., 1947).

48. Oscar Handlin, "Education and the European Immigrant, 1820–1920," in *American Education and the European Immigrant, 1840–1940*, ed. Bernard J. Weiss (Urbana: University of Illinois Press, 1982), 112.

49. Ewa Morawska, *For Bread with Butter: The Life-Worlds of East Central Europeans in Johnstown, Pennsylvania, 1890–1940* (Cambridge: Cambridge University Press, 1985), 269.

50. Andrew T. Kopan, *Education and Greek Immigrants to Chicago, 1982–1973: A Study in Ethnic Survival* (New York: Garland Press, 1990), 108, 242.

51. Leonard Dinnerstein and David M. Reimers, *Ethnic Americans,* 4th ed. (New York: Columbia University Press, 1999), 43.

52. Robert Bell, "Public School Education of Second Generation Japanese in California," *Educational Psychology* 1 (1935): 20.

53. Julia Richman, "The Immigrant Child," *Journal of Proceedings and Addresses of the Forty-Fourth Annual Meeting, Asbury Park and Ocean Grove, New Jersey, July 3–7, 1905* (Winona, Wis.: National Education Association, 1905), 120.

54. Ravitch, *The Great School Wars,* 244.

55. Frances A. Kellor, "The Education of the Immigrant," *Educational Review* 48 (1914): 24.

56. Morawska, *For Bread with Butter,* 269.

57. Joel Perlmann, "Historical Legacies: 1840–1920," in *English Plus: Issues in Bilingual Education,* ed. Courtney B. Cazden and Catherine E. Snow, special issue, *Annals of the American Academy of Political and Social Science* 508 (March 1990): 36.

58. Kellor, "Education of the Immigrant," 30.

59. Adele Marie Shaw, "Evening Schools for Foreigners," *World's Work,* 9, no. 3 (January 1905): 5738.

60. Howard C. Hill, "The Americanization Movement," *American Journal of Sociology* 24, no. 6 (May 1919): 620; Shaw, "The True Character," 4204–21.

61. Hartmann, *Movement to Americanize,* 98–101.

62. Noah Pickus, *True Faith and Allegiance: Immigration and American Civic Nationalism* (Princeton, N.J.: Princeton University Press, 2007), 82–83.

63. Cremin, *Transformation of the School,* 60–64.

64. John Dewey, "Nationalizing Education," *National Education Association Journal of Addresses and Proceedings, Twenty-Fourth Annual Meeting, July 1–8,* 54 (1916): 185.

65. Jane Addams, "Immigration: A Field Neglected by the Scholar," convocation address, University of Chicago, 1904, reprinted in *Immigration and Americanization: Selected Readings,* ed. Philip Davis (Boston: Ginn and Co., 1920), 3–22.

66. Horace Mann, "Twelfth Annual Report (1848)," in Lawrence A. Cremin, *The Republic and the School: Horace Mann and the Education of Free Men* (New York: Teachers College Press, 1957), 87; Rosemary C. Salomone,

Visions of Schooling: Conscience, Community, and Common Education (New Haven, Conn.: Yale University Press, 2000), 17.

67. Rivka Shpak Lissak, *Pluralism and Progressives: Hull House and the New Immigrants, 1890–1919* (Chicago: University of Chicago Press, 1989), 123–131.

68. Orm Overland, *Immigrant Minds, American Identities: Making the United States Home, 1870–1930* (Chicago: University of Illinois Press, 2000), 39–40.

69. Ibid., 116–119.

70. "Eminent Citizens Join Patriot Band," *New York Times,* October 17, 1915, 1.

71. Nathan Glazer, "Assimilation Today: Is One Identity Enough?" in *Reinventing the Melting Pot: The New Immigrants and What It Means to Be American,* ed. Tamar Jacoby (New York: Basic Books, 2004), 62.

72. Frances Kellor, *Straight America* (New York: Macmillan, 1916), 37–38, 10–11.

73. "Teaching English to Factory Employees," editorial, *Detroit News,* September 6, 1915, 4.

74. U.S. Bureau of Education, *Report to the Secretary of the Interior for 1918* (Washington, D.C.: U.S. Government Printing Office, 1918), 88.

75. Stephanie Nicole Robinson, *History of Immigrant Female Students in Chicago Schools, 1900–1950* (New York: Peter Lang, 2004), 63.

76. U.S. Bureau of Education, *Americanization as a War Measure: Report of a Conference Called by the Secretary of the Interior* (Washington, D.C.: U.S. Government Printing Office, 1918), 14–16, 36, 43.

77. Hartmann, *Movement to Americanize,* 133.

78. U.S. Bureau of Education, *Report to the Secretary of the Interior for 1918* (1918), 88.

79. Hartmann, *Movement to Americanize,* 217.

80. Geoffrey Stone, *Perilous Times: Free Speech in Wartime* (New York: W. W. Norton, 2005).

81. Arthur S. Somers, "Americanism and the Americanization Problem," address delivered to the National Security League, New York City, September 26, 1918, 6–7.

82. U.S. Bureau of Education, *Americanization as a War Measure,* 27.

83. Department of the Interior, Bureau of Education, *Proceedings, Americanization Conference* (Washington, D.C.: U.S. Government Printing Office, 1919), 27–30 (address of P. P. Claxton, Commissioner of Education).

84. Ibid., 218 (address of Dr. Nathan Peyser, Director, Educational Alliance).

85. Ibid., 227 (address of Albert Mamatey, President, Slovak League).

86. Ibid., 234 (address of H. A. Miller, Professor of Sociology and Director, Mid-European Union, Oberlin College).

87. M. E. Ravage, "Standardizing the Immigrant," *New Republic,* May 1919, 145–147.

88. Frances A. Kellor, "What Is Americanization?" *Yale Review* 8 (January 1919): 288.

89. South Dakota, Session Laws, 1919, 45.

90. Indiana, Session Laws, 1919, ch. 8, p. 45; Harry Rider, "Americanization," *American Political Science Review* 4, no. 1 (February 1920): 111–112.

91. W. L. Harding, "Language Proclamation," from Iowa War Proclamations in *Iowa and War*, ed. B. F. Shambaugh (Iowa City: State Historical Society, 1919), 43–47.

92. Aneta Pavlenko, "'Languages of the Enemy': Foreign Language Education and National Identity," *International Journal of Bilingual Education and Bilingualism* 6, no. 5 (2003): 321.

93. John D. Fitz-Gerald, "National Aspects of Modern Language Teaching in the Present Emergency," *Modern language Journal* 3, no. 2 (November 1918): 62.

94. Arnold H. Leibowitz, "Language and the Law: The Exercise of Political Power through Official Designation of Language," in *Language and Politics*, ed. William M. O'Barr and Jean F. O'Barr (The Hague: Mouton, 1976), 451.

95. Thompson, *Schooling of the Immigrant*, 288.

96. South Dakota, Session Laws, 1919, 45.

97. *Meyer v. Nebraska*, 262 U.S. 390 (1923). (See Chapter 6.)

98. Einar Haugen, *Bilingualism in the Americas: A Bibliography and Research Guide* (Montgomery: University of Alabama Press, 1956), 80–84. (See Chapter 8.)

99. John Kulamer, "Americanization: The Other Side of the Case," *Atlantic Monthly*, March 1920, 423.

100. Thompson, *Schooling of the Immigrant*, 121–122.

101. "Plan to Make All Americans Real Americans," *Chicago Daily Tribune*, April 14, 1919, in U.S. Department of Labor, Immigration, and Naturalization Service, Americanization Section, record group 85, National Archives, file no. 27671/2680.

102. Peter Roberts, *The Problem of Americanization* (New York: Macmillan, 1920), v.

103. Carol Aronovici, "Americanization: Its Meaning and Function," *American Journal of Sociology* 25, no. 6 (May 1920): 714–715.

104. David B. Roediger, *Working toward Whiteness: How America's Immigrants Became White* (New York: Basic Books, 2005), 19.

105. John F. McClymer, "The Americanization Movement and the Education of the Foreign-Born Adult, 1914–25," in Weiss, *American Education*, 111.

106. John Higham, *Send These to Me: Immigrants in Urban America* (Baltimore: Johns Hopkins University Press, 1974), 53.

107. Arthur S. Link, *Woodrow Wilson and the Progressive Era, 1910–1917* (New York: Harper Torchbooks, 1954), 60–61.

108. Calvin Coolidge, State of the Union Address, December 6, 1923, in *Gutenberg Project EBook of State of the Union Addresses by Calvin Coolidge*, 10, www.gutenberg.org.

109. "Immigration from Leading Sources, as Affected by Restriction Laws," www.freerepublic.com.

110. Madison Grant, "America for Americans," *Forum,* December 1925, 351.

111. Henry Pratt Fairchild, *The Melting-Pot Mistake* (Boston: Little, Brown, and Co., 1926), 245, 261.

112. Henry H. Curran, "The New Immigrant," *Saturday Evening Post,* August 15, 1925, 25.

113. Geoffrey Gorer, *The American People: A Study of National Character* (New York: W. W. Norton, 1948), 25–26.

114. Marcus Lee Hansen, "The Problem of the Third Generation Immigrant," republication of the 1937 address (Rock Island, Ill.: Swenson Swedish Immigration Research Center and Augustana College Library, 1987), 12.

115. June Ganatir Alexander, *Ethnic Pride, American Patriotism: Slovaks and Other New Immigrants in the Interwar Period* (Philadelphia: Temple University Press, 2004), 224.

116. Roger Waldinger, "The 21st Century: An Entirely New Story," in Jacoby, *Reinventing the Melting Pot,* 81–82.

117. John Higham, "Cultural Responses to Immigration," in Smelser and Alexander, *Diversity and Its Discontents,* 54.

118. "U.S. 'Melting Pot' Is Seen as Failure," *New York Times,* December 25, 1938, sec. 2, p. 11.

119. Louis Adamic, "Thirty Million New Americans," *Harper's Magazine,* November 1934, 688–690.

120. Ronald K. Goodenow, "The Progressive Educator, Race and Ethnicity in the Depression Years: An Overview," *History of Education Quarterly* 15, no. 4 (Winter 1975): 374–375; David Tyack, *Seeking Common Ground: Public Schools in a Diverse Society* (Cambridge, Mass.: Harvard University Press, 2003), 79–81.

121. Nicholas V. Montalto, *A History of the Intercultural Educational Movement, 1924–1941* (New York: Garland Press, 1982), 123, 147.

122. Michael Olneck, "Symbolism and Ideology," *American Journal of Sociology* 98, no. 2 (February 1990): 153–154, 159.

123. Francis J. Brown, "New Tensions and Cultural Minorities," address delivered at the joint luncheon of the Adult Education Division of the National Education Association and the National Council on Naturalization and Citizenship, St. Louis, Missouri, February 28, 1940, 4.

124. Richard Alba and Victor Nee, *Remaking the American Mainstream: Assimilation and Contemporary Immigration* (Cambridge, Mass.: Harvard University Press, 2003), 110–117.

125. This change in language and presumably attitude is clear in my own family's documentation. Whereas my grandfather's naturalization certificate from 1932 separately designated his "race" as "Italian (So.)," the north-south distinction being "racially" significant, his "color" as "white," and his "former nationality" as "Italian," noticeably absent from my grandmother's certificate in 1949 was any mention of race, color, or region. It merely stated her "former nationality" as Italian. And while my grandmother was of noticeably darker skin tone than my grandfather, the immi-

gration clerk who happened to have an Italian surname deemed that she too was of "fair complexion."

Examining these documents for the first time brought to mind writer Louise DeSalvo's similar observations regarding her own Italian grandmother's naturalization papers issued during the war. By that time, race had disappeared from the certificate yet her grandmother was still designated as "white" of color and "dark" of "complexion," or as DeSalvo says, "dark white" despite her very fair skin which was clear from the photo appended to the document. (Louise DeSalvo, "Color: White/Complexion: Dark," in *Are Italians White? How Race Is Made in America,* ed. Jennifer Guglielmo and Salvatore Salerno [New York: Routledge, 2003], 25.) Apparently the nuances of skin color were in the eyes of the immigration clerk while the applicant unquestioningly certified that the "description given above" was "true." These gradual changes in the certificate from pre-war, to wartime, to postwar no doubt reflected a progressively changed attitude on the part of the government.

126. Alejandro Portes and Rubén G. Rumbaut, "Introduction: The Second Generation and the Children of Immigrants Longitudinal Study," *Ethnic and Racial Studies* 28 (November 2003): 985.

127. Nancy Foner and Richard Alba, "The Second Generation from the Last Great Wave of Immigration: Setting the Record Straight," *Migration Information Source* (Washington, D.C.: Migration Policy Institute, October 2006), 1.

128. Alejandro Portes and Rubén G. Rumbaut, *Immigrant America: A Portrait,* 3rd ed. (Berkeley: University of California Press, 2006), 892–893.

3. The New Immigrants

1. "Flushing Rejoices as Subway Opens," *New York Times,* January 22, 1928, 28.

2. Joseph Berger, "A Group as Diverse as the Borough Itself," *New York Times,* August 1, 2004, B1.

3. Internationals Network for Public Schools, www.internationalsnps.org.

4. Anthony J. DeFazio, "Language Awareness at the International High School," in *Encyclopedia of Language and Education,* vol. 6, ed. Leo Van Lier and David Corson (Dordrecht: Kluwer Academic, 1997), 103.

5. Michele Fine, Professor, City University of New York, who studied the International Schools in New York City, quoted in Trevor Hunnicutt, "School Provides Haven for Teens New to English: Oakland International High School Is Just for Immigrants," *San Francisco Chronicle,* August 3, 2008, B1; see also Michelle Fine, Brett Stoudt, and Valerie Futch, *The Internationals Network for Public Schools: A Quantitative and Qualitative Cohort Analysis of Graduation and Dropout Rates* (New York: Graduate Center, City University of New York, 2005).

6. Interview with Burt Rosenberg, former Principal, International High School, Long Island City, New York, May 5, 2003.

7. Lyndon B. Johnson, "Remarks at the Signing of the Immigration Bill, Liberty Island, New York," October 3, 1965, The American Presidency Project, www.presidency.ucsb.edu.

8. John F. Kennedy, "Letter to the President of the Senate and to the Speaker of the House of Representatives on the Immigration Laws," July 23, 1963, The American Presidency Project, www.presidency.ucsb.edu.

9. *Brown v. Board of Education,* 347 U.S. 484 (1954).

10. Hearings before the Subcommittee on Immigration and Naturalization of the Committee on the Judiciary, U.S. Senate, on S. 500, 89th Cong., 1st sess., February 1965, 3 (statement of Sen. Edward M. Kennedy).

11. Ibid., 65 (statement of Secretary of State Dean Rusk).

12. Audrey Singer, "Immigrant Gateways: Faces of the Next Cities" (presentation at Urban Libraries Council, Cleveland, Ohio, May 4, 2007) (Washington. D.C.: Brookings Institution, Metropolitan Policy Program, 2007).

13. Michael Hoefer, Nancy Rytina, and Christopher Campbell, *Estimates of the Unauthorized Population Residing in the United States: January 2006* (Washington, D.C.: Office of Immigration Statistics, U.S. Department of Homeland Security, August 2007).

14. Michael Fix, Margie McHugh, Aaron Matteo Terrazas, and Laureen Laglagaron, *Los Angeles on the Leading Edge* (Washington, D.C.: Migration Policy Institute, April 2008), 21.

15. *A Description of the Immigrant Population* (Washington. D.C.: Congressional Budget Office, November 2004), 1–6.

16. Jeffrey S. Passel and D'Vera Cohn, *U.S. Population Projections: 2005–2050* (Washington, D.C.: Pew Research Center, February 2008), 9–10.

17. Mark E. Pfeifer, "Cambodian, Hmong, Lao and Vietnamese Americans in the 2005 American Community Survey," *Journal of Southeast Asian American Education and Advancement* 3 (2008): 2.

18. Ibid., 7–9; Randy Capps, Michael Fix, Julie Murray, Jason Ost, Jeffrey S. Passel, and Shinta Herwantoro, *The New Demography of America's Schools* (Washington, D.C.: Urban Institute, September 2005), 11–12; Andrew Wainer, *The New Latino South and the Challenge to Public Education* (Los Angeles, Calif.: Tomas Rivera Policy Institute, November 2004), 8–10.

19. Audrey Singer, introduction to *Twenty-First Century Gateways: Immigrant Incorporation in Suburban America,* ed. Audrey Singer, Susan W. Hardwick, and Caroline B. Bretell (Washington, D.C.: Brookings Institution Press, 2008), 14–17.

20. Ford Fessenden, "The New Crossroads of the World," *New York Times,* August 27, 2006, New Jersey Section, 14.

21. U. S. Government Accountability Office, *Information Sharing Could Help Institutions Identify and Address Challenges Some Asian Americans and Pacific Islander Students Face* (Washington, D.C.: USGAO, July 2007), 17, fig. 4; *Facts, Not Fiction: Setting the Record Straight* (New York: New York University and the College Board, 2008).

22. Mary C. Waters, *Ethnic Options: Choosing Identities in America* (Berkeley: University of California Press, 1990), 157–158.

23. Rachel Moran, "Bilingual Education, Immigration, and the Culture of Disinvestment," *Journal of Gender, Race, and Justice* 2 (1999): 207.

24. "Modern Mobility Blurs Definition of 'Home,'" April 5, 2006, www.cnn.com.

25. Naz Rassool, "Sustaining Linguistic Diversity within the Global Cultural Economy: Issues of Language Rights and Linguistic Possibilities," *Comparative Education* 40, no. 2 (May 2004): 204.

26. Linda Basch, Nina Glick Schiller, and Cristina Szanton Blanc, *Nations Unbound: Transnational Projects, Postcolonial Predicaments, and Deterritorialized Nation-States* (Amsterdam: Gordon and Breach Science, 1995), 7.

27. Jeremy Rifkin, *The European Dream: How Europe's Vision of the Future Is Quietly Eclipsing the American Dream* (New York: Tarcher/Penguin, 2004), 258.

28. Nina Glick Schiller and Georges E. Fouron, "Terrains of Blood and Nation: Haitian Transnational Social Fields," *Ethnic and Racial Studies* 22, no. 2 (March 1999): 347.

29. Jason DeParle, "World Banker and His Cash Return Home," *New York Times,* March 18, 2008, A1.

30. Manuel Orozco and Rebecca Rouse, "Migrant Hometown Associations and Opportunities for Development: A Global Perspective," *Migration Information Source* (Migration Policy Institute, Washington, D.C.), February 1, 2007, 1, www.migrationinformation.org.

31. See Nadje Al-Ali and Khalid Koser, eds., *New Approaches to Migration? Transnational Communities and the Transformation of Home* (New York: Routledge, 2002).

32. Dilip Ratha, Sanket Mohapatra, K. M. Vijayalakshmi, and Zhimel Xu, *Remittance Trends 2007: Migration and Development Brief 3* (Washington, D.C.: World Bank, November 29, 2007), 2–3; Muzaffar A. Chisti, "The Phenomenal Rise in Remittances to India: A Closer Look," *MPI Policy Brief* (Migration Policy Institute, Washington, D.C.), May 2007, 1.

33. *Global Economic Prospects 2006: Economic Implications of Remittances and Migration* (Washington, D.C.: International Bank for Reconstruction and Development/ World Bank, 2006), 89.

34. Sarah Gammage, "El Salvador: Despite End to Civil War, Emigration Continues," *Migration Information Source* (Migration Policy Institute, Washington D.C.), July 2007, www.migrationinformation.org.

35. Robert Suro, *Remittance Senders and Receivers: Tracking the Transnational Channels, Report of the Pew Hispanic Center* (Washington, D.C., November 24, 2003), 5, 13.

36. "Fewer Latin Americans Sending Money Home from the United States, Survey Finds," press release, Inter-American Development Bank, April 30, 2008.

37. Nathan Glazer, "Assimilation Today: Is One Identity Enough?" in *Rein-*

venting the Melting Pot: The New Immigrants and What It Means to Be American, ed. Tamar Jacoby (New York: Basic Books, 2004), 63.

38. Often discussed as if they were interchangeable, nationality and citizenship are distinguishable. *Nationality* refers to the legal relationship between an individual and the state of origin, affiliation, or loyalty. It includes both citizens and noncitizens. It can also refer to membership in a community sharing a national identity, culture, or ethnicity even without a state, such as the Basques who enjoy semi-autonomous status within Spain. *Citizenship* grants individuals the right to participate in the political life of the state, typically by voting in national elections or standing for election to political office.

39. Peggy Levitt and Rafael de la Dehesa, "Transnational Migration and the Redefinition of the State: Variations and Explanations," *Ethnic and Racial Studies* 26, no. 4 (July 2003): 594–595.

40. Ginger Thompson, "Mexico's Migrants Profit from Dollars Sent Home," *New York Times,* February 23, 2005, A1.

41. Peter H. Schuck, "The Re-Evaluation of American Citizenship," *Georgetown Immigration Law Journal* 12, no. 1 (1997): 11.

42. Jeffrey S. Passel, *Growing Share of Immigrants Choosing Naturalization,* Report of the Pew Hispanic Center, Washington, D.C., March 28, 2007.

43. Stephen Castles, "Migration, Citizenship, and Education," in *Diversity and Citizenship Education,* ed. James A. Banks (New York: Jossey-Bass), 17.

44. See, generally, Robert Smith, "Diasporic Memberships in Historical Perspective: Comparative Insights from the Mexican, Italian and Polish Cases," *International Migration Review* 37, no. 3 (2003): 724–759.

45. Barbara Schmitter, "Sending States and Immigrant Minorities—The Case of Italy," *Comparative Studies in Society and History* 26, no. 2 (April 1984): 328.

46. Jorge Durand, Douglas S. Massey, and Emilio A. Parrado, "The New Era of Mexican Migration to the United States," *Journal of American History* 86, no. 2 (September 1999): 526–527.

47. Raúl Delgado-Wise and Luis Eduardo Guarnizo, "Migration and Development: Lessons from the Mexican Experience," *Migration Information Source* (Migration Policy Institute, Washington, D.C.), February 1, 2007, www.migrationinformation.org.

48. "Plazas Comunitarias: An Educational Program for Mexicans Living Abroad," Office of the Institute for Mexicans Abroad, Consulate General of Mexico in Atlanta.

49. "Concurso 'Éste es mi Mexico,'" (winner selection), Institute of Mexicans Abroad, October 4, 2007, www.ime.gob.mx.

50. Aaron Terrazas and Michael Fix, *The Binational Option: Meeting the Instructional Needs of Limited English Proficient Students* (Washington, D.C.: Migration Policy Institute, November 2009), 29.

51. Jorge A. Vargas, *Nationality, Naturalization and Dual Nationality under Mexican Law,* Legal Studies Research Paper Series, Research Paper No. 07-103 (May 2007), 30, www.ssrn.com.

52. Robert Courtney Smith, *Mexican New York: Transnational Lives of New Immigrants* (Berkeley: University of California Press, 2006), 284–285.

53. "New York Mogul Takes Business Home," *Buscador,* July 29, 2001, www.fox.presidencia.gob.mx.

54. See Glazer, "Assimilation Today," in Jacoby, *Reinventing the Melting Pot,* 69–71.

55. Antonio Olivo, "Mexican President Pledges to Boost Economy," *Chicago Tribune,* February 12, 2008, 2.

56. Yossi Shain, *Marketing the American Creed Abroad: Diasporas in the U.S. and Their Homelands* (Cambridge: Cambridge University Press, 1999), 170.

57. Peggy Levitt and Rafael de la Dehesa, "Transnational Migration and the Redefinition of the State: Variations and Explanations," *Ethnic and Racial Studies* 26, no. 4 (July 2003): 587–588.

58. Bella Feldman-Bianco, "Multiple Layers of Time and Space: The Construction of Class, Race, Ethnicity, and Nationalism among Portuguese Immigrants," in *Towards a Transnational Perspective on Migration,* ed. Nina Glick Schiller, Linda Basch, and Cristina Blanc-Szanton (New York: New York Academy of Sciences, 1992), 149.

59. Ewa Morawska, "Exploring Diversity in Immigrant Assimilation and Transnationalism: Poles and Russian Jews in Philadelphia," *International Migration Review* 38, no. 4 (Winter 2004): 1393–95.

60. Roger D. Waldinger, *Between "Here" and "There": Immigrant Cross-Border Activities and Loyalties,* On-line Working Paper Series, CCPR-054-06 (Los Angeles: University of California, California Center for Population Research, August 2006), 16.

61. Peggy Levitt and Mary C. Waters, introduction to *The Changing Face of Home: The Transnational Lives of the Second Generation,* ed. Peggy Levitt and Mary C. Waters (New York: Russell Sage Foundation, 2004), 9.

62. Telephone interview with Oscar Medina, English Language Learner Services Coordinator, San Diego County Office of Education, October 13, 2005.

63. Nancy Foner, "Second Generation Transnationalism, Then and Now," in Levitt and Waters, *Changing Face of Home,* 250.

64. Rubén Rumbaut, "Severed or Sustained Attachments? Language, Identity, and Imagined Communities in the Post-Immigrant Generation," in Levitt and Waters, *Changing Face of Home,* 90.

65. Georges E. Fouron and Nina Glick-Schiller, "The Generation of Identity: Redefining the Second Generation within a Transnational Field," in Levitt and Waters, *Changing Face of Home,* 194.

66. Nazli Kibria, "Of Blood, Belonging, and Homeland Trips: Transnationalism and Identity among Second-Generation Chinese and Koreans," in Levitt and Waters, *Changing Face of Home,* 310.

67. Interview with Madhulika Khandelwa, Director, Asian American Center, Queens College, Queens, New York, May 5, 2007.

68. Marcelo Suárez-Oroczo and Carola Suárez-Oroczo, "Some Conceptual Considerations in the Interdisciplinary Study of Immigrant Children," in

Immigrant Voices: In Search of Educational Equity, ed. Enrique (Henry) T. Trueba and Lilia I. Bartolemé (Lanham, Md.: Rowman and Littlefield, 2000), 29.

69. Philip Kasinitz, Mary C. Waters, John H. Mollenkopf, and Merih Anil, "Transnationalism and the Children of Immigrants in Contemporary New York," in Levitt and Waters, *Changing Face of Home,* 119.

4. Language, Identity, and Belonging

1. "Calls in Louisiana to Require English at Commencement," *New York Times,* June 30, 2008, A17.
2. Charles Taylor, "The Politics of Recognition," in *Multiculturalism: Examining the Politics of Recognition,* ed. Amy Gutmann (Princeton, N.J.: Princeton University Press, 1994), 33–34.
3. Henri Tajfel, *Differentiation between Social Groups* (London: Academic Press, 1978), 63.
4. Erik H. Erikson, *Childhood and Society* (New York: W. W. Norton, 1950), 242.
5. Philip Gleason, "American Identity and Americanization," in *Harvard Encyclopedia of American Ethnic Groups* (Cambridge, Mass.: Harvard University Press, 1980), 31, citing Erik H. Erikson, "Autobiographic Notes of the Identity Crisis," *Daedalus* 99, no. 4 (1970): 747–748.
6. Erikson, "Autobiographic Notes," 748 (emphasis added).
7. Mary Jane Rotheram and Jean S. Phinney, introduction to *Children's Ethnic Socialization: Pluralism and Development,* ed. Jean S. Phinney and Mary Jane Rotheram (Newbury Park, Calif.: Sage, 1987), 12–13.
8. Bela Feldman-Bianco, "Multiple Layers of Time and Space: The Construction of Class, Ethnicity, and Nationalism among Portuguese Immigrants," in *Towards a Transnational Perspective on Migration: Race, Class, Ethnicity, and Nationalism Reconsidered,* ed. Nina Glick, Linda Basch, and Cristina Blanc-Szanton (New York: New York Academy of Sciences, 1992), 145.
9. Jhumpa Lahiri, *The Namesake* (New York: Houghton Mifflin, 2003), 49–50.
10. Edward Sapir, "Language," in *Edward Sapir: Selected Writings in Language, Culture, and Personality,* ed. David G. Mandelbaum (Berkeley: University of California Press, 1949), 15–17 (article reprinted from *Encyclopedia of the Social Sciences* [New York: Macmillan, 1933], 9:155–169).
11. Michael Ignatieff, *Blood and Belonging: Journeys into the New Nationalism* (New York: Farrar, Strauss and Giroux, 1993), 10.
12. Benjamin Lee Whorf, *Language, Thought, and Reality* (Cambridge, Mass.: MIT Press, 1956); George Herbert Mead, *Movements of Thought in the Nineteenth Century* (Chicago: University of Chicago Press, 1936).
13. Aneta Pavlenko, "Bilingualism and Thought," in *Handbook of Bilingualism,* ed. Judith F. Kroll and Annette M. B. De Groot (Oxford: Oxford University Press, 2005), 536.

14. Steven Pinker, *The Stuff of Thought: Language as a Window into Human Nature* (New York: Viking, 2007), 125, 244–246, 248. See also Lera Boroditsky, "Linguistic Relativity," in *Encyclopedia of Cognitive Science*, ed. Lynn Nadel (London: Macmillan Press, 2003), 917–921.
15. Harold Schiffman, *Linguistic Culture and Language Policy* (New York: Routledge, 1966), 58.
16. Jack M. Balkin, *Cultural Software: A Theory of Ideology* (New Haven, Conn.: Yale University Press, 1998), 24; Adeno Addis, "Cultural Integrity and Political Unity: The Politics of Language in Multilingual States," *Arizona Law Review* 33 (Fall 2001): 727.
17. Andrée Tabouret-Keller, "Language and Identity," in *The Handbook of Sociolinguistics*, ed. Florian Coulmas (Oxford: Blackwell, 1997), 317.
18. John J. Gumperz, *Discourse Strategies* (Cambridge: Cambridge University Press, 1982), 58–99.
19. Aneta Pavlenko, "Bilingual Selves," in *Bilingual Minds: Emotional Experience, Expression and Representation*, ed. Aneta Pavlenko (Clevedon, England: Multilingual Matters, 2006), 29.
20. Jean-Marc Dewaele, "Perceived Language Dominance and Language Preference for Emotional Speech," in *First Language Attrition: Theoretical Perspectives*, ed. Barbara Schmid, Monika S. Kopke, Merel Keijzer, and Susan Dostert (Amsterdam: John Benjamins, 2007), 101.
21. David Luna, Torsten Ringberg, and Laura A. Peracchio, "One Individual, Two Identities: Frame Switching among Bilinguals," *Journal of Consumer Research* 35 (August 2008): 279–293.
22. Michèle Koven, *Selves in Two Languages: Bilinguals' Verbal Enactments of Identity in French and Portuguese* (Amsterdam: John Benjamins, 2007), 72, 238.
23. Jean Portante, "Strange Language. Let's Say It's a Whale. . . ," *UNESCO Courier* 1 (2008), www.unesco.org/courier.
24. Harold Schiffman, "Language, Primordialism and Sentiment," in *Languages of Sentiment: Cultural Constructions of Emotional Substrates*, ed. Gary B. Palmer and Debra J. Occhi, vol. 18 of *Advances in Consciousness Research* (Amsterdam: John Benjamins, 1999), 25–26.
25. Pierre Bourdieu, *Language and Symbolic Power*, ed. John B. Thompson, trans. Gino Raymond and Matthew Adamson (Cambridge, Mass: Harvard University Press, 1991), 66–67.
26. John Earl Joseph, *Language and Identity: National, Ethnic, Religious* (New York: Palgrave Macmillan, 2004), 168–169.
27. Tabouret-Keller, "Language and Identity," 315–317.
28. Amado A. Padilla, "Psychology," in *Handbook of Language and Ethnic Identity*, ed. Joshua A. Fishman (Oxford: Oxford University Press, 1999), 113.
29. Joseph, *Language and Identity*, 225.
30. Pierre Bourdieu, "The Economics of Linguistic Exchanges," *Social Science Information* 16 (1977): 648.
31. Dmitri Priven, "Grievability of First Language Loss: Towards a Reconcep-

tualisation of European Minority Language Education Practices," *International Journal of Bilingual Education and Bilingualism* 2, no. 1 (2008): 103.

32. Wallace E. Lambert, "Culture and Language as Factors in Learning and Education," paper presented at the Annual Convention of the Teachers of English to Speakers of Other Languages, Denver, Colo., March 1974), ERIC document 096 820, www.eric.ed.gov; Lambert, "Effects of Bilingualism on the Individual," in *Bilingualism: Psychological, Social and Educational Implications*, ed. Peter A. Hornby (New York: Academic Press, 1977), 19.

33. Joshua Fishman, *Reversing Language Shift: Theoretical and Empirical Foundations of Assistance to Threatened Languages* (Clevedon, England: Multilingual Matters, 1991), 60.

34. David Crystal, *Language Death* (Cambridge: Cambridge University Press, 2000), 45.

35. "Pourquoi le plurilinguisme?" *Charte européenne du plurilinguisme* (Paris: Observatoire européean du plurilinguisme, 2005), 3.

36. Thijl Sunier, "National Language and Mother Tongue," in *Civil Enculturation: Nation-State, School and Ethnic Difference in the Netherlands, Britain, Germany and France,* ed. Werner Schiffauer, Gerd Baumann, Riva Kastoryano, and Steven Vertovec (New York: Berghahn Books, 2004), 147–163.

37. Mairead Nic Craith, *Europe and the Politics of Language: Citizens, Migrants and Outsiders* (New York: Palgrave Macmillan, 2006), 32.

38. Will Kymlicka, *Politics in the Vernacular: Nationalism, Multiculturalism and Citizenship* (Oxford: Oxford University Press, 2001), 312.

39. Tabouret-Keller, "Language and Identity," 319–320.

40. Michael Collins, "Alexander Wants Workplaces to Be English-Only," *Knoxville News Sentinel,* February 18, 2008, www.knoxnews.com.

41. *Equal Employment Opportunity Commission v. Salvation Army,* No. 07-CA-10620 (WGY), consent decree (D. Mass. November 6, 2008).

42. Britta Schneider, *Linguistic Human Rights and Migrant Languages* (Frankfurt am Main: Peter Lang, 2005), 26.

43. Guus Extra and Kutlay Yagmur, *Urban Multilingualism in Europe: Immigrant Minority Languages at Home and School* (Clevedon, England: Multilingual Matters, 2004), 15.

44. Jean-Jacques Rousseau and Johann Gottfried Herder, *On the Origin of Language: Two Essays,* trans. John H. Moran and Alexander Gode (Chicago: University of Chicago Press, 1986), 5.

45. Benedict Anderson, *Imagined Communities: Reflections on the Origins and Spread of Nationalism,* 2nd ed. (London: Verso, 1991).

46. E-mail correspondence from Harold Schiffman, Professor Emeritus of Dravidian Linguistics and Culture, University of Pennsylvania, July 30, 2008.

47. Kenneth L. Karst, *Belonging to America* (New Haven, Conn.: Yale University Press, 1989), 99.

48. John Ogbu, "Variability in Minority School Performance: A Problem in

Search of an Explanation," *Anthropology and Education Quarterly* 28 (1987): 312–334; Will Kymlicka, *Multicultural Citizenship: A Liberal Theory of Minority Rights* (Oxford: Oxford University Press, 1995), 97–101; Stephen May, *Language and Minority Rights: Ethnicity, Nationalism and the Politics of Language* (Essex, England: Pearson Education, 2001), 86–87.

49. Ogbu, "Variability," 321.

50. Yasir Suleiman, "Constructing Languages, Constructing National Identities," in *The Sociolinguistics of Identity,* ed. Tope Omoniyi and Goodith White (London: Continuum, 2006), 59.

51. Jeffra Flaitz, ed. *The Ideology of English: French Perceptions of English as a World Language* (Berlin: Mouton de Gruyter, 1988), 9.

52. John Walsh and Wilson McCleod, "An Overcoat Wrapped around an Invisible Man? Language Legislation and Language Revitalization in Ireland and Scotland," *Language Policy* 7 (2008): 25–27.

53. Kari Lydersen, "Preserving Languages Is About More Than Words," *Washington Post,* March 16, 2009, A07.

54. Adeno Addis, "Constitutionalizing Deliberative Democracy in Multilingual Societies," *Berkeley Journal of International Law* 25 (2007): 132 n. 65; Juli S. Charkes, "For the Return Trip, a Dose of Irish Heritage," *New York Times,* Sunday, October 21, 2007, Westchester Section, 1, 7.

55. Joseph, *Language and Identity,* 225.

56. James Coleman and Thomas Hoffer, *Public and Private High Schools* (New York: Basic Books, 1987), 223.

57. Alasdair MacIntyre, *After Virtue* (South Bend, Ind.: Notre Dame University Press, 1981), 201.

58. Padilla, "Psychology," 116.

59. Shirin Hakimzadeh and D'Vera Cohn, *English Language Usage among Hispanics in the United States* (Washington, D.C.: Pew Hispanic Center, November 29, 2007), 13.

60. Edward George Hartmann, *The Movement to Americanize the Immigrant* (New York: Columbia University Press, 1948), 22–23.

61. Jane Addams, "Foreign Born Children in the Primary Grades," *National Education Association Journal of Proceedings and Addresses of the Twenty-Sixth Meeting* (1897): 106–110.

62. Jane Addams, "Immigrants and Their Children," in *Twenty Years at Hull House* (New York: Macmillan, 1910), 231–258.

63. U.S. Immigration Commission Reports, vol. 23, San Francisco (1911), cited in *Education in the United States: A Documentary History,* vol. 1, ed. Sol Cohen (New York: Random House, 1974), 152.

64. Leonard Covello, *The Heart Is the Teacher* (New York: McGraw-Hill, 1958), 44.

65. See, e.g., Oscar Handlin, "Education and the European Immigrant, 1820–1920," in *American Education and the European Immigrant, 1840–1940,* ed. Bernard J. Weiss (Urbana: University of Illinois Press, 1982), 5.

66. Robert Putnam, *Bowling Alone: The Collapse and Revival of American Community* (New York: Simon and Schuster, 2000), sec. 4.

67. Interview with Deycy Avita, Education Reform Program Coordinator, New York Immigration Coalition, New York City, June 7, 2007.

68. Grace Cho and Stephen Krashen, "The Negative Consequences of Heritage Language Loss and Why We Should Care," in *Heritage Language Development*, ed. Stephen D. Krashen, Lucy Tse, and Jeff McQuillan (Culver City, Calif.: Language Education Associates, 1998), 33–36.

69. Louis-Jean Calvet, *La guerre des langues et les politiques linguistiques* (Paris: Hachette, 1999), 104–105.

70. Carola Suárez-Oroczo and Marcelo M. Suárez-Oroczo, *Learning a New Land: Immigrant Students in American Society* (Cambridge, Mass.: Belknap Press, 2008), 372.

71. Carola Suárez-Orozco and Marcelo M. Suárez Orozco, *Children of Immigration* (Cambridge, Mass.: Harvard University Press, 2001), 74, 106.

72. Lily Wong-Fillmore, "Loss of Family Languages: Should Educators Be Concerned?" *Theory into Practice* 39, no. 4 (Autumn 2000): 206.

73. Lily Wong-Fillmore, "When Learning a Second Language Means Losing the First," *Early Childhood Research Quarterly* 6 (1991): 343.

74. Cho and Krashen, "Negative Consequences," in Krashen et al., *Heritage Language Development*," 33–34.

75. Grace Cho, Kyung-Sook Cho, and Lucy Tse, "Why Ethnic Minorities Want to Develop Their Heritage Language: The Case of Korean-Americans," *Language, Culture and Curriculum* 10, no. 2 (1997): 108.

76. Interview with Jessica O'Donovan, Director of Programs for English Language Learners, Port Chester School District, Rye Brook, New York, December 5, 2006.

77. Alejandro Portes and Lingxin Hao, "*E Pluribus Unum*: Bilingualism and Loss of Language in the Second Generation," *Sociology of Language* 71, no. 4 (October 1998): 285.

78. Grace Cho, "The Role of Heritage Language in Social Interactions and Relationships: Reflections from a Language Minority Group," *Bilingual Research Journal* 24, no. 4 (Fall 2000): 333–348; Leanne Hinton, "Trading Tongues: Loss of Heritage Languages in the United States," *English Today* 15, no. 4 (October 1999), 21–30.

79. Alejandro Portes and Rubén G. Rumbaut, *Immigrant America: A Portrait*, 3rd ed. (Berkeley, Calif.: University of California Press, 2006), 277.

80. Robert Taylor, "The Role Language Plays in One's Search for Self," review of *Hunger of Memory* by Richard Rodriguez, *Boston Globe*, March 10, 1983, 1.

81. Richard Rodriguez, *Hunger of Memory: The Education of Richard Rodriguez* (New York: Bantam Books, 1983), 21, 25–27, 32.

82. Mary Ann Zehr, "Scholars Mull the 'Paradox' of Immigrants," *Education Week*, March 18, 2009, 1.

83. Russell W. Rumberger and Katherine A. Larsen, "Toward Explaining Differences in Educational Achievement among Mexican American Language Minority Students," *Sociology of Education* 71 (1998): 68–92; Carl L. Bankston III and Min Zhou, "Effects of Minority-Language Literacy on the Academic Achievement of Vietnamese Youth in New Orleans," *Sociology*

of Education 68 (1995): 1–17; Ricardo D. Stanton-Salazar and Sanford M. Dornbusch, "Social Capital and the Reproduction of Inequality—Information Networks among Mexican-Origin High School Students," *Sociology of Education* 68 (1995): 116–135; Margaret Gibson, *Accommodation without Assimilation: Sikh Immigrants in an American High School* (Ithaca, N.Y.: Cornell University Press, 1988); Roberto M. Fernandez and Francois Nielsen, "Bilingualism and Hispanic Scholastic Achievement: Some Baseline Results," *Social Science Research* 14 (1986): 43–70.

84. Cynthia Feliciano, "The Benefits of Biculturalism: Exposure to Immigrant Culture and Dropping out of School among Asian and Latino Youths," *Social Science Quarterly* 82, no. 4 (December 2001): 866–879.

85. Paul Smokowski, Rachel L. Buchanan, and Martica L. Bacalao, "Acculturation and Adjustment in Latino Adolescents: How Cultural Risk Factors and Assets Influence Multiple Domains of Adolescent Mental Health," *Journal of Primary Prevention* 30 (2009): 371–379.

86. Alejandro Portes and Rubén G. Rumbaut, *Legacies: The Story of the Immigrant Second Generation* (Berkeley, Calif.: University of California Press, 2001), 274; Alejandro Portes and Lingxin Hao, "The Price of Uniformity: Language, Family and Personality Adjustment in the Immigrant Second Generation," *Ethnic and Racial Studies* 25, no. 6 (November 2002): 908.

87. Chris Woodruff, *English Proficiency across Generations: Evidence and Consequences, Final Report* (San Diego: University of California Linguistic Minority Research Institute, December 2007).

88. Andrew T. Kopan, *Education and Greek Immigrants to Chicago, 1982–1973: A Study in Ethnic Survival* (New York: Garland Press, 1990), 108, 242.

89. Theresa Hsu Chao, "Chinese Heritage Community Language Schools in the United States," *CAL Digest*, June 1997, 213–214; Evelyn Shih, "Heritage Language Schools Help Bind Families of Immigrants," NorthJersey .com, October 15, 2006.

90. Russell Working, "Immigrant Influx to Chicago Suburbs Spawns Foreign Language Schools for Kids," *Chicago Tribune*, January 4, 2008, 4.

91. Eun Kyung Kim, "Language Gap Affects Young Bosnians at School, Home," *St. Louis Post-Dispatch*, March 8, 2006, www.STLtoday.com.

92. Interview with Juliet Choi, Staff Attorney, Asian American Justice Center, Washington, D.C., November 7, 2005.

93. Carol J. Compton, "Heritage Language Communities and Schools: Challenges and Recommendations," in *Heritage Languages in America: Preserving a National Resource*, ed. Joy Kreeft, Donald A. Ranard, and Scott McGinnis (McHenry, Ill.: Center for Applied Linguistics and Delta Systems, 2001), 145–165.

94. Marcelo M. Suárez-Orozco, "Everything You Ever Wanted to Know about Assimilation but Were Afraid to Ask," *Daedalus* 129, no. 4 (Fall 2000), 20.

95. Interview with Peter Kwong, Professor of Political Science, Hunter College, New York City, May 14, 2007.

96. Min Zhou and Susan S. Kim, "Community Forces, Social Capital, and Educational Achievement: The Case of Supplementary Education in the Chi-

nese and Korean Immigrant Communities," *Harvard Educational Review* 76, no. 1 (Spring 2006): 22.

97. Yangguang Chen, "Contributing to Success: Chinese Parents and the Community School," in *Multilingual Learning: Stories from Schools and Communities in Britain*, ed. Jean Conteh, Peter Martin, and Leena Helavaara Robertson (Staffordshire, England: Trentham Books, 2007), 84.

98. Cho, "Role of Heritage Language"; Hinton, "Trading Tongues."

99. Charkes, "For the Return Trip," 1, 7.

100. Guadalupe Valdes, "Heritage Language Students: Profiles and Possibilities," in Kreeft et al., *Heritage Languages in America*, 38–39.

101. Mary Ann Zehr, "'Heritage Speakers': Loss of a Treasure?" *Education Week*, April 6, 2006, 24.

102. See also Lucy Tse, "Ethnic Identity Formation and Its Implications for Heritage Language Development," in Krashen, et al., *Heritage Language Development*, 15–29; Jean S. Phinney, "Stages of Ethnic Identity in Minority Group Adolescents," *Journal of Early Adolescence* 9, nos. 1–2 (1989): 34–49.

103. Kiran Desai, *The Inheritance of Loss* (New York: Grove Press, 2006); "Kiran Desai: Exclusive Interview," *The Man Booker Prizes* (interview by Sophie Rochester, 2007), www.themanbookerprize.com.

104. Madhulika S. Khandelwal, *Becoming American, Being Indian: An Immigrant Community in New York City* (Ithaca N.Y.: Cornell University Press, 2002), 43.

5. Rights, Ambivalence, and Ambiguities

1. *Brown v. Board of Education*, 347 U.S. 484 (1954); Rosemary C. Salomone, *Equal Education under Law: Legal Rights and Federal Policy in the Post-"Brown" Era* (New York: St. Martin's Press, 1986), 78–79.

2. Tove Skutnabb-Kangas and Robert Phillipson, "Linguistic Human Rights, Past and Present," in *Linguistic Human Rights: Overcoming Linguistic Discrimination*, ed. Tove Skutnabb-Kangas and Robert Phillipson (Berlin: Mouton de Gruyter, 1994), 71.

3. *Strauder v. West Virginia*, 100 U.S. 303 (1890). See also *Hernandez v. Texas*, 347 U.S. 475 (1954).

4. *Report of the Commissioner of Education*, 1919, 43, cited in Kenneth B. O'Brien, "Education, Americanization and the Supreme Court: The 1920s," *American Quarterly* 13 (1961): 163.

5. *Meyer v. State*, 187 N.W. 100, 102 (Nebraska 1922), rev'd, 262 U.S. 390 (1923).

6. *Brief and Argument of the State of Nebraska, Defendant in Error, Meyer v. Nebraska and Nebraska District of Evangelical Lutheran Synod of Missouri, Meyer v. Nebraska*, 262 U.S. 390 (1923), 13–15.

7. *Meyer*, 262 U.S. at 402.

8. *Lochner v. New York*, 198 U.S. 45 (1905).

9. *Meyer*, 262 U.S. at 400.

10. Ibid., 401.

11. William Ross, *Forging New Freedoms: Nativism, Education, and the Constitution, 1917–1927* (Lincoln: University of Nebraska Press, 1994), 131.

12. Ellwood P. Cubberly, "The American School Program from the Standpoint of the Nation," *N.E.A. Proceedings* 61 (1923): 181; I. N. Edwards, "State Educational Policy and the Supreme Court of the United States," *Elementary School Journal* 26 (1925): 25.

13. Arthur Miller, *Western Democrat* (New York: Wilfred Funk, 1940), 209.

14. *Pierce v. Society of Sisters,* 268 U.S. 510, 535–536 (1925).

15. *Farrington v. Tokushige,* 273 U.S. 284, 298 (1927).

16. Martha Minow, *Making All the Difference: Inclusion, Exclusion, and American Law* (Ithaca, N.Y.: Cornell University Press, 1990), 27.

17. *Meyer,* 262 U.S. at 402.

18. For a well-reasoned argument supporting that view, see Barbara Bennett Woodhouse, "'Who Owns the Child?' *Meyer* and *Pierce* and the Child as Property," *William and Mary Law Review* 33 (1992): 995–1122.

19. *Planned Parenthood v. Casey,* 505 U.S. 833, 851 (1992); see also *Stanley v. Illinois,* 405 U.S. 645 (1972); *Quilloin v. Walcott,* 434 U.S. 246 (1978); *Parham v. J. R.,* 442 U.S. 594 (1979); *Santosky v. Kramer,* 455 U.S. 745 (1982); *Washington v. Glucksberg,* 521 U.S. 702 (1997).

20. *Troxel v. Granville,* 530 U.S. 57, 65–66 (2000).

21. For a comprehensive discussion of *Meyer v. Nebraska,* see Ross, *Forging New Freedoms.*

22. *Brown,* 347 U.S. at 393, citing *McLaurin v. Oklahoma State Regents,* 339 U.S. 637 (1950).

23. *Brown,* 347 U.S. at 494.

24. Minow, *Making All the Difference,* 27.

25. *Brown,* 347 U.S. at 493.

26. See Jack M. Balkin, "Rewriting *Brown:* A Guide to the Opinions," in *What Brown v. Board of Education Should Have Said,* ed. Jack M. Balkin (New York: New York University Press, 2001), 56–59.

27. See *Griswold v. Connecticut,* 381 U.S 479 (1965); *Roe v. Wade,* 410 U.S. 113 (1973).

28. Terry Eastland and William Bennett, *Counting by Race* (New York: Basic Books, 1979), 6.

29. House of Representatives, Report No. 143, 89th Cong., 1st sess., 1965 (statement of Francis Keppel, U.S. Commissioner of Education).

30. Charles F. Abernathy, "Title VI and the Constitution: A Regulatory Model for Defining Discrimination," *Georgetown Law Journal* 70 (1981): 28–32.

31. 45 Code of Federal Regulations § 80.3 (b) (2) (2008).

32. 42 U.S.C. § 2000d (Supp. 2008).

33. *Hearings before the Subcommittee on Education of the Committee on Education and Labor, House of Representatives, on H.R. 9840 and H.R. 10224,* 90th Cong., 1st sess. (June 1967), 49 (statement of Commissioner of Education Harold Howe II).

34. See John Gardner to Capitol Hill, LBJ Library, University of Texas at Aus-

tin, cited in Hugh Davis Graham, *The Uncertain Triumph: The Kennedy and Johnson Years* (Chapel Hill: University of North Carolina Press, 1984), 158.

35. *Hearings before the Subcommittee on Education of the Committee on Education and Labor, House of Representatives, on H.R. 9840 and H.R. 10224,* 90th Cong., 1st sess. (June 1967), 91 (statement of Rep. Augustus F. Hawkins).

36. Gail P. Kelly, "Contemporary American Policies and Practices in the Education of Immigrant Children," in *Educating Immigrants,* ed. Joti Bhatnagar (New York: St. Martin's Press, 1981), 216.

37. See, e.g., Wallace R. Lambert and G. Richard Tucker, *Bilingual Education of Children* (Rowley, Mass.: Newbury House, 1972); William F. Mackey, *Bilingual Education in a Binational School* (Rowley, Mass.: Newbury House, 1972).

38. Chester C. Christian Jr., "The Acculturation of the Bilingual Child," *Modern Language Journal* 49, no. 3 (March 1965): 162 (quoting from the oral summary of the conference proceedings read by John W. Macy Jr., Chairman, United States Civil Service Commission).

39. Robert F. Roeming, "Bilingualism and the Bilingual Child—A Symposium: Foreword," *Modern Language Journal* 49, no. 3 (March 1965): 143.

40. National Education Association, *The Invisible Minority,* Report of the NEA-Tucson Survey on the Teaching of Spanish to the Spanish-Speaking (Washington, D.C.: NEA, 1966).

41. *Las Voces Nuevas del Sudoeste: A Symposium on the Spanish-Speaking Child in the Schools of the Southwest, Tucson, Arizona, October 30–31, 1966* (Tucson, Ariz.: National Education Association, Committee on Civil and Human Rights of Educators of the Commission on Professional Rights and Responsibilities, 1966).

42. *Hearings before the Special Subcommittee on Bilingual Education of the Committee on Labor and Public Welfare,* 90th Cong., 1st sess. (May 1967), 18–19 (statement of Senator Ralph Yarborough).

43. *Congressional Record,* 90th Cong., 1st sess., vol. 113, pt. 25, S. 34703, December 1, 1967 (statement of Senator Ralph Yarborough).

44. "Two Proposals for a Better Way of Life for Mexican-Americans of the Southwest," *Congressional Record* 17 (1967), 600 (statement of Senator Ralph Yarborough).

45. *Hearings before the General Subcommittee on Education of the Committee on Education and Labor, House of Representatives on H.R. 9840 and H.R. 10224,* 90th Cong., 1st sess. (June 1967), 57, 103 (statement of Hon. Harold Howe II, U.S. Commissioner of Education).

46. Rachel Moran, "The Politics of Discretion: Federal Intervention in Bilingual Education," *California Law Review* 76 (1988): 1261.

47. Amendments to the Elementary and Secondary Education Act of 1965, Title VII, §§ 702–703, Bilingual Education Programs, Pub. Law 90-247, 90th Cong., 1st sess., 1968.

48. Ibid., §704.

49. Joshua Fishman, "The Politics of Bilingual Education," in *Bilingual Schooling in the United States: A Sourcebook for Educational Personnel,* ed. Francesco Cordasco (New York: McGraw-Hill, 1976), 141–149.

50. John C. Molina, "National Policy on Bilingual Education: An Historical View of the Federal Role," in *Bilingual Education,* ed. Hernan La Fontaine, Barry Persky, and Leonard Golubchick (Wayne, N.J.: Avery, 1978), 17.

51. *1971 Manual for Title VII Applicants and Grantees,* U.S. Department of Health, Education, and Welfare, quoted in Noel Epstein, *Language, Ethnicity, and the Schools* (Washington, D.C.: Institute for Educational Leadership, 1977), 20.

52. Frank Carlucci, Undersecretary for Education, "Departmental Position on Bilingual Education," HEW memorandum, December 2, 1974, in *Bilingual Education: An Unmet Need* (Washington, D.C.: General Accounting Office, May 1976), appendix 2, pp. 55, 56.

53. Ibid., citing *Conference Report on H.R. 69* (Pub. Law 93-380), 148.

54. United States Commission on Civil Rights, *Toward Quality Education for Mexican Americans* (Washington, D.C., 1974), iii.

55. *Hearings before the General Subcommittee on Education of the Committee on Education and Labor, House of Representatives, on H.R. 1085, H.R. 2490, and H.R. 11464* (May 1974), 404 (statement of Lily Fok, Assistant Coordinator, Title VII Bilingual Project, P.S. 2, New York City).

56. Ibid., 407 (testimony of the Hellenic American Neighborhood Action Committee of New York City).

57. Herman Badillo, *One Nation, One Standard* (New York: Sentinel, 2006), 61–63.

58. *Hearings before the Subcommittee on Education of the Committee on Labor and Public Welfare, United States Senate, on S. 1539,* 93rd Cong. 1st Sess. (October 1973), 2591 (testimony of Senator Alan Cranston, D-California).

59. Bilingual Education Act, 1974 Reauthorization, § 703 (4).

60. Ibid., § 703 (1).

61. Ibid., § 704 (4) (B).

62. Austin Scott, "Bilingual Education Gains," *Washington Post,* September 22, 1974, F4.

63. Stephen S. Rosenfeld, "Bilingualism and the Melting Pot," *Washington Post,* September 22, 1974, A18.

64. Joseph M. Montoya, "Bilingual Education" (opinion), *Washington Post,* October 22, 1974, A20.

65. Albert Shanker, "Bilingual Education: Not 'Why' But 'How,'" *New York Times Sunday Magazine,* November 3, 1974, 233.

66. Letter from Albert Shanker, President, American Federation of Teachers, to Irving Anker, Chancellor, New York City Board of Education, reprinted in, "UFT Responds to Anker Memorandum on Goals of Consent Decree," *New York Teacher,* January 26, 1975, 1.

67. *Hearings before the General Subcommittee on Education of the Committee on Education and Labor, House of Representatives on H.R. 1085, H.R. 2490, and H.R. 11464,* 93rd Cong. 2nd sess. (March 1974), 208 (statement of James Harris, President-Elect, National Education Association).

68. Badillo, *One Nation, One Standard,* 71.
69. Richard Ruiz, "Orientations in Language Planning," in *Language Diversity: Problem or Resource?* ed. Sandra Lee McKay and Sau-ling Cynthia Wong (New York: Newbury House, 1988), 9.
70. *Code of Federal Regulations,* vol. 45, § 80.3 (b) (2) (2008).
71. "Policies on Elementary & Secondary School Compliance with Title VII of the Civil Rights Act of 1964," *Federal Register,* 33, 58 (March 23, 1968): 4955–4956.
72. "Identification of Discrimination and Denial of Services on the Basis of National Origin," *Federal Register,* 35, 139 (July 18, 1970): 11 595; for a thorough discussion of the 1970 memorandum, see Martin F. Gerry, "Cultural Freedom in the Schools: The Right of Mexican-American Children to Succeed," in *Mexican Americans and Educational Change,* ed. Alfredo Castaneda et al. (New York: Arno Press, 1974), 226–253.
73. Andrew Barnes, "Schools Accused of Denying Equal Bilingual Education," *Washington Post,* January 21, 1972, A2.
74. *Revisiting the Lau Decision: 20 Years After* (Oakland, Calif.: ARC Associates, 1994), 6 (statement of Edward D. Steinman, attorney representing Kinney Kinmon Lau).
75. L. Ling-chi Wang, "Lau v. Nichols: History of a Struggle for Equal and Quality Education," in *Counterpoint: Perspectives on Asian America,* ed. Emma Gee (Los Angeles, Calif.: Asian American Studies Center, University of California, 1976), 242.
76. Terrence G. Wiley, "Accessing Language Rights in Education: A Brief History of the U.S. Context," in *Language Policies in Education,* ed. James W. Tollefson (Mahwah, N.J.: Erlbaum, 2002), 55; *Constitution of 1879 as Amended 1943, Statutes,* 55th Legislature, 1943, 470, reprinted in *Education in the United States: A Documentary History,* vol. 5, ed. Sol Cohen (New York: Random House, 1974), 2978; State of California Statutes, 59th Legislature, 1947, 1792, reprinted in Cohen, *Education in the United States,* 5:2979.
77. W. Henry Cooke, "The Segregation of Mexican-American School Children in Southern California," *School and Society* 67 (1948): 417–421.
78. *Report of the Special Committee of the Board of Supervisors of San Francisco,* reprinted in Cohen, *Education in the United States,* 3:1769.
79. *Resolution of the San Francisco School Board,* reprinted in Cohen, *Education in the United States,* 4:2971.
80. Robert A. Carlson, *The Quest for Conformity: Americanization through Education* (New York: John Wiley, 1975), 71.
81. *Hearings before the General Subcommittee on Education of the Committee on Education and Labor, House of Representatives on H.R. 1085, H.R. 2940, and H.R. 11464,* 93rd Cong., 2nd sess. (May 1974), 51 (prepared statement of L. Ling-chi Wang, Lecturer in Asian Studies, University of California, Berkeley, and Director, Chinese for Affirmative Action).
82. Dexter Waugh and Bruce Koon, "Breakthrough for Bilingual Education," *Civil Rights Digest* (Summer 1974): 24.

83. Telephone interview with L. Ling-chi Wang, Professor Emeritus of Asian American Studies, University of California at Berkeley, October 18, 2005.

84. L. Ling-chi Wang, "Addressing Xenophobia and Insecurity: Bilingual Education in the Age of Globalization" (paper presented to the New York City Board of Education Teacher Academy, March 27, 2004).

85. Wang, "Lau v. Nichols," in Gee, *Counterpoint*," 241.

86. Garance Burke, "Ambivalent in Any Language, Subject of Landmark Bilingual Case Uncertain of Role," *Boston Globe,* July 22, 2002, A1.

87. Telephone interview with Edward Steinman, Professor of Law, Santa Clara University School of Law, October 13, 2005.

88. *Lau v. Nichols,* Order Denying Request for En Banc Consideration, 483 F. 2d 791, 794 (9th Cir. 1973).

89. Ibid., 797–798.

90. Ibid., 796 n. 11, quoting *Meyer v. Nebraska,* 262 U.S. at 402.

91. Ibid., 799.

92. *Pennsylvania Association for Retarded Children (PARC) v. Pennsylvania,* 343 F. Supp. 279 (E.D. Pa. 1972) (consent decree); *Mills v. Board of Education,* 348 F. Supp. 866 (D.D.C. 1972).

93. Telephone interview with Edward Steinman, October 13, 2005.

94. *Lau v. Nichols,* Order Denying Request for En Banc Consideration, 483 F. 2d at 805–806 (Hufstedler, C.J., dissenting).

95. Tom I. Romero, "MALDEF and the Legal Investment in a Multi-Colored America," *Berkeley La Raza Law Journal* 18 (2007): 144.

96. *Memorandum for the United States as Amicus Curiae, Lau v. Nichols,* 18, quoting *Brown v. Board of Education,* 347 U.S. 483, 493 (1954), citing *McLaurin v. Oklahoma State Regents,* 399 U.S. 637 (1950) and *Sweatt v. Painter,* 339 U.S. 629 (1950).

97. *San Antonio Independent School District v. Rodriguez,* 411 U.S. 1 (1973).

98. Ibid., at 37.

99. *Brief for the Petitioners, Lau v. Nichols,* 8, 24–25, 11.

100. *San Antonio Independent School District v. Rodriguez,* 411 U.S. at 37.

101. Transcript of Oral Argument, *Lau v. Nichols,* at 8 (statement of Edward Steinman).

102. Letter of Justice Harry A. Blackmun to Justice William O. Douglas, December 26, 1973; letter from Justice William H. Rehnquist to Justice William O. Douglas, December 28, 1973; letter from Chief Justice Warren Burger to Justice William O. Douglas, January 2, 1974; Conference Notes, Justice William O. Douglas, December 14, 1973 (papers of Justice William O. Douglas, Box 1652, *Lau v. Nichols*) available at Library of Congress, Washington, D.C.

103. *Keyes v. School District No. 1,* 413 U.S. 189 (1973).

104. Memorandum of Justice Harry A. Blackmun, November 26, 1973 (papers of Justice Blackmun, Box 184, *Lau v. Nichols*), available at Library of Congress, Washington, D.C.; Justice Lewis Powell, Conference Notes, December 14, 1973 (papers of Justice Lewis F. Powell), available at Law Library, Washington and Lee School of Law.

105. Telephone interview with Edward Steinman, October 13, 2005.

106. *Lau v. Nichols*, 414 U.S. 563, 568 (1974).

107. *Brown*, 347 U.S. at 493 (1954), quoting *McLaurin v. Oklahoma State Regents*, 339 U.S. 637 (1950).

108. *Lau v. Nichols*, 414 U.S. at 566 (emphasis added).

109. Ibid.

110. Charles F. Abernathy, "Legal Realism and the Failure of the 'Effects' Test for Discrimination," *Georgetown Law Journal* 94 (2006): 279.

111. *Lau v. Nichols*, 414 U.S. at 565.

112. See *Brown v. Board of Education* (Brown II), 349 U.S. 294 (1955).

113. Waugh and Koon, "Breakthrough for Bilingual Education," 21.

114. Ibid., 20.

115. Ibid., 21.

116. Wang, "Lau v. Nichols," in Gee, *Counterpoint*, 243; Waugh and Koon, "Breakthrough for Bilingual Education," 20; *Revisiting the Lau Decision*, 5–6 (statement of L. Ling-chi Wang, community leader for the *Lau* lawsuit).

117. Burke, "Ambivalent in Any Language," A1.

118. Telephone interview with L. Ling-chi Wang, October 18, 2005.

119. Plaintiff's Response to Order to Show Cause, *Lau v. Hopp*, No. C 70-627 LHB (N.D. Cal. January 30, 2007), 2–4; Declaration of Mary Hui, Ed.D in Support of Plaintiffs' Response to Order to Show Cause, *Lau v. Hopp*, No. C 70-627 LHB (January 30, 2007); Order Modifying Consent Decree, *Lau v. San Francisco Unified School District*, No. C70-0627 CW (N.D. Cal. September 11, 2008); see, generally, Rachel F. Moran, "The Story of *Lau v. Nichols*: Breaking the Silence in Chinatown," in *Education Law Stories*, ed. Michael A. Olivas and Ronna Greff Schneider (New York: Foundation Press, 2007), 110–157.

120. Telephone interview with L. Ling-chi Wang, October 18, 2005.

121. Ruddie A. Irizarry, *Bilingual Education: State and Federal Legislative Mandates* (Los Angeles, Calif.: National Dissemination and Assessment Center, California State University, 1978), 39–128 (California, 1976; Colorado, 1975; Connecticut, 1977; Indiana, 1976; Louisiana, 1975; Maine, 1977; Minnesota, 1977; New Jersey, 1975; Utah, 1977; Wisconsin, 1975).

122. *Serna v. Portales Municipal Schools*, 499 F.2d 1147 (10th Cir. 1974) (setting aside the constitutional question and deciding the case on Title VI); *Aspira v. Board of Education of the City of New York*, 394 F. Supp. 1161 (S.D.N.Y. 1975) (consent decree); *Morgan v. Kerrigan*, 401 F. Supp. 216 (D. Mass. 1975), aff'd 523 F.2d 917 (1st Cir. 1976) (part of desegregation plan ordered for Boston public schools); *Bradley v. Milliken*, 402 F. Supp. 1096 (E. D. Mich. 1975) (part of desegregation plan for Detroit public schools).

123. S. MacPherson Pemberton, *A Better Chance to Learn: Bilingual Bicultural Education* (Washington, D.C.: U.S. Commission on Civil Rights, 1975).

124. "Departmental Position on Bilingual Education," memorandum from Frank Carlucci, Undersecretary for Education to the Assistant Secretary for Education, December 2, 1974, in *Bilingual Education, An Unmet Need: Office of Education, Report to Congress* (Washington, D.C.: U.S. General Accounting Office, 1976), 55.

125. U.S. Department of Health, Education, and Welfare, Office for Civil Rights, *Task Force Findings Specifying Remedies for Eliminating Past Educational Practices Ruled Unlawful under Lau v. Nichols* (Washington, D.C., 1975).

126. Noel Epstein, *Language, Ethnicity, and the Schools: Policy Alternatives for Bilingual Bicultural Education* (Washington, D.C.: George Washington University, Institute for Educational Leadership, 1977), 15.

127. Department of Health, Education, and Welfare, Memorandum to Regional Offices, April 8, 1976, quoted in Noel Epstein, "Bilingual Aid Clarified," *Washington Post,* April 19, 1976, A1; Nancy Hicks, "H.E.W. Clarifies Bilingual Policy," *New York Times,* April 20, 1976, A15.

128. Thomas Toch, "The Emerging Politics of Language," *Education Week,* February 8, 1984, 1, 14 (statement of Martin Gerry); Noel Epstein, "Bilingual Pupil Aid Clarified," *Washington Post,* April 19, 1976, A1.

129. Bayard Rustin, "The Dangers of Ethnic Separatism," *New York Times Sunday Magazine,* July 6, 1975, 125.

130. *Aspira v. Board of Education of the City of New York,* 394 F. Supp. 1161 (S.D.N.Y. 1975) (consent decree).

131. *Revisiting the Lau Decision,* 10 (statement of Edward A. De Avila).

132. Herbert Teitelbaum and Richard J. Hiller, "Trends in Bilingual Education and the Law," in La Fontaine, et al., *Bilingual Education,* 46.

133. *Northwest Arctic School Dist. v. Califano,* No. A-77-216 (D. Alaska September 29, 1978) (consent decree).

134. Salomone, *Equal Education under Law,* 99–100.

135. Marjorie Hunter, "U.S. Education Chief Bars Bilingual Plan for Public Schools," *New York Times,* February 3, 1981, A1.

136. 20 U.S.C. § 1701 et. seq. (2008).

137. 20 U.S.C. § 1703(f) (2008).

138. *Address to the Nation on Equal Educational Opportunities and School Busing,* 90 Pub. Papers 425, 426 (March 16 1972).

139. H.R. Rep. No. 92-1335, at 6 (1972).

140. *Castaneda v. Pickard,* 648 F.2d 989 (5th Cir. 1981).

141. Ibid., 1008–09.

6. Backlash

1. Malcolm N. Danoff et al., *Evaluation of the Impact of the ESEA Title VII Spanish/English Bilingual Education Programs, Study Design and Interim Findings,* vol. 1 (Washington, D.C.: American Institutes for Research, 1977); see also, ibid., vol. 3, *Two Year Impact Data, Educational Process, and In-Depth Analysis* (1978).

2. Rosemary C. Salomone, *Equal Education under Law: Legal Rights and Federal Policy in the Post-"Brown" Era* (New York: St. Martin's Press, 1986), 89–90.

3. See Tracy C. Gray, "Response to the AIR Study, Evaluation of the Impact of ESEA Title VII Spanish/English Bilingual Education Programs," memoran-

dum (Washington, D.C.: Center for Applied Linguistics, April, 18, 1977); James Crawford, *Hold Your Tongue: Bilingualism and the Politics of "English Only"* (Reading, Mass.: Addison-Wesley, 1992), 219–220.

4. Noel Epstein, *Language, Ethnicity and the Schools: Policy Alternatives for Bilingual-Bicultural Education* (Washington, D.C.: Institute for Educational Leadership, 1977), 1; see also Noel Epstein, "The Bilingual Battle: Should Washington Finance Ethnic Identities?" *Washington Post,* June 5, 1977, C1.

5. Epstein, *Language, Ethnicity and the Schools,* 19–20.

6. Joshua A. Fishman, "A Gathering of Vultures, the 'Legion of Decency,' and Bilingual Education in the USA," *NABE News* 2 (1978): 13–16.

7. David Vidal, "Bilingual Instruction Is Thriving," *New York Times,* January 30, 1977, E9 (statement of Dr. Joshua A. Fishman, professor, Yeshiva University).

8. Rachel F. Moran, "Language and the Law in the Classroom: Bilingual Education and the Official English Initiative," in *Perspectives on Official English,* ed. Karen L. Adams and Daniel T. Bank (Berlin: Mouton de Gruyter, 1990), 288.

9. *Hearings on H.R. 15 before the Subcommittee on Elementary, Secondary, and Vocational Education of the Committee on Education and Labor,* House of Representatives, 95th Cong., 1st sess., June 1977, 335–338 (statement of Professor Gary Orfield, University of Illinois at Urbana).

10. David Lopez, "Bilingualism and Ethnic Change in California," in *Language, Nation, and State: Identity Politics in a Multilingual Age,* ed. Tony Judt and Denis Lacorne (New York: Palgrave Macmillan, 2004), 81.

11. Bilingual Education Act, 1978 Reauthorization Act, § 703 (1).

12. Ibid., § 703 (4).

13. Ibid., § 703 (a)(4)(B).

14. *Strength through Wisdom: Report of the President's Commission on Foreign Language and International Studies* (Washington, D.C.: HEW, Office of Education, 1979), quoted in J. David Edwards, Ashley L. Lenker, and Dara Kahn, "National Language Policies: Pragmatism, Process, and Products," *NECTFL Review* 63 (Fall/Winter 2008/2009): 16.

15. President Ronald Reagan, *Remarks at the Mid-Winter Congressional City Conference of the National League of Cities,* Public Papers of Ronald Reagan, March 21, 1981, www.reagan.utexas.edu/archives/speeches/1981/81mar.htm.

16. Keith A. Baker and Adriana A. de Kanter, *Bilingual Education: A Reappraisal of Federal Policy* (Lexington, Mass.: Lexington Books, 1983), 33–86.

17. See, Wallace E. Lambert and G. Richard Tucker, *Bilingual Education of Children: The St. Lambert Experiment* (Rowley, Mass.: Newbury House, 1972); Merrill Swain and Sharon Lapkin, *Bilingual Education in Ontario: A Decade of Research* (Toronto: Minister of Education, Ontario, 1981).

18. G. Richard Tucker, "Implications for U.S. Bilingual Education: Evidence

from Canadian Research," *Focus* (National Clearinghouse on Bilingual Education) 2 (February 1980).

19. Russell N. Campbell and Tracy C. Gray, "Critique of the U.S. Department of Education Report on Effectiveness of Bilingual Education: Review of the Literature," memorandum (Washington, D.C.: Center for Applied Linguistics, June 8, 1981).

20. Thomas Toch, "The Emerging Politics of Language," *Education Week,* February 8, 1984, 1, 16.

21. Bilingual Education Act, 1984 Reauthorization, §704 (a) (4).

22. James J. Lyons, *NABE News* 8, no. 2 (Winter 1985): 22.

23. Address by William J. Bennett, United States Secretary of Education, to the Association for a Better New York, New York City, September 26, 1985, reprinted in *La Raza Law Journal* 1 (1983–1986): 219–220; Theodore Roosevelt, "The Children of the Crucible," September 9, 1917, reprinted in *Annals of America, 1916–1928: World War and Prosperity,* vol. 14 (Chicago: Encyclopedia Britannica, 1968), 129–131.

24. James Crawford, introduction to *Language Loyalties: A Source Book on the Official English Controversy,* ed. James Crawford (Chicago: University of Chicago Press, 1992), 4.

25. Alina Tugend, "Uniform Bilingual Rules Lacking, Report Finds," *Education Week,* June 19, 1985, 13, 16.

26. Bilingual Education Act, 1988 Reauthorization, §7021 (d).

27. Bilingual Education Act, 1994 Reauthorization, §7102 (a).

28. Ibid., § 7102 (a).

29. Ibid., § 7102 (c) (2).

30. See, e.g., Rosalie Pedalino Porter, *Forked Tongue: The Politics of Bilingual Education* (New York: Basic Books, 1990).

31. Lynn Schnaiberg, "In Questioning Bilingual Ed., Hispanic Parents Join Backlash," *Education Week,* February 28, 1996, 11.

32. 42 U.S.C. §1973b (f) (4) (2008).

33. U.S. English website, www.us-english.org.

34. Memo from John Tanton to WITAN IV Attendees, October 10, 1986, reprinted in Southern Poverty Law Center, *Intelligence Report* (Summer 2002), www.splcenter.org.

35. English First website, www.englishfirst.org.

36. *Ruiz v. Hull,* 957 P. 2d 984 (Arizona 1998).

37. ProEnglish website, www.proenglish.org.

38. "The Puppeteer," Southern Poverty Law Center, *Intelligence Report* (Summer 2002), www.splcenter.org.

39. John Vinson, "Europhobia the Racism of Anti-Racists," *Social Contract* 8, no. 4 (Summer 1998): 1.

40. Anita Huslin, "On Immigration, a Theorist Who's No Fence-Sitter," *Washington Post,* November 26, 2006, D01. See also "The Tanton Files," Southern Poverty Law Center, *Intelligence Report* (Winter 2008) www.splcenter.org.

41. Spanish-American League Against Discrimination (SALAD) Education

Committee, "Not English Only, English *Plus!*" unpublished manuscript, October 4, 1985.

42. "Statement of Purpose," English Plus Information Clearinghouse, 1987, www.languagepolicy.net.

43. Mary Carol Combs, "English Plus: Responding to English Only," in Crawford, *Language Loyalties,* 224.

44. Raymond Tatalovich, *Nativism Reborn? The Official Language Movement in the American States* (Lexington: University Press of Kentucky, 1995), 18, 23.

45. *English Plus Resolution,* H. Con. Res. 3, 111th Cong., 1st sess. (2009).

46. James Crawford, "California Vote Gives Boost to 'English-Only' Movement," *Education Week,* April 1, 1987, 27.

47. "English Language Unity Act Introduced in the 111th Congress," press release, U.S. English, February 11, 2009.

48. Joshua A. Fishman, "'English Only': Its Ghosts, Myths, and Dangers," *International Journal of the Sociology of Language* 74 (1988): 133.

49. *Plyler v. Doe,* 457 U.S. 223 (1982).

50. *League of United Latin American Citizens v. Wilson,* 1998 WL 141325 (C.D. Cal. March 13, 1998).

51. Cal. Educ. Code § 305 (West. Supp. 2008).

52. James Crawford and Stephen Krashen, *English Language Learners in American Classrooms: 101 Questions, 101 Answers* (New York: Scholastic, 2007), 45; Jim Cummins, "Bilingual Education," in *Language Education,* ed. Jill Bourne and Euan Reid (London: Kogan Page, 2003), 3–21.

53. Margot Hornblower, "The Man behind Prop. 227," *Time,* June 8, 1998, 56.

54. Cal. Educ. Code 1999, ch. 3, §§ 300–340 et seq.; Ariz. Rev. Stat. Tit. 15, 2000, ch. 7, §§ 15-751–755; Mass. Gen. Laws 2000, pt. I, tit. XII, ch. 71A.

55. Lance T. Izumi, Rachel S. Chaney, and Jennifer L. Nelson, *English Immersion or Law Evasion? A 10th Anniversary Retrospective on Proposition 227 and the "End" of Bilingual Education* (San Francisco: Pacific Research Institute, 2008), 9.

56. Wayne E. Wright and Daniel Choi, "The Impact of Language and High-Stakes Testing Policies on Elementary School English Language Learners in Arizona," *Education Policy Analysis Archives* 14, no. 13 (May 22, 2006): 20.

57. Telephone interview with Oscar Medina, English Learner Services Coordinator, San Diego County Office of Education, October 13, 2005.

58. "Immigrant Parents Demand Their Rights under Proposition 227," press release, Californians Together, March 5, 2002, www.californianstogether .org.

59. Ariz. Rev. Stat. Tit. 15, ch. 7, §§ 15-751–755 (2000); Mass. Gen. Laws, pt. I, tit. XII, ch. 71A (2002).

60. Christine Rossell, "The Near End of Bilingual Education," *Education Next* 3, no. 4 (Fall 2003): 48–49.

61. Cal. Educ. Code, Article 8, Sec. 335; Ariz. Rev. Stat., Title 15, Ch. 7, Sec. 5.

62. *Valeria v. Wilson,* 307 F.3d 1036, 1041–42 (9th Cir. 2002), petition for rehearing denied, *Valeria v. Davis,* 320 F.3d 1014 (9th Cir. 2003).

63. *Valeria v. Wilson,* 307 F.3d at 1041–42.

64. *Valeria v. Davis,* 320 F.3d at 1019 (Pregerson, C.J., dissenting).

65. English Language Acquisition, Language Enhancement, and Academic Achievement Act, Pub. Law 107-110, §§ 3001 et seq. (2002).

66. Ibid., §3102 (7).

67. Ibid., §3301 (8).

68. "Improving the Academic Achievement of the Disadvantaged," *Federal Register* 71, 177 (September 13, 2006): 54, 187–94.

69. California Department of Education, *2007 Dataquest,* www.data1.cde.ca.gov/dataquest.

70. Crawford and Krashen, *English Language Learners in American Classrooms,* 32–33.

71. Institute for Language and Education Policy, *No Child Left Behind: A Failure for English Language Learners* (talking points), www.elladvocates.org.

72. Carl Campanile, "Higher 'Degree' of HS Kids Seek GED," *New York Post,* June 21, 2004, 2.

73. Kate Menken, *English Language Learners Left Behind: Standardized Testing as Language Policy* (Clevedon, England: Multilingual Matters, 2008), 95.

74. *English Language Learners' Provisions of the No Child Left Behind Act: Summary of a Roundtable Discussion* (Washington, D.C.: Center for Education Policy, March 20, 2007); Guillermo Solano-Flores, "Who Is Given Tests in What Language by Whom, When, and Where? The Need for Probabilistic Views of Language in the Testing of English Language Learners," *Educational Researcher* 37, no. 4 (May 2008): 189–199.

75. Lynn Shafer Wilner, Charlene Rivera, and Barbara D. Acosta, *Descriptive Study of State Assessment Policies for Accommodating English Language Learners* (Arlington, Va.: George Washington University, Center for Equity and Excellence in Education, October 2008), 7, 48.

76. James Crawford, "A Diminished Vision of Civil Rights" (Commentary), *Education Week,* June 6, 2007, 39.

77. Jim Cummins, speech before the annual conference of the California Teachers of English to Speakers of Other Languages Association, San Diego, July 25, 2007, quoted in Meteor Blades, "Jim Cummins Demolishes NCLB's Ideology and Practice," *Daily Kos,* July 26, 2007, www.dailykos.com.

78. *Hearings Before the House Education and Labor Committee, Early Childhood, Elementary and Secondary Education Subcommittee,* 110th Cong., 1st Sess. (March 23, 2007), 30–33 (prepared statement of Peter Zamora, Washington, D.C. Regional Counsel, Mexican American Legal Defense and Educational Fund).

79. Sean Cavanaugh and Kathleen Kennedy Manzo, "NAEP Gains: Experts Mull Significance," *Education Week,* October 3, 2007, 1, 16–17; Sam

Dillon, "Math Scores Rise, but Reading Is Mixed," *New York Times*, September 26, 2007, 20.

80. Janet M. Hostetler, "Testing Human Rights: The Impact of High-Stakes Tests on English Language Learners' Right to Education in New York City," *New York University Review of Law and Social Change* 30 (2006): 495–501.

81. See James Crawford, "Obituary: The Bilingual Education Act, 1968–2002," *Rethinking Schools* 16, no. 4 (Summer 2002): 1.

82. Mary Ann Zehr, "NCLB Seen as Damper on Bilingual Programs," *Education Week*, May 9, 2007, 5, 12 (statement of Sandra Mendez, Principal, Pioneer Bilingual Elementary School, Lafayette, Colorado).

83. Ibid.

84. Ibid.

85. Proceedings and Debates of the 107th Cong., 1st Sess., *Congressional Record*, 147 (May 22, 2001), H2396-02 (statement of Congressman Ruben Hinojosa).

86. Rodolfo O. de la Garza, Louis DeSipio, F. Chris Garcia, and Angelo Falcon, *Latino Voices: Mexican, Puerto Rican, and Cuban Perspectives on American Politics* (Boulder, Colo.: Westview Press, 1991), table 7.19, p. 99.

87. Steve Farkas, Ann Duffet, and Jean Johnson with Leslie Moye and Jackie Vine, *Now That I'm Here: What America's Immigrants Have to Say about Life in the U.S. Today* (New York: Public Agenda, 2003), 52.

88. Matt A. Barreto and Sylvia Manzano, "Commentary: Poll Is Reality Check on Latino Vote," *CNN Politics.com*, www.edition.cnn.com.

7. More Wrongs than Rights

1. *Lau v. Nichols*, 414 U.S. 563 (1974).

2. *Castaneda v. Pickard*, 648 F.2d 989 (5th Cir. 1981); "Policy Update on Schools' Obligations toward National Origin Minority Students with Limited-English Proficiency (LEP Students)," memorandum from Michael L. Williams, Assistant Secretary for Civil Rights to OCR Staff, September 27, 1991.

3. *Guardians Association v. Civil Service Commission*, 463 U.S. 582 (1983); see also *Regents of the University of California v. Bakke*, 438 U.S. 265 (1978) (holding that Title VI rights are coterminous with those guaranteed under the Fourteenth Amendment equal protection clause, which requires proof of discriminatory intent).

4. *Alexander v. Sandoval*, 532 U.S. 275 (2001).

5. Rachel F. Moran, "Undone by Law: The Uncertain Legacy of *Lau v. Nichols*," *UCLMRI Newsletter*, Summer 2004, 5.

6. *Teresa P. v. Berkeley Unified School District*, 724 F. Supp. 698 (N.D. Cal. 1989).

7. *Valeria v. Wilson*, 12 F. Supp. 2d 1007, 1018 (N.D. Cal. 1998).

8. *United States v. Texas*, 680 F.2d 356 (5th Cir. 1982); *Gomez v. Illinois State Board of Education*, 811 F.2d 1030 (7th Cir. 1987).

9. *Flores v. Arizona*, 172 F. Supp. 2d 1225, 1238 (D. Ariz. 2000).

10. See Eric Haas, "The Equal Educational Opportunity Act 30 Years Later: Time to Revisit 'Appropriate Action' for Assisting English Language Learners," *Journal of Law and Education* 34, no. 3 (2005): 361–387.

11. *Washington v. Davis*, 426 U.S. 229 (1976); *City of Boerne v. Flores*, 521 U.S. 507, 520 (1997).

12. Telephone interview with Roger Rice, November 16, 2006.

13. Ibid.

14. Michael A. Rebell, "Equal Opportunity and the Courts," *Phi Delta Kappan* 89, no. 6 (February 2006): 432–439.

15. *Horne v. Flores*, 129 S.Ct. 2579 (2009).

16. *Flores v. Arizona*, 172 F. Supp. 2d 1225 (D. Ariz. 2000).

17. Ibid., 1239.

18. *Flores v. Arizona*, 480 F. Supp. 2d 1157, 1161 (D. Ariz. 2007).

19. *Flores v. Arizona*, 516 F.3d 1140, 1169 (9th Cir. 2008), as amended on denial of rehearing and rehearing en banc (April 17, 2008).

20. *Speaker of the Arizona House of Representatives and President of the Arizona Senate v. Flores*, 516 F. 3d 1140 (9th Cir. 2008), *Petition for Writ of Certiorari* (U.S., September 1, 2008) (No. 08-824), 38.

21. Ibid., 30.

22. *Flores v. Arizona*, 516 F. 3d at 1174.

23. *Horne v. Flores*, 129 S.Ct. 2579, 2602–03 (2009).

24. Ibid. at 2588–89.

25. Ibid. at 2587.

26. Ibid. at 2589, quoting *Castaneda v. Picard*. 648 F. 2d. 989, 1009 (5th Cir. 1981).

27. Ibid. at 2600.

28. Ibid. at 2588 n.1.

29. Ibid. at 2601.

30. Ibid. at 2623 (Breyer, J., dissenting).

31. Ibid. at 2614 (Breyer, J., dissenting).

32. Associated Press, "Some Experts Questioning Arizona Instruction Method," *Arizona Daily Star,* August 4, 2008, www.azstarnet.com (statement of Jeff McSwan, Professor, Arizona State University; statement of Patricia Gandara, Professor and Co-Director, The Civil Rights Project, University of California at Los Angeles).

33. *Plyler v. Doe*, 457 U.S. 202 (1982).

34. *United States v. Texas*, 572 F. Supp. 2d 726 (E.D. Texas, 2008).

35. Mary Ann Zehr, "Federal Court Ruling Prods Texas on ELLs," *Education Week*, July 29, 2008, 29, 45 (statement of Diane August, co-editor of report of the National Literacy Panel on Language Minority Children and Youth); Michelle J. Nealy, "Two English-Language Learner Programs Come Under Fire," *Educational Equity, Politics and Policy in Texas*, August 19, 2008 (statement of Dr. Elena Izquierdo, Associate Professor, University of Texas at El Paso), www.texasedequity.blogspot.com.

36. *Horne v. Flores*, 129 S.Ct. at 2631 (Breyer, J., dissenting), quoting Cristina

Rodriguez, "Language and Participation," *California Law Review* 94 (2006): 693.

37. *Meyer v. Nebraska,* 262 U.S. 390 (1923); *Troxel v. Granville,* 530 U.S. 57 (2002).
38. See *San Antonio Independent School District v. Rodriguez,* 411 U.S. 1 (1973).
39. *Plyler v. Doe,* 457 U.S. 202 (1982).
40. Katherine Leal Unmuth, "25 Years Ago: Tyler Case Opened Schools to Illegal Migrants," *Dallas Morning News,* June 11, 2007, 1A.
41. Michael A. Olivas, "*Plyler v. Doe,* the Education of Undocumented Children, and the Polity," in *Immigration Law Stories,* ed. David A. Martin and Peter H. Schuck (New York: Foundation Press, 2005), 201.
42. Ibid., 221–222, 234, 230, 211.
43. Wayne King, "Texas Governor Says Problem with Court Compliance Ruling Is No Problem," *New York Times,* June 16, 1982, D22.
44. "Teaching Alien Children Is a Duty" (editorial), *New York Times,* June 16, 1982, A30.
45. Unmuth, "25 Years Ago."
46. *The Costs of Illegal Immigration to Texans; The Costs of Illegal Immigration to Californians* (Washington, D.C.: Federation for American Immigration Reform), www.fairus.org.
47. Telephone interview with Roger Rice, November 16, 2006.
48. Roger L. Rice and Jane E. López, *Ensuring an Adequate Education for English Language Learner Students in New York* (New York: New York Immigration Coalition, May 2008), 61.
49. Telephone interview with Peter Roos, former Director, META, May 8, 2007.
50. Thomas Toch, "The Emerging Politics of Language," *Education Week,* February 8, 1984, 1, 14 (statement of Martin Gerry, former Director, Office for Civil Rights, U.S. Department of Health, Education, and Welfare); the Individuals with Disabilities Education Improvement Act, Pub. Law 108-446, 108th Cong., 20 U.S.C. § 1400 et seq. (2007).
51. See *Board of Education of the Hendrick Hudson Central School District v. Rowley,* 458 U.S. 176 (1982).

8. Setting the Record Straight

1. Rudolf Pintner and Ruth Keller, "Intelligence Tests for Foreign Children," *Journal of Educational Psychology* 13 (1922): 214–222; O. J. Saer, "The Effects of Bilingualism on Intelligence," *British Journal of Psychology* 14 (1923): 25–28.
2. Marguerite E. Malakoff, "The Effect of Language of Instruction on Reasoning in Bilingual Children," *Applied Psycholinguistics* 9 (1988): 17.
3. Margaret Mead, "The Methodology of Racial Testing: Its Significance for Sociology," *American Journal of Sociology* 31, no. 5 (1926): 657–667.
4. Jules Ronjat, *Le developpement du langage observé chez un enfant bilingue*

(Paris: Champion, 1913); Werner F. Leopold, *Speech Development of a Bilingual Child*, 4 vols. (Evanston, Ill.: Northwestern University Press, 1939–1949).

5. Elizabeth Peal and Wallace Lambert, "The Relation of Bilingualism to Intelligence," *Psychological Monographs: General and Applied* 76 (1962): 1–123.

6. Colin Baker, *Foundations of Bilingual Education and Bilingualism*, 4th ed. (Clevedon, England: Multilingual Matters, 2006), 144–164; Josiane F. Hamers and Michael H. A. Blanc, *Bilingualism and Bilinguality*, 2nd ed. (Cambridge: Cambridge University Press, 2000), 87–88; Marjorie Faulstich Orellana, *Translating Childhood: Immigrant Youth, Language, and Culture* (New Brunswick, N.J.: Rutgers University Press, 2009), 114.

7. Jim Cummins, *Language, Power, and Pedagogy: Bilingual Children in the Crossfire* (Clevedon, England: Multilingual Matters, 2000), 173–200; Courtney B. Cazden, "Play and Metalinguistic Awareness: One Dimension of Language Experience," *Urban Review* 7 (1974): 23–39; see also Mila Schwartz, Esther Geva, and David L. Share, "Learning to Read in English as Third Language: The Cross-Linguistic Transfer of Phonological Processing Skills," *Written Language and Literacy* 10, no. 1 (2007): 25–52.

8. Charlotte Hoffman and Jehannes Ytsma, eds., *Trilingualism in Family, School and Community* (Clevedon, England: Multilingual Matters, 2004).

9. Rosalie Pedalino Porter, *Forked Tongue: The Politics of Bilingual Education* (New York: Basic Books, 1990), 119; Christine H. Rossell and Keith Baker, "The Educational Effectiveness of Bilingual Education," *Research in the Teaching of English* 30 (1996): 7–74.

10. Ellen Bialystock, "Language and Literacy Development," in *The Handbook of Bilingualism*, ed. Tej K. Bhatia and William C. Ritchie (Malden, Mass.: Blackwell, 2004), 597–598.

11. Ellen Bialystock, "Metalinguistic Dimensions of Bilingual Proficiency," in *Language Processing in Bilingual Children*, ed. Ellen Bialystock (Cambridge: Cambridge University Press, 1991), 113–140; Ellen Bialystock, *Bilingualism in Development: Language, Literacy, and Cognition* (Cambridge: Cambridge University Press, 2001), 194, 218.

12. Ellen Bialystock, "Consequences of Bilingualism for Cognitive Development," in *Handbook of Bilingualism: Psycholinguistic Approaches*, ed. Judith F. Kroll and Annette M. B. De Groot (Oxford: Oxford University Press, 2005), 428.

13. Ellen Bialystock, "Cognitive Effects of Bilingualism: How Linguistic Experience Leads to Cognitive Change," *International Journal of Bilingual Education and Bilingualism* 10, no. 3 (2007): 220.

14. Gitit Kavé, Nitza Eyal, Aviva Shorek, and Jiska Cohen-Mansfield, "Multilingualism and Cognitive State in the Oldest Old," *Psychology and Aging* 23, no. 1 (2008): 70–78.

15. Ellen Bialystock and Kenji Hakuta, *In Other Words* (New York: Basic Books, 1981), 122; see also Sandra Ben-Zeev, "The Effects of Bilingualism

in Children from Spanish-English Low Economic Neighborhoods on Cognitive Development and Cognitive Strategy," *Working Papers on Bilingualism* 14 (1977): 83–122; Sandra Ben-Zeev, "The Influence of Bilingualism on Cognitive Strategy and Cognitive Development," *Child Development* 48, no. 3 (September 1977): 1009–18; Agnes Melinda Kovács, "Beyond Language: Childhood Bilingualism Enhances High-Level Cognitive Functions," in *Cognitive Aspects of Bilingualism,* ed. Istvan Kecskes and Liliana Albertazzi (Dordrecht: Springer, 2007), 301–323.

16. Baker, *Foundations,* 145–146.
17. Fred Genesee, G. Richard Tucker, and Wallace E. Lambert, "Communication Skills in Bilingual Children, *Child Development* 46 (December 1975): 1014; Ajit K. Mohanty, *Bilingualism in a Multilingual Society: Psycho-Social and Pedagogical Implications* (Mysore, India: Central Institute of Indian Languages, 1994).
18. Carol W. Pfaff, "Sociolinguistic Problems of Immigrants," *Language in Society* 10 (1981): 155–188; Christian R. Lemmon and Judith P. Goggin, "The Measurement of Bilingualism and Its Relationship to Cognitive Ability," *Applied Psycholinguistics* 10 (1989): 133–155.
19. Cummins, *Language, Power, and Pedagogy,* 173–200.
20. Rafael M. Diaz, "Bilingual Cognitive Development: Addressing Three Gaps in Current Research," *Child Development* 56 (1985): 1387.
21. See, generally, Kenji Hakuta, *Mirror of Language: The Debate on Bilingualism* (New York: Basic Books, 1986).
22. Catherine Snow, "Cross-Cutting Themes and Future Research Directions," in *Developing Reading and Writing in Second-Language Learners: Lessons from the Report of the National Literacy Panel on Language-Minority Children and Youth,* ed. Diane August and Timothy Shanahan (New York: Routledge, 2008), 282.
23. Robert Rueda, "Metalinguistic Awareness in Monolingual and Bilingual Mildly Retarded Children," *NABE Journal* 8 (1984): 55–68.
24. Cummins, *Language, Power and Pedagogy,* 192.
25. Bialystock, "Consequences of Bilingualism," 428.
26. David Crystal, *Language Death* (Cambridge: Cambridge University Press, 2000), 44.
27. Russell Gersten and Scott Baker, "What We Know about Effective Instructional Practices for English-Language Learners," *Exceptional Children* 66 (2000): 454–470; Fred Genesee, Kathryn Lindholm-Leary, William M. Saunders, and Donna Christian, *Educating English Language Learners: A Synthesis of Research Evidence* (Cambridge: Cambridge University Press, 2006).
28. Robert E. Slavin and Alan Cheung, "A Synthesis of Research on Language of Reading Instruction for English Language Learners," *Review of Educational Research* 75, no. 2 (Summer 2005): 247–284; Kellie Rolstad, Kate Mahoney, and Gene V. Glass, "The Big Picture: A Meta-Analysis of Program Effectiveness Research on English Language Learners," *Educational*

Policy 19, no. 4 (2005): 572–594; Genesee et al., *Educating English Language Learners;* Diane August et al., "Instruction and Professional Development," in August and Shanahan, *Developing Reading and Writing,* 134–140.

29. James Crawford, "More Evidence from the National Literacy Panel," *Language Learner* (November/December 2005): 10.

30. Diane August and Timothy Shanahan, *Developing Literacy in Second-Language Leaners: Report of the National Literacy Panel on Language-Minority Children and Youth* (Mahwah, N.J.: Erlbaum, 2006).

31. Wayne P. Thomas and Virginia P. Collier, *A National Study of School Effectiveness for Language Minority Students' Long-Term Academic Achievement* (Santa Cruz, Calif.: Center for Research on Education, Diversity and Excellence, 2002).

32. D. Kimbrough Oller and Rebecca E. Eilers, eds., *Language and Literacy in Bilingual Children* (Clevedon, England: Multilingual Matters), 2002.

33. Claude Goldenberg, "Teaching English Language Learners: What the Research Does—and Does Not—Say," *American Educator* (Summer 2008): 12.

34. Kathryn Lindholm-Leary, *Dual Language Education* (Clevedon, England: Multilingual Matters, 2001); Elizabeth R. Howard and Julie Sugarman, *Realizing the Vision: Fostering Effective Programs and Classrooms* (Washington, D.C.: Center for Applied Linguistics, 2007).

35. Telephone interview with Julie Lambert, Bilingual Migrant Education Consultant, California Department of Education, July 19, 2007.

36. Oyster Bilingual School, www.oysterbilingualschool.com; Veronica Fern, "Oyster School Stands the Test of Time," *Bilingual Research Journal* 19, nos. 3–4 (Summer/Fall 1995): 497–512.

37. Maria E. Torres-Guzmán, "Dual Language Programs: Key Features and Results," *Directions in Language and Education* 14 (Spring 2002): 7.

38. Donna Christian, Christopher L. Montone, Kathryn J. Lindholm, and Isolda Carranza, *Profiles in Two-Way Immersion Education* (McHenry, Ill.: Center for Applied Linguistics and Delta Systems, 1997), 1–2.

39. Maria Sacchetti and Tracy Jan, "Bilingual Law Fails First Test," *Boston Globe,* May 21, 2006, A1.

40. Roger Rice and Jane Lopez, "Silence on the English Learners' Gap," commentary, *Boston Globe,* August 4, 2008, A15. See also, Rosann Tung et al., *English Learners in Boston Public Schools: Enrollment, Engagement and Academic Outcomes, AY2003–AY2006, Final Report* (Boston: Mauricio Gaston Institute for Latino Community Development and Public Policy, 2009).

41. Thomas B. Parrish, et al., *Effects of the Implementation of Proposition 227 on the Education of English Learners, K-12: Findings from a Five-Year Evaluation* (Washington, D.C., and San Francisco: American Instutes for Research and WestEd, 2006); Elizabeth G. Hill, *A Look at the Progress of English Learner Students* (Sacramento, Calif.: Legislative Analyst's Office, 2004); Elizabeth G. Hill, *Update 2002–2004: The Progress of English Learner Students* (Sacramento, Calif.: Legislative Analyst's Office, 2006).

42. Wayne E. Wright and Chang Pu, *Academic Achievement of English Language Learners in Post Proposition 203 Arizona* (Tempe: Language Policy Research Unit, Educational Policy Studies Laboratory, Arizona State University, 2005).

43. Kate Mahoney, Jeff MacSwan, and Marilyn Thompson, *The Condition of English Language Learners in Arizona: 2005* (Tempe: Education Policy Studies Laboratory, Arizona State University, 2005).

44. Mary Ann Zehr, "NAEP Scores in States That Cut Bilingual Ed. Fuel Concern on ELLs," *Education Week,* May 14, 2008, 10.

45. "Gingrich Backs English Official Language Push," *CNSNews.com,* January 25, 2007, www.cnsnews.com; Paul Kita, "Push for Official Language Would Challenge Bilingual Schools," *AxcessNews.com,* January 25, 2007, www.axcessnews.com.

46. Miranda E. Wilkerson and Joseph Salmons, "'Good Old Immigrants of Yesteryear' Who Didn't Learn English: Germans in Wisconsin," *American Speech* 83, no. 3 (Fall 2008): 259–283.

47. Will Kymlicka, *Politics in the Vernacular: Nationalism, Multiculturalism, and Citizenship* (Oxford: Oxford University Press, 2001), 169.

48. Margie McHugh, Julia Gelatt, and Michael Fix, *Adult English Language Instruction in the United States: Determining Need and Investing Wisely* (Washington, D.C.: Migration Policy Institute, National Center on Immigrant Integration Policy, July 2007), 6–7.

49. James Thomas Rucker, *Waiting Times for Adult ESL Classes and the Impact on English Language Learners* (Los Angeles: NALEO Educational Fund, 2006), 4.

50. Daniel González, "English Classes for Immigrants Fall Short of Demand," *Arizona Republic,* August 18, 2007, A1.

51. "Official English Legislation: Bad for Civil Rights, Bad for America's Interests, and Even Bad for English," testimony of James Crawford, Director, Institute for Language and Education Policy, before the House Subcommittee on Education Reform, July 26, 2006, 3, www.languagepolicy.net.

52. Tara Goldstein, "'Nobody Is Talking Bad,'" in *Gender Articulated: Language and the Socially Constructed Self,* ed. Kira Hall and Mary Bucholtz (New York: Routledge, 1995), 379.

53. The Latino Coalition, *National Survey of Hispanic Adults,* October 2, 2006, www.TheLatinoCoalition.com.

54. Shirin Hakimzadeh and D'Vera Cohn, *English Usage among Hispanics in the United States* (Washington, D.C.: Pew Hispanic Center, November 29, 2007), 4; *Hispanic Attitudes toward Learning English,* fact sheet (Washington, D.C.: Pew Hispanic Center, June 7, 2006), 1.

55. *Now That I'm Here: What America's Immigrants Have to Say about Life in the U.S. Today* (New York: Public Agenda, 2003), 1–2.

56. Lucy Tse, *"Why Don't They Learn English?" Separating Fact from Fallacy in the U.S. Language Debate* (New York: Teachers College Press, 2001), 22.

57. Richard Alba, John Logan, Amy Lutz, and Brian Stults, "Only English by the Third Generation? Loss and Preservation of the Mother Tongue among

the Grandchildren of Contemporary Immigrants," *Demography* 39, no. 3 (August 2002): 467–484.

58. Hakimzadeh and Cohn, *English Usage,* 13–17.

59. Alejandro Portes and Rubén Rumbaut, *Immigrant America: A Portrait,* 3rd ed. (Berkeley: University of California Press, 2006), 277.

60. Amy Goldstein, "A Journey in Stages: Assimilation's Pull Is Still Strong, but Its Pace Varies," *Washington Post,* January 16, 2000, A01.

61. Enrique Fernandez, "The Erosion of Espanol," *Miami Herald,* March 2, 2008, www.miamiherald.com.

62. Eric Gorski, "Hispanic Congregations Adding English Services to the Mix," *Nashua Telegraph,* August 25, 2007, 2.

63. *Changing Faiths: Latinos and the Transformation of American Religion* (Washington, D.C.: Pew Forum on Religion and Public Life, April 2007), 54.

9. Looking Both Ways

1. Jeremy Rifkin, *The European Dream: How Europe's Vision of the Future Is Quietly Eclipsing the American Dream* (New York: Tarcher/Penguin, 2004), 250–251.

2. *Statistics in Focus: First Demographic Estimates for 2006* (Luxembourg: Eurostat, April 2007).

3. *Europe in Figures: Eurostat Yearbook, 2006–2007* (Luxembourg: Eurostat, 2007).

4. Marie Price and Lisa Benton-Short, "Counting Immigrants in Cities across the Globe," *Migration Information Source* (Washington, D.C.: Migration Policy Institute, January 2007).

5. *Hearings before the Senate Committee on Foreign Relations,* 109th Cong., 2nd Sess. (April 5, 2006), 1–2 (testimony of Daniel Fried, Assistant Secretary for European and Eurasian Affairs).

6. Rogers Brubaker, *Citizenship and Nationhood in France and Germany* (Cambridge, Mass.: Harvard University Press, 1992), 184.

7. Jane Kramer, "Taking the Veil," *New Yorker,* November 22, 2004, 59.

8. C. Educ. Art. L. 141-5-1 (2004).

9. Jon Henley, "Something Aggressive about Veils, Says Chirac," *Guardian* (London), December 6, 2003, 19.

10. Brubaker, *Citizenship and Nationhood,* 1–18.

11. Craig S. Smith, "Immigrant Rioting Flares in France for Ninth Night," *New York Times,* November 5, 2005, A1.

12. Craig S. Smith, "France Has an Underclass, but Its Roots Are Still Shallow," *New York Times* (Sunday *Week in Review*), November 6, 2005, 3, quoting Manuel Valls, member of the French parliament and Mayor of Ivry, a suburb south of Paris.

13. Rifkin, *The European Dream,* 259–260.

14. Richard Bernstein, "A Continent Watching Anxiously Over the Melting Pot," *New York Times,* December 15, 2004, A4.

15. Sarah Wildman, "Europe Rethinks Its 'Safe Haven' Status," *Christian Science Monitor,* May 24, 2006, 7.

16. Richard Bernstein, "A Quiz for Would-Be Citizens Tests Germans' Attitudes," *New York Times,* March 29, 2006, A4.

17. *The Netherlands: Discrimination in the Name of Integration* (New York: Human Rights Watch, May 2008).

18. Anna Triandafyllidou, *Immigrants and National Identity in Europe* (London: Routledge, 2001), 69.

19. Nahal Toosi, "It's Harder to Define Nationality in Today's Germany," *Milwaukee Journal Sentinel,* June 26, 2005, 1.

20. "Act to Control and Restrict Immigration and to Regulate the Residence and Integration of EU Citizens and Foreigners (Immigration Act) of July 30, 2004" (English translation), reprinted in *Federal Law Gazette,* pt. 1, 41 (August 5, 2004); "Speaking the Language of Integration," *Deutsche Welle,* October 21, 2005, www.dw-world.de.

21. "German Immigration Issues," transcript of interview of Otto Schily, German Federal Minister of the Interior, with Joanne Myers, Carnegie Council Breakfast Meeting, November 21, 2005, www.cceia.org/resources.

22. Niamh Nic Shuibhne, *EC Law and Minority Language Policy* (The Hague: Kluwer Law International, 2002), 22.

23. "Language Use in the EU," *EurActiv.com,* November 24, 2006, www.euractiv.com.

24. Message from Mr. Koichiro Matsura, Director-General of UNESCO, on the celebration of 2008, International Year of Languages, May 11, 2007, www.unesco.org.

25. *Europeans and Their Languages,* Summary (Brussels: European Commission, February 2006), 3–4.

26. *Summary of the First Report on the Activities of the Working Group on Languages, July 2002–June 2003* (Brussels: European Commission, 2003), 3.

27. European Parliament and Council of the European Union, "Recommendation of the European Parliament and of the Council on Key Competencies for Lifelong Learning," *Official Journal of the European Union* 394 (December 2006): 10–18, www.eur-lex.europa.eu.

28. *High Level Group on Multilingualism, Final Report* (Luxembourg: Commission of the European Communities, 2007), 9–10.

29. *Languages Mean Business: Companies Work Better with Languages* (Brussels: European Commission, Directorate-General for Education and Culture, 2008).

30. *A Rewarding Challenge: How the Multiplicity of Languages Could Strengthen Europe* (Brussels: European Commission, Directorate-General for Education and Culture, 2007), 11.

31. *Multilingualism: An Asset for Europe and a Shared Commitment* (Brussels: European Commission, September 2008), 4.

32. "Orban: Multilingualism 'Cost of Democracy' in EU," *EurActiv.com,* November 12, 2008, www.euractiv.com.

33. Nathalie Baïdak and Theodora Parveva, *Key Data on Teaching Languages at School in Europe* (Brussels: Education, Audiovisual and Culture Executive Agency, P9 Eurydice, November 2008), 35–36, fig. B4.

34. "No Extra Cash for Languages 'until 2013,'" *EurActiv.com,* September 19, 2008, www.euractiv.com.

35. MENON Network EEIG, *Multilingualism: Between Policy Objectives and Implementation,* executive summary (Brussels: European Parliament, 2008), iii–iv.

36. "Plurilinguisme et identités européennes," in *Charte européenne du plurilinguisme* (Paris: Observatoire européenne du plurilinguisme, 2005), 5 (my translation).

37. Jean Claude Beacco and Michael Byram, *Guide for the Development of Language Education Policies in Europe: From Linguistic Diversity to Plurilingual Education,* executive version (Strasbourg: Council of Europe, 2003), 18.

38. Britta Schneider, *Linguistic Human Rights and Migrant Languages* (Frankfurt am Maim: Peter Lang, 2005), 33.

39. Baïdak and Parveva, *Key Data,* 69 fig. C7, 46 fig. B9.

40. *Encarta World English Dictionary,* s.v. "assimilate," www.encarta.msn.com.

41. *Universal Declaration of Linguistic Rights,* www.linguistic-declaration.org (emphasis added).

42. *The Hague Recommendations Regarding the Education Rights of National Minorities and Explanatory Note,* www.osce.org.

43. E-mail correspondence from Fernand de Varennes, Associate Professor of International Law and Human Rights, Murdoch University School of Law, Australia, August 12, 2008.

44. *Common Basic Principles for Immigrant Integration Policy in the EU,* November 2004, www.iccsi.ie.

45. Adrian Favell, *Philosophies of Integration: Immigration and the Idea of Citizenship in France and Britain,* 2nd ed. (New York: Palgrave Macmillan, 1998), 62.

46. Alec G. Hargreaves, *Immigration, "Race" and Ethnicity* (New York: Routledge, 1999), 195–196.

47. Rosa Santibáñez et al., "Equitable Education and Immigrant Education," in *Social Integration and Mobility: Education, Housing and Health* (Lisbon: Universidade de Lisboa, Centro de Estudos Geograficos, 2005), 73.

48. Lisane Wilken, "The Development of Minority Rights in Europe," in *The Tension between Group Rights and Human Rights: A Multidisciplinary Approach,* ed. Koen de Feyter and George Pavlakos (Portland, Ore.: Hart, 2008), 101–102.

49. Irish Constitution, art. 8

50. Italian Const., art. 6, trans. and ed. A. Tschentsher, in *International Constitutional Law* (last modified September 7, 2008), www.servat.unibe.ch/icl; Law no. 482, 297 Gazz. Uff., December 20, 1999, art. 4–6, www.parlamento.it.

51. Spanish C.E. [Constitution] art. 3, trans. and ed. A. Tschentsher, in *Interna-*

tional Constitutional Law (last modified September 7, 2008), www.servat
.unibe.ch/icl.

52. Welsh Language Act, 1993; Gaelic Language (Scotland) Act, 2005,
    (A.S.P.7).

53. *Euromosaic: Regional and Minority Languages in the New Member States*
    (Brussels: Office for Official Publications of the European Communities,
    2004).

54. *Council Directive 77/486/EEC of July 1977 on the Education of the
    Children of Migrant Workers: Integrating Immigrant Children into Schools
    in Europe* (Brussels: Eurydice, 2004), 8.

55. *U.N. Convention on the Rights of the Child,* Art. 8; Art. 30, November 20,
    1989.

56. E-mail correspondence from Fernand de Varennes, August 12, 2008.

57. Wilson McLeod, "An Opportunity Avoided? The European Charter for Re-
    gional or Minority Languages and UK Language Policy," in *The European
    Charter for Regional or Minority Languages: Legal Challenges and Oppor-
    tunities* (Strasbourg: Council of Europe, 2008), 215.

58. Fernand de Varennes, "Language Protection and the European Charter for
    Regional or Minority Languages: Quo Vadis?" in *The European Charter
    for Regional or Minority Language,* 26–27.

59. Directorate General for Internal Policies of the Union, *Multilingualism: Be-
    tween Policy Objectives and Implementation* (Brussels: European Parlia-
    ment, 2008), vi.

60. Robert Phillipson, Mart Rannut, and Tove Skutnabb-Kangas, introduction
    to *Linguistic Human Rights: Overcoming Linguistic Discrimination,* ed.
    Tove Skutnabb-Kangas and Robert Phillipson (Berlin: Mouton de Gruyter,
    1995), 5.

61. Joshua A. Fishman, "On the Limits of Ethnolinguistic Democracy," in
    Skutnabb-Kangas and Phillipson, *Linguistic Human Rights,* 54.

62. Duncan Wilson, "From Freedom of Education to Equality through Educa-
    tion," paper prepared for the Council of Europe conference to mark the
    5th anniversary of the entry into force of the *Framework Convention,*
    Strasbourg, October 30–31, 2003, 17.

63. De Varennes, "Language Protection," 31.

64. Tove Skutnabb-Kangas, "The Right to Mother Tongue Medium Educa-
    tion—The Hot Potato in Human Rights Instruments," plenary address pre-
    sented at Il Simposi Internacional Mercator: Europe 2004: Un Nou Marc
    per a Totes Les Llengues? February 27–28, Tarragon-Catalunya, Spain, 6.

65. Guus Extra and Kutlay Yagmur, *Urban Multilingualism in Europe: Immi-
    grant Minority Languages at Home and at School* (Clevedon, England:
    Multilingual Matters, 2004), 90; Fernand de Varennes, "Language Rights
    as an Integral Part of Human Rights," *International Journal on Multicul-
    tural Societies* 3, no. 1 (2001): 22.

66. Sue Wright, "Language and Power: Background to the Debate on Linguistic
    Rights," *International Journal on Multilingual Societies* 3, no. 1 (2001),
    44–54.

67. Alain Fenet, "Difference Rights and Language in France," in *Language,*

Nation, and the State: Identity Politics in a Multilingual Age, ed. Tony Judt and Denis Lacorne (New York: Palgrave Macmillan, 2004), 47.

68. Michel de Certeau, Dominique Julia, and Jacques Revel, *Une politique de la langue: La revolution française et les patois* (Paris: Gallimard, 1975), 170.

69. Robert Phillipson, *Challenging Language Policy* (New York: Routledge, 2003), 47.

70. Davyth Hicks, "France: Deputies Vote for 'Regional' Language Recognition amidst Strong UN Criticism," *Eurolang,* May 27, 2008, www .eurolang.net.

71. Davyth Hicks, "Meet the French, Strong Supporters of Regional Languages," *Eurolang,* June 25, 2008, www.eurolang.net.

72. Angelique Chrisafis, "Local Language Recognition Angers French Academy," *Guardian,* June 17, 2008, (statement of Philippe Jacq, Director of l'Office de la language bretonne), www.guardian.co.uk.

73. Anne Judge, *Linguistic Policies and the Survival of Regional Languages in France and Britain* (New York: Palgrave Macmillan, 2007), 125.

74. Douglas A. Kibbee, "Minority Language Rights: Historical and Comparative Perspectives," *Intercultural Human Rights Law Review* 3 (2008): 127.

75. Glyn Williams, *Sustaining Language Diversity in Europe: Evidence from the Euromosaic Project* (Basingstoke, England: Palgrave Macmillan, 2005), 82.

76. See Glyn Williams, *Sustaining Language Diversity in Europe* (New York: Palgrave Macmillan, 2005), 72–89.

77. Dmitri Priven, "Grievability of First Language Loss: Towards a Reconceptualisation of European Minority Language Education Practices," *International Journal of Bilingual Education and Bilingualism* 11, no. 1 (2008): 96, 103.

78. Ingrid Gogolin and Hans Reich, "Immigrant Languages in Federal Germany," in *The Other Languages of Europe: Demographic, Sociolinguistic and Educational Perspectives,* ed. Guus Extra and Durk Gorter (Clevedon, England: Multilingual Matters, 2001), 192–214; Dominique Caubet, "Maghrebine Arabic in France," in Extra and Gorter, *The Other Languages of Europe,* 261–277.

79. Extra and Yagmur, *Urban Multilingualism in Europe,* 17–18.

80. See, The TIES (The Integration of the European Second Generation) Project, www.tiesproject.eu.

81. Michael Clyne, "Why Germany Needs a Coordinated Pluralistic Language Policy," in *Multilingual Europe: Reflections on Language and Identity,* ed. Jane Warren and Heather Merle Benbow (Newcastle upon Tyne: Cambridge Scholars, 2008), 9.

82. Gayle Christensen and Petra Stanat, *Language Policies and Practices for Helping Immigrants and Second-Generation Students Succeed* (Washington, D.C.: Migration Policy Institute, September 2007).

83. Santibáñez et al., "Equitable Education," 78–79.

84. *Integrating Immigrant Children into Schools in Europe,* 52.

85. *Education in a Multilingual World,* Education Position Paper (Geneva: UNESCO, 2003), 15.

86. Ingelore Oomen-Welke and Guido Schmitt, "Teaching the Mother Tongue in Germany, in *Teaching the Mother Tongue in a Multilingual Europe,* ed. Witold Tulasiewicz and Anthony Adams (London: Continuum, 1998), 144.

87. *Integrating Immigrant Children into Schools of Europe,* 51–52; *Migrants, Minorities and Education: Documenting Discrimination and Integration in 15 Member States of the European Union* (Luxembourg: European Monitoring Centre on Racism and Xenophobia, 2004), 74–78; Baïdak and Parveva, *Key Data,* 103.

88. *European Convention on the Legal Status of Migrant Workers,* Article 15 (1977).

89. *Integrating Immigrant Children into Schools in Europe: Germany* (Brussels: Eurydice, 2004).

90. Clyne, "Why Germany Needs," 11–12.

91. Sigrid Luchtenberg, "Bilingualism and Bilingual Education and Their Relationship to Citizenship from a Comparative German-Australian Perspective," *Intercultural Education* 13, no. 1 (2002): 52.

92. Clyne, "Why Germany Needs," 8.

93. Maria Böhmer, "The National Integration Plan—A Contribution of Germany towards Shaping a European Integration Plan," www.citiesofmigration .ca.

94. Fulya Özerkan, "Domestic Support for Turkish Courses," *Hurriyet Daily News,* December 2, 2008, www.hurriyet.com.tr.

95. Françoise Convey, "Teaching the Mother Tongue in France," in *Teaching the Mother Tongue in a Multilingual Europe,* 113–114.

96. See Christine Hélot, "Bilingual Education in France: School Policies versus Home Practices," in *Forging Multilingual Spaces: Integrated Perspectives on Majority and Minority Bilingual Education,* ed. Christine Hélot and Anne-Marie de Mejía (Clevedon, England: Multilingual Matters, 2008), 203–227.

97. Christine Hélot and Andrea Young, "Bilingualism and Language Education in French Primary Schools: Why and How Should Migrant Languages Be Valued?" *International Journal of Bilingual Education and Bilingualism* 5, no. 2 (2002), 99.

98. Christine Hélot, "Language Policy and the Ideology of Bilingual Education in France," *Language Policy* 2 (2003): 257–258.

99. Hélot, "Bilingual Education in France," 217.

100. Hélot, "Language Policy," 267; Françoise Lorcerie, "L'Islam dans les cours de 'langue et culture d'origine': Le procès," *Revue européenne des migrations internationales* 10, no. 2 (1994): 5–43.

101. Peter Broeder and Guus Extra, *Language, Ethnicity and Education: Case Studies on Immigrant Minority Groups and Immigrant Minority Languages* (Clevedon, England: Multilingual Matters, 1999), 78.

102. Monica Loewenberg and Bob Wass, "Provisions for the Development of the Linguistic Proficiency of Young Immigrants in England and Wales and

France: A Comparative Study," *Comparative Education* 33, no. 3 (1977): 404.

103. E-mail correspondence from Christine Hélot, University Professor, University of Strasbourg, January 19, 2009.

104. Hélot, "Language Policy," 267–268.

105. Tove Skutnabb-Kangas, *Linguistic Genocide in Education—Or Worldwide Diversity and Human Rights?* (Mahwah, N.J.: Erlbaum, 2000), 619–622; Hugo Baetens Beardsmore, "The European School Model," in *European Models of Bilingual Education,* ed. Hugo Baetens Beardsmore (Clevedon, England: Multilingual Matters, 1993), 121–123; website of Schola Europea, www.eursc.org.

106. *The Gallup Coexist Index 2009: A Global Study of Interfaith Relations* (2009), 19, www.muslimwestfacts.com.

107. Stéphanie Giry, "France and Its Muslims," *Foreign Affairs* 85, no. 5 (September/October 2006): 103.

108. Thijl Sunier, "National Language and Mother Tongue," in *Civil Enculturation: Nation-State, School and Ethnic Difference in the Netherlands, Britain, Germany, and France,* ed. Werner Schiffauer, Gerd Baumann, Riva Kastoryano, and Steven Vertovec (New York: Berghahn Books, 2004), 162.

109. Sigrid Luchtenberg, "Ethnic Diversity and Citizenship Education in Germany," in *Diversity and Citizenship Education,* ed. James A. Banks (New York: Jossey-Bass, 2007), 256.

110. Krystyna M. Bleszynska, "Constructing Intercultural Education," *Journal of Intercultural Education* 19, no. 6 (December 2008): 540–541.

111. Sabine Mannitz, "Regimes of Discipline and Civil Conduct in Berlin and Paris," in Schiffauer et al., *Civil Enculturation,* 170–174.

112. Strengthen and Unite Communities with Civics Education and English Skills Act of 2009, H.R. 3249, 111th Cong., 1st sess. The Senate version, S. 1478, calls for an "office of citizenship and new Americans."

113. U.S. Department of Homeland Security, *Building an Americanization Movement for the Twenty-First Century: A Report to the President of the United States from the Task Force on New Americans* (Washington, D.C.: U.S. Government Printing Office, 2008), 2.

114. *E Pluribus Unum Prizes,* Migration Policy Institute, National Center on Immigration Policy, www.migrationinformation.org.

115. *E Pluribus Unum: The Bradley Project on America's National Identity* (Chicago: Bradley Foundation, June 2008); Jacob L. Vigdor, *Measuring Immigrant Assimilation in the United States* (New York: Manhattan Institute, May 2008).

116. Tove Skutnabb-Kangas, "Linguistic Diversity, Human Rights and the 'Free Market,'" in *Language: A Right and a Resource: Approaching Linguistic Human Rights,* ed. Miklós Kontra, Robert Phillipson, Tove Skutnabb-Kangas, and Tibor Várady (New York: Central European University Press, 1999), 204–205.

117. Hans H. Reich, "Developments in Ethnic Minority Language Teaching within the European Community," in *Ethnic Minority Languages and Edu-*

cation, ed. Koen Jaspaert and Sjaak Kroon (Amsterdam: Swets and Zeitlinger, 1991), 165.

118. Guus Extra, "Comparative Perspectives on Immigrant Minority Languages in Multicultural Europe," in *Maintaining Minority Languages in Transnational Contexts,* ed. Ann Pauwels, Joanne Winter, and Joseph Lo Bianco (New York: Palgrave Macmillan, 2007), 52–53.

119. Kevin Robins, *The Challenge of Transcultural Diversities, Final Report* (Strasbourg: Council of Europe, March 2006).

10. A Meaningful Education

1. Samuel P. Huntington, "The Hispanic Challenge," *Foreign Policy* 141 (April 1, 2004): 45.

2. Paul Simon, "Beef Up the County's Foreign Language Skills," *Washington Post* (opinion), October 23, 2001, A23.

3. National Security Education Program, *National Briefing on Language and National Security* (College Park, Md.: National Foreign Language Center, January 2002), 12 (statement of Everette Jordan, U.S. Department of Defense).

4. U.S. House of Representatives, Committee on Armed Services, *Building Language Skills and Cultural Competencies in the Military: DOD's Challenge in Today's Educational Environment* (November 2008); *Defense Language Transformation Roadmap* (Washington, D.C.: Department of Defense, January 2005).

5. *Education for Global Leadership: The Importance of International Studies and Foreign Language Education for U.S. Economic and National Security* (Washington, D.C.: Committee for Economic Development, 2006), 3.

6. Fareed Zakaria, *The Post-American World* (New York: W. W. Norton, 2008).

7. Donald J. Hernandez, Nancy A. Denton, and Suzanne Macartney, "School-Age Children in Immigrant Families: Challenges and Opportunities for America's Schools," *Teachers Collage Record* 111, no. 4 (March 2009): 629.

8. Kenneth L. Karst, "Paths to Belonging: The Constitution and Cultural Identity," *North Carolina Law Review* 64 (1986): 359; see also Giovanna Guerzoni and Daniela Soci, "School Communities and Children's Rights," in *The Tension between Group Rights and Human Rights: A Multidisciplinary Approach,* ed. Koen de Feyter and George Pavlakos (Portland, Ore.: Hart, 2008), 193–206.

9. Alan Wolfe, "The Costs of Citizenship: Assimilation v. Multiculturalism in Liberal Democracies," *Responsive Community* (Summer 2003): 27, 29.

10. David A. Hollinger, *Postethnic America,* rev. ed. (New York: Basic Books, 2000), 216–217.

11. Robert D. Putnam, "Community-Based Social Capital and Educational Performance," in *Making Good Citizens: Education and Civil Society,* ed. Diane Ravitch and Joseph P. Viteritti (New Haven, Conn.: Yale University Press, 2001), 58–59.

Index